FRANCE

A NATION OF PATRIOTS

FRANCE

A NATION OF PATRIOTS

BY

CARLTON J. H. HAYES

PROFESSOR OF HISTORY IN
COLUMBIA UNIVERSITY

NEW YORK
COLUMBIA UNIVERSITY PRESS
1930

PRINTED IN THE UNITED STATES OF AMERICA
BY THE PLIMPTON PRESS · NORWOOD · MASS.

PREFACE

THIS volume really belongs to two different series of researches which American scholars have recently made into European social developments since the World War. In the first place, it is one of the *Social and Economic Studies of Post-War France*, prepared under the auspices of the Columbia University Council for Research in the Social Sciences; and as such it aims to expound and explain a national psychology which has inspired Frenchmen to effect and maintain an extraordinary degree of national unity and national optimism not only during the awful military strain of 1914–1918 but also during the unparalleled economic stresses of the decade of reconstruction from 1919 to 1929.

Secondly, this volume is, in fact if not in name, one of the series of *Studies in the Making of Citizens*, which has been guided and edited by Professor Charles E. Merriam of the University of Chicago and the other volumes of which — those on Germany, Great Britain, Russia, Italy, Austria-Hungary, Switzerland, the United States, etc. — are being published by the University of Chicago Press. The present volume deals specifically with the means by which Frenchmen of the present day are rendered supremely patriotic, the agencies by which French national psychology is fashioned and fortified.

Much of the present volume is devoted to an exposition of the patriotic national rôle of the French State and government, of the educational and military systems, of the churches, the press, radio, and cinema, of patriotic societies, and of national symbols and ceremonies. Such agencies of patriotic national propaganda are, of course, not peculiar to France. They exist in every civilized country. And the author wishes to state most emphatically that whatever may appear to the casual reader of the following pages as evidence perhaps of a menacing nationalism in France can be matched by equally incriminating evidence in the case of the

v

United States or of Germany or of Italy. No " holier-than-thou "
attitude is assumed in respect of France.

The purpose of this study is strictly scientific. It is neither anti-
French nor pro-French. It seeks merely to describe, with the utmost objectivity, what French national psychology is and how it is
communicated. It is communicated, as has been said, by agencies
which are not peculiar to France but which rather are common
to many countries in our modern age. What makes a distinctive
content of French national psychology is historical circumstance,
and this is sketched in the first chapter following. Thereafter
is shown (Chapters II–IX) how agencies, common to many nations, operate in France on peculiar French traditions to com-
municate to most Frenchmen what, on the whole, may be termed
French national psychology. In the last three chapters (X–XII)
are indicated the regionalisms in Alsace-Lorraine and elsewhere in
France and the relationship of Frenchmen to internationalism,
which form integral parts of, and condition, French national psychology and the making of patriotic Frenchmen. As appendices
are provided (1) a digest of typical textbooks used in French
schools, (2) a guide to associations of school-teachers, and (3)
guides to the French press. The comment therein made on particular newspapers and textbooks is intended to be informational
and objective; the reader who imagines that it is designed to prove
the " nationalism " of the French should investigate for himself
the newspapers and textbooks of other peoples. It should be repeated that the French are not more " nationalistic " than any
other people in a like stage of economic and social development.

The investigations on which the findings of this book are based
were carried on in France from 1926 to 1928 by the author and a
staff of able and devoted assistants for whom the Carnegie Endowment for International Peace provided comfortable working quarters at its European Center, 173 Boulevard Saint-Germain, Paris.
The investigations covered wide fields, including some that had not
hitherto been much tilled; and the author, in assuming responsibility for the results, is only too well aware of their unavoidably
sketchy and impressionistic character and of the manifold errors
and misapprehensions of detail which may have crept into them

through pressure of time or difficulties of language. Whatever merit this book possesses is attributable to the staff of assistants and to the contacts made with the French Government and with a very large number of individual Frenchmen, directly or indirectly through the good offices of Dr. Nicholas Murray Butler, the Director, and Dr. Earle B. Babcock, the Assistant Director, of the Dotation Carnegie, and of Dr. Horatio N. Krans, the Associate Director of the American University Union, in Paris.

To certain members of the staff, the author is under special obligations. Mr. Shepard B. Clough interviewed representatives of all the patriotic and international societies mentioned in Chapters VIII and XII; he spent several months in Alsace-Lorraine, gathering the information for Chapter X; he prepared memoranda for parts of Chapters V and XI. Miss Vera Mikol made an intensive study of French newspapers and magazines, radio and cinema; Chapters VI and VII, and Appendices C, D, and E are almost wholly the product of her pen. Miss Tamara Abelson (now Mrs. David Talbot Rice) collected a good deal of useful information about French symbols and ceremonies, and she, together with Mr. William C. Buthman and a group of French secretaries, made a digest of national comments in the French press from 1919 to 1927. Mr. Buthman centered his attention on newspapers and organizations of the " Right," particularly on the Action Française.

The number of Frenchmen to whom this study is indebted is legion. It is simply impossible to mention all the governmental officials, all the teachers and army officers and churchmen and journalists and officers of private societies and business men who were interviewed and who supplied aid or counsel. It must here suffice to acknowledge special assistance in certain particulars, from M. Paul Painlevé, Minister of War, and M. Édouard Herriot, Minister of Public Instruction, who gave gracious counsel respectively concerning the French army and concerning the French schools; from M. Camille Bloch, Director of the Musée de la Guerre at Vincennes, who made available its great collection of French newspapers; from Professor Jean Marx, of the École des Chartes and the French Foreign Office, and from M. Luchaire of the Institut International de Coopération Intellectuelle, both of whom made helpful suggestions about the whole undertaking.

Every one of the thousand and more Frenchmen who were interviewed in connection with this study evinced the utmost courtesy and a very real desire to be helpful. No obstacle was put in the way of a full and free investigation, either by governmental officials or by private individuals or groups. The French are patriotic; some of them are "nationalist"; but their patriotism, even their "nationalism," does not preclude an engaging degree of internationalism. Their attitude in the present instance to the author and his fellow American investigators will be reciprocated, it is to be hoped rather than asserted, by citizens of the United States when they shall be descended upon and cross-examined about things nearest and dearest to them by a group of French scholars.

CARLTON J. H. HAYES

August 15, 1929.

CONTENTS

ix

CHAPTER I

INTRODUCTION: THE FRENCH NATIONALITY

I

FRENCHMEN of the past generation have borne the chief military shock of the greatest war in human history and afterwards a succession of economic shocks which would normally seem sufficient of themselves to ruin any country. That Frenchmen have borne all these shocks with fortitude, and that throughout the crisis of war and the less spectacular but still trying crises of peace they have displayed a high degree of cohesion, of unity of thought and action, of a truly national sentiment and will, has elicited expressions of respect from all quarters of the world.

The manner in which Frenchmen faced the war and the manner in which they have faced post-war problems have alike been conditioned in large part by the fact that Frenchmen constitute a distinctive nationality with well marked national habits and with what may properly be termed a national psychology. Indeed, no other modern nationality (save, perhaps, the English) possesses a common consciousness more deeply rooted or more stubbornly enduring than the French.

Foreign visitors have often noted external signs of French homogeneity — the relative uniformity of the French countryside; the striking similarity in social usage of each provincial city to every other; the constantly repeated pattern of manners and customs through the length and breadth of France. Doubtless such external signs have been grossly exaggerated and in certain respects invented, but however mythical they may be, they symbolize a truth, the truth that the natives are essentially a singularly homogeneous nationality. All Frenchmen take it for granted that they are Frenchmen. All Frenchmen take it equally for granted that France is the leader and champion of the world's civilization. This is not to say that Frenchmen are not inveterate individualists. In fact they differ profoundly among themselves and even quarrel bitterly with one another over questions of politics, economics, and religion. But these questions are open questions, subordinate to the closed faith which all French factions and all French individuals repose in France. Frenchmen love their native land above everything else. Republicans, royalists, socialists, communists, all are basically patriotic; all are so devoted to realizing their ideal of France that their quarrelling over ways and means tends to assume the nature of the worst family rows.

Supreme devotion to one's nationality has been termed nationalism. French writers, however, almost unanimously object to the word nationalism as descriptive of general French national psychology. They associate the word with ostentatious boastfulness, with chauvinism and jingoism, with greedy designs against other lands and other peoples. They may accuse Germany of being nationalist, or even Italy. But they insist that France is not nationalist. They admit that a small fraction of Frenchmen, such as, for example, the " Action Française," may be temporarily nationalist, but they shrug their shoulders at the suggestion that Frenchmen as a whole or in considerable numbers have any sympathy with nationalism.

In a certain sense, this is most reasonable. Everything depends upon one's conception of nationalism. The French are so national, they take their nationality and their national patriotism so much for granted, and withal they are so polite, that they are pretty largely saved from the artificial boastfulness and crude ostentation which may characterize a people less sure of itself. They are so certain of meriting foreign praise that they can comfortably refrain from praising themselves. They can likewise be sincere and eager internationalists, for they assume that a whole world of nations must revolve around France. If, then, we use the word nationalism to designate the basic quality of French national psychology, the reader should rigorously bear in mind that we mean by it simply the supreme devotion which Frenchmen bear to their nationality and to their *patrie*, without any connotations whatsoever of militarism or imperialism or spread-eagleism.

National feeling has not always existed in France, nor did it come suddenly into being. It has been the product of a slow, historical evolution. Traces of it begin to appear in French literature of the Middle Age; they become clearer in the later phases of the Hundred Years' War; and they reach the dignity of royal roads under the Bourbon monarchy.[1] It is the French Revolution, however, which inaugurates the type of supreme national loyalty that has broadened and deepened during the course of the nineteenth century and eventually produced the special national psychology with which we are here concerned.

The history of the development of national spirit in France has been the history of the overcoming of centrifugal forces in the life of the nation by centripetal forces. Down to the latter part of the eighteenth century, down to the Great Revolution, centripetal forces existed and tended to draw all Frenchmen together in common bonds of language, government, religion, tradition, and social usage, but they were counterbalanced in large degree by centrifugal forces which operated to break France into disparate provinces, dialects, and castes. It was the mission of the Revolution to depress the centrifugal forces and to construct or project engines of popular propaganda which, as they have since been put to work, have steadily exalted centripetal forces at the expense of the centrifugal in national thought and action.

2

Centrifugal forces have not been wholly banished from the France of to-day. They were too much and too long an inherent part of the country's history to be overcome in a mere century and a half of counter-propaganda since the Revolution. They have been lessened and transformed, but they still exist.

[1] See Henri Hauser, *Le Principe des Nationalités, ses Origines historiques* (Paris, Alcan, 1916); René Johannet, *Le Principe des Nationalités* (Paris, Nouvelle Librairie Nationale, 1923); A. Aulard, *Le Patriotisme français de la Renaissance à la Révolution* (Paris, Chiron, 1921); and H. F. Stewart and Paul Desjardins, *French Patriotism in the Nineteenth Century* (Cambridge, University Press, 1923).

They comprise several categories. First may be mentioned the territorial divisions, the localisms and provincialisms. France, it should be recalled, acquired its present territorial extent in Europe only very gradually. Beginning with a little district around Paris — the Île-de-France — long lines of French kings, through feudal wars, through foreign wars, through Crusades, through diplomacy and marriage, through stratagem and statesmanship, brought district after district, and province after province, into subjection to them and into union with France. Languedoc was thus acquired in the thirteenth century, Normandy in the fourteenth, Gascony and Brittany and Burgundy in the fifteenth, Navarre in the sixteenth, Franche-Comté and Alsace in the seventeenth, and Lorraine and Corsica in the eighteenth. Every one of these districts, and innumerable others which were similarly annexed, had previously had fairly long periods of separate or quasi-independent existence, and their populations had severally developed local traditions and local patriotisms of a commanding sort. An event of war or a decree of a king could not make all these populations change their traditions or enlarge their patriotism in the twinkling of an eye. They did become Frenchmen in time, but they retained — and still retain — at least a secondary attachment to their respective provinces and *pays*.[2]

Secondly, there are linguistic divisions. The French language of to-day has developed from a Gallo-Roman dialect of the Île-de-France, and has spread with the expansion of the French State, as the language of the government, the courts, the army, the schools, commerce, and polite society and literature, through all the annexed areas, south, north, west, and east. But it has not altogether supplanted as vulgar speech the rival Gallo-Roman dialects which it encountered and to which the natives have clung with maternal tenacity and in some of which, notably Provençal, modern provincial littérateurs have sought to revive a glorious non-French literature. Nor has the French language obliterated quite different languages which were once the official languages of whole provinces and are still the common vernaculars of large

[2] See Chapters X and XI, below.

numbers of peasants — the Celtic Breton in Brittany, the Teutonic Flemish in Artois and German in Alsace, the Basque in the Pyrenees, and an Italian dialect in Corsica. All Frenchmen now know French, but some of them are bilingual and possess a sentimental attachment to their patois, to their " little language." [3]

Thirdly, there are social cleavages. For centuries, so long as there was a privileged nobility and a privileged clergy, there existed in every province and in France as a whole veritable states within the state, enshrining social inequality and pursuing divergent social aims and policies. As the Abbé Siéyès put it a hundred and forty years ago, it was " the classes against the nation." The Great Revolution abolished feudalism and serfdom and sheared the clergy and the nobility of exceptional rights and formal privileges; it labored zealously to assert and maintain egalitarianism among all Frenchmen, legal equality, social equality, and, so far as possible, economic equality. But nobles and clergymen might lose their privileged position in law and even much of their property; they could not be completely divested in a century, at least in their own minds, of the social preëminence and prestige which their predecessors for a millennium had enjoyed.

Besides, it should be remembered that the bourgeoisie in the France of the old régime was in fact if not in theory a privileged class. This class of untitled traders, financiers, and professional men was something of a caste; it furnished much of the money and many of the brains for private enterprise and public undertakings, and in return it was granted economic concessions and honored with public offices of trust and responsibility. It was the bourgeoisie, moreover, which decisively influenced and directed the course of the French Revolution and which ever since has magnified, and in turn been magnified by, the success of the Revolution. And with the introduction of machinery and large-scale production into France in the nineteenth century, the same class has found new means of fortifying its predominant position in the life of the nation. But if nowadays a risen bourgeoisie can

[3] For a discussion of contemporary linguistic regionalism in France, see Chapter XI, below.

enjoy social contacts with a fallen nobility and even on occasion
with a dispossessed clergy, it can be troubled and vexed by the
grumblings and mutterings of the class of urban workingmen and
proletarians whose numbers have been steadily augmented by the
widening employment of machinery and large-scale production.
To earlier cleavage between " privileged " and " unprivileged,"
has succeeded in France, as elsewhere, the cleavage between capitalist and proletarian, with effects economic, social, and national.

Until the Great War, France was predominantly agricultural,
that is to say, the majority of Frenchmen earned their livelihood
directly on and from the soil.[4] Most of the majority, moreover,
were peasant proprietors, and these, with the bourgeoisie, were
special beneficiaries of the French Revolution and influential in
shaping the national development of France throughout the nineteenth century. They were a balance-wheel between dispossessed
aristocrats and propertyless proletarians. And both through
their own efforts and through the assistance which the bourgeoisie
gave for services rendered, they came to occupy an almost privileged position in the national economy: they were protected by
bounties and tariffs, and when it was a matter of direct taxation
they were treated most exceptionally.[5] Since the war, however,
France has undergone something of an industrial revolution, so
that now probably a majority of the French population live in
urban centres and are dependent directly on manufacturing
or commerce.[6] This means that French agriculture, and with it
French peasant proprietorship, has declined relatively if not
absolutely. It also signifies that the social cleavage in France
between town and country, between farmer and day-laborer, is
likely to grow more, rather than less, acute.

    [4] W. F. Ogburn and W. Jaffé, *The Economic Development of Post-War France*,
Vol. III of *Social and Economic Studies of Post-War France* (New York, Columbia
University Press, 1929), pp. 8–10, 183.

    [5] R. M. Haig, *The Public Finances of Post-War France*, Vol. I of *Social and
Economic Studies of Post-War France* (New York, Columbia University Press,
1929).

    [6] W. F. Ogburn and W. Jaffé, *op. cit.*, pp. 203–205.

3

Social cleavage, linguistic division, and provincialism must not be stressed too much. Modifying and moderating them are centralizing factors of extended duration and great strength — national institutions and national traditions.

Foremost among the national institutions are those of politics and religion. The long line of French kings, from Louis VI in the twelfth century to Louis XIV in the eighteenth century, not only enlarged their territories by annexation, but also made steady progress toward their consolidation and unity by superimposing upon feudal and other local governments the governors, the laws, the courts, the language, the coinage, the tax-collectors, the army, of a national centralized State. A certain amount of confusion between national and local authority naturally resulted, but it was largely dissipated during the French Revolution, when everywhere throughout France local governmental institutions were abolished or subordinated to those of the nation. What was begun by the fanatical idealism of the Revolution was consummated by the practical discipline of the soldier Napoleon, and it has remained intact to the present day. The French State of the Third Republic centres in the capital of the nation even more than did the French State of the Bourbon monarchy. The old provinces which under the monarchy retained some degree of local autonomy have been supplanted since the Revolution by départements and arrondissements, highly artificial in construction and relatively devoid of independent traditions. And the prefects and sub-prefects who really rule these newer local divisions are appointed by the central government and constitute more efficient eyes and ears for the Republican ministry at Paris than did Richelieu's "intendants" for the King at Versailles. Politically speaking, the contemporary French government is one of the most highly centralized, the most formally national, governments on the face of the earth.[7]

Of religion, too, France possesses institutions which have had great unifying potency. The nation is appropriately called the

[7] For further discussion of this subject, see Chapter II.

" eldest daughter " of the Roman Catholic Church, for the Frankish people were the first of the non-Roman peoples to accept the Faith of the Popes and, what is more significant for our present purposes, to effect the organization of a national hierarchy throughout Gaul. Indeed, ecclesiastical unity of France antedated and paved the way for political unity. For centuries the vast mass of inhabitants of the whole country were Catholics, governed in spiritual matters and to some extent in temporalities by a group of bishops who thought of themselves not only as agents of the Bishop of Rome but also as mouthpieces of the Gallican, French Church. It is true that Protestantism made some headway in France in the sixteenth century and that agnosticism and skepticism made even greater progress in the eighteenth century. It is likewise true, during the nineteenth and twentieth centuries, that Frenchmen have been sharply divided in their opinions of the Catholic Church and that the almost continuous conflict between " clericals " and " anti-clericals " has added a new divisive element to French life. But these truisms should not obscure two main points: first, that the earlier unifying work of the Church has rendered possible and natural the later centralizing achievement of the State; and second, that the early and long-continued practice of Catholic Christianity by the whole nation chiefly explains the marked homogeneity in social usage and custom of contemporary Frenchmen. A large percentage of present-day Frenchmen may reject the authority and the dogmas of the Catholic Church and may absent themselves from its sacraments and services, but they cannot altogether escape the implications of a Catholic tradition which many generations of their ancestors implanted in the nation. Church holidays are national holidays; and social usages associated originally with ecclesiastical observance of birth, death, and marriage are now national customs.[8]

Centralized government and Catholic Christianity are perhaps the chief, but by no means the only, enduring traditions of the French nation. There is an important military tradition, a tradition of national courage and *élan*, a tradition which has been

[8] For details concerning the Church in France, see Chapter V.

built up through the centuries under the aegis of such commanders
as Charlemagne, Du Guesclin, Bayard, Henry IV, Turenne, Condé,
and Napoleon, down to Foch and Pétain, Joffre and Galliéni.[9]

There is also a missionary and colonial tradition, dating from
the Crusades and exemplified by the medieval Saint-Louis as well
as by countless French explorers and missionaries and traders
who builded in the seventeenth century a colonial empire in India
and the New World and in the nineteenth century a vaster imperial
domain in Africa and Asia.

There is likewise a twofold economic tradition. On the one
hand is the tradition of France as the country par excellence of
the olive and the mulberry-tree, of grainfield and vineyard, the
country of hard working, close-fisted peasants, and, paradoxically,
the country of the good-natured rural Jacques Bonhomme. On the
other hand is the tradition of France as the country par excellence
of delicate manufactures and hand-work, of fashionable clothing
and articles of luxury, the country of the fastidious urban
boulevardier.

Even more significant has been, since the time of the Grand
Monarch, the cultural tradition of France, the tradition that the
French nation set the styles for the whole world's manners, clothing, dancing, and cooking, the tradition that the French language
is the clearest, most precise language in the world, the natural
language of international diplomacy and cosmopolitan society,
and the tradition of the continuously great French literature and
art of modern times. Indeed, the French Academy, as the cus-
todian of the nation's cultural tradition, has been since the time
of Richelieu and Mazarin, under Republic as persistently as under
Monarchy, an institution comparable in its national rôle to State
and Church.

All these traditions and all the institutions which enshrine them
have been common heritage of the French people; together they
help to explain how the French nationality has been created and

[9] See Chapter IV. The geographical position of France has had much to do
with prompting a national desire for " security " and with establishing the military
tradition which has promoted national consciousness. This point is discussed below,
pp. 65–66, 93.

what have been its distinguishing features. And yet of themselves they are not enough. Any nation might possess common traditions of culture, economics, expansion, and war, might once have adhered to the same church, and might still be directed by a centralized state, and with many, with even a majority, of such a nation loyalty to the nationality might not be deemed the highest loyalty. For no nation lives exclusively on tradition, and the break-up of old institutions and old modes of thought is a natural phenomenon in a changing world. Contemporary France is bound by tradition as much, and as little, as any other country of the present age. And France, perhaps beyond any other country, has experienced a revolution of institutions and modes of thought.

The Great French Revolution at the close of the eighteenth century, despite its exalting of the nation at the expense of provinces and localities, was (and still is) a divisive force in French life. It overthrew the traditional monarchy and set up a new-fangled republic; it laid violent hands on the Church; it dispossessed the nobles; it substituted for such traditional national heroes as Saint-Louis and Jeanne d'Arc revolutionary heroes like Danton and Carnot. In fine, it established a new synthesis of French patriotism, the synthesis which we may term Jacobin patriotism. And Jacobin patriotism has been in the ascendant in France most of the time since the Revolution.

But nobles and churchmen and royalists there were at the time of the Revolution, and most of them did not take kindly to Jacobinism. Their like have persisted in France to the present day, abominating Jacobinism and all its works, and priding themselves on being "counter-revolutionaries." They, too, are patriotic Frenchmen, but the synthesis of Counter-Revolutionary patriotism contains ingredients differently compounded from that of Jacobin patriotism. And between pure Jacobin patriotism (which is now a sect, represented chiefly by French Freemasonry and the "League of the Rights of Man") and pure Counter-Revolutionary patriotism (which now is also a sect, represented most militantly by the "Action Française") are innumerable varieties of French patriotism shading and merging from one extreme to the other.

In certain respects there has been less real unity of thought among Frenchmen since the Revolution than before. Agriculture and with it the agricultural mind no longer exert the overwhelmingly predominant influence which they exerted in earlier ages. Conspicuous now and conflicting at times with the agricultural mind are the bourgeois mind, the socialist mind, and the communist mind. And all these minds create and entertain divergent concepts of French patriotism. Then, too, overlapping the diverse economic minds are conflicting cultural minds. Contemporary French literature embodies such divergent views of patriotism as those of Romain Rolland and Maurice Barrès. There are anti-clerical and anti-Christian patriotisms; there are Royalist Catholic and Republican Catholic and Democratic Catholic patriotisms; there are Radical and Conservative patriotisms; that which extols and that which denounces the revival of provincial and local loyalties. In other words, there is no longer a single basic philosophy of religion and government; there are several such philosophies, each with a considerable following of Frenchmen and each in conflict with the others.

4

Yet the fact remains, as impressive as it is paradoxical, that in the present age, far more truly than ever before in French history, all Frenchmen are supremely loyal to France and, in this sense, are nationalist. There can be no doubt of the fact. What is the explanation?

It is to be explained in part by a curious achievement of French intellectuals in seeking and finding during the past century the lowest common denominator of the various French philosophies and patriotisms. Carnot, one of the finest and most practical of the Jacobin patriots of the Great Revolution, came to realize that Jacobinism was not and could not be the faith of all his fellow countrymen, and in the statesmanlike memoir which in 1814 he addressed from his retirement to the restored Bourbon king, Louis XVIII, who symbolized at least in theory the Counter-Revolution, the Jacobin wrote:

What will be the great motive of all individual efforts? What will give them a uniform tendency toward one and the same end? It can be, obviously, only a strong noble passion, and this passion can be only the love of country. This love, then, must be given birth; a national spirit must be created. This is what we lack, and what we lack to such an extent as almost to prevent us from thinking it. No one among us, so to speak, understands how one can sacrifice one's own interest to the general interest or forget one's self for the safety and glory of the country. . . . In England all private fortunes are linked to the public fortune. There everyone is vitally concerned that the commonwealth suffer no harm or loss. Consequently, the great majority of that nation necessarily support the government, and the opposition-party is quite weak. . . . That is why there is in England a national spirit. . . . In France there is more egoism, little or no national spirit. And yet there must be a national spirit in France, for it is only great passions which make great nations. With one, it is liberty; with another, it is conquest; with another, it is religious fanaticism. With us, it ought to be love of the soil which has given us birth. In other words, it ought to be the love of the fatherland. Such ought to be the character of the national spirit which suits the French people; it is the love of the soil, collectively considered, its integrity, its improvement, its political independence. The disposition of our minds carries us naturally toward this common goal; Frenchmen have always been very strong in their own homes; and it is as difficult for foreigners to maintain themselves with us as for Frenchmen to establish themselves at a distance from their firesides.[10]

Carnot struck a note which could evoke a sympathetic response from all sorts of Frenchmen. But he was by no means unique. A whole host of French intellectuals of his time and subsequent busied themselves with touching similar chords and with improvising entire sonatas of truly national appeal. Royalists and revolutionaries, republicans and reactionaries, clericals and anti-clericals, vied with one another in protestation of love of the fatherland, and gradually, through the labors of littérateurs, historians, and publicists, republicans learned to recognize that kings had loved France, royalists discovered love of France in republicans, anti-clericals came to honor clericals who had been patriotic, and clericals to forgive some anti-clericals. Among historians, for example, an outright Protestant like Guizot, a

[10] Lazare Carnot, *Mémoire adressé au Roi en juillet 1814* (Brussels, 1814).

radical like Mignet, a Liberal turned Catholic like Thierry, and, most of all, a romantic patriot like Michelet, were representative of the process which went on in the nineteenth century. It was, so to speak, a weaving together, for the masses, of old and new traditions. It involved the acceptance of the centralized State as a waxing achievement and glory of France, of the Catholic Church as an early creator and past glory of France, of the Great Revolution as a modern re-creator and new glory of France. It meant the coupling of Saint-Louis and Danton, of Bossuet and Voltaire, of Louis XIV and Napoleon, of Renan and Pasteur, as national heroes. For they all loved France. And the moral of it was that every individual Frenchman who honored one or another of such national heroes, should pattern his public life, in a national sense, after his particular hero and accordingly should evince in national crises a patriotism which would transcend all differences of party, profession, and philosophy that might distinguish him from fellow countrymen.

The work of French intellectuals, during a half century after Napoleon, established the ideal that all Frenchmen *should be* supremely loyal to France. But the result has perhaps surpassed the expectation. At any rate, the reality has equalled the ideal. All Frenchmen *are* supremely loyal to France. And the explanation of this fact is attributable only in part to achievements of French intellectuals in discovering common denominators of various French philosophies and patriotisms. It is attributable even more to the invention and skilled use of new engines of education and propaganda by means of which the common denominators have been impressed on the minds of all Frenchmen while everything else has been slurred over and blurred.

The democratic centralized State, as renovated by the Revolution and perfected in the course of the last century, has been, with its elaborate bureaucracy, its extending suffrage, and its increasing powers, one of these engines. Other engines were newly devised at the time of the Revolution and closely articulated with the centralized State — the system of state-supported, state-directed, compulsory universal schooling, and the system of compulsory universal conscription and training of soldiers and sailors.

Outside of the foregoing official and compulsory agencies of national education and propaganda, but nicely supplementing and reënforcing them, are a considerable number of private or semi-private agencies. There are the churches, for example, Catholic and Protestant, and such religious institutions as the Jewish synagogues and the Masonic lodges: none of these is novel but most of them, in novel ways, have labored to hold their numbers by vying with one another in the preaching of national patriotism. There are, moreover, the popular newspapers, magazines, cinemas, and radios, quite new in nature and quite intent on securing ever larger audiences; the proprietors of most of the new journalism, patriotic themselves, emphasize in their productions what they think will afford the greatest happiness to the greatest number of Frenchmen, namely, national patriotism. There are, too, formal societies and associations of professional patriots that conduct special propaganda of this kind among intellectuals or among the masses by means of pamphlets, lectures, and public demonstrations; even the newer organizations of youth and sport have been given a national complexion. There is, besides, the continuing and intensifying national rôle of French literature and art. There are, finally, alike under state auspices and under private auspices, a multitude of monuments and buildings, of symbols and ceremonies, which are daily reminders to Frenchmen and to foreign visitors that France is a nation and that national heroes deserve well of the fatherland.

The following chapters of this book will deal at length with all these engines and agencies for the making, in the present generation, of supremely loyal national Frenchmen: the government and the bureaucracy, the army and navy, the educational system, the churches, journalism and publicity, the patriotic societies, art and literature, symbols and ceremonies. From such a detailed study it is hoped that the reader will be in a better position to appreciate not only how French national psychology has latterly been shaped but also what it is, its general content, and its manner of pondering the problems of the Great War and the ensuing peace. However, lest the reader gather therefrom the mistaken idea that the engines and agencies of national propaganda have operated identically and have produced uniformly national Frenchmen, it has been thought desirable to add special chapters, recalling and reëmphasizing the fact that Frenchmen are still individualist, factional, and partisan, and that, alongside of the common denominator of the patriotism which all or most of them cherish, flourish numerous subsidiary and conflicting patriotisms to the stimulation of which some of the mentioned engines and agencies contribute.

Here may be remarked a very important point. The current supreme loyalty of Frenchmen to their country — French nationalism, if we may so style it — is an artificial, not a natural creation. It depends exclusively neither on physical heredity nor on geographical environment; it does not conform to canons of biology or botany.

The French people, biologically speaking, are not a single pure race. They are a much mixed conglomeration of three chief races of Europe — Alpines, Nordics, and Mediterraneans; roundheads, tall blond long-heads, and short brunet long-heads — with no one knows how many strains of prehistoric races. It is customary to think of America as the melting pot of assorted stocks, but France has been such a pot for countless centuries and its inhabitants have been so long inured to racial intermixture that they do not nowadays rebel, like some Americans, against the addition to their pot of a few more alien scraps. They have faith in their artifice. They know that, through it, what goes into the pot as white or blond or brunet, or yellow or black, will come out French.

Nor are the " natural frontiers " of France more than a literary convention and an artifice of statecraft. Ancient Gaul, under Roman domination, extended from the Alps to the Ocean and from the Pyrenees to the Rhine, but France as a political entity has never, except for a moment in the Napoleonic era, embraced the same area, while France as a cultural unit has steadily encountered within geographical France both a German culture and a Celtic culture. Moreover, the physical geography of the land which admittedly is and has long been French includes mountains, sea-coasts, river valleys, fertile plains, and relatively barren plateaus; and if physical geography were the main determinant of national character, then there would be not one French nation but at least five.

No, French nationalism is not exclusively or chiefly a product of physical geography or of racial heredity. It is the product of historical human cultural forces. It rests on traditions of politics, religion, language, war, invasion, conquest, economics, and society, which have been fashioned by peculiar and often fortuitous circumstances and which have been preserved and synthesized by great writers and other intellectuals. The work of the intellectuals, however, has been artificial; others might have made another and different synthesis. And what is most artificial about the whole phenomenon of contemporary French nationalism is the fact that it has been consciously taught to, and thereby imposed upon, the mass of Frenchmen. France has had enough history during the past fifteen or twenty centuries to enable an objective and scientific historian to find precedent for almost any line of action which he and his compatriots might take at the present day. But the masses in France, as elsewhere, are not objective scientific historians; they receive on faith what they are taught about the past, and the past of France has been rendered by publicists and popularizers highly conventional, highly artificial.

Frenchmen, then, are a nationality, with a national psychology which has real roots in ancient, medieval, and modern tradition but which in latter times has artificially been pruned and trained in order to produce the perfect flower of supreme national loyalty.[11]

[11] For illustrative material on topics discussed in this and the following chapter, the following recent books may be found useful in one way or another: Sisley Huddleston, *France* (London, Ernest Benn, 1926); Raymond Recouly, *The Third Republic,* English translation by E. F. Buckley (New York, Putnam, 1928); Alexandre Zévaès, *Histoire de la Troisième République, 1870–1926* (Paris, Anquetil, 1926); Firmin Roz, *Comment faire connaître la France à l'Étranger* (Paris, Plon, 1922); Robert Cornilleau, *De Waldeck-Rousseau à Poincaré: Chronique d'une Génération, 1898–1924* (Paris, Spes, 1927); Joseph Denais, *Pour que la France vive!* (Paris, Spes, 1926); Jules Rassak, *Psychologie de l'Opinion et de la Propagande politique* (Paris, Rivière, 1927); O. M. Hueffer, *French France* (New York, Appleton, 1929).

CHAPTER II

THE GOVERNMENT AND THE BUREAUCRACY

I

HISTORICALLY, the political State has been the most obvious and the most continuously effective maker of France. Since the time of Clovis and the Franks in the fifth century there has been an independent government in the land, and ever since that time " France " has signified the territorial jurisdiction of this independent government, and the inhabitants subject to it have been transformed into " Frenchmen." " France " for centuries was much more restricted in area and population than it is to-day; its expansion was very gradual, and the districts and peoples incorporated one by one in it were first subjected to the common government and afterwards, through the operation of this common government, became " French." As late as the eighteenth century the Bourbon kings in solemn proclamations referred to " our peoples," but the goal of the labors of the old régime was already pretty well achieved; the Revolution which closed the century erased the phrase " our peoples " and wrote large on all its documents the words " the French people." The Revolution merely registered an accomplished fact: the French nation, the French nationality, had come into existence and was coterminous with the territorial sway of the French central government.

The French central government since 1789 has undergone a bewildering number of kaleidoscopic changes of form. An absolute monarchy in 1789, it became a liberal monarchy in 1791; a republic in 1792, with one constitution in 1795 and another in 1799; an empire in 1804; a constitutional monarchy in 1814; a more liberal monarchy in 1830; a republic, for the second time, in 1848; a restored empire in 1852; a republic, for the third time, in

1870, at first, curiously enough, under royalist influence, and only after 1879 completely under republican control. These rapid changes of form, together with the swift changes of ministry which have characterized the Third Republic, have made a far deeper impression on the superficial observer than their real significance can justify. Basically, they are changes of form and name. At most they are external expressions of an internal alteration of emphasis on peculiarly enduring traditions of French government. It is most unfortunate that the large number of superficial observers, especially those abroad, and even some observers who ought to know better, have been so transfixed by external changes that they have failed to perceive the abiding internal nature of French political institutions or to judge aright the continuous functions which they perform. If there were enlightened public opinion on this point, there would be less talk about the volatility of the French and more about their constancy and conservatism.

As a matter of fact, there are several great traditions which for centuries have been linked, ever more closely, with the political government, and these traditions can be set forth with little or no reference to the form or personnel of the government, whether it be royalist, imperial, or republican, or whether its ministry be headed by Monsieur Poincaré or by Prince de Polignac or by Cardinal Mazarin. First is the tradition of centralization, the tendency to reduce local and provincial autonomy to the minimum and to bring every individual Frenchman into immediate political relationship with the central government. Between the national capital, whether at Paris or at Versailles, and the subjects or citizens, there must be no intermediary in the nature of a semi-sovereign local division, such as a state, a county, a township, a school-district, or a municipality. Local self-government never developed in France as in England and America, and whenever it threatened to develop it was warred against and eventually controlled and perverted by the creation of a new set of superior central agents. The " intendants " of Cardinal Richelieu's invention, the " commissioners " of the Revolution's devising, and the " prefects " and " sub-prefects " that were created by Napoleon and have since endured, have been of one kind: they have been the authoritative emissaries of the central government which appointed them; its spies as well as its agents, and they have been also the official foes of local self-government, the vetoers of its legislation and the destroyers of its initiative. Just as under the monarchy the building of a bridge or the repair of a church had to be approved by an intendant, who in turn had to obtain permission from the central government at Versailles, so now under the republic the repair of a church or the erection of a public monument must be requested of a prefect whose decision must depend upon instructions from the central government at Paris. This surely is centralization both in theory and in practice. It is nothing new. It is traditional with French government.

Another tradition of French political government, associated with centralization, is what the French themselves call *étatisme*. This has two aspects, the veneration, almost the worship, of the State (that is, the central government of the State) as the source of national light and life, and the ascription to the State of the right, nay, the duty, of regulating many details of collective and individual enterprise. The tradition dates from the Bourbon monarchy. The honor which Frenchmen paid to the majesty of the court of Louis XIV, the deference with which they viewed the sun as the Grand Monarch's symbol of himself and his government, was equalled only by their acquiescence in the elaborate economic regulations of a Colbert and in the chronic interference of the king himself in matters ecclesiastical, artistic, and social. The habits of Frenchmen in these respects had been slowly acquired, but, once acquired, they were not to be lost or materially altered. They withstood the storms of political and social revolution and have lasted on, in undiminished vigor, to the present day. In the popular mind, the exact object of veneration, the precise source of authority, has been a bit changed since the eighteenth century; it is no longer the king; it is the nation itself. Actually, however, a nation, like a king, must have a government, and what once the people expected from a royal national government they now expect from a republican national government. They still expect the State (that is, the central government of the State) to interfere actively in matters economic, ecclesiastical, cultural, and social, in the whole range of public and private life and activity, and they still venerate the idea, if not always the personal representatives, of state omnipotence.

In some ways the tradition of *étatisme* has been stronger under the modern Republic than under the earlier Monarchy. The State during the Great Revolution broke down finally a considerable number of competing institutions and practices, notably those of feudal and noble privilege and those of communal and guild right, and by its suppression of lingering independence on the part of the Church it inaugurated a new era of " secularization," that is, the transfer to itself of many functions, educational, economic, and charitable, which had formerly been exercised by semi-private religious corporations. Regulation of domestic relations, registration of vital statistics, control of schooling, are some of the matters which have been transferred from Church to State, and the transfer, the " secularization," has conformed to, and strengthened, the tradition of *étatisme*.

Among the traditional functions of the centralized French State should especially be noted an interesting survival or revival of the ancient Roman tradition of the State's providing its citizens with bread and circuses. The " bread " as dispensed in contemporary France is quite metaphorical and does not differ in kind from what we are familiar with in the United States or in Germany or in almost any other modern nation; it consists of tariffs, bounties, public works, and all those devices by which the State seeks to increase the wealth of the nation and actually enriches individual citizens. But the " circuses," though also somewhat metaphorical, symbolize a French tradition which is fundamentally different from anything that obtains in English-speaking countries. It is the tradition of state direction and subsidizing of the fine arts. State patronage of architects, littérateurs, scientists, sculptors, painters, and actors has been practised on a fairly large scale in France since the time of Francis I, early in the sixteenth century; it reached large proportions under Louis XIV; and it has been consistently maintained by all the diverse governments of the last hundred and forty years. The French Academy, with its affiliated organizations, has always been subsidized by the State, and is in part a most dignified cultural agency of the central government. The State, moreover, supports and directs all the universities and technical schools in the country; all university-professors are functionaries of the central government. The State, too, maintains the chief libraries and almost all the museums and art-galleries. Besides, the State builds and subventions the opera-houses and certain theatres, and partially defrays the expense of their productions. The State even undertakes the repair of a large number of ecclesiastical edifices which it designates as of historical, national, or artistic importance, and so strong is the general tradition that anti-clerical governments have not been backward in performing such indirect service to religion. For the supervision of its manifold cultural activities, the central government possesses, on a par with the ministries of foreign affairs, war, finance, and agriculture, a ministry charged in part with the supervision of the fine arts.

The long-continued direct fostering of the arts and sciences by the central government has undoubtedly helped greatly to establish a French national art of great importance and rich content. But it has had the natural effect of discouraging considerable private initiative and checking such numerous personal benefactions as have latterly been a much discussed mark of English and particularly of American cultural development. It is probable that the French system, at least in the past, has operated, far more effectively than the Anglo-American, to exalt the position of artists and the standing of scholars and to promote the esthetic accomplishment of the few and the esthetic appreciation of the masses. In the field of natural and applied science, however, it is possible that the Anglo-American tradition of private initiative and private support is now producing more varied and more valuable fruits than is the French tradition of state-help and state-direction. At any rate, individual Frenchmen are so habituated to the expectation of state support of cultural undertakings that they are reluctant, if the thought ever occurs to them, to make donations from their private fortunes for the erection or equipment of universities, libraries, or laboratories, for the endowment of professorial salaries or student scholarships, or for the encouragement of research. This reluctance, for better or for worse, is a national tradition in France, and one connected with the centralization and *étatisme* of the French State. But should the State itself be threatened with disaster, private talents and property may be voluntarily offered to the national Treasury. In the "Save the Franc" movement of the latter part of 1926 French artists — and even some foreigners — sold their works for the benefit of the depleted coffers of the State, and many loyal citizens, rising to the highest pinnacle of self-sacrifice in peace-time, renounced their claim to funds due them on government bonds or made donations of actual cash.

2

The fostering of a national culture, *étatisme*, and centralization: these are abiding traditions of the French State alike of the Old Régime and of post-revolutionary governments. In addition, there are several state-traditions which are now fairly well established but which are not so old, which hardly antedate the Revolution, and which have become national by rather painful stages.

One of these newer traditions is the idea that it is the business of the State to guarantee " liberty, equality, and fraternity." " Liberty, equality, fraternity " was the formula which the French Jacobins of revolutionary days proclaimed as the goal of their efforts and which they solemnly painted on public buildings and churches in capital letters which can still be seen and read. By "liberty" they meant certain "natural rights" of man, rights inherent in every individual to freedom of belief, speech, writing, worship, and association. By "equality" they meant the destruction of feudalism and privilege and the assurance of equal treatment of all citizens by the government and before the law. By "fraternity" they signified a mystical union of all French hearts in the common cause of national betterment and originally too an idealistic union of all nations and peoples in the transcendent common cause of human betterment. But the same Jacobins, true to another and earlier tradition, affirmed in their " Declaration of the Rights of Man and of the Citizen " that it belonged to the revolutionary State to define and delimit the practical exercise of individual liberty, social equality, and national fraternity; and since then, every French government, according to its particular shade of revolution or counter-revolution, of Jacobinism or anti-Jacobinism, has industriously interpreted in its own way the famous formula, stressing now one and now another of its parts. The constitutional monarchy stressed liberty; the two empires emphasized equality; the second and particularly the third republics have paid some attention to equality but more to liberty and fraternity. Altogether there can be little doubt that to-day France approaches nearer the goal of " liberty, equality, and fraternity " than ever before and nearer than almost any other Great Power in the world. What started as a Jacobin dogma has ended as a national ambition. Throughout the process, however, it has been the central government which has guided the fraternity, measured the equality, and determined the liberty, of Frenchmen. In France there has been no institution analogous to the Supreme Court in the United States for the defense of the individual against encroachment by the State, nor has there been in France any pressing popular demand for such an institution. The French tradition in respect of the State is too strong in the opposite direction.

A second of the newer traditions of the French State is political democracy. This also dates in its original theoretical promulgation from the Revolution, but its practical realization has been the outcome of a subsequent century of halting half-measures punctuated by popular protests and Parisian riots. The restored Bourbon monarchy of 1814 recognized that it could not uproot all Jacobinism from France; one of the revolutionary tenets which it accepted and made its own was the principle that the legislature (at least the lower chamber) should be elected by the people on the basis of " one man, one vote," but, like most of the earlier revolutionaries, it thought of the " people " as property-owners and taxpayers and imposed a heavy property qualification on the exercise of the suffrage. The liberal monarchy of Louis Philippe lowered the property qualification, and the Second Republic, in 1848, abolished it altogether. The Second Empire, while employing universal manhood suffrage directly for its plebiscites or referenda and indirectly for the election of certain legislative bodies, so manipulated it as partially to nullify it. Only under the Third Republic, in accordance with the constitutional laws enacted by an Assembly in which Royalists had the majority, was universal manhood suffrage finally and definitely established as the regular means of choosing the Chamber of Deputies. Even to-day, full political democracy is distrusted in France: women have not been granted the suffrage; the senators are chosen by indirect election; and the President of the Republic is elected by the Senate and Chamber rather than by a popular electorate. Nevertheless, despite adverse criticism and denunciation of it by reactionary groups, political democracy is now more firmly believed in and practised in France than in any other country of continental Europe. It is now a tradition of the French State.

Still another newer tradition of the French State is republicanism. Taking rise in the stormiest period of the Revolution, its progress during the nineteenth century encountered many more vicissitudes than did the parallel growth of political democracy. Many royalists could compromise with democracy but hardly with republicanism. In the long run, however, the logical fruition of democracy was not monarchy but republic, and in measure as democracy was broadened and deepened, the number of French republicans increased. The Second Republic lasted only from 1848 to 1852; the Third Republic, proclaimed by a handful of zealots in 1870, survived the royalist Assembly which wrote its democratic constitution, and since 1879 has been guided and controlled by confirmed Republicans. Royalists have remained to the present day, but they are now a small minority of the total population and are to be encountered only in places where veneration of the Old Régime is either a habit or a fashion. The mass of Frenchmen are at last republican, and they have definitely stamped upon the contemporary State the tradition of republicanism.

A fourth significant state-tradition of the newer sort lies in the French custom of operating democracy and republicanism not by such a system of well organized political " parties " as obtains in English-speaking countries but by an indigenous medley of fragmentary political " groups," a custom, it may be remarked incidentally, almost universal throughout continental Europe and not peculiar to France. In France it has been traditional since the Revolution. It has been a natural political expression of general French individualism and of specific French groupings differentiated from one another by geography, economics, and philosophy. There never has been a single Republican Party in France arrayed against a single Royalist Party. Some Royalists — the so-called " Legitimists " — have been thoroughgoing reactionary counter-revolutionaries; others have been " liberal," that is, willing to compromise with the principle of democracy and to subscribe to the formula of liberty, equality, and fraternity; still others have " rallied " more or less cordially to the support, or at any rate the toleration, of the Republic. On the other hand some Republicans — the so-called " Radicals " — in the pursuit of what they deemed to be the present Jacobinism have been militantly anti-clerical; others have been willing to ignore, if not to champion, the Church. Some have sought to use the Republic as a special instrument for the protection of private property and bourgeois interests; others have desired to employ it as a means of improving the material condition of the lower classes; some have viewed it as a stepping-stone to socialism or communism. Because of historical circumstances, southern districts of France are strongholds of Radical Republicanism, and Legitimist Royalism is still entrenched in Brittany. Elsewhere there is the utmost confusion in the shadings of political belief, and everywhere is the complicating tendency of Frenchmen to follow personal leaders regardless of political platforms. Altogether, then, it has resulted that no political " groups " possess well knit countrywide organizations or have had much permanence or continuity, and that most " groups " represent at the maximum particular popular shadings and tendencies and at the minimum miscellaneous supporters of particular politicians. There is one set of " groups " in the Chamber of Deputies, and another in the Senate; there is a new shuffling and sometimes a new creation of " groups " after, rather than before, every general election. And the central Government is always a coalition-government; it must depend for electoral and legislative support on a temporary juncture of perpetually shifting " groups."

One might suppose that the " group " system (or lack of system) would weaken the central government, paralyze democracy, and eventually undermine the old traditions of centralization and *étatisme*. Such has not proved to be the case in France. To the contrary, it has but strengthened the State and supplemented the other state-traditions. There can hardly be in France the personal, hereditary loyalty of large aggregations of the population to a particular political party, such as Englishmen owe to a Liberal or a Conservative Party or Americans to a Republican or a Democratic Party, and it may be that the lack of such loyalty in France helps Frenchmen to be the more loyal to the State; they do not have to reconcile state-loyalty with a competing, and possibly conflicting, party-loyalty. Besides, the very necessity under which French political leaders find themselves of effecting coalitions and agreements and blocs among a variety of " groups," tends to develop in them a habit of minimizing divergencies and stressing what the " groups " have in common, even when all they have in common is devotion to the fatherland. In this way have been formed, during and since the Great War, " sacred unions " and " national blocs "; leaders of the constituent " groups " in the Parliament, and the voters behind them back home, are usually alive to the need of subordinating their several demands to the exigencies of a truly national policy. Futhermore it should be observed that the group-system is especially productive of a large class of shrewd, cleverly manipulating professional politicians, whose common vocation is the exalting of the centralized State.

Before taking leave of the traditions, old and new, of the French State, mention should be made of the ceremonial character of French public life. It is a reflection, of course, of the proverbial politeness and ceremonialism of the nation's private life. It is itself an old tradition, which reached its greatest elegance and pomp in the Versailles court of Louis XIV, Louis XV, and Louis XVI. It has since declined; but if the contemporary French Republic is less showy and ostentatious in court-functions than the British monarchy, it is vastly more ceremonial than the American democracy. Indeed, some foreign visitors and even some Frenchmen have thought it a pity that France became a republic; her national habit, they say, is so much better adapted to monarchical display. In any event, affairs of the French State to-day, as of yore, and republican, as formerly royalist, are conducted in the " grand manner," in stately old palaces, by a graduated hierarchy of officials and functionaries and lackeys with adornment of gold lace and gleaming swords. With much the same pomp and magnificence as the princely occupants of other days, the President of the Senate resides in the Luxembourg Palace and the President of the Chamber in the Palace of the Bourbons. This, too, is a state-tradition of abiding significance.

3

The French State, we have pointed out, has traditional attributes. It is centralized; it is respected; it performs many functions; it fosters national art as well as national economics; it interprets " liberty, equality, fraternity "; it is democratic; it is republican; it operates in the " grand manner." But what essentially is it? And precisely how does it " make " Frenchmen?

The State may be conceived of as a metaphysical being, an idealized embodiment of a popular " soul," a mysterious supernatural agency of eternal national destiny; and as such it frequently finds lodgment in finite human minds and thereby acquires a considerable quasi-religious significance. But for our present purposes, it will prove more profitable to be somewhat realistic and to view the State as a kind of business corporation, of which all the citizens are stockholders and a large number of them are agents and directors. Especially let us fix our attention upon these directors and agents; collectively they constitute the officialdom, the bureaucracy, of the State.

The directors are the hundreds of elected legislators and the

score of ministers and undersecretaries. Each of these gentlemen
performs some special function, debating and shaping legislation,
or directing a department of the Government, and all of them
make a regular practice of delivering to their constituents (the
stockholders) a good deal of oratory, proclaiming the great services which they themselves are rendering both to the constituents
and to the fatherland. For not least among the duties of directors
is that of preparing and spreading reports of the company's business and particularly of inspiring the confidence of stockholders
in the company's greatness. In France, as elsewhere, the ministers and legislators in the main, are, from the very nature of
things, official and professional missionaries of patriotism.

Under the ministry and the legislature, are a host of secondary
officials, agents, functionaries, clerks, and flunkeys — the vast
civil service of the French State, the bureaucracy proper. There
is, for example, the President of the Republic who in theory is
most certainly not a " secondary official," but in fact is mainly
a figurehead, an agent of the legislature and the ministry; he is
supposed to be, like a constitutional king, above and beyond
partisan politics, the temporary personification of the unity and
sovereignty of the nation, the layer of cornerstones, the receiver
of foreign emissaries, the utterer of finely phrased patriotic
platitudes; he is actually a first-class state-functionary, and
as such he is supplied with palaces, with liberal funds for entertainment, and with numerous and more or less ornamental sub-
functionaries.

The most important sub-officials are the prefects and sub-
prefects and the permanent staff of the several ministries. The
latter direct the personnel and influence the policy of the central
government pretty continuously, despite rapid change of ministers; they tend to reconcile political differences, to stress national
interests, and to promote the stability of the State and the
continuity of its policies. The prefects and sub-prefects are
agents of the Ministry of the Interior in the local divisions of the
country, in the départements and arrondissements respectively;
their function is to secure the uniform enforcement of national
laws throughout France and to prevent any locality from develop-

ing policies at variance with those of the national State.[1] The members of the permanent staff of the ministries may be relatively obscure and may seldom come into official contact with large numbers of the common citizenry, but the prefects and sub-prefects can never conceal their importance from the popular gaze; these are marked men, with showy badges of office, and with the duty of presiding at all manner of local meetings and of conferring with all manner of local individuals that have any imaginable connection with the activities of the State.

Each minister and prefect has a whole corps of sub-directors and heads of departments, office-staff, field-agents, bookkeepers, stenographers, filing-clerks, curators, doormen, janitors, and errand-boys. There is the Minister of Finance with such a corps of civil servants, assessing and collecting taxes throughout the entire country, keeping elaborate accounts, disbursing funds, superintending the currency, engaging in public and private banking, and studying the economic condition of the nation collectively and individually. There is the Minister of the Interior, with another such a corps of civil servants, appointing and instructing the prefects and sub-prefects, passing upon local ordinances and upon applications for local improvements, and conducting or supervising local administration. There is the Minister of Justice, with still another such a corps of civil servants, appointing the judges, admitting lawyers to the bar, registering and codifying the laws, and exercising an oversight of all the law-courts of the land both criminal and civil. There is the Minister of Foreign Affairs, the Minister of Agriculture, the Minister of Commerce, the Minister of Labor, the Minister of Education and the Fine Arts, the Minister of Posts and Telegraphs, and, latterly, the Minister of Pensions and the Minister of Devastated Regions, each with yet other corps of civil servants. Altogether these eleven corps constitute a large army, every one of whose soldiers, from the lowest errand-boy up through grades of tax-clerk and tax-collector, prefect and undersecretary, to minister and even

---

[1] Uniformity is emphasized by the application throughout France of hard-and-fast codes of civil and administrative law. Convenient editions of the Codes are those of Dalloz (1927).

to the very exalted President of the Republic, is sworn to supreme loyalty to France. This gives some idea of what we mean, essentially, by the French State. But it is not all.

The French State requires every able-bodied young Frenchman to serve for a time in army or navy, and during their period of military service all Frenchmen are directly subject to a staff of regular army or navy officers who, together with a large number of civilian employees, are directed respectively by a Minister of War and a Minister of Marine.[2] The French State, moreover, requires every French child, boy and girl, to attend school for a specified period; and most French children attend schools which are built, equipped, manned, and conducted under the immediate auspices of a Minister of Public Instruction. The Ministers of War and Marine direct a military personnel which is certainly as numerous as the civil personnel of the combined ministries mentioned above. And the Minister of Public Instruction, through his control not only of primary schools but also of secondary schools and of universities and other higher institutions of learning, possesses, in the hundreds of supervisors, in the thousands of professors of university and lycée, and in the tens of thousands of primary teachers, and in the millions of students, an educational army which surpasses in number and probably in national influence the personnel directed by the Ministers of War and Marine.

Counting the public schools and the army as parts of the French State, it is safe to say that at any given time at least one out of every twenty French citizens is a state functionary, a state bureaucrat. And there can be no doubt that at all times the one-twentieth of the citizens who are state employees exert a disproportionately great influence upon the other nineteen-twentieths. Besides, it should be remembered that when general elections occur, every Frenchman over twenty years of age is a qualified voter and every Frenchman over twenty-four years of age a potential state official;[3] that for several years of childhood most

---

[2] Veterans of army and of navy, moreover, enjoy certain preferential treatment in appointment to, and promotion in, the civil bureaucracy. See Ministère de la Guerre, *Bulletin Officiel no. 36: Emplois civils et militaires reservés aux militaires des armées de terre et de mer* (Paris, Lavauzelle, 1927).

[3] Of the 10,000,000 qualified voters in France, 1,200,000 were candidates for

Frenchmen are school-wards of the State; and that for a later period of youth and on into manhood almost all Frenchmen are army-wards of the State.

4

The French State thus has ample means of exerting a preponderant influence upon its citizens and of molding them into Frenchmen. It dominates the schooling of the French youth from kindergarten to university; it prescribes what they shall be taught, who shall teach them, and what methods shall be employed; it uses the public educational system for patriotic and national ends. Likewise it uses the army and the navy for patriotic and national ends, for it supplements the schooling of French boys by training them as soldiers or sailors. Moreover its multiform and numerous civil bureaucracy comes into contact with the individual Frenchman and Frenchwoman almost constantly from the cradle to the grave: in registering births, in performing marriages, in licensing attorneys and physicans and undertakers, in recording deaths, in wielding police power, in assessing and collecting taxes, in adjucating disputes, in punishing crime, in holding elections.

Indirectly the French State helps to make Frenchmen by supervising and coöperating with semi-private national agencies. Newspapers, for example, are subject to state control, even to prosecution and possible suppression by the State, and, although the State is nowadays very tolerant of journalistic dissent, the mere possibility of suppression tends to render dissenting newspapers somewhat wary of carrying too far any adverse criticism. The State publishes an official journal of its own, and the wide powers and multitudinous activities of the State provide more

---

communal office in 1929. Every village, town, and city in the country — 37,984 communes in all — was electing a mayor and a communal council. Each commune, no matter how tiny it is, elected ten councillors; and of the 1,200,000 candidates throughout France, about 400,000 actually were elected. In some places every voter was an officeholder. In the hamlet of Riboux, in the département of Var; where there were only eight voters, two officeholders had to be borrowed from a neighboring village.

material of general interest for the ordinary newspaper than can be supplied from any other source; the result is that state news bulks relatively large in all newspapers. Then, too, on the staff of the average French newspaper, as proprietor or publisher or editor or contributor, is some statesman or state official — a deputy or senator, a minister or departmental head — who gives political tone to the publication. Frequently, in almost all newspapers, are special articles from retired army-officers, university professors, or Academicians, all of whom are, or have been, closely connected with the State: they too are likely to be semi-official in character and national in effect.

Again, the churches exist more or less on the sufferance of the State, and in France they are quite accustomed to a kind of working partnership with the State. The bishop and the prefect, the curé and the sub-prefect, may not agree in politics and may bitterly disagree about philosophy and religion, but they are traditional competitors in national good works. Since the Revolution, all church property has been deemed to be national, that is, state property. From the time of Napoleon to the year 1905 — over a century — the State paid the salaries of Catholic priests, Protestant pastors, and Jewish rabbis; and, despite the contemporary separation of the churches from the State, the ordinary Frenchman is still disposed to regard the bishop and the curé, the pastor and the rabbi, no less than the prefect and the sub-prefect, as functionaries of the State. And many clergymen still act as if they were state functionaries. Moreover, all the churches have traditionally inculcated in their followers loyalty and obedience to secular authority, that is, to the State; and the French clergy as a whole to-day is intensely patriotic. The churches, like most of the newspapers, can be relied upon by the State to assist it in its task of " making " Frenchmen.

With the hundreds of national and patriotic societies which flourish in France, the State is indirectly associated. It not only tolerates but encourages them; and it is usual to find the President of the Republic or one of the ministers or members of Parliament acting as honorary president of such a society and an influential group of state employees belonging to it. Associations of war-veterans, associations for the promotion of French interests abroad, societies for national action in the sphere of economics, education, religion, or art, societies for the furtherance of athletics and sport, societies for charitable and philanthropic purposes, societies for the support of political " groups " or political programmes: these are largely patronized by the State, and, in return, these largely serve the State.

The State, moreover, by its patronage of national culture and particularly by its use of monuments and memorials, of symbols and ceremonies, is reminding all the inhabitants of France almost daily of itself — its past history, its present greatness, and its future destiny. There are the palaces and museums and offices long associated in the popular mind with the State and its functions. There are the streets and avenues and public squares, frequently named by the State in honor of men who have most faithfully served it. There are the triumphal arches, the statues, and the other monuments raised to the glory of statesmen and the State's warriors or scholars. There are the state cemeteries, the state parks and gardens, the state playgrounds. There are, too, the displays of flags and bunting, the parades and processions, the solemn tours of official dignitaries, by means of which the State adds a colorful personal touch to its popular appeal for national unity and national supremecy.

The French State, with its bureaucracy, is the central coördinator of national training and national life.[4] It is the basic maker of Frenchmen. All other agencies of national propaganda are directed or supervised by it.

The individual Frenchman, no matter what may be his economic or cultural environment, no matter what may be his familiar or local traditions or his political predilections, is constantly, throughout his life, made aware by the State, directly or indirectly, that he is a Frenchman, marked off from all other nationalities and owing supreme loyalty to France. His birth is recorded by a state official; he probably attends during his most impressionable

---

[4] For further details concerning the French government, see Vol. VI of this series: Lindsay Rogers, *The French Parliamentary System* (New York, Columbia University Press, 1929).

years a state school; he must serve in the armed forces of the State; he is married by a state official; he hears speeches by state officials and votes for state officials; he pays taxes to the State and participates in demonstrations sponsored by the State; if he reads a newspaper or attends church or joins a national association or engages in competitive athletics or takes an outing or visits a library or an art-gallery, he is reminded on every such occasion of the existence and the mission of the State; he cannot walk in town or ride in the country without encountering state monuments, state laws, and state officials; his obsequies will be regulated by the State.

It is hardly to be wondered at that persons who experience such a regimen should develop a considerable amount of like-mindedness. Not even the centralized French State has been (or is likely to be) able to overcome all human differences among its citizens and to fuse diverse personalities into a uniform type of Frenchman. But, although differences of physique, mind, education, occupation, and outlook on life are still quite obvious in France, and although French individualism is still very much a reality, the State has certainly succeeded in superimposing on individual differences a common national consciousness, something approaching a national psychology. All Frenchmen, Communists and Royalists as well as bourgeois Republicans, regard France differently from other countries; France is theirs; and they respect the traditions and prize the achievements of what is theirs more highly than what is another's. It is the French State, more than anything else, which has given them this attitude. It is the French State, more than anything else, which has made them Frenchmen.

In the two succeeding chapters we shall examine more closely the means by which two great agencies of the State — school training and military training — are being employed for the making of Frenchmen and the shaping of French national psychology. Thereafter, we shall take up in turn certain other, and semi-private, agencies operating to a similar end.

CHAPTER III

THE EDUCATIONAL SYSTEM

I

THE French State, being almost if not quite coextensive with the French nationality,[1] and possessing the traditions and performing the functions which have already been sketched, is the great central and coördinating fashioner of national psychology in France. Its civil arm — the arm of the functionaries and bureaucrats — brings the State into immediate and manifold contact with all Frenchmen and consists of an imposing official body of exemplars and apostles of French patriotism. The military arm — the army and navy — prepares all Frenchmen for national defense and is at once an instrument and an end of the propagation of national sentiment among the inhabitants of France. All French soldiers and sailors, however, and all French functionaries and bureaucrats, indeed all Frenchmen and all Frenchwomen have, with negligible exceptions, attended French schools; and these schools constitute the most pervasive and ubiquitous means of forming a truly French national psychology.[2]

Since the Great Revolution, at the end of the eighteenth century, it has been an ambition of French patriots that a formal education should be given every French child, under state direction or control, and that such education should be compulsory, gratuitous, and patriotic. This ambition the Third French Republic since 1870 has fully realized. A law of February 27, 1880, erected a Higher Council of Public Instruction, presided over

[1] Linguistically considered, the French nationality includes sizeable groups in Switzerland, Belgium, and Canada.

[2] See C. Richard, *L'Enseignement en France: Organisation répertoire des Établissements*, Vol. III of *Bibliothèque de l'Office National des Universités et Écoles Françaises* (Paris, Colin, 1925).

35

by the Minister of Public Instruction and composed largely of functionaries dependent upon him, and entrusted to it the supervision of all public and private schools in the country. A law of June 16, 1881, abolished all fees and tuition charges in public primary schools. A law of March 28, 1882, required all French children to attend public or private primary school between the ages of six and thirteen, abolished religious instruction in the public schools, and defined the content of primary education. A law of March 20, 1883, obliged every town and village to construct and maintain a public primary school. A law of June 20, 1885, granted liberal subventions by the State for the support of primary education throughout the country. A law of October 30, 1886, elaborated the program of primary education, always in a patriotic direction, and the provisions for state inspection and control of schools and teachers.[3]

In theory, education is free in France. In fact, however, the vast majority of French boys and girls between the ages of six and thirteen attend the public primary schools which are maintained by the State and which are dominated in their curricula, textbooks, and teaching-staff by that representative of the State who is known as the Minister of Public Instruction. No country in the world has a more highly centralized and autocratic system of national education than France.

It is true that there are private schools in France — " free schools " the French call them. These are mainly Catholic, and parents may comply with the law of compulsory attendance by sending their children between the ages of six and thirteen to private rather than to public school. However, the " free schools " are not entirely free of state direction and control: the State prescribes the educational qualifications of their teachers,

[3] The most convenient compilations of French educational laws and decrees are those of A. Wissemans, *Nouveau Code de l'Instruction primaire*, 27th ed. (Paris, Hachette, 1923) and *Code de l'Enseignement secondaire*, 4th ed. (Paris, Hachette, 1920). See also Joseph Soleil, *Le Livre des Instituteurs: Traité complet des Devoirs et des Droits des Membres de l'Enseignement: Administration, Législation, Jurisprudence de l'Enseignement primaire public et privé à tous les degrés*, 4th ed. (Paris, Le Soudier, 1927), and, for historical background of the legislation, 1881-1886, A. Rambaud, *Histoire de Jules Ferry* (Paris, Plon, 1904).

forbids (since 1904) members of religious orders to teach in them, exercises a censorship over their textbooks, and, in general, supervises all their activities. In the Catholic free schools, unlike the state public schools,[4] religious instruction may be given, but even in the matter of the catechisms by means of which religious instruction is ordinarily imparted, the Minister of Public Instruction has power to interfere and has actually employed his authority to ban particular catechisms.[5] Besides, the State obliges all young persons who wish to attend higher institutions of learning or to enter the learned professions to pass examinations which it sets and conducts on the basis of the curriculum of its own schools, and this obligation rests upon graduates of private schools as well as upon those of public schools. The result is that the curriculum of the " free " schools is largely patterned after that of the state schools, and consequently the former are hardly less concerned than the latter with the inculcation of national patriotism.[6]

Then, too, it should be remembered that the financial resources of the State are in back of the public schools but not of the private schools and that parents who choose to send their children to free schools must pay not only their share of taxes for the support of the public schools but a supplementary sum for the maintenance of the private school of their choice. Financial considerations and the " herd-instinct " are important factors in explaining the preponderance of the public over the private schools.

The relative number of students in the two types of French schools is set forth at five-year intervals from 1886 to 1911 and

---

[4] The French educational laws of 1881–1886 have not been applied fully to Alsace-Lorraine, and in these recovered provinces religious instruction is still given in the public schools. See Chapter X, below, pp. 264–268.

[5] *Catéchisme a l'Usage du Diocèse d'Aix,* imprimé par ordre de Mgr. L'Archévêque d'Aix, Arles et Embrun (Bar-le-Duc, 1890), banned by arrêt of July 21, 1892; *Catéchisme du Diocèse de Rennes* (1891) and *Catéchisme du Diocèse de Luçon* (Paris, Dumoulin, 1892), both banned by arrêt of January 4, 1893.

[6] See E. Pouget, *Guide de l'École libre, Législation et Jurisprudence,* 2d ed. (Paris, Hatier, 1925); and Lande, *Manuel pratique des Écoles libres,* 12th ed. (Paris, Société Générale d'Éducation, 1927). See also G. Weill, *Histoire de l'Idée laïque en France au XIXᵉ Siècle* (Paris, Alcan, 1925).

annually since 1921 in the following table, compiled from official sources: [7]

TABLE I

Year	Students in State Public Primary Schools	Students in Church Private Primary Schools	Total of Students in Primary Schools
1886	3,598,007	1,919,134	5,517,141
1891	3,760,601	1,833,282	5,593,883
1896	3,768,650	1,764,861	5,533,511
1901	3,864,189	1,662,611	5,526,800
1906	4,476,302	1,090,580	5,566,882
1911	4,592,634	1,062,160	5,654,794
1921	3,561,000	891,000	4,452,000
1922	3,763,000	851,000	4,614,000
1923	3,393,000	817,000	4,210,000
1924	3,175,000	798,000	3,973,000
1925	3,061,000	767,000	3,828,000

It will be noted that the number of students in private primary schools amounted in 1886 to about a third of the total, and in 1925 to about a fifth.

The French national system of primary schools — public and private — has undoubtedly accomplished one purpose for which it was devised: it has taught almost all Frenchmen to read and write the French language. This is indicated by the constantly lowering illiteracy of army conscripts: 38.66 per cent in 1851; 16.12 per cent in 1881, 9.42 per cent in 1891; 5.63 per cent in 1901; 4.26 per cent in 1911; and 3.51 per cent in 1922.

2

Hardly less doubtfully has the educational system trained almost all Frenchmen for patriotic national citizenship. By order of the Minister of Public Instruction of July 27, 1882, and January 18, 1887, primary instruction is organized on a uniform basis, so that everywhere one goes in France one finds the same program of studies followed by teachers and pupils. The latest (and relatively slight) modification of the program of studies oc-

[7] *Statistique Générale de la France.*

curred on an order of the Minister of Public Instruction under date of February 23, 1923. In accordance with these ministerial orders from 1882 to 1923, every French child between the ages of six and thirteen is required to take thirty hours of class-room work a week (exclusive of home-study) in a primary school, apportioned as follows: [8]

TABLE II

	PREPARATORY SECTION: CHILDREN AGED 6–7	"ELEMENTARY COURSE:" CHILDREN AGED 7–9	"MIDDLE COURSE:" CHILDREN AGED 9–11	"HIGHER COURSE:" CHILDREN AGED 11–13
1. Instruction in Morals and French Citizenship.	1¼ hours	1¼ hours	1¼ hours	1½ hours
2. Reading the French Language.	10	7	3	2½
3. Writing the French Language.	5	2½	1½	¾
4. Studying the French Language.		5	7½	7½
5. French History and Geography.	2½	2½	3	3
6. French Songs.	1¼	1	1	1
7. Military and other Physical Exercises.	1¾	2	2	2
8. Mathematics.	2½	3½	4½	5
9. Science.	1¼	1½	2½	2½
10. Design.	1	1	1	1
11. Manual Training.	1½	1	1	1½
12. Recreations.	2	1¾	1¾	1¾
Total.	30 hours	30 hours	30 hours	30 hours

The first seven of these twelve subjects of study in primary schools are " national " subjects, that is, they are susceptible of specific patriotic interpretations and uses. Therefore, for our present purposes, we may group the first seven together as " na-

[8] These figures indicate the requirements for boys. For girls they are the same except that a little less emphasis is put upon language-studies and a little more on manual training, that is, on needlework. See *Plan d'Études et Programmes des Écoles primaires élémentaires et Instructions du 20 juin 1923* (Paris, Vuibert, 1926); and P. H. Gay and O. Mortreux, *Programmes officiels des Écoles primaires élémentaires, 1923–1924: Textes officiels: Répartition mensuelle et hebdomadaire*, 2d ed. (Paris, Hachette, 1927).

tional " subjects, and the remaining five as " non-national " subjects and thus indicate the relative emphasis put on them in all the primary schools of France:

TABLE III

	PREPARATORY SECTION: CHILDREN AGED 6-7	"ELEMENTARY COURSE:" CHILDREN AGED 7-9	"MIDDLE COURSE:" CHILDREN AGED 9-11	"HIGHER COURSE:" CHILDREN AGED 11-13
"National" Subjects	21¾ hours	21¼ hours	19¼ hours	18¼ hours
"Non-National" Subjects.	8¼	8¾	10¾	11¾
Total	30 hours	30 hours	30 hours	30 hours

The national Government, through the Minister of Public Instruction, prescribes in great detail what shall be the content of the subjects taught in the primary schools, with the result that textbooks in any given subject do not differ radically from one another, and with a further result that a teacher has relatively slight freedom to develop or interpret his subject according to his own ideas. For example, in accordance with the latest prescriptions of the Minister of Public Instruction, those of February 23, 1923, it has been ordered that the history taught for two and a half hours a week in the preparatory course for children aged six to seven shall consist of forty lessons (one a week during the school-year) as follows: (1) the struggle of the Gallic chieftain Vercingetorix against Julius Caesar; (2) Saint Genevieve as protectress of Paris against early Germans; (3) Charlemagne as patron of science and of schools; (4) Roland and his fighting prowess at Roncevaux; (5) Godfrey of Bouillon as a French Crusader; (6) King Philip Augustus and his defeat of the English at Bouvines; (7) King Louis IX and his captivity and death; (8) the patriotism of the citizens of Calais during the Hundred Years' War; (9)-(10) Du Guesclin, hero of the Hundred Years' War, his childhood, captivity, and ransom; (11)-(15) Jeanne d'Arc, her childhood, her interview with the king at Chinon, her military exploits at Orléans, her presence at Reims, and her trial and death at the hands of the English; (16) Christopher Columbus as an exemplar of perseverance; (17) Bernard Palissy as a model of unselfishness; (18) Bayard for his fidelity " to king and fatherland "; (19)–(21) King Henry IV, his boyhood, his generosity, and his death; (22) Colbert; (23) Riquet; (24) La Fontaine; (25) Turenne; (26) Montcalm; (27) Benjamin Franklin; (28) Parmentier; (29) La Fayette and his departure for America; (30) Bara, a model heroic child; (31) Drouot, a model poor and studious child; (32) General Hoche; (33) Carnot; (34) Jacquard; (35) Napoleon; (36) Ferdinand de Lesseps, the builder of the Suez Canal; (37) David Livingstone; (38) Pasteur; (39) Marshal Galliéni, saviour of Paris in 1914; and (40) Guynemer, type of valiant French aviator during the Great War. It will be noted that only three out of the forty lessons treat of non-French heroes (Columbus, Franklin, and Livingstone) and that of the remaining thirty-seven devoted to French national heroes, twenty-eight deal with military personages and nine with exponents of works of peace.

According to the same ministerial prescriptions of 1923, history in the " elementary course " for children aged seven to nine consists of " the main facts and dates in the history of France to 1610," with special reference to " ancient Gaul, the German invasions, the Middle Age, the formation of national unity, the great Discoveries, the Renaissance, and the Reformation; " history in the " middle course " for children aged nine to eleven comprises " the main facts and dates in the history of France since 1610," with attention to the Absolute Monarchy, the end of the Old Régime, the Revolution, the Consulate and Empire, the Restoration, the Constitutional Monarchy, the Second Republic, the Second Empire, the Third Republic, and the War of 1914–1918; while history in the " higher course " for children aged eleven to thirteen gives " very summary notions of antiquity (Egypt, the Jews, Greece, and Rome) " and a fuller treatment of " great questions of French history in their relation to general history." Moreover, for each of these courses in history there are detailed ministerial instructions as to precisely what shall be covered month by month and week by week.

It is similar with preparatory, elementary, middle, and higher

courses in morals and French citizenship and in the French language. For example, in the prescribed program for instruction in
morals and French citizenship, it is provided somewhat more generally for pupils in the preparatory course that they shall be given
" very simple talks," " moral fables," " biographies of famous
men," and lessons in the " formation of good habits (propriety,
order, exactness, politeness etc.)," and for pupils in the elementary courses that they shall be given " familiar talks," " moral
fables and stories," and " readings with explanations; " while it
is provided more rigorously for pupils in the middle course that
they shall be instructed for seven months each year in specific
personal virtues and for the remaining two months in duties
toward family and fatherland; and for pupils in the higher course
it is required that they be taught both the personal and social virtues and the framework and functioning of French government
simultaneously throughout the nine months of the school-year.
The month's work on duties toward the fatherland, prescribed for
the middle course of children aged nine to eleven, is elaborated as
follows: First Year, first week, " The fatherland: what constitutes it: our territory, our nation "; second week, " What we owe
it: our security, our well-being, our language, our ideas "; third
week, " Our attachment to it: homesickness of exiles: pride of
being French "; fourth week, " Defense of fatherland and respect for its laws: our national heroes "; Second Year, first week,
" Likeness of fatherland to family: physical and moral resem-
blance of citizens, common interests, traditions "; second week,
" The fatherland as an achievement of our ancestors: their suffering for it: love of fatherland is respect for ancestors "; third week,
" Reconciliation of love of family and love of fatherland: family
formed and prospers within the fatherland: family enjoys security thanks only to national solidarity "; fourth week, " Duties
toward fatherland: in time of war, devotion even to death: in time
of peace, performance of all civic duties: respect for other
nations."

It is hardly necessary to proceed farther with a detailed account of the state prescriptions as to precisely what shall be
taught year by year, month by month, and day by day, in all

the subjects in all the courses in all the primary schools of France. Certain generalizations will here suffice. Not only do " national " subjects outweigh " non-national " subjects of instruction throughout the seven years of compulsory primary instruction, in number of hours spent upon them, but also the " national " subjects are treated, with the possible exception of the "non-national " subject of mathematics, as the more basic and therefore according to more detailed governmental prescriptions. Most of the " national " subjects are national in fact as well as in name: they possess a largely patriotic content and they must be taught in a conspicuously national manner.

Instruction in morals and citizenship deals with traditional morals of Frenchmen and trains for French national citizenship: exemplars of personal and social virtues are almost invariably French heroes or heroines, and while minor attention is devoted in the higher course to some study of local government in France, local loyalties are never encouraged and internationalism is not mentioned.

In respect of language it is the French national language, not any local speech or dialect, which is read, written, and studied, and this instruction serves not only to familiarize all French boys and girls with the same French poems and stories but also to indoctrinate them with romantic literary notions of French patriots and their noble, usually heroic, deeds. French alone may be the medium of instruction in the primary schools of France; no foreign language is taught in them; [9] and few, if any, examples of classical or popular foreign literature, even of the literature of neighboring Italians, Spaniards, Englishmen, or Germans, are read in French translation in these French schools.

Instruction in history is almost exclusively instruction in French national history: the preparatory year is concerned with French national heroes; the two years of the elementary course outline the history of France to 1610; the two years of the middle

[9] An exception to this generalization must be made in the case of the recovered provinces of Alsace-Lorraine, where German is taught in the primary schools, but even in Alsace-Lorraine the medium of all primary instruction must be French. See Chapter X, below.

course sketch the history of France since 1610; and the last two years of the higher course re-tell a continuous story of France with a little attention to her foreign relations. No French child under thirteen learns anything in school about the history of the next-door nations of Italy, Spain, Germany, or England, except as, in the higher course, he or she may be taught something about them incidental to an account of their wars with France.

Instruction in geography, which accompanies instruction in history, deals in the elementary course with " geographical terms," " forms of the Earth," and " very summary notions of French geography "; in the middle course, with " the geography of France and her colonies "; and in the higher course, with " Europe," " the great countries of the world," and " a review of the geography of France and her colonies."

Singing is taught throughout the seven years of primary education, and the songs sung are principally French songs and patriotic songs. Physical exercise is also prescribed throughout the seven years of primary education, and though some of it certainly has no nationalist character or implications, it includes the first systematic preparation, by means of simple military marching and formation, of the future soldiers of the French national army. Altogether, the official programs of French primary education are calculated to render all Frenchmen patriotic as well as literate.

Not all French children attend the public primary schools. A considerable number, as we have seen, attend private (Catholic) primary schools, but the programs of study in these schools are almost identical with those in force in the public schools, with the exception of a program of religious instruction, which can be used, and often is used, in the private schools to exalt the rôle of Christianity and the Church in France, to set forth the Christian mission of France, and thus indirectly to serve as an additional means of stimulating French patriotism. Besides, some French children between the ages of six and thirteen receive their primary education in the lycées and collèges, which are chiefly secondary schools but which customarily offer primary instruction also. In 1924–1925 there were 54,182 boys and girls in the primary courses of state-directed lycées and collèges. But the programs of the primary courses of these institutions are likewise almost identical with the programs in force in the public primary schools.

So-called " maternal " or " infant " schools — kindergartens, we would call them — for children between the ages of two and six precede the primary schools. Some are private, that is, Catholic; but most of them are public. In 1924–1925 the enrollment at public maternal schools amounted to 328,416, and at private maternal schools to 38,381. The programs of study in these schools are not nearly so rigid and uniform as the programs in the primary schools, properly so-called, but there can be no doubt that they are utilized, among other purposes, for implanting in children at a very early age the rudiments of national patriotism.

Beyond the primary schools, properly so-called, are " higher primary schools " for children between the ages of thirteen and sixteen. These schools are public, under the immediate control of the Minister of Public Instruction, and are reckoned as part and parcel of the French system of primary education; in 1924–1925 they were attended by 71,463 boys and girls. Their program of study, as prescribed by ministerial orders of January 18, 1887, and August 18, 1920, provides for a three-year course differentiated in the last two years into a " general section," an " agricultural section," an " industrial section," a " commercial section," and a " household section "; there is a considerable amount of vocational training and a requirement of a foreign language in most of the sections, but about a third of the instruction in all sections is in the " national " subjects of morals and citizenship, French language, history, and geography.[10] The program of morals and citizenship for the three years is as follows: (1) morals of individual life, family, school, profession, and society; (2) historical and moral foundations of the French nation, solidarity of generations and continuity of national life, the national ideal and its progressive realization, patriotism, defense of country's integrity and respect for its laws, the State, and international rela-

---

[10] See *Plan d'Études et Programmes des Écoles primaires supérieures de Filles* (Paris, Vuibert, 1925); and *Plan d'Études et Programmes des Écoles primaires supérieures de Garçons,* 4th ed. (Paris, Vuibert, 1926).

tions; (3) elements of private law and political economy. The program of instruction in the French language provides for a continuous course in French literature with prescribed readings from Molière, Racine, La Fontaine, Voltaire, Chateaubriand, Victor Hugo, Lamartine, Michelet, Daudet, etc. The program of history is as follows: (1) history of France from 1500 to 1774; (2) history of France from 1774 to 1851; (3) history of France and notions of general history from 1852 to 1920. The accompanying program of geography is: (1) notions of general geography and the non-European world; (2) geography of Europe; (3) geography of France and her colonies, and France in the world.

Paralleling and going beyond the " higher primary schools " are the state lycées and collèges.[11] These are private in that they charge tuition-fees, but they are public in that the State directs and subventions them. They give elementary instruction, similar to that given in the public primary schools, but their main function is to offer a seven-year course of secondary education for young men and women between the ages of thirteen and twenty.[12] This course, as laid out by ministerial orders of 1902 and 1924–1925, provides for one section with Latin throughout the seven years, a second section with Latin and Greek during the last three years, and a third section without Greek or Latin but with compensatory study of a modern foreign language. All sections involve compulsory study of a modern foreign language, mathematics, and natural science. And for all sections throughout the seven years the " national " subjects of French literature, history, and geography are required, these subjects consuming from a fourth to a half of the students' class-room hours. According to the governmental program of June 3, 1925, the subjects of historical instruction for each of the seven years are as follows: first year (6th Class), ancient Orient and Greece; second year (5th Class), ancient Roman history; third year (4th Class), European

---

[11] See G. Weill, *Histoire de l'Enseignement secondaire en France, 1802–1920* (Paris, Payot, 1921).

[12] See *Enseignement secondaire: Horaires, Programmes, Instructions, 1925* (Paris, Colin, 1925); *Horaires et Programmes de l'Enseignement secondaire des Garçons*, 2d ed. (Paris, Vuibert, 1925); *Plan d'Études et Programmes de l'Enseignement secondaire des jeunes Filles*, 9th ed. (Paris, Vuibert, 1926).

history with special attention to French history from the end of
the fifth century to the Hundred Years' War; fourth year (3d
Class), European history with special attention to French history
during the fourteenth, fifteenth, and sixteenth centuries; fifth
year (2d Class), European history with special reference to
French history during the seventeenth and eighteenth centuries;
sixth year (1st Class), European history with special reference
to French history from the end of the Old Régime to the middle
of the nineteenth century; seventh year (Classes of Philosophy
and Mathematics), European history with special reference to
French history since the middle of the nineteenth century and
with emphasis upon the actual institutions of the French people.
The subjects of geographical instruction are similarly prescribed
for each of the years as follows: (1) general geography, America,
and Australia; (2) Asia, Oceanica, and Africa; (3) France and
her colonies; (4) Europe; (5) physical and anthropological
geography; (6) France; (7) principal economic World Powers.

3

All the foregoing means that a boy or girl who goes through the
French educational system up to the University is instructed year
after year from six to twenty in French language and literature,
in French history, and in French geography. Such a child is introduced to French national heroes at the tender age of six; covers
French history in a four-year program through the elementary
and middle courses of the primary schools, and again covers
French history in the two-year program of the higher course of
the primary schools. If he continues in higher primary school,
he covers for a third time in a three-year course French history
since 1500; if, on the other hand, he pursues his studies in a lycée
or collège, he gets two years of ancient history and then five years
of European history which always centers in French history and
ends with an appreciation of French institutions. The same child,
in his geographical studies, must study and re-study the geography of France and her colonies every year of the seven years of
primary school and during the last year of higher primary school
or in the third and sixth years of lycée or collège. And when one

remembers the year-by-year instruction in training for French citizenship throughout the ten years of primary and higher primary schools and the reading of patriotic French prose and verse and the singing of patriotic French songs throughout the seven years of primary school, one is in a position to recognize that the French educational system is admirably adapted from start to finish to the task of making future French citizens know and love their fatherland, their own national State. But one is in a position also to perceive that the thoroughness of the training in knowledge and love of France is secured at the expense of ignorance of other, even neighboring, national states. Nowhere in the seven years of primary education does the French boy or girl acquire any special knowledge of any non-French language, literature, history, government, or culture. Everything is viewed, according to the prescribed official programs, through French national eyes.

It is true that in the higher primary schools as well as in the lycées and collèges foreign languages and literatures are taught; that in the secondary education of lycée and collège much general history — ancient, medieval, and modern — is given, and major attention is devoted to foreign languages and natural science, philosophy, and mathematics, rather than to French national subjects. But it is also true that while almost all Frenchmen have attended primary schools, in which national studies are stressed, relatively few have graduated from higher primary school, lycée, or collège, where national studies are less emphasized.

Only primary education for children between the ages of six and thirteen is compulsory in France, and indeed the mass of French boys and girls leave school at or before the end of the higher course of the primary schools. A small percentage of boys and girls enter upon the three-year course of the higher primary schools or upon the seven-year course of secondary education in the lycées and collèges. And an even smaller percentage graduate from or follow the courses of higher education in the universities. In the year 1924–1925, for example, there were 366,797 pupils in public and private maternal schools; 3,828,000 in public and private primary schools; and 54,182 in the elementary courses of state lycées and collèges; a total of 4,248,979 children in elementary primary education, all presumably under fourteen years of age. During the same year there were 71,463 pupils in higher primary schools; 115,659 in the secondary courses of State lycées and collèges; 10,367 in primary normal schools; 34,785 in technical and professional schools; and an estimated number of 150,000 in secondary private schools; a total of 382,274 young persons, presumably over thirteen years of age, in higher primary and secondary education, or a trifle less than nine per cent of the number in elementary primary education. The number at the universities for the same year was 44,170, or, roughly, eleven per cent of the number in higher primary and secondary schools and one per cent of the number in elementary primary schools.

Much the same lesson may be drawn from a study of the educational statistics of army conscripts. All young Frenchmen have to serve in the French army, and at the time of their enrollment — usually at the age of twenty, though in certain cases older up to twenty-five and even to twenty-seven — they are obliged to submit their general educational qualifications. The statistics of the Class of 1924 are as follows:

TABLE IV

	Total	For Every Thousand	
1. Unable to read or write	13,838	59	89
2. Able to read but not to write	7,074	30	
3. Able to read and write	136,396	580	
4. Possessing certificate of elementary primary studies, showing satisfactory completion of elementary primary schooling	63,682	271	851
5. Possessing certificate of higher primary studies, showing satisfactory completion of higher primary schooling	2,413	10	
6. Possessing elementary brevet, showing satisfactory completion of nine years of schooling	2,942	12	
7. Possessing higher brevet, showing satisfactory completion of eleven years of schooling	1,819	8	60
8. Possessing baccalaureate, showing satisfactory completion of secondary education	3,826	16	
9. Possessing diplomas of higher education	588	2	
10. Possessing other diplomas	2,747	12	
Total	235,325	1000	1000

It will be seen that the first two categories comprise young men who have had little or no schooling and who constitute 8.9 per cent of the total; that categories 5–10 comprise those who have had higher primary or secondary training and who constitute 6 per cent of the total; and that the remaining categories 3–4 embrace the bulk of conscripts — 85.1 per cent — who have had in whole or in part only elementary primary schooling. In other words, over five-sixths of Frenchmen — and doubtless of Frenchwomen too — are exposed to the strongly nationalist curriculum of primary education and not to the broader and more humanitarian training of later education. Most leaders of French public life are drawn from the 6 per cent, that is, from categories 5–10 listed above, but the rank and file of the French nation are products exclusively of the primary schools.

4

It is not only the governmental programs which render school instruction generally national and patriotic but also, more specifically, the textbooks by which these programs are elaborated and carried into effect by teachers and pupils. Textbooks are extraordinarily important in the French schools, and there is a marked tendency on the part of teachers not merely to use textbooks as supplements to class-room instruction but to follow them pretty slavishly and even to require pupils to memorize fairly lengthy extracts from them.

Numerous textbooks exist, and a large number of the publishing houses of Paris have competing series of texts for all grades in history, geography, morals and civics, language and literature, as well as in mathematics, science, etc. There are Catholic texts and " anti-clerical " texts, and texts used in both public and private schools. Some freedom is allowed to teachers in the choice of textbooks, but no textbook may be used in any public school unless it has been approved by the Minister of Public Instruction, and certain textbooks have been formally banned by the national educational authorities from all schools or at least from public schools. Besides, the Catholic bishops in France have banned from their private schools certain textbooks used in the public schools.

In an appendix to this volume we have presented brief commentaries on some eighty-eight more or less typical textbooks.[18] Distributed by subjects, fifty-three are textbooks of history; fourteen, of morals and civics; one, of geography; one, of military instruction; one, of philosophy; and eighteen are readers. Distributed by grade, fifty-five are used in elementary primary schools; twenty-three in higher primary and secondary schools; and ten in both. All these textbooks, we think, are typical. Most of them are published by the larger and more important Parisian houses, such as Hachette, Alcan, Belin, Colin, Gedalge, Delagrave, Delalain, de Gigord, Masson, etc., and are very widely used. A few are not so widely employed now, but have been included because of their extensive use before the Great War, and their resulting influence on the generation which made and survived the war. A few others, chiefly brief histories or readers of the Great War, have been selected as typical of a large class of writings which flourished abundantly in the French schools just after the war but which are now decidedly on the wane.

We have been at some pains to make our whole selection truly representative, to include both Catholic and non-Catholic texts, both "militarist" and "pacifist" texts. Altogether, we have examined all the texts which were reviewed by the " Dotation Carnegie pour la Paix Internationale " in its interesting and valuable *Enquête sur les Livres scolaires d'après-Guerre*, published in 1925, and, in addition, a score or two of other texts. In every case we have sought to use the most up-to-date editions.

The reader is referred for more detailed discussion of each of these representative French textbooks to the appropriate appendix, where they are listed and arranged alphabetically (by authors) in order of the school-grade for which they were severally prepared: (1) for children, aged six to seven, in the preparatory course; (2) for children, aged seven to nine, in the elementary course; (3) for children, aged nine to eleven, in the middle course;

---

[18] See Appendix A, " Digest of Typical Textbooks in French Schools for Instruction in History, Morals and Civics, Geography, and Reading," pp. 343–399.

(4) for children, aged eleven to thirteen, in the higher course, of the elementary primary schools; (5) for adolescents, aged thirteen to sixteen, in the higher primary schools; (6) for young persons, aged thirteen to twenty, in the secondary schools (lycées and collèges) ; and (7) a few miscellaneous supplementary texts. Here it will suffice to present certain generalizations of our detailed study of French " national " texts.

First of all, we are impressed by the striking similarity in content, style, and format of all texts of the same subject for the same grade, and by the closeness with which every text follows the official program. What differences exist in content, or, better said, in emphasis, are chiefly differences in the treatment of the French Revolution and the Republic and of the Catholic Church in historical textbooks. The majority of these books extol the French Revolution, exalt the Republic and its work, especially its national and educational work, and touch only lightly on the Church. A minority criticise the Revolution, minimize the achievements of the existing political régime, and praise the Church. An even smaller minority tend to decry or denounce Catholicism and to make of humanitarianism a veritable substitute religion in contemporary France.

Secondly, we are impressed by the distinctly national tone of almost all the books. From our study of the official programs and our knowledge that the textbooks are based on the official programs, we expect to find the textbooks national. But our expectations are more than fulfilled. The texts, in general, are even more national than the official programs. Nearly all the texts seem to be written not merely to acquaint boys and girls with the history, language, and institutions of the country in which they live but also to make them love it with emotional pride and religious zeal. There are differences in emphasis, as we have remarked, among historical textbooks, but there are few if any differences among them in the ultimate purpose of developing in their respective readers a greater devotion to " sweet France " or " beautiful France." The majority of such texts exalt the French Revolution as a product of French genius and a revivifier of French civilization; a minority praise the Church as an expression of French genius and a missioner of French civilization; a smaller minority regard the Church as a handicap to French genius, and humanitarianism as the final flower of French civilization. The means are different, but the end is the same. It is French genius which is discussed, French civilization which is extolled.

Thirdly, we are impressed by the moralizing tendency of textbooks in history, reading, and civics. There is occasional moralizing along Christian lines, and rare moralizing toward a simply humanitarian or pacifist goal, but most often present is a moralizing about the preëminent services of France to the world and the paramount duties of Frenchmen to France. We gather from these textbooks that the preëminent services of France to the world are personal liberty, equality, national solidarity, democracy, manners, art, learning, religion, morals, and science. We gather also that the paramount duties of Frenchmen are willingness to sacrifice their lives in military defense of their fatherland, to love its soil, to honor its dead heroes, to esteem large families, and, incidentally, to observe its laws. We note conspicuously among the services of France its excellent unselfish colonial undertakings, and among the duties of Frenchmen their obligation to know and prize the French colonial empire.

Fourthly, we are impressed by the preponderant attention which is given in most historical textbooks and in most readers to happenings of war, and in most texts on morals and civics to national preparedness for war. Occasionally an historical text criticises adversely some French military undertaking, and it is almost a vogue with ardent Republican authors to denounce the ambitious militarism of Napoleon Bonaparte, which, as one writer says, "ruined France and caused her to lose the frontier of the Rhine which the Convention [that is, the First Republic] had given her." [14] Occasionally a reader includes among its selections an indictment of war, and two readers which we have examined refrain from any reference to fighting. Occasionally, too, a book on morals and civics, while pointing out the national

[14] Aulard and Debidour, *Récits familiers sur les Grands Personnages et les Faits principaux de l'Histoire nationale*, 13th ed., p. 57.

duty of self-defense, distinguishes between defensive and offensive war and discusses international responsibility for peace. But these are exceptions and not the rule, at least among textbooks used in the elementary primary schools. Among textbooks used by pupils over thirteen years of age in the higher primary and the secondary schools relatively less space is accorded to war and more to social, economic, and cultural events. Even here, however, war receives considerable attention, and France is represented as being invariably in the right in all international disputes.

Fifthly, we are impressed by the prevailing treatment of the Great War in all manner of "national" textbooks. Of course, some texts, from the nature of their subject-matter, do not treat of the Great War at all; such, for example, are certain books on morals, politeness, ancient and medieval history, philosophy, geography, etc. A few others, from the conscious choice of their authors, either do not refer to the Great War or endeavor obviously to treat of it with judiciousness; such are certain readers which consist of pretty and familiar stories and fanciful descriptions, all of pacific character; such too are certain historical texts, notably two or three used in the higher course or in secondary school, and marked by apparent fairmindedness. But the majority of readers and texts of modern history used in the elementary primary schools, together with numerous supplementary books, are characterized by several nationalist tendencies: they hold Germany, and Germany only, responsible for the war; they discuss previous aggressions of Germany against France and do not speak of any aggression ever committed by France; they picture Germany as "barbarous," "warlike," and "brutal," and France as "great," "pacific," "just," and "generous"; they stress German "atrocities" during the war and French "heroism"; they dwell on French suffering and sacrifice; they mention assistance which France received from her allies but attribute the main cause of Germany's defeat to French leadership, bravery, and brains; they glorify the victory, and the recovery of Alsace-Lorraine; they pronounce the treaty of Versailles a peace of justice and declare that as France has won the war so it remains for her "to win the peace"; they leave an impression that Germany is still strong and crafty, that she is bent upon revenge, and that, while the League of Nations may be a promise of a better day in the distant future, the only means right now of thwarting the German menace is for France to rely upon her own military might.

Sixthly, we are impressed most of all by what French textbooks as a whole do not say. By their omissions they make it difficult for a French youth to be critical of French institutions or conduct, or to know of any services rendered to the world by modern foreign nations, or to understand how or why a foreign people should love its fatherland and serve its national government. One does not acquire, at least from elementary primary textbooks, any special knowledge of any non-French language, literature, history, government, or culture. Nor does one gain any idea of the complexity of individual differences and party-strife within a foreign country, for all primary texts tend to personify and thus to simplify every foreign nation and to convey to the student the impression, for example, that all Germans always have been and still are of one mind and heart in furthering whatever " Germany " has done or is supposed to be planning to do. It is the same in the case of " France." By means of simplification and personification, all party-differences, social differences, and local differences are omitted or glossed over in the interest of national solidarity and in the name of the fatherland one and indivisible.

5

We have now spoken of the national organization of the French schools and of the programs of study and the textbooks used in them. It remains to say something of the teaching-staff. For it is the teachers who carry the governmental prescriptions into effect, who expound and interpret the textbooks, and who exert a special influence, secondary only to the influence of the family, upon the children of the French nation.

The teaching-staff of the public national schools of France is an army in itself. In 1924–1925 there were 44,323 men and

76,414 women [15] engaged in teaching in the public maternal and elementary primary schools: a total of 120,737 teachers of public primary education. In addition, there were 3,439 teachers in the higher primary schools, 1,036 teachers in the primary normal schools, and an uncertain number of teachers in private primary schools, in secondary schools both public and private, and in institutions of higher learning.

Public primary teachers, who constitute the mass of the French teaching-staff, are state functionaries and are appointed by national officials from persons who meet certain legal requirements. The candidates must be French citizens, at least eighteen years of age; they may not be clergymen or in receipt of any remuneration or gratuity from a church, and they may not engage in commercial or industrial professions or hold major administrative positions; they must possess certain educational qualifications. All must possess the higher brevet, showing satisfactory completion of the seven years of compulsory elementary schooling and four years beyond in higher primary or secondary schools; in addition, the lower grade of teachers, the so-called *stagiaires,* must have completed at least one year's study in a primary normal school, while the higher grade of teachers, the so-called *titulaires,* must have obtained a " certificate of pedagogic aptitude," showing satisfactory completion of courses equivalent to those of the normal and higher primary schools.

In other words, every primary teacher in France, for seven years, as a child, has followed the strongly nationalist program and has studied the markedly nationalist textbooks of the elementary primary schools, and, in adolescence, has been exposed for three or four years to the somewhat broader and less nationalist training of the higher primary school, lycée, or collège, and, then, as immediate preparation for teaching, has had from one to three years of training in a primary normal school. In France there are 170 of these normal schools — 85 for men, and 85 for women

[15] It is interesting to note that until 1902 the number of men-teachers considerably exceeded the number of women-teachers, but that since then the number of women-teachers has steadily increased while the number of men-teachers has correspondingly declined.

— one for each sex in almost every département in the country. They are maintained by the State; their teachers are appointed by the Minister of Public Instruction; and their students, admitted only in such numbers as the probable vacancies in the primary teaching-staff would seem to warrant, are subsidized by the State.

The program of studies for the primary normal schools is as carefully and elaborately prescribed by the Minister of Public Instruction as that for the elementary schools previously discussed. The latest revision of the program, a revision of 1921, calls for seven hours of class-room work a week for three years, in the " national " subjects of history and French; seven hours, in mathematics and science; two hours, in pedagogical psychology and sociology; two hours, in a modern foreign language; eleven hours, in music and vocational studies; and a varying amount of practice-teaching.[16] The three-year program of history presents a survey of world history: (1) ancient and medieval history; (2) modern history to 1815, with some source-readings and with special attention to French history; and (3) modern history since 1815, closing with a study of the rôle of France in the world. The accompanying three-year program of French prescribes study of French composition and grammar and the reading in French translation of literary masterpieces, of which about two-thirds are by French writers and one-third by non-French writers, the latter consisting, in addition to several ancient Greeks and Romans, of Ariosto, Cervantes, Shakespeare, and Goethe.

It will be noted that the teacher-training in the normal schools, according to the official programs, is not particularly nationalist. The historical textbooks used in them, moreover, are of the same grade as those used in the higher primary and secondary schools and as such are considerably less nationalist than the general run of historical texts employed in the elementary primary schools. Primary teachers, as a group, can hardly be expected to free

[16] See *Plan d'Études et Programmes d'Enseignement des Écoles normales primaires d'Instituteurs et d'Institutrices* (Paris, Delalain, 1922); Bernard, *Comment on devient un Éducateur* (Paris, Nathan, 1924) ; P. Lapie, *Pédagogie française* (Paris, Alcan, 1920); Lucien Poincaré, *Education, Science, Patrie* (Paris, Flammarion, 1926).

themselves entirely from the influence of their national environment or from specifically nationalist influences of their early
training in home, school, and society. But it must be said that
the normal schools do not seek to reëmphasize or strengthen the
nationalist training already received; on the contrary, they aim
chiefly to give professional and vocational guidance of a utili-
tarian sort, and, wherever they touch on " national " subjects,
they tend to broaden the horizon and to afford a glimpse of the
world as well as a view of France. Nevertheless, in the actual
teaching of most subjects in the normal school, much emphasis is
put upon the national duties and obligations of prospective
teachers in the elementary schools, and if these teachers are
pointed toward a mission of humanitarianism rather than of militarism, their mission is fundamentally conceived of as national.

6

Considerations of the above sort may account for the fact
that a large number of primary public-school teachers in France
are " radical," if not downright " pacifist," and at the same time,
in a certain sense, nationalist. For example, the organization
known as the "National Syndicate of Public-School Teachers
of France and her Colonies" ("Syndicat National des Institutrices et Instituteurs de France et ses Colonies "), which claims
(1927) a membership of 78,000 men and women teachers in the
public elementary primary schools, is distinctly radical: founded
in 1901 under the title of " Fédération des Amicales d'Instituteurs," it was reorganized in 1920 under its present name as a
trade-union and was affiliated in 1925 with the Socialist " Confédération Générale du Travail." It is strikingly pacifist as well
as radical: in 1924 its Congress adopted the following resolutions:

(1) Instruction in history should remain a part of the curriculum
of the elementary schools, for it is necessary in order to train the child
to be an enlightened worker and an informed citizen of tomorrow, instructed as to his rights and conscious of his duties; (2) Such instruction should be truthful and should repudiate the falsehoods which too
often dishonor it; (3) Instruction in history should try to show human
evolution toward progress and justice and to pay chief attention to the
economic and social life of the past, showing the rôle which France

has played in this evolution and indicating what France owes to other peoples and what she has given to the world; it should be absolutely pacifist and should reject everything that might tend to instill in the young a hatred for foreigners; it should have no other object than to teach truth and human fraternity, and thereby to prepare the child for a greater, indeed for an international, society. . . .

And to carry these resolutions into effect, the same Congress directed a special committee to prepare and publish two new textbooks: " (1) for children, a brief history of man and human progress, composed of a few salient facts marking the different stages in the progress of humanity; and (2) for adults, a history of peoples, labor, and civilization, impregnated with love of humanity, hatred of war, and passion for justice, and with the great hope of peace on earth by means of the workers of all nations." But with all its pacifism and radicalism the Syndicate is pronouncedly national and even nationalist: it advocates unceasingly the *école unique* for France, that is, the extension of a centralized governmental monopoly of all primary education by abolishing primary instruction in the semi-private lycées and collèges; it is anti-Catholic and fights the private schools; it demands (since 1922) the abolition of religious instruction in the public schools of Alsace-Lorraine and the introduction into the recovered provinces of the centralized national lay system of French primary education; and among the resolutions adopted by its Congress in 1924 is this, that "one should try to stress as much as possible general or national history rather than local history."

An even more radical group of French teachers, though very much smaller and less influential, is the "Federation of Educational Unions" ("Fédération des Syndicats de l'Enseignement") an international Communist organization, founded in 1919, in close relationship with Moscow. The Federation advocates working-class internationalism and the dictatorship of the proletariat; it denounces "imperialism"; and it declares that "the history taught in the schools ought to become authentic, that is, ought to be the history of class struggles." The Federation carries on a campaign against chauvinist textbooks, often quoting the words of Anatole France, "burn all books which teach hate," and has recently published an historical textbook embodying its peculiar ideas. At the same time, the Federation opposes private schools of all sorts and champions the *école unique* and a more uniform, an even more highly centralized, system of public schools throughout France.

A large number of French primary teachers do not adhere to the Communist " Federation " or to the Socialist " National Syndicate," and among the numerous members of the latter there are doubtless some who pay little heed to its counsels and resolutions. The more moderate views of a large number (probably the majority) of the teachers are expressed by such an organization as the " National Union of Members of Public Instruction " (" Union Nationale des Membres de l'Enseignement Public "), founded in 1925 and open to secondary and university, as well as to primary, teachers. On the question of chauvinist textbooks, a special committee of the National Union reported in 1927, in part as follows:

The Committee has examined the question of bellicose texts. It finds that there actually are texts which were hurriedly written in the fever of the war and which do not always treat of events with the serenity which is to be expected from educators nor with the documentation which the historical method demands. These books ought to be recast or withdrawn from circulation. . . . At the same time it is not to be denied that Germany wanted, prepared, and began the World War and that in waging it she resorted to all manner of barbarous practices so long as she thought she could win. To deny this would be to ignore the pre-war German literature which preached aggression and in advance justified atrocities. Note, for instance, among this type of literature, the works of General Bernhardi. On the other hand, it is not chauvinism for a text to carry extracts from Maurice Barrès, Moselly, or Bazin. It is not chauvinism to relate the heroic deeds of our soldiers or to affirm the valor of our leaders. There is something above militarism and pacifism; that something is love of truth and the strict application of historical method.

There are several other organizations of teachers [17] : some for public primary teachers; some for teachers in secondary schools

[17] In Appendix B, following the digest of typical textbooks, will be found a list of the more important teacher-organizations, with brief mention of the character and principal activities of each. This list has been prepared in consultation

and universities; some for private-school teachers. The last named are likely to be nationalist in the sense of being intensely patriotic to the French nation, but they are quite anti-nationalist in the sense of being opposed to the *école unique* or any other extension of centralized national monopoly of education and in favor of educational autonomy of Alsace-Lorraine and a larger measure of educational freedom throughout France. Most of the teacher-organizations of all kinds are far more interested, however, in the economic betterment of their individual members and in the pedagogical and scientific improvement of the profession than in questions of war and peace, nationalism and internationalism. The ordinary teacher, no matter how skeptical he or she may be of certain details in this or that textbook, is basically patriotic and can be counted on to conduct French boys and girls, without shock, along the path of national studies clearly marked for them by the central governmental authorities of the French national State and to utilize as aids in their course such textbooks as are at hand.

Yet many public-school teachers in France are dissatisfied with the chauvinism which has characterized probably a majority of the textbooks, and, backed by several important teacher-organizations and by a gradually moderating state of public opinion since the war, they have demanded and secured the writing of a few new textbooks and the revision of certain old ones, almost invariably with a view to expurgating extreme nationalism and stressing the League of Nations and other factors and agencies of internationalism. It appears now (1929) that French textbooks, particularly those of history and geography, are, in the main, less bellicose and less emotional than the corresponding textbooks of ten or twenty years ago.[18]

---

with M. LeBrun, Director of the Musée Pédagogique, and M. Bellette, secretary of the Bureau International des Fédérations Nationales du Personnel de l'Enseignement Secondaire Public.

[18] This has just been pointed out and emphasized by M. J. Prudhommeaux, in an essay (1928) supplementary to the *Enquête sur les Livres scolaires d'après-Guerre* which he edited and published through the Dotation Carnegie in 1923. See also Troisième Congrès International d'Éducation Morale, *L'Esprit international et l'Enseignement de l'Histoire* (Paris, Delachaux & Niestle, 1923).

Amendment of textbooks in the direction of greater internationalism and pacifism has been accomplished, however, against energetic protests of nationalist groups inside, and more often outside, the teaching profession. Certain patriotic societies and certain newspapers, both royalist and republican,[19] have been markedly critical of the more recent developments. The attempt of the Communist federation of teachers to bring out an " unpatriotic " textbook of French history has met with pronounced opposition in private and official circles.[20]

The French Government has pursued in this matter, during the last three or four years, a middle course. On the one hand, it has at least tacitly acquiesced in the revision of textbooks and on several occasions has actually taken steps to discourage chauvinism in the schools. On the other hand, it has repeatedly used its authority to discipline Communist or other " unpatriotic " teachers and has given no sign of any intention to revise the program and curriculum of the public-school system in an international direction. Two random quotations from French newspapers in the month of April, 1927, may illustrate the twofold attitude of the Minister of Public Instruction. The first is from *Le Matin* of April 8:

M. Herriot, Minister of Public Instruction, having caused an examination to be made by his officials into the case of M. Laurent, in charge of a course at the Lycée of Épinal, who delivered at Châtel-sur-Moselle a partisan speech at the obsequies of a militant Communist, has decided to proceed with his deposition from the office of professor. He will be demoted to a collège according to the usual procedure. The Cabinet Council ratified yesterday the proposal of M. Herriot.

The second quotation is from *Le Quotidien* of April 14:

A Deputy asked in writing the following question of the Minister of Public Instruction: " Are there any official texts, instructions, or

[19] Typical of such newspapers are *L'Action Française, Le Figaro, L'Écho de Paris,* and *Le Temps. Le Temps,* for example, has carried a series of leading editorials during the past two or three years on " Pacifisme scolaire," finding fault with the very modest *Enquête* of M. J. Prudhommeaux, criticizing the pacific resolutions of teacher-organizations, denouncing in unmeasured terms Communist agitation in the schools, and calling upon the Government to suppress pacifist propaganda.

[20] This textbook is referred to above, p. 60, and in Appendix A, p. 361 below.

circulars relative to the teaching of the war of 1914–1918 in primary schools? Is it not desirable to restrain certain chauvinistic incitements in the schools? " M. Herriot replied that no complaint had reached him of any chauvinist incitement in the schools.

Revision of textbooks and direct action on the part of school-teachers may gradually affect to a considerable extent the subject-matter taught in the French schools and the manner in which it is taught. It is probable, in fact, that a kind of internationalism will enter more and more through the French schools into French popular consciousness, into French national psychology.

But so long as the educational system of France endures in its present form, with its extreme centralization and its extreme dependence on the State, and with the avowed and generally accepted purpose of training children for French citizenship, it will continue in the future the work which it has so successfully performed during the past two generations, the work of " making " patriotic Frenchmen, the work of transforming a large aggregation of individuals into a compact mass that, regardless of how it may differ about innumerable other matters, is one in its cherishing of French traditions and in its supreme loyalty to France and to the French national State.

CHAPTER IV

THE ARMY AND NAVY

I

THE vast educational system which the French State directs aims to make patriotic Frenchmen of all the children of the country. The system of armaments which the French State maintains seeks to confirm the national patriotism of the young men of the country by training them to be guardians of internal peace and repellers of foreign invasion.[1]

Far older than the tradition of public schooling in France is the tradition of national fighting. Ever since the time of Clovis in the fifth century, ever since there has been a " France," fighting or preparedness for fighting has been a fairly constant attribute of the country and its people, and multitudinous have been the persons whom modern French patriots extol as national military heroes: Clovis, Charles Martel, Charlemagne, Hugh Capet, Godfrey of Bouillon, Louis VI, Louis VII, Philip Augustus, Louis IX, Du Guesclin, Joan of Arc, Francis I, Bayard, Guise and Coligny, Henry IV, Turenne, Vauban, Louis XIV, Marshal Saxe, Dumouriez, Carnot, the great Napoleon and his numerous Marshals, Macmahon, Joffre, Foch, Pétain, Galliéni. The historian Lemontey, writing over a hundred years ago, declared that " an invincible horror of all foreign domination " and " a love of war and an intoxication of success " were inherent French traits which were to be found equally under the grossness of barbarian customs, in the enthusiasm of the age of chivalry, and among the refinements of elegant civilization.[2] Another French historian,

---

[1] See *Sur le Front de France: Almanach du Combattant* (Paris, Éditions du Combattant, annually).

[2] P. E. Lemontey, *Essai sur l'Établissement monarchique de Louis XIV* (1818). *Oeuvres*, 5 vols. (1829), Vol V, pp. 5-9.

writing at about the same time, was even more precise: " The Frenchman, warlike by temperament, conqueror by origin, fighter by habit, flattering himself, from century to century, from reign to reign, that France would succeed in dominating Europe, attached himself to France by this sentiment; at least this sentiment was, of all ties, the strongest." [3]

Since the close of the Hundred Years' War, in the fifteenth century, the French State has maintained a standing professional army and a regular armed navy; and since the French Revolution, in the latter part of the eighteenth century, the State has assumed that national defense is a national duty of all its citizens, that every able-bodied Frenchman is liable for service in the State's army or navy. And this assumption has been constant, even if its effectiveness has altered, under the various governments which have headed the French State in the nineteenth and twentieth centuries. It has been as much a tenet of Republicans as of Royalists, and of Socialists and Radicals as of Conservatives.

The principle of universal compulsory military service is deeply imbedded in the minds of contemporary Frenchmen. It seems to be the fairest and most logical way, the way most in harmony with the Revolutionary ideals of equality and fraternity, if not of liberty, of supporting the heavy burden of national armaments. That national armaments must be maintained and supported in some way, is likewise a principle with the large majority of Frenchmen, a principle resting on historic tradition and long experience. It was, to a high degree, the national army which created " France " and which has made " Frenchmen." It was, and is, the national army which has preserved the independence and assured the international prestige of France.

France, after all, is a country on the continent of Europe, almost completely surrounded by foreign nationalities — Spanish, Italian, English, and German — and these nationalities more than once in the past have actually warred against France and invaded its territories, and potentially one or another of them may do so

[3] G. H. Roques, " Abbé de Montgaillard," *Revue chronologique de l'Histoire de France depuis la Première Convocation des Notables jusqu'au Départ des Troupes étrangères, 1787–1818* (1820), p. 614.

again in the future. In the case of Frenchmen, with their restricted country and their powerful encompassing neighbors, there is a much more natural and pragmatic reliance on a large army than in the case of Americans, with their extensive country and their few and relatively weak neighbors. Besides, France had once, and now has again, a great overseas colonial empire, and as she lost the first through military and naval weakness, so it is natural that she should seek to retain and develop the second through military and naval strength. Altogether, national "security," with all its implications, is a passionate desire of Frenchmen, and the armaments which, it is hoped, will guarantee it are known to heighten the Frenchman's loyalty to his nationality and his State. No wonder that the French State cherishes its military arm and expends more money on it than on its educational arm.

French faith in armaments has not been shaken by the experiences of the twentieth century, not even by the creation of the League of Nations. French public opinion retains a tenacious grasp on the classical arguments for national military preparedness. Paul Painlevé, a " Radical-Socialiste " and the Minister of War in the Poincaré Cabinet, expressed them clearly before the Chamber of Deputies in 1926:

Despite the work of international concord which France has so assiduously aided, she cannot but be concerned with her own security. This concern is not only a legitimate one but it is an essential element of European stability. Notwithstanding our hope in the efficacy of treaties of arbitration among the peoples of the world and of projects for the reduction of armaments, France in the present state of affairs would commit an imprudent act which might be fatal if she did not hold herself ever ready to do her duty to keep the peace.

To secure the maximum of the nation's resources in men, munitions, and means of production against an eventual aggression, and at the same time to keep order in our colonies and in foreign regions under our charge, is a dual task which no Government should avoid. . . .

France is charged with maintaining order in her overseas possessions, especially in Northern Africa, indispensable for the realization of her mission of civilizing others . . .[4]

[4] Paul Painlevé, *Projet de loi sur l'organisation générale de l'armée* (Chambre des Députés, Session de 1926, No. 2500), pp. 1–2, 5.

The French people as a whole are indeed so thoroughly convinced of the necessity of strong armed forces for national defense, for the "civilization" of colonies, spheres of influence, and protectorates, and for the assurance of internal order that they have acquiesced in the maintenance since the Great War of an army twice the size of any of their neighbors' and a navy equal to Italy's. It is true that there has been a considerable reduction in term of service and number of soldiers on active duty. The survivors of the vast numbers mobilized for the Great War were gradually and mainly disbanded after the Armistice; the term of active training and service for all able-bodied young Frenchmen, which had been fixed in 1913 at three years, was reduced in 1923 to eighteen months, and again in 1928 to one year; and the number of men in the active army correspondingly decreased from 813,029 in 1921 to 733,873 in 1926 and to 590,-000 in 1929.[5]

In fact, the general military law of 1928, sponsored by the prominent Socialist, Paul-Boncour, and piloted by the Radical Minister of War, Paul Painlevé, goes farther than any of its innumerable predecessors in emphasizing the popular responsibility for national defense and the State's autocracy in assuring it.[6] "In times of war," the act provides, "all Frenchmen and all French subjects, as well as all legally constituted bodies, are to participate . . . in the defense of the country or in the maintenance of the country's material life and morale" (art. 1). Under the provisions of the act, the Government is now (1929) organizing, through the several ministries, the "economic, social, intellectual, and moral" resources of the nation and coördinating them with the army and navy (arts. 3 and 4). Of "moral resources" M. Painlevé has written:

It was the admirable morale of the country which allowed us to endure without flinching the surprises of the first days in August and

---

[5] These figures are taken from the *Annuaire Statistique* (Paris, Imprimerie Nationale). They are based upon the provisions of the budget. The Ministry of War reports annually to the Parliament on the military force, but these reports are not published.

[6] Paul-Boncour, *Rapport fait sur l'organisation générale de la nation pour le temps de guerre* (Chambre des Députés, Session de 1927, No. 4018), p. 56.

September, 1914, and then the privations of 1917 and 1918, and finally to hold on a " quarter of an hour " longer than our adversary and to win the war. Too much care cannot be taken in case of another conflict to maintain the moral forces of the nation at the highest possible pitch. This task cannot be performed without the coöperation of all good citizens, particularly without the aid of propaganda, the educational system, and the press.[7]

Under the existing law, when war is declared, the State may contract for or requisition industries, may exploit mines, may take over all private business, may use inventions (art. 10), may demand the coöperation of trade-unions and other societies (the churches, patriotic societies, Masonic lodges, etc.), and may require the active service of any or all Frenchmen (art. 11).

2

The idea of bringing every ounce of the nation's strength into play in case of war is not essentially novel. It is only an extension of the peace-time principle of universal obligatory military service for men, which has been in continuous operation in France for more than fifty years and during the entire history of the Third Republic. At the present time every male citizen must become a soldier, no exception being made for conscientious objectors or for persons who would hire substitutes. Only criminals and the physically unfit can escape the draft, but even here the line is not sharply drawn, a great many of the latter being used in auxiliary services and some of the former being sent to Africa to serve in battalions of light infantry.

Every year a census is made of the young men in France who are nineteen years of age or who will attain that age during the course of the year. A list of such young men in each town is published before the first of June. If any of them believe that they are physically unfit they present themselves for an examination. All men declared fit for military service are called to arms the year following the census, that is, at the age of twenty. They are divided into two contingents, those having been born prior to

[7] *Projet de loi sur l'organisation générale de la nation pour le temps de guerre* (Chambre des Députés, Session de 1925, No. 1879), pp. 25–26.

June 1 being called in May and those born after June 1 being called in November.[8] Provision is made, however, for voluntary enlistment at the age of eighteen, and for the postponement of service up to the age of twenty-five in the case of an individual who can show that for reasons of family support, studies, apprenticeship, business affairs, or residence abroad it is not feasible that he serve earlier. Special provision is likewise made for medical, dental, veterinary, and pharmaceutical students, who need not serve before the age of twenty-seven, and for other students, who are permitted to postpone their service for six months so that they may complete the school-year. Two brothers are not required to serve at the same time; and professional sailors serve their time in the navy rather than in the army.

Sailors' names are put on lists ("*l'inscription maritime*") and records are kept of their voyages. They are liable to call for active naval service between the ages of eighteen and fifty, but in times of peace they serve at the same age and for the same length of time as soldiers. If the *inscription maritime* does not provide a sufficient number of men, the Minister of Marine may demand a quota from the yearly military contingent or may accept voluntary enlistments.

French citizens in the colonies are subject to the same military laws as citizens in France.[9] Special laws, however, apply to the indigenous native populations, the requirements varying from colony to colony. In Tunis, Algeria, and Morocco, the natives serve either as voluntary recruits, reënlisted men, or drafted men.[10] In French East Africa and French Equatorial Africa, the normal method of recruitment is by voluntary enlistment, but during the Great War the draft was resorted to as a temporary

[8] Law of April 1, 1923, art. 11. The law of 1928 has changed the age of service from twenty to twenty-one years. This change was recommended by medical men, especially after the experiences of the Moroccan War, in which boys of twenty did not prove strong enough for the severe physical strain. See Paul Bernier, *Rapport fait au nom de la commission de l'armée rélatif au recrutement de l'armée* (Chambre des Députés, Session de 1927, No. 4659), p. 58.

[9] Law of April 1, 1923, art. 98.

[10] See decree of Sept. 8, 1926 as regards Algeria; art. 4, law of Feb. 13, 1923 as regards Morocco; and Charles Rabany, *Le Recrutement de l'Armée* (Paris, Berger-Levrault, 1923), p. 780, as regards Tunis.

expedient. In Senegal, the French military laws are applied to the communes of Dakar, St. Louis, Rufisque, and Gorée and to the descendants of citizens of these towns. In Indo-China, soldiers are recruited by voluntary enlistments and by draft. In almost all of the other colonies there are small groups of native soldiers who serve with the colonial troops. There is also, for colonial service, the famous French Foreign Legion, composed of two regiments whose personnel is an international medley of adventurers and soldiers of fortune.[11]

The system of recruitment which exists in France provides about 270,000 men per class, that is, per year, as may be gathered from the following table:

TABLE V

Class of 1924	Male births in 1904	444,000
	Young men in military census	346,723
	Young men fit for service	293,393
Class of 1925	Male births in 1905	439,000
	Young men in military census	346,887
	Young men fit for service	294,955
Class of 1926	Male births in 1906	436,500
	Young men in military census	350,036
	Young men fit for service	288,688

Although the birth rate in France is steadily decreasing, infant and adolescent mortality is also decreasing, so that up to 1934 the yearly contingent will be above 255,000. From 1934 to 1939 the classes of young men who were born during the war will be called upon to serve, and the contingent of 1936 will decrease to as low as 112,000.[12] Means of bridging this period are already under consideration. It may be accomplished by gradually reducing the age of service to nineteen years or by increasing the length of obligatory training.

As has already been pointed out, the numerical strength of the French army has steadily decreased since the World War, the

[11] Charles Rabany, op. cit., pp. 503–504, 776–779.
[12] Paul Bernier, Rapport relatif au recrutement de l'armée (Chambre des Députés, Session de 1927, No. 4659), pp. 23–24.

budget having provided for 813,029 in 1921 and for 734,813 in 1926. According to a parliamentary report, there were 733,873 men in the army on July 1, 1926. They were obtained by means of the following kinds of recruitment:

TABLE VI[13]

First half of the 1925 class	128,645	
Second half of the 1925 class	134,126	
First half of the 1926 class	100,185	
Enlisted men	31,781	
Reënlisted men of whom 24,335 were *gendarmes* (provincial police) and 2,822 were *gardes républicains* (special Parisian police)	85,538	480,275
Foreigners	18,818	
Native North Africans	96,449	
Native Colonials	46,383	
Irregulars	10,989	172,639
Total men		652,914
Officers		31,572
Total under Minister of War		684,486
Troops in Indo-China, French East Africa, French Equatorial Africa, Madagascar, Pacific Islands, West Indies, and Cameroun, under Minister of Colonies		49,387
Grand Total		733,873

The naval forces for 1926 numbered 4,169 officers and 55,998 men.[14]

Now that the period of obligatory service is reduced to one year, the total force will be considerably decreased. But in order partially to offset this decrease, the law of 1928 has authorized an increase of the number of professional soldiers from 75,000 to 106,000. The army, under the law of 1928, will comprise, in addition to 361,000 Frenchmen (professional or conscripted), 90,000 native North Africans and 85,000 native colonials. This will mean that .925 per cent of the population of France, .96 per cent of the population of Algeria, .92 per cent of that of Tunis, and a smaller percentage of that of the other colonies will be under arms.

[13] These figures are taken from Paul Bernier, *Rapport relatif au recrutement de l'armée,* pp. 13–14.

[14] *Annuaire Statistique, 1925,* " Effectifs de l'armée de mer d'après le projet de budget," p. 297.

The military law of August 7, 1913, which remained in force almost ten years, provided for three years' obligatory service in the active army, eleven years in the reserve of the active army, seven years in the territorial army, and seven years in the reserve of the territorial army. The law of 1923 reduced the period of active service to one year and a half, instituted a period of *disponibilité* of two years, a period of first reserve of sixteen years and a half, and a second reserve of eight years. Although the Army Commission of the Chamber of Deputies has admitted that nine months are enough to train a Frenchman to be a soldier on account of his "intelligence, spirit of initiative, and faculty of assimilation," the law of 1928 provides for a year's period of active service, for three years in the *disponibilité*, sixteen years in the first reserve, and eight years in the second reserve. The period of active service was not reduced any lower because it was thought that to do so would be to reduce the army too much.

The periods of reserve which have been mentioned indicate the order in which men will be called to arms in case of war. Moreover, men who are in the *disponibilité* and the first reserve are subject to supplementary annual training which must not exceed nine weeks.[15]

During the three years' period of service men were allowed a furlough of one hundred and twenty days, exclusive of Sundays and holidays, but when the period was reduced to eighteen months the furlough was decreased to twenty-five days with the possibility of thirty-five as a reward for good behavior. On the other hand, men who are punished by imprisonment for more than one week are forced to serve as many days extra as they have been in prison.

Provision is made for the voluntary enlistment of men after the age of eighteen, such recruits being freed from obligatory service provided they stay in the army at least as long as the time required of drafted men. Considerable effort is made to encourage reënlistment and to this end men are offered increased pay and bonuses, and are promised a professional training in

[15] The law of April 1, 1923, made the maximum period eight weeks, but the law of 1928 increased it to nine.

some trade if they serve at least five years, a sum of money on leaving the army after five years, a pension after fifteen years, and the possibility of one of the many governmental positions reserved for military men.

The French active army consists at the present time (1929) of (1) " metropolitan " troops, (2) " colonial " troops, and (3) a " *force mobile.*" The metropolitan troops are regulars who serve in France and in the French colonial empire of North Africa; they comprise French soldiers, native soldiers of North Africa, and the Foreign Legion. The colonial troops include the soldiers, French and native, who are drafted in the colonies (outside of North Africa), together with a certain number of soldiers from France itself who would normally belong to the metropolitan troops but who are attached to the colonial troops for purposes of solidarity and strength.[16] The *force mobile,* as created by a special law of July 13, 1927, is composed of a select group, mainly native French and professional, whose duty it is to be ever ready on a moment's notice to resist a sudden foreign attack and thereby to enable the slower and more general mobilization of the whole French army to proceed in order.

It was formerly the custom to despatch the older men in each conscript-class to points distant from their homes. In 1911, however, this custom was abandoned, and the location of all conscripts was determined by lot. By the law of 1923, it was provided that married men and men who had had some preliminary military training should serve as near to their homes as possible. Despite these changes, it is still usual for most conscripts to serve away from the locality of their birth, for there is a natural tendency to concentrate troops on the eastern frontier and in large cities and the State recognizes that young men are likely to develop a higher loyalty to France as a whole in measure as they

16 This does not necessarily mean that all Frenchmen in the colonial troops are sent to distant colonies. It would be manifestly absurd, for instance, to send a one-year conscript from France to Indo-China, inasmuch as the trip there and back would consume a large part of his term of service. Frenchmen in the colonial troops are usually stationed at Cherbourg or Toulon or in North Africa and are sent elsewhere only in case of emergency. See Charles Rabany, *op. cit.,* pp. 505–506.

are moved away from their homes and brought into close association with others from all parts of the country.

The " metropolitan " territory, comprising France and Algeria, is divided by the law of 1927 into military " regions," which take the place of the former " *corps d'armée.*" Each region has a commander who superintends the recruitment, training, supply, and other services of the army in his jurisdiction. Each region has normally one " division," subdivided into regiments and companies. The regiment is the most important unit of organization from the standpoint of general morale and individual loyalty: it cherishes particular traditions of past prowess; it possesses a special flag, on which are embroidered the names of famous battles in which it has fought; and the soldier's uniform bears on the lapel the number of the regiment to which he belongs.

3

Most of the conscripts have had no military training when they enter the army, although in view of the present short term of service attempts are being made to give them preliminary instruction. The Army Commission of the Chamber of Deputies is of the opinion that children should be put through a definite program of physical education and that specifically military instruction should begin two years before their period of service. Even the Socialist group in the Chamber would make this preliminary training obligatory.[17]

Up to the present time, however, the task of imparting preliminary military training to boys has been left to private societies. Of these there are in France some 8,000,[18] of which two thousand, representing a membership of 341,000, are federated in the " Union des Sociétés d'Éducation Physique et de Préparation au Service Militaire de France et des Colonies " ; 1,764, with 500,000 members, are united in the " Union des Sociétés de Gymnastique "; others are grouped in the " Fédéra-

---

[17] Paul Bernier, *op. cit.*, pp. 69–71.

[18] Estimate given in *Vers l'Armée,* the official monthly organ of the Fédération Nationale des Sociétés d'Éducation Physique et de Préparation au Service Militaire de France et des Colonies, Jan.–Feb. 1926, p. 1818.

tion Nationale des Sociétés d'Éducation Physique " ; and still others are independent and separate.

The preliminary military instruction usually consists of physical training, the use of arms, and moral and civic education. Under the last heading the boys are taught their " duties to France ":

1. France, our country, is one of the most beautiful and one of the richest countries in the world. It is the country of justice and right. All the generous ideas which make human beings better and happier originated in France.

2. I love my country more than myself because it is she who instructs me, protects me, and guarantees to me all the comforts which I enjoy.

3. My duty towards her consists in obeying her laws, working for her prosperity, and defending her unto death.[19]

Every year in July a great military and athletic field day is held at Paris in the Jardin des Tuileries for the purpose of giving boys and youths a chance to show the results of their preliminary military training. The Government actively encourages this work: it allows the boys who pass elementary examinations after a certain period of preliminary training to select upon their entry into the army the regiment in which they prefer to serve; it gives them the chance of becoming corporals after four months; and it permits them to have ten days' extra furlough.

Furthermore, the Government since 1923 has established a two years' military course in the higher institutions of learning, in order to give French university students a military foundation which will permit them to enter the reserve officers' training corps during part of their period of service and eventually to become reserve officers.[20] This course has been made obligatory in some nineteen schools (École des Chartes, Ecole Normale Supérieure,

[19] Commandant Réal, *Manuel de Préparation militaire élémentaire*, 150th thousand (Épinal, Paul Kahn, 1927), p. 5. See also Louis Vuillemin, *Manuel de Préparation militaire*, 13th edition (Paris, Charles Lavauzelle, 1927), p. 107 *et seq;* and Lieut.-Col. Coste, *L'Éducation physique en France* (Paris, Lavauzelle, n.d.).

[20] See Léon Vignal, *L'Officier de Réserve: ses Droits, ses Prérogatives, ses Devoirs, ses Obligations* (Paris, Charles Lavauzelle, 1927).

École Normale Primaire Supérieure, École Coloniale, etc.) and optional in nearly all the French institutions of higher learning (Universities of Paris, Aix, Algiers, Bordeaux, Strasbourg, etc., École Libre des Sciences Politiques, Écoles Dentaires, etc.)

The instruction in these official military courses is confined largely to technical matters, but according to the government program it includes in the first year three lectures on the Great War. In one of the handbooks prepared for this course may be found the following statement:

> Whatever Germany may pretend, it is to-day formally proved and established:
> That she willed the war;
> That she began it, in her own time, in the most culpable fashion;
> That she wilfully thwarted all attempts which were made to stop it;
> That she violated French territory before the declaration of war;
> Therefore, that she remains for all time responsible for this World War which she willed, prepared, provoked, and imposed.[21]

Despite the efforts of the Government to encourage preliminary military training and despite the strenuous efforts of numerous patriotic societies to stimulate and support it, the large majority of conscripts in every class begin their active service in the army without special knowledge of military affairs. The result is that the army itself gives to most Frenchmen all the military training which they have.

As far as possible the conscripts are attached to services in which they may severally utilize the professional education which they have received as civilians, and this practice is now increasingly stressed because of the short time available for training. The training itself is very largely in the technical arts of war. Throughout the period of army training, however, emphasis is put on " moral education," on discipline, on honor, and on the inculcation of respect for the flag and duty to the nation. Nearly all of this instruction is given verbally, but soldiers' and non-commissioned officers' handbooks give a good indication of its

[21] *Memento d'Instruction militaire générale a l'Usage des jeunes gens suivant les Cours de la Préparation militaire supérieure, Fascicule* No. 2 (Paris, Charles Lavauzelle, 1927), p. 6.

nature. One of these books, an official publication of the Ministry of War, chosen at random from among a great many, imparts the following information:

THE FLAG

For every Frenchman the flag represents France. It bears on one side the two words: " Honor and Country " [Honneur et Patrie], which is the motto of the French army and the rule of every honest man. On the other side are inscribed the principal battles in which the regiment has honored itself and which all the soldiers ought to know in memory of their predecessors. . . .

All military men must salute the flag. All civilians who spontaneously uncover before it do their duty as Frenchmen.

THE FATHERLAND

The Fatherland [La Patrie] is the native soil. It is the land of our fathers which we should leave to our sons with all that it holds: our hearts and our tombs.

It is the country of France, with its mild climate, its shores, its plains, and its mountains. It is the sphere of our daily life: our houses, our fields, our workshops, our factories. It is everything which we feel in common: sufferings and joys, remembrances and affections, disappointments and hopes.

It is the creative genius of the race, its cult of beauty and of glory, its ideal of justice, its beliefs, its laws and its customs. It is the clarity of the French language. It is everything which our ancestors have acquired after centuries of effort and endurance: our institutions, our liberties and our rights, our security and our independence. It is our whole history with its triumphs and with its reverses.

For this heritage which we receive at birth, we ought in return to love our Fatherland, to serve it faithfully, to submit to its laws, and to take up arms to defend it when it is attacked. Its greatness and its force, realized by the union of all its energies, are the guardians of our property.

The love of the Fatherland is the source of all virtues. It lifts the soldier to the heights by inspiring him to sacrifice his life. This love is innate in every Frenchman who feels the heart-beat in his breast. One must, however, have crossed the frontiers, lived in other climates, and followed roads which are not those of France in order really to know what attaches us to our native land. We suffer when far from our Fatherland, and when we return to it we are like an invalid who has been restored to health. Our enemies themselves know how sweet it is to live here, how beautiful, fertile, and attractive it is.

A famous foreigner could say: every man has two fatherlands, his own and France. We should be proud of the French Fatherland, which has always been the leader of human conscience and dignity. It has sponsored the noblest ideas and has poured out without measure its gold and its blood for altruistic causes. Its brilliant genius, so attractive and so seductive, the true home of intelligence and feeling, radiates over the whole world the glory of the French name.[22]

Besides the direct attempts which are made to imbue soldiers with ardent patriotism, there are factors in military life which operate indirectly in the same direction. Merely to dress a man in a uniform gives him a feeling of personal importance and *esprit de corps*. Then to have him march in the famous review at Longchamps on July 14, or along the Champs-Elysées on November 11, between columns of cheering citizens, behind a streaming tricolor, keeping step to martial strains, and led by officers on nervous mounts, is to raise the average human being into the realm of emotional patriotism. Men in uniform are apt to be flattered by the ladies and petted by the populace. If they wear decorations such as the Croix de Guerre or even a simple fourragère, their patriotic significance is intensified.

In addition to the foregoing factors, the young soldier usually gets a patriotic stimulus from visiting the cities and viewing the wonders of his country, which if he were not a soldier he might never be able to know. And in daily disciplined contact with a large number of other young soldiers from quite diverse parts of France, he commonly loses a good deal of his localism and provincialism and acquires a corresponding accession of national feeling. Many a young soldier, moreover, must be influenced, consciously or unconsciously, by the especially patriotic training and example of the army officers who are over him and who are themselves professional military functionaries of the centralized national State.

[22] *Manuel du Gradé d'Infanterie* (Paris, Berger-Levrault, 1927), pp. 43–45.

4

The direction and control of the armed forces of France is centered in the " Conseil Supérieur de la Défense Nationale," which is composed of the President of the Republic (as presiding officer), the President of the Council of Ministers, the Ministers of War, Marine, Colonies, Foreign Affairs, Finance, Interior, and Public Works, and, in a consultative capacity, the Vice-President of the " Conseil Supérieur de la Guerre " and the Vice-President of the " Conseil Supérieur de la Marine." [23]

The high command of the army is vested in the Superior Council of War, composed of the Minister of War, the Marshals of France (the highest military grade in the army), and twelve generals of division. The Vice-President of this Council is commander-in-chief of the French forces in time of war. The corresponding authority for the navy is the Superior Council of Marine, composed of the Minister of Marine and six vice-admirals. Under these bodies is the regular hierarchy of officers more or less common to all armies and navies: generals, colonels, majors, captains, and lieutenants of the active army and of the reserve; and vice-admirals, captains, commanders, ensigns, etc., of the navy.

For the training of officers, the State maintains a large number of special schools of various grades. The most elementary is the École Militaire Enfantine Hériot at La Boissière (Seine-et-Oise), a primary school for orphans of military men. Most of the boys in this institution pass on to one or another of the preparatory military schools (" Écoles Militaires Préparatoires "), where they are joined by sons of other military men and by other boys whose parents are bent upon fitting them for an army career.

The " preparatory " schools are seven in number: four " écoles de base " (grounding schools) at Rambouillet (Seine-et-

---

[23] The Conseil Supérieur de la Défense Nationale was created by decree of April 3, 1906 and was reorganized by decree of Nov. 17, 1921. The Conseil Supérieur de la Guerre was created by law of July 27, 1872 and reorganized by decree of April 6, 1906. The Conseil Supérieur de la Marine was reorganized Sept. 12, 1924.

Oise), Les Andelys (Eure), Billon (Puy-de-Dôme), and Sainte-Hippolyte-du-Fort (Gard), which give the "higher course" of the elementary primary schools and the first year of the higher primary schools; two " *écoles de perfectionnement* " at Autun (Saône-et-Loire) and at Tulle (Corrèze), which afford a secondary education, the former emphasizing topography and fencing, and the latter stressing mechanical and electrical training; and finally the school known as the "Prytanée Militaire" at La Flèche (Sarthe), of the same grade as a lycée, which prepares boys directly for the great military schools. At eighteen years of age a pupil in any of these seven "preparatory" schools must enlist in the army or reimburse the State the cost of his instruction.

The next group of schools consists of the so-called " *écoles de formation.*" It includes the great military schools for training students to become commissioned officers, the officers' training schools for non-commissioned officers who have worked their way up from the ranks, and the special technical schools for artillery, aviation, tanks, etc. The great military schools are L'École Polytechnique at Paris, L'École Spéciale Militaire at Saint-Cyr-l'École (Seine-et-Oise), and L'École du Service de la Santé Militaire (for prospective officers in the medical corps) at Lyons. The first two are peculiarly important for this study because it is in them, along with Saint-Maixent,[24] that most officers receive their training.

L'École Polytechnique, an institute of technology, trains military engineers, and L'École Spéciale Militaire at Saint-Cyr trains field officers. Entrance to both schools is by means of competitive examinations. Candidates for the former must be between seventeen and twenty years of age and for the latter between eighteen and twenty-one. The period of attendance is two years, the graduates of Saint-Cyr being required to enlist in the army for at least six years. Graduates of L'École Polytechnique may enter civil life after one year's service in the army and if they choose to do so they then become reserve officers. Saint-Cyr attracts the sons of a great many families rich in military and aristocratic traditions. One has but to read the list of gradu-

[24] Men who have risen from the ranks are trained at Saint-Maixent.

ates published annually in the *Journal Officiel* to realize this fact. Nevertheless, there are many scholarships which permit sons of poor families to receive a military education at Saint-Cyr. As a result of the competitive examinations of 1924, the Minister of War granted 220 complete scholarships, with outfit, 3 without outfit, 10 half-scholarships with outfit, and 4 half-scholarships with half-outfit. Even for those students who receive no direct aid from the State, the cost of a year's training is relatively low, having been raised in 1924 from 1,000 to 1,400 francs (exclusive of outfit). Despite the low cost, there have been since the war only about two candidates for each available place, whereas in 1889 there were six. One result has been a decline in the calibre of students. Another result has been a " crisis of recruitment " which constitutes a grave military problem of the post-war period. It is doubtless to be explained in large part by the fact that army officers are very badly paid.[25]

The Polytechnic and Saint-Cyr do not furnish a sufficient number of officers to staff the large French army; and the deficiency has to be made up by another group of institutions which are open to non-commissioned officers who have worked their way up from the ranks. There are seven such institutions: L'École Militaire d'Infanterie at Saint-Maixent (Deux-Sèvres), L'École Militaire de Cavalerie at Saumur (Maine-et-Loire), L'École Militaire d'Artillerie at Poitiers (Vienne), L'École Militaire du Genie, L'École Militaire de l'Aéronautique, l'École de Gendarmerie at Versailles, and l'École d'Administration Militaire at Vincennes. They provide an opportunity for men to become officers who are unable to pass the entrance examinations at the "great schools." Sons of military families often take advantage of this opportunity, if they fail to obtain admission to Saint-Cyr or to the Polytechnic. The course lasts one year, graduates becoming commissioned officers.

The third category of the *"écoles de formation"* are the " schools of application," whither officers may go for practical training. There are eight such schools: Le Centre d'Études d'Infanterie, Le Centre d'Études des Chars de Combat, Le Centre

25 See below, pp. 86–87.

d'Études Aéronautiques, and L'École d'Application du Génie at Versailles, L'École d'Application d'Artillerie, L'École d'Application du Service de Santé Militaire at Paris, and L'École d'Application du Service de Santé des Troupes Coloniales at Marseilles. Besides these schools there are seventeen of a more special and technical nature dealing with such matters as artillery fire, rifle fire, defense against aerial attacks, liquid fire, etc., and still others known as " écoles de perfectionnement " which exist for reserve officers who attend lectures at them about twice a month.[26]

Officers are prepared in special schools for the high command of the army. L'École Supérieure de Guerre at Paris trains men for the general staff in a two years' course.[27] At Metz there is Le Centre d'Études Tactiques d'Artillerie which instructs officers in the use of artillery. And at Paris is Le Centre des Hautes Études Militaires where a selected group of about thirty officers (generals or colonels) are instructed each year in strategy and manœuvres and where officers may study the political, social and economic aspects of war. This is one of the highly exceptional schools which are not open to foreigners.

A similar but smaller group of schools exists for naval training. L'Établissement des Pupilles de la Marine (located at Villeneuve near Brest) trains boys from thirteen to fifteen years of age in the elements of naval warfare. The naval counterpart of Saint-Cyr is L'École Navale at Brest. Students having completed here the two years of instruction, enlist in the navy as ensigns for six years. An opportunity to become officers is afforded sailors who work their way up in the service at L'École des Élèves Officiers de Marine. In order to give the graduates of L'École Navale and those of L'École Polytechnique who enlist in the navy and even those of L'École des Élèves Officiers a practical training, there are a number of special and technical schools. At the top are two institutions at Paris: L'École de Guerre Navale, to prepare officers for the general staff; and Le Centre des Hautes

---

[26] For further details, consult C. Richard, *L'Enseignement en France* (Paris, Armand Colin, 1925), pp. 503–507.

[27] See A. Marchand, *Méthode de Préparation à l'École supérieure de Guerre* (Paris, Charles Lavauzelle, n.d.).

Études Navales, to train a limited number of men for the high command of the navy.[28]

It is almost impossible to determine how many pupils there are each year in all of the military and naval schools, but it is certain that almost all of the 31,572 army officers and the 4,169 naval officers in service in 1926 [29] passed through at least one of these schools.

It is also very difficult to ascertain how much time is devoted in the military and naval schools specifically to the formation of a peculiarly French national psychology. It is certain that the officer-teachers are vigorously patriotic, and that the textbooks used in the military and naval schools are even more nationalist than those employed in the public schools. The occasional publication of lectures delivered in army schools doubtless gives further indication of the general spirit which pervades such schools and dominates the training of their students, the future officers of the French army and as such the leaders and trainers of millions of young men. A fairly typical example of this kind of publication is afforded by the lectures delivered at Saint-Maixent in 1910 and at Saint-Cyr in 1911 by Lieutenant Jean Taboureau, Assistant Professor of Professional Morale at Saint-Cyr, and published in 1911. From these lectures, the following illustrative extract is taken:

Who will oppose the criminal work [of anti-patriotic trade-unionists]? The philosophers? The publicists? The teachers, the professors? Yes, without doubt. But you also, gentlemen, born educators of soldiers; on you devolves the mission of fashioning in the young men of France a military soul, that is to say, a French soul.

Therefore prepare yourselves to fight anti-patriotism. In this new struggle the perfected machine of modern warfare is of no avail. One must adopt other methods. You ought no longer to be animated by the noble fury of the combatant blindly bent on the destruction of his enemies. You should have the holy ardor of the apostle. Trade-unionist workers with anti-patriotic tendencies whom you may by chance encounter are not enemies to be slain: they are hearts to be won, and

---

[28] For further details see C. Richard, *op. cit.*, pp. 512–522.

[29] These figures are taken from Paul Bernier, *Rapport relatif au recrutement de l'armée*, pp. 13–14, and from *Annuaire Statistique, 1925* (Paris, Imprimerie Nationale), pp. 295, 297.

the finest conquest which you can make in respect of them is to lead them to share your patriotic faith. . . .

You will say to the anti-patriots, or rather you will prove to young soldiers, that without society, that is, without a fatherland, human life is obviously cramped in its activity, menaced in its development, and threatened even in its existence. But how can this society, without which man is unable to live a full life, how can it attain its fullest development — the happiness of its members — if the members do not observe a minimum of moral conduct? If they are disloyal, lazy, or unjust, society dies. . . .

To the children of the mother-country you will explain that to serve France is a way of collaborating in the good of humanity and for us Frenchmen the best way. To love France, her earth, her waters, her forests, her mountains, the sea which bathes her coasts, the sky which lights her, the steeples of her villages, her towns feverish with movement and noise, her cities darkened by the smoke of factories, her art as logical and harmonious as that of Greece and as vigorous as that of Rome; to love her language, her alert spirit, and her politeness which makes her one of the most gracious nations of the world, is for one to remain faithful to his race, to his ancestors, whether humble or glorious, to his family, to his blood, and to himself.[30]

Commissioned officers of the armed forces constitute a remarkably homogeneous class, almost a caste. Their solidarity is a natural outcome of the circumstances that many of them are sons of officers, that all of them have received a special education and have developed an *esprit de corps* in military schools, that they continue throughout their career to be marked off from the ordinary run of civilians by uniforms, by common professional interests, and by particular traditions and peculiar usages. The State treats them as especially honorable functionaries, but, at the same time, emphasizes their exceptional position and class-consciousness by depriving them of the right to vote and by forbidding them to publish books, to make public speeches, to attend meetings of a political character, or to join societies, without the express authorization of the Minister of War.[31] They may not even marry without the permission of the Minister of

[30] Lieutenant Jean Taboureau, *Le Sophisme antipatriotique, Réplique aux Syndicalistes* (Paris, Charles Lavauzelle, 1911), pp. 36–38.

[31] See the law of April 1, 1923, art. 1, and the decree of May 30, 1924, on discipline in the army.

War.[32] They are the servants of the Government of the day; they are also, above quarrelling parties and changing governments, the official representatives of the France of the past and the future.

There are some societies which commissioned officers are encouraged to join and which have in general a pronounced military and patriotic character. There is, for instance, the Legion of Honor, which, though not exclusively military, is largely so; the Minister of War is allowed to nominate a thousand new members every year; and almost every Grand Chancellor of the Legion since its establishment in Napoleonic times has been an army officer. There are, too, the alumni associations of the several military and naval schools.[33] There are, moreover, for the fostering of the preliminary military training of the youth of the nation, certain societies to which army officers are permitted to adhere. Finally, the Ministry of War has authorized the establishment of officers' clubs, such as "Le Cercle Militaire" in Paris where regular officers may enter into close social relationship with their fellows. Among the even more significant societies for reserve officers, the most important are "La Société des Officiers de Complément de France" and "L'Union Nationale des Officiers de Réserve."[34] The statement of aims of the former of these reserve organizations indicates the general nature of most of the societies to which military and naval officers belong: "We aim to maintain among reserve officers the good fellowship of the

[32] Decrees of June 16 and August 28, 1808, suspended during the Great War but renewed April 28, 1921. Even non-commissioned officers may not marry without the permission of the Council of Administration of their Corps. A similar rule obtains for naval officers. *Circular of the Minister of Marine*, September 20, 1885.

[33] Among them are: "La Saint-Cyrienne," 12 rue de Bellechasse, Paris (General des Garets, president); "La Saint-Maixentaise," 15 rue César-Franck, Paris (General Dataille, president); "L'Association Amicale des Anciens Élèves des Écoles Militaires Préparatoires et des Anciens Enfants de Troupe," 17 Avenue de l'Opéra, Paris (M. Pastre, president); and "L'Association Amicale des Anciens Élèves du Prytanée Militaire de la Flèche," 185 rue de Grenelle, Paris (General Eon, president).

[34] The former maintains headquarters at 26 Galerie Montpensier, Paris, and publishes a monthly organ, *L'Horizon*. The latter has its headquarters at 17 Avenue de l'Opéra, Paris, and publishes a monthly organ, *L'Officier de Réserve*.

battlefields, to preserve and honor the memory of the heroic dead, and to perpetuate among our members, along with the cult of honor and patriotism, the traditions of military valor, bravery, and self-sacrifice."

The position of army officers in France since the Great War is not altogether enviable. It is true that military prestige, which a Louis XIV and a Napoleon won for France but which suffered eclipse in the disaster of 1870, was regained and magnified during the World War, and that it not only has brought lasting glory to a Joffre, " the victor of the Marne," to a Pétain, " the soul of Verdun's defense," to a Foch, " the master mind of the Allies' command," to the remembrance of a Galliéni and many another veteran officer, but it has also shed a reflected glory upon all contemporary French officers. Yet French officers are now worse off, economically, than at any other time since the Great Revolution. During the vast struggle of 1914–1918 very many men became officers, and upon the conclusion of hostilities a relatively large number of them remained in service. This fact, coupled with the ensuing general decrease in the size of the army, has resulted in the delaying of promotion. Besides, the salaries of army and navy officers have always been rather low, and since the Great War the nominal raising of such salaries has not nearly kept pace with the actual decline in value of the franc. In 1927 second lieutenants received, depending upon their duties, the number of their children, and the length of their service, from 865 to 1,533 francs a month; captains, from 962 to 1,911 francs; colonels, from 3,435 to 3,694 francs; and generals of divisions, from 5,659 to 5,748 francs.[35] It is obvious that a service which pays at the top only some $230 a month is not a very attractive one for ambitious young men of limited means. There is no doubt that a very large number of officers of the French army and navy have remained at their posts at great personal financial sacrifice, and only because of sheer sentiment, professional or patriotic (and probably both). There can hardly be any more

[35] Decree and Ministerial Instruction of January 23, 1927, published in *Soldes et Indemnités* (Paris, Charles Lavauzelle, 1927), pp. 52–54. The American equivalent is based on stabilized rates.

convincing proof than this of the supreme national loyalty to France which has been implanted in the armed force and which actuates its officers.

5

What is the patriotic and nationalist effect of compulsory military training upon the whole rank and file of Frenchmen? It is impossible to guage it with any precision. Some persons go so far as to assert that compulsory military training has effects which are predominantly contrary to nationalism, that it fills the majority of Frenchmen with dislike and distaste for the army and for the social and political order which requires heavy armaments. Without assenting to such extreme assertions, we must point out, in fairness and justice, that compulsory military training as practised in France does not make an entire nation of militarists, and that, on the contrary, it is attended by open dissent and criticism on the part of a considerable number of persons who have undergone it. Indeed, contemporary France has its full share of pacifists and anti-militarists.[36]

In considering certain limitations upon the nationalist effectiveness of French compulsory military training, the reader should bear in mind at the outset that Frenchmen are human and that it is a fairly frequent trait of humanity to resent, if not to resist, whatever is compulsory. This thought suggests a first and fundamental, but somewhat vague, general limitation.

Secondly, the life of conscripts in the French army is not exactly a continuous round of gayety nor is it wholly conducive to idealistic reflection on the beauties and grandeur of the fatherland. There is a vast deal of drudgery and a vast deal of boredom. There is likewise a vast deal of economic worry, even economic distress. Not only is the normal economic life of the country interrupted and the earning-power of individuals arrested by removing all twenty-year-old youths from productive and remunerative employment and cloistering them for a year or more as wards of the State, but the young men themselves suffer

[36] For an account of the peace-societies in France, see Chapter XII, pp. 333–337, below.

thereby no little inconvenience and hardship. Conscripts, during their term of active service, receive a wage of twenty-five centimes (one cent) a day, which certainly does not suffice to supply them with any luxuries. To be sure, they are given food, such as it is,[37] and clothing and tobacco and a place to sleep. Many of the barracks, however, are old and damp, and most of them are located in cities with all the urban temptations for young men suddenly free from the control of family and friends. Men who have families dependent upon them are required, when they enter service, to leave their charges to the care of the State; and the State undertakes to provide for such needy families at the daily rate of one franc sixty centimes each, with an additional sixty centimes for one child, seventy for two, eighty for three, and an additional franc for four.[38] It frequently happens, because of bureaucratic red-tape, that a dependent family may not receive any money until months after the breadwinner has left home and joined his regiment; and men have sometimes deserted from the army in order to support their impoverished families. Professional soldiers fare scarcely better than conscripts. A sergeant, for example, in his first five years of service receives only 3,948 francs ($158) a year aside from small allowances and the right to a bonus upon entering civil life. Most soldiers have considerable spare time but they are not permitted to utilize it for any outside remunerative work.

In view of the hardships and annoyances of army life, it is but natural that many young Frenchmen begin their term of military service with reluctance and end it with a great sense of relief. The ordinary private soldier must have a good deal of inertia or a good deal of patriotic sentiment to endure compulsory military training.[39]

Still another — a third — type of limitation upon the nationalist rôle of the French military system arises from propaganda conducted both without and within the armed forces by groups of extreme " left-wing " Frenchmen, Socialist and Com-

---

[37] A Ministerial Circular of March 18, 1927, prescribed that five francs (twenty cents) be spent on each soldier's food each day.

[38] These rates are of July, 1927.

[39] See Monteilhet, *Les Institutions militaires de la France,* pp. 305 *et seq.*

munist, with the purpose of effecting radical reforms in the system
or of counteracting particular sorts of national propaganda in
the army.

French Socialists before the Great War displayed divergent
tendencies in their attitude toward the army and navy and toward compulsory military training. One group enthusiastically
supported Jean Jaurès's idea of " The New Army " (" L'Armée
Nouvelle "), the idea that the principle of compulsory military
training should be retained and extended and should be supplemented, in case of national danger, by the conscription of all the
material and spiritual resources of the country. This group
criticized the existing army-system on the ground that it unjustly
imposed burdens upon the proletariat and none upon capital.
Jaurès and his followers did not assail armed force as such; they
sought rather to render it in every respect more thoroughly and
more intensely national.

On the other hand many Socialists were frankly anti-militarist,
partially because of the international tradition of Marxian Socialism and partly because of the frequent use of troops by the
French Government to suppress strikes and to overawe workingmen. In March 1907 the Government tried to replace strikers
in electrical works with soldiers; in July 1908 three workers
were killed by soldiers during a strike of the building trades; in
1907 soldiers were sent to repress disorders at Narbonne, with resulting loss of life; and in the summer of 1910 M. Briand, himself
a leader of the " Left " but head of the Ministry, called railway
strikers to arms and then sent them back to work as soldiers.[40]
This policy naturally aroused marked hostility to the army on
the part of some workers; and in the years immediately preceding
the Great War " pacifist " Socialists were very active with pen
and voice.

Since the Great War and the formation of a pro-Bolshevist
Communist Party in France, the Socialist political party
(S.F.I.O.) has tended to support the Jaurès doctrines of " The
New Army." Paul-Boncour, the Socialist leader, was largely

[40] Charles Seignobos, Histoire de France contemporaine, Vol. VIII, edited by
Ernest Lavisse (Paris, Hachette), pp. 260–261, 276.

responsible for the preparation of the Army Act of 1928, which has already been discussed,[41] and his Socialist colleagues in the Parliament voted for it. The " Confédaration Générale du Travail," the Socialist trade-union organization, has not strictly followed the lead of the Socialist parliamentarians, however: it has urged a measure of gradual disarmament and has criticized the act of 1928.

The Communists, because of their close relationship with revolutionary Russia and their admiration for its " Red Army," are not anti-militaristic and do not oppose the theory of armed force. Rather, they hold that workers should learn the arts of war so that when the opportunity for the proletarian revolution presents itself in France they will be prepared to destroy the forces of capitalism. To this end the Communist papers, *L'Humanité, La Caserne* (a special sheet for soldiers), *La Page de Jean de Gouin* (for sailors), and *Le Conscript* (for newly drafted men), advise their readers to go through the required training but to win all the converts possible to the cause of the proletariat. This is also the doctrine of the Communist veteran associations, " L'ARAC " and " L'Union Fraternelle des Marins et Anciens Marins."

The State has dealt severely with those who have contributed to Communist propaganda in the army and navy. Marcel Cachin was condemned to imprisonment for one year and to a fine of 2,000 francs for " inciting military men to disobedience " by his articles in *L'Humanité*. Camille Renault, manager of *La Caserne*, Gaston Bernard, manager of the Arabic edition of *La Caserne*, and others have been condemned for like offenses.[42]

But after making full allowances for the propaganda of revolutionary Communists and pacifist Socialists, for the hardships of officers and men, and for the human reaction against anything compulsory, the fact remains that no political or social group in France contemplates with any seriousness the speedy abolition of compulsory military training. It is not a political or social issue. On the contrary, it is a national issue. The mass of

---

[41] See above, pp. 67–68.
[42] See *L'Humanité*, April 24 and 29 and May 11–12, 1927.

Frenchmen have come to view the army and navy as national institutions which must be supported by the whole nation; and anyone who might seek to destroy them utterly would be deemed certainly an anti-social Frenchman and probably a madman. There might be differences of opinion about details of organization, recruitment, term of service, and many other matters affecting the armed forces. There might be more serious differences of opinion about the use to which the army should be put. There would be essentially no difference of opinion about the principle that the army must be a truly national army.

For the mass of Frenchmen recognize rightly that the army is, actually or potentially, an agency of national training second in importance only to the educational system. Thousands, perhaps millions, of French conscripts during the past half-century have at least temporarily been inconvenienced and even disillusioned by certain aspects of military life; some doubtless during their term of service have developed a repugnance to discipline and drill and patriotic preachment and have grown less nationalist. On the vast majority of Frenchmen, however, compulsory military training simply must leave an indelibly national and patriotic stamp. National patriotism has created the French army of to-day; and this army labors to strengthen national patriotism in France. The national army is directed by the centralized national State and officered by men who have been trained in the nationalist environment of state military schools. Every year the officers prepare some 250,000 young Frenchmen to give their lives for their country and teach them how to take the lives of other young men who are equally ready to sacrifice themselves for their respective nations. The preparation is technical in large part, but it is also nationalist; and during their period of service young Frenchmen are once again, beyond their formal schooling, indoctrinated with the glories of France and the righteousness of her mission, and the indoctrination this time is coupled with guns and cannon. The conscript is usually away from home and his provincial habitat; his travelling, his associations, his experiences, his uniform, his new environment, all enlarge his view and enable him to visualize France as a whole.

Compulsory military training helps to " make " patriotic Frenchmen, even though some Frenchmen are not fully conscious of
the process.

National armaments do not cease their nationalizing influence
when a conscript completes the minimum term of active service
in army or navy. Every Frenchman remains a soldier in reserve
and is liable to be called upon to perform a limited amount of
military service for several succeeding years. Every Frenchman is eligible for membership in one or another military society
— an association of former conscripts, a veterans' association,
or an association of reservists.[43] Every Frenchman, boy as well
as adult, female equally with male, witnesses throughout life, on
every side, monuments and memorials to the soldier dead of
France, military parades and demonstrations, the cult of the
" unknown soldier," military flags and uniforms,[44] laudatory comment in textbooks about the army, speeches by statesmen about
the army, articles in the press about the army — all the multiple
forms under which the " making " of patriotic Frenchmen is
forwarded by the State's military arm.

It may be well at this point to close our survey of the French
army and navy with a quotation from a personal letter which
a high-minded French army officer, a wounded veteran of the
Great War, addressed to the author in 1927. The quotation may
serve to illustrate the emotional, almost religious, character of
the French patriotism of the average army officer and at the
same time to remove any misapprehension that army-patriotism
necessarily involves " militarism " or " nationalism " in the bad
sense of these words:

We Frenchmen love the great moral being that is our France.
Above all, we veterans, who have seen her soil ravaged, her forests
sacked, her factories destroyed. Does not a son cherish his sick mother?
We know, better than anyone, the horrible suffering borne by her
honest, industrious, brave people. We love our France for her heroic
qualities, her virtues, her vigor, her will to live and to hold aloft the

---

[43] For an account of military associations, see Chapter VIII on National
Societies, pp. 220–223, below.

[44] National symbols and ceremonies, many of which are military, are discussed in Chapter IX, pp. 229–251, below.

torch of civilization. We are proud of her natural wealth and of her marvellous past.

Is not France, as a great writer has put it, " the finest realm after the Kingdom of Heaven? " Her history is made up of catastrophes but also of admirable victories. There are indeed Bouvines and Sedan, but there are also Jena and Verdun: France goes into an abyss only to rise the higher.

The lovableness of our France, her manifold riches, her unique beauties, her treasures collected by our ancestors, fascinate and irresistibly attract the foreign tourist, painter, and littérateur who admire her and even the artisan of other lands who works here under free and social laws.

France, strong in her might, remains, however, solicitous of her security. She nourishes no aggressive design. But this great country, which has the bloodiest, as well as the most beautiful, history of any country in the world, has indeed the intangible right to have a " revolver-pocket " if not a " browning " in it. Our Catalaunian Plains cannot keep their natural color when they are engulfed from the east. Our riches may still provoke jealousy, may still engender covetousness. France has demonstrated that she wishes to live on good terms with all peoples, but her geographical position exposes her to sudden blows. 1914 must not be repeated.

We Frenchmen testify particularly to affectionate friendship with Americans, to whom we owe everything. Lafayette and Washington forged the ring of Franco-American friendship; the Sammies on the Vesle and the Poilus at Verdun have consecrated it in battle-blood.

We Frenchmen certainly love peace, but when we are forced to it war does not frighten us. We take precautions, that is all.

Nevertheless, personally, I, a French officer, who have fought the War, can say to you, although it may seem paradoxical to you, that I desire a close union, if not an alliance, between the two great military and warrior peoples — France and Germany. Perfectly so, between the Gauls and the Teutons; both have issued from Frankish tribes. If these two nations live in good relations with each other, peace is assured. The majestic Rhine should be only a hedgerow which separates the fields of two good farmers, quite occupied with their harvests, their fruits, and their flowers. It should not be a subject of eternal discord. . . .

CHAPTER V

THE CHURCHES

I

FRENCHMEN, as we have seen, have a national State to which they must belong. They are expected to obey its laws and its officials, to undergo a special schooling prescribed by it, and to serve in its army or navy. They are imbued in childhood and youth with loyalty to it, in many instances with such a supreme and emotional loyalty to it as to partake of the nature of religion. In fact, most Frenchmen are devotees, consciously or unconsciously, of a veritable religion of national patriotism.

The French State itself, with its civil bureaucracy, with its educational system, and with its military training, is at once the most obvious and the most important agency for " making " patriotic Frenchmen and for indoctrinating them with at least a quasi-religious fidelity to France. But it is not the only agency. Others there are, semi-public and semi-private, recognized and partially restricted by the State, it is true, but not wholly or in detail directed by the State; and of these voluntary and largely independent agencies, traditional religious organizations are the most significant.

France is traditionally a Christian country, and the mass of its inhabitants have been for centuries baptized members of the Christian Church. In France, State and Church had practically the same membership for so long a time that it became customary for Frenchmen to think of themselves as Christians and for Christians to think of themselves as French. For a very long time, moreover, a close legal relationship existed between Church and State: officials of the former were functionaries of the latter; State maintained Church; Church supported State.

Throughout the Middle Age, the French Church was one; it was the Gallican section of the Roman Catholic Church; and it expressed and emphasized the growing unity of the French national State. Subsequently, ecclesiastical schism arose. Rival Protestant churches emerged in the sixteenth century. Jewish dissenters reëstablished themselves in the country. And the development of agnosticism and skepticism found a quasi-ecclesiastical expression in the eighteenth century in the rise of French Freemasonry. Centuries of ecclesiastical unity and religious uniformity, however, had already done their work; and in the nineteenth and twentieth centuries the coexistence of Catholicism, Protestantism, Judaism, and Freemasonry in France has proved divisive only in detail; in a broad way each of these movements has vied with the other in making patriotic Frenchmen and teaching them to be supremely loyal to France. It is the business of the present chapter to suggest various ways in which the Catholic Church, the Protestant churches, the Jewish synagogues, and the Masonic lodges perform a nationalizing mission.

2

The Catholic Church is outstandingly important in numbers, in tradition, and in contemporary influence. All Frenchmen (freethinkers and Freemasons, Protestants and Jews, as well as practising Catholics) who read the history or the great literature of their country, who view its greatest monuments, or who walk in the streets or ride on the open road, encounter constant reminders of the Catholic Church. One has to search in France for a Protestant temple or a Jewish synagogue, and one is mildly surprised when one finds it; one sees daily so many Catholic churches that one is not at all surprised to discover another. The chief holy days of the Catholic Church are still legal holidays of the whole nation, and everybody's vital " crises " of birth, marriage, and death are still generally observed by rites at least reminiscent of a Catholic past.

Of the actual number of communicants of the Catholic Church in contemporary France there are no reliable statistics. Catholic estimates put the number at between twenty-eight and twenty-nine millions out of a total population of forty millions.[1] Undoubtedly a considerably smaller number comprise the " devout faithful " who regularly go to confession and receive communion. We can say that, at least for a majority of Frenchmen, Catholic customs, if not Catholic creeds and sacraments, constitute a centripetal force of no mean importance.

The administration of the Catholic Church in France is conducted, under the supreme authority of the Pope, by a hierarchy of seventeen archbishops and seventy bishops, with some twenty-six auxiliary and titular bishops. Under the hierarchy are about 32,000 secular priests and a considerable, but indefinite, number of members of religious orders, monks and nuns, together with a fairly large number of laymen and women who, because they devote all their time to services of the Church as secretaries, sacristans, teachers, or journalists, may be counted as part of the sizable staff that carries on Catholic propaganda in France.[2]

All this staff is patriotic as well as Catholic. With almost negligible exceptions, its members have received their schooling and undergone military training in France; they are acutely conscious of the function which their Church has performed during past centuries in creating and solidifying the French nation; they know that in glorifying the history of their country, they are glorifying the past achievements of the Catholic Church, and *vice versa* that in praising the work of the Church they are extolling France; and, particularly nowadays, when they find themselves in more or less unfavorable competition with a State Government which arrogates to itself the supreme direction of the form and content of French patrioism, they tend naturally to redouble their efforts to remind their compatriots that the

---

[1] R. P. Dassonville, " La France, Pays de Mission," *Dossiers de l'Action Populaire,* Oct. 25, 1926, pp. 273–284; L'Abbé Pyotte, " Le Problème des Non-Baptisés," *ibid.,* April 25, 1926, pp. 113–124.

[2] *Cf. Almanach Catholique Français* (Paris, Bloud & Gay), an annual directory published under the auspices of the " Catholic Committee of French Friendships Abroad." See also Abbé R. Aigrain, *Ecclesia: Encyclopédie populaire de Connaissances religieuses* (Paris, Bloud & Gay, 1927) ; and Mgr. Gibier, *La France Catholique organisée* (Paris, Téqui, 1925).

Catholic Church has been, and ever should be, the fashioner of the purest and the best French patriotism.[3]

French Catholic leaders of the nineteenth and twentieth centuries, especially under the Third Republic, have been prone, in their attitude toward the Government and the State, to make a very nice distinction, the full significance of which must be grasped by everyone who would seek a sound understanding of the seeming paradox that certain Frenchmen who are most loyal to the national State can be most critical of its Government. It is an integral and traditional tenet of Catholic doctrine that Christians must obey the lawful commands of their temporal rulers and must be thoroughly loyal to the State. It is a peculiarly deep-seated conviction of French Catholics that so long as the Government of the French State was formally and expressly Catholic, so long as both State and Government gave direct aid and support to the Church, the carrying into effect of Catholic teaching on relations of Church and State was blessed with great advantage to both. But since the Great Revolution at the close of the eighteenth century, the Government of the French State has often been, from the viewpoint of French Catholic leaders, inimical to the Church and therefore inimical to the best interests of the State. Accordingly, they have tended to draw a line between the State, that is, the Nation, which is always good, and the Government, that is, the Ministry of the day, which may be and frequently is very bad. They have usually counselled their followers, in accordance with Catholic principles, to tolerate and endure the Government, no matter how bad it may be, but they have been disposed, particularly under the Republican régime of the last fifty years, to bestow enthusiasm on the State and not on the Government.

It is hardly to be wondered at that Catholic leaders should have been scandalized by certain aspects of a Revolution which despoiled the Church of its property, which persecuted and put

[3] In this connection, note should be made of two books by eminent French Catholics: one by Paul Feron-Vrau, the most influential Catholic journalist, entitled *Dieu et la France* (Paris, Maison de la Bonne Presse, 1923); and the other by Mgr. Gibier, Bishop of Versailles, *Patrie*, fourth edition (Paris, Téqui, 1926).

to death a large number of clergymen, and which deprived the Church of a multitude of its historic functions in society, education, and charity. Nor is it surprising, on one hand, that scandalized Catholic leaders should have cherished throughout the nineteenth century a devotion to the monarchy and to the social institutions and customs of pre-revolutionary times and a desire to reëstablish them, or, on the other hand, that devotees of the French Revolution, especially Jacobin Republicans, should have retained a lurking suspicion of Catholic leaders and should have sought further to curb the influence of " clericalism."

On the whole, the republican Jacobin leaders have been more successful than the royalist Catholic leaders in securing followers. It must be that a considerable number of professed and practising French Catholics who have been willing to take their religion from the Church have been unwilling to take their politics from Church-leaders. For all the general elections in France since 1875 have been favorable to republicanism; all the ministries since 1878 have been tinged with Jacobinism; and every Parliament since 1879 has enacted or maintained a growing amount of " anti-clerical " legislation.

Towns and cities, under the auspices of republican prefects, began in 1879 to prohibit Catholic public processions. In 1880 the Society of Jesus, along with some three hundred other religious congregations, was dissolved. Religious instruction in the public schools was abolished in 1882. In 1884 civil marriage was made compulsory, and civil divorce was legalized. In 1886 priests were forbidden to teach in public schools.

In 1892 Pope Leo XIII solemnly admonished French Catholics to beware of the dangers attending their intransigeant attitude in politics and to " rally " to the acceptance of the Republican régime in their country " as the actual Government of the nation." Some French Catholic leaders heeded the papal admonition and " rallied " from royalism to republicanism. But a larger number, proving themselves to be more Catholic than the Pope, more Gallican than international, remained royalist in fact if not in name and redoubled their criticism of the " corrupt and infidel " republican Government. Followed the Dreyfus affair, in which many Catholic leaders aligned themselves with professional anti-Semites, militarists, and royalists. Followed, too, a revulsion of popular feeling in favor of the Republic and its Jacobin leaders. Followed, finally, another wave of "anti-clerical" legislation.[4]

In 1901 an Associations Act dissolved and expelled from France all religious congregations of monks and nuns which were not specially licensed by the Government; and the licenses granted by the Government were extremely few. The same act struck a severe blow at the Catholic educational system by forbidding any religious congregation to maintain a school or to engage in teaching. In 1904 the Government ruptured diplomatic relations with the Vatican; and the Separation Act of 1905 abrogated the Concordat which Napoleon had negotiated with the Papacy in 1801 and which had regulated the relations of Church and State in France for more than a century.

The Separation Act took away from the Church almost the last vestiges of the official sanction and financial assistance which the French State, in modern times as in the Middle Age, had traditionally accorded it as the embodiment of the religion of a majority of the French citizens. The Act suppressed the special governmental department charged with the supervision of public worship; it removed the bishops and priests from the category of state functionaries, and by ceasing to pay their salaries it threw them for support upon private charity and voluntary contributions. Moreover, it ordered the removal of religious emblems from public buildings and the abolition of chaplaincies in the army and navy. It transferred Church property used for charitable purposes and all other Church property not necessary for religious worship to public and State establishments serving similar ends. Besides, the Act asserted the right of the Government to investigate at any time the finances of the Church and provided that the Church might not receive gifts by legacy but only through collections and pew-rent. Finally the Act

[4] See Georges Weill, *Histoire de l'Idée laïque en France au XIXᵉ Siècle* (Paris, Alcan, 1925); and M. l'Abbé Bourceret, *Cinquante Années de Laïcité* (Paris, Bonne Presse, 1926).

vested the ownership of church-buildings in the State and authorized their use by the Church only on condition that its temporal and business affairs should be managed by "associations of worship" almost wholly free from control by the clergy.

This last stipulation was contrary to Catholic discipline, and the Pope in August 1906 forbade French Catholics to form "associations of worship." The resulting chaos in the relations of Church and State was temporarily dispelled by the Government's receding from its extreme position and by the enactment in January 1907 of an amendment to the Separation Act, authorizing the Catholic Church to continue its use of church-buildings without the formation of "associations of worship."

During the twenty years from 1908 to 1928, especially during and after the War, the Catholic Church in France has probably grown stronger, rather than weaker. At any rate, its relations with the Government have not been quite so strained as formerly, and there has been much talk of a Catholic "revival." Several factors have contributed to this end: the heroic part taken by Catholic priests and prominent Catholic laymen in the military defense of France; the obviously growing sincerity of professions of loyalty to the Republic on the part of Catholic leaders; the popular sympathetic reaction to an impoverished and hard-pressed clergy, who nowadays must serve the Church not for financial or social position but for the sake of conscience; the acquisition of Alsace-Lorraine with a large proportion of zealous and well organized Catholics; the newer tendency on the part of Catholic leaders to go direct to the people rather than to the Government; and the perfecting and extension of instruments of popular propaganda.[5]

The Chamber of Deputies of 1919-1924 seemed less disposed to press the State's quarrel with the Church than had its Republican predecessors. The Concordat of 1801, destroyed for the rest of France, was retained for Alsace-Lorraine, and these newly regained provinces were exempted from the operation of the other "anti-clerical" legislation of the Third Republic. Diplomatic relations between the French Government and the Vatican, which

[5] See Paul Lesourd, Le Catholicisme en France (Paris, Giraudon, 1927).

had been ruptured since 1904, were formally resumed in 1921. Jeanne d'Arc was canonized by the Church on May 16, 1920, and on June 24 of the same year the Chamber voted unanimously that the second Sunday in May should be a national holiday in her honor. More important, members of religious congregations, that had been expelled from France in 1901, returned in considerable numbers during and after the war, and, despite the fact that their return was strictly illegal, they have not usually been molested by the Government.[6] Questions of church-property, which had been raised by the Separation Act of 1905, seemed to be in a fair way to solution when Pope Pius XI authorized the formation of " associations of worship," each to be composed of a bishop and laymen and to function " under the authority of the Bishop, in communion with the Holy Father, and in conformity with the constitution of the Catholic Church," and when the Council of State recognized the legality of such " associations." [7]

It is true that, following the victory of the left-wing political groups in the general election of 1924, the Government of M. Herriot announced its intention of enforcing the Associations Act, ending normal diplomatic relations with the Vatican, and extending the operation of " anti-clerical " legislation to Alsace-Lorraine. This time Catholic leaders were able to arouse a popular opposition so strong and so effective that it was responsible in part for the fall of the Herriot Government in April 1925. The *status quo* was maintained, and the general election of 1928 returned a Chamber of Deputies somewhat less Radical and a little more Catholic. M. Doumergue, the President of the Republic, comes from a Protestant family; M. Poincaré, the prime minister, is not a practising Catholic; but there is now (1929) no sign of any early resumption of an acute conflict between the Government and the Catholic Church in France.

The Catholic Church in France is almost certainly more influ-

[6] Paul Lesourd, *Le Catholicisme en France* (Paris, Giraudon, 1927), pp. 34–36. See also Jacob Dupont, " Le Parti Prêtre et ses Progrès," *L'Acacia*, Sept. 1927, p. 13 *et seq.* A law of 1929 formally legalized the return of some of these congregations.

[7] Dec. 13, 1923. The papal encyclical, *Maximam gravissimamque*, was issued on Jan. 18, 1924.

ential to-day than twenty years ago. But now, as then, its chief influence is to be measured less in terms of politics than in spiritual
and cultural values. Its leaders have failed to prevent the enactment, or to secure the formal repeal, of a considerable mass of
anti-clerical laws; they have succeeded, however, in holding to
the sacraments and services of the Church a large number of
Frenchmen, and this, they insist, is their primary concern; and,
incidentally, they have contributed to the strengthening among
the " faithful " of the sentiment of national patriotism.

The Catholic cause in France is served by numerous agencies
of popular propaganda. All such agencies are first and foremost
religious in object: they aim to preserve and promote the Catholic
religion. Some of them stress political action. Some emphasize
social or economic action. Some represent intellectual and cultural interests. But all of them, secondarily to their religious
object, inculcate loyalty to the nation and the State and glorify
the past and labor for the future of the fatherland.

First among the agencies of Catholic propaganda are the
clergy themselves, the bishops and priests, who by sermons, conferences, letters, books, and personal contact and conversation
exert varied and far-reaching influence. These men are patriots
as well as priests; they have been reared and educated in a patriotic environment; and they naturally confirm the patriotism
which the laity have developed in school and army.

Secondly, there is the Catholic press. Such important Parisian dailies as *Le Figaro, L'Écho de Paris, Le Gaulois, L'Avenir,
Le Journal des Débats,* whilst not professedly or ostentatiously
Catholic, oppose " anti-clericalism " and cater to Catholic readers; and all of them are distinctly nationalist. The outstanding
Catholic daily is *La Croix,* published at Paris by a Catholic
syndicate and printed with local supplements in one hundred and
four different places throughout the country: it is militantly
Catholic and strenuously patriotic, and has a large circulation.[8]
Catholic periodical literature includes a number of weeklies,
such as *La Jeune République, Le Petit Patriote, La Vie Ca-*

---

[8] The provincial press includes several important Catholic dailies, notably
L'Ouest Éclair of Rennes and *L'Express du Midi* of Toulouse.

tholique, etc. It includes less frequent publications, such as *Le Correspondant* (political fortnightly), *Les Études* (general monthly), *Les Lettres* (literary monthly), *Les Dossiers de l'Action Populaire* (fortnightly of social reform), *La Démocratie* and *Le Mouvement* (monthlies), etc. There are also *L'Almanach Catholique Français,* an annual directory, and *La Documentation Catholique,* a weekly bulletin of official documents. And there are the Catholic publishing houses (Éditions Spes, La Bonne Presse, Bloud et Gay, etc.), the presses of which produce a continuous stream of Catholic (usually patriotic) pamphlets and books.

Thirdly, Catholic schools, despite much " anti-clerical " legislation against them, are still important in keeping alive in France the Catholic tradition of religion and patriotism. In France, outside of Alsace-Lorraine, the Catholic Church maintained in 1924–1925 some 12,000 elementary schools, with an attendance of 767,000 children;[9] and in Alsace-Lorraine a majority of the public schools are Catholic. Besides, the Church maintains a large number of secondary schools, with an estimated attendance (in 1924–1925) of 80,000 boys and 100,000 girls,[10] and several institutions of higher learning, which, though they may not under state law confer degrees or be called universities, compete with the state universities in preparing young men and women for the professions. The attendance at these Catholic " Institutes " totalled in 1924–1925 about 3,600.

Fourthly, there are definitely propagandist societies of many kinds among French Catholics. There is, for instance, the National Catholic Federation ("La Fédération Nationale Catholique,") commonly referred to as the F. N. C.,[11] formed under the presidency of General de Castelnau after the electoral victory of the " anti-clerical " parties of the Left in 1924 in order to combat

---

[9] *Annuaire Statistique, 1926,* p. 24. See also J. P. Niboyet, *Répertoire pratique de Droit et de Jurisprudence d'Alsace et Lorraine* (Paris, Recueil Sirey, 1925), Vol. II, p. 782, and A. Albaret, *L'Enseignement public et privé* (Paris, Spes, 1927), p. 40. Catholic schools are discussed in Chapter III, pp. 36–37, 44, above.

[10] See the article by Maurice Charny in *La Défense laïque,* May, 1926.

[11] Headquarters; 36 rue de Montparnasse, Paris. Its action is seconded by a veterans' organization: La Ligue de Défense des Droits de Religieux Anciens Combattants (DRAC).

hostile legislation. It has published a weekly sheet, *Correspondance Hebdomadaire de la F. N. C.*, has distributed thousands of pamphlets, and has staged mammoth mass-meetings, including assemblies of 50,000 men at Falgoët (Finistère), December 8, 1924; 30,000 at St. Brieuc, February 1, 1925; 80,000 at Nantes, March 1, 1925; 50,000 at Angers, March 8; 100,000 at Landerneau (Finistère), October 5: 30,000 at Bordeaux, July 11; 40,000 at Pontchâteau (Loire-Inférieure), September 5; etc.[12] Less spectacular but perhaps more significant is the Patriotic League of Frenchwomen ("La Ligue Patriotique des Françaises"), which champions Catholicism, patriotism, and social welfare and boasts that its propaganda reaches 600,000 women and 33,000 girls; the Catholic Association of French Youth ("L'Association Catholique de la Jeunesse Française"), with a membership of 120,000 in 3,200 local branches; the National Federation of Catholic Students ("La Fédération Nationale des Étudiants Catholiques"), with 6,000 members; and a considerable number of miscellaneous associations of professional men, writers, artists, etc.

A special category of French Catholic organizations have been very active in the field of economic and social reform. Every year a week's national congress (a *semaine sociale*) of Catholic intellectuals and labor-leaders is held in one or another city. All the time a propagandist organization ("L'Action Populaire") is studying and instructing French Catholics generally about the application of Christian principles to labor problems and specifically about trade-unionism, industrial coöperation and profit-sharing, social insurance, etc.; it reaches a large public by means of its pamphlets, books, periodicals, study-outlines, and lectures. There is likewise a national organization of Catholic trade-unionists ("La Confédération Française des Travailleurs Chrétiens"), founded in 1919 and now (1929) embracing a membership of 80,000.

Catholic societies, schools, press, and clergy constitute in

[12] Yves de la Brière, *La Fédération Nationale Catholique après la Deuxième Année d'Existence* (Paris, F. N. C., 1927), p. 11. See also *Objectifs: 1927–1928* (Paris, F. N. C., 1927), 3 vols.

France so many major agencies of popular propaganda which are religious but which are also national and patriotic. Last but not least is still another such agency — the missionary activity of French Catholics abroad.

France for centuries has made a disproportionately large contribution of men and money to Catholic foreign missions. In 1900 about seventy per cent of all Catholic missionaries were French; and despite the adverse effects of " anti-clerical " legislation and the war, France still supplies the whole Catholic Church with some 16,000 missionaries, more than half of the total number supplied by all the countries of the world.[13] Moreover, French Catholics have contributed since the war about twelve million francs a year of the seventy-five millions collected by the major missionary societies of the Church, about an eighth of the fifty-two millions collected by minor societies, and some twenty millions in the form of revenue from missionary publications and exhibits, private resources of individual missionaries, etc. — an estimated grand total of thirty-five million francs.

Missionary endeavor of French Catholics has always been primarily religious, but it has had special national significance. What La Salle and Marquette and the other French Jesuit missionaries did for France, as well as for Catholicism, in America in the seventeenth century, and what Lavigerie did similarly in Africa in the nineteenth century, established a tradition which is exemplified in Africa and Asia and Oceania at the present time by the corps of 16,000 French Catholic missionaries. These missionaries are educated and trained mainly in France, and wherever they go they carry with them the French language, French customs and traditions, and a lively French patriotism. They have been, and are, forerunners or companions of French traders and soldiers and empire-builders. Incidentally, at least, they exalt the international prestige of their native land.

Missionary activity of French Catholics is an asset, not only

<hr>

[13] These figures and the following estimates of financial expenditures are taken from J. P. Piolet, " Du Budget des Missions étrangères," *La Revue d'Histoire des Missions* (Paris, Spes, June 1, 1926), and Bernard Arens, *Manuel des Missions Catholiques* (Louvain, Éditions du Museum Lessianum, 1925), pp. 264–277.

of the Catholic Church, but also of the French State, and almost every French Government, no matter how "anti-clerical" it may be at home, is likely to lend a helping hand to "clericals" abroad. The vehemently "anti-clerical" Government which sponsored the Associations Act of 1901 and expelled most religious orders and congregations from France, expressly allowed three orders most active in training foreign missionaries to remain in the country and to retain their property and schools.[14] Catholic missions receive no direct subsidy from the State except in respect of certain hospitals and the Catholic university at Beirut, and occasionally an "anti-clerical" colonial governor annoys and handicaps the local missionaries.[15] In the main, however, as M. Poincaré reminded the Parliament in 1923, the Government deems it a national duty to encourage French Catholic missionaries in the work of "radiating French civilization."[16]

A somewhat different kind of missionary propaganda is conducted by the "Catholic Committee of French Friendships Abroad" ("Comité Catholique des Amitiés Françaises à l'Étranger").[17] This organization was effected during the war "to defend the reputation of France in foreign Catholic circles, to learn about foreign Catholics, and to interest French Catholics in Catholic movement abroad." During the war, it sent several delegations on visits to allied and neutral countries and distributed six million French books and pamphlets in foreign lands. Since the war, it has maintained a press service reaching two hundred publications a week and has awarded thirty scholarships to foreign students to enable them to study in France.

The Catholic Church in France, in its inculcation of national patriotism, pays special veneration to the patronal saints of the nation: Saint Louis,[18] Saint Jeanne d'Arc, and Saint Michel.

[14] The three are: Foreign Missions (Les Missions Étrangères), 128 rue du Bac, Paris; Holy Ghost Fathers (Les Pères du Saint Esprit), 30 rue Lhomond, Paris; and the Lazarists (Les Lazaristes), 95 rue de Sèvres, Paris. Several other missionary orders were "authorized" by act of the French Parliament in 1929.

[15] Such was notably the case of General Sarrail in Syria in 1924–1925.

[16] See Almanach Catholique Français (Paris, Bloud et Gay, 1924), p. 89; and Charles Daniélou, Les Affaires étrangères (Paris, Feguière, 1927).

[17] Headquarters: 3 rue Garancière, Paris.

[18] See Marius Sepet, Saint Louis, 11th ed. (Paris, Lecoffre, 1924).

Especially around Jeanne d'Arc has grown up a cult which is at once religious and nationalist. Nearly every Catholic place of worship has a shrine dedicated to her, and nearly every city has a statue erected to her memory. A national shrine, " La Chapelle Sainte Jeanne d'Arc," was built at Rouen in 1921, and a great basilica is now (1929) projected for the site of her martyrdom. A monthly publication and several special societies labor to extend and deepen the popular devotion to the sainted national heroine.[19] With Saint Jeanne is usually linked Saint Michel, it being the belief of many French Catholics that the victory of the Allies in the Great War was achieved through his intercession. To Saint Michel a national basilica has been erected at Paris, and here Mass is said daily for soldiers who died for the fatherland.

The cult and liturgy of the Church are put to the service of national patriotism in other ways. Mass is said pretty generally on almost all patriotic occasions. Particularly on Armistice Day, November 11, religious services are held in thanksgiving for the deliverance of the nation and in memory of the soldier dead; on this day the great basilica of the Sacred Heart in Paris is the scene of an imposing religious and patriotic rite.

It must not be assumed of French Catholics any more than of Frenchmen generally that patriotism and national loyalty necessarily imply chauvinism and intolerance. Indeed, the organizations of French Catholics striving for international accord and peace are impressive in number and influence. One of the most important of such organizations is " The Young Republic " (" La Jeune République "), which, under the leadership of Marc Sangnier, and with papal approbation, conducts an active campaign against extreme nationalism. It has a membership of 5,000, holds annual congresses, and publishes a weekly, *La Jeune République*, with a circulation of 15,000, and a monthly, *La Démocratie*, with a circulation of 2,000.[20]

[19] Chief among such societies are Les Chevaliers de Jeanne d'Arc, Le Comité d'Hommage National à Jeanne d'Arc, and Le Comité du Mémorial Jeanne d'Arc. The publication is *La Revue Nationale Jeanne d'Arc*, edited by Jean Sarril, at 41 avenue d'Orléans, Paris.

[20] See Georges Hoog, *Histoire, Doctrine, Action de la Jeune République* (Paris,

There is also a French branch of the " Catholic Union of International Studies " ("L'Union Catholique d'Études Internationales "), an international Catholic organization, with headquarters at Fribourg in Switzerland and with the purpose of " studying international problems in the light of Christian principles and instructing Catholics in the work undertaken by the League of Nations and problems before it." A kindred organization is the " League of French Catholics for International Justice " (" La Ligue des Catholiques Français pour la Justice Internationale "), sponsored by the French hierarchy and publishing a quarterly magazine, *Justice et Paix*.[21]

Both within and without these and numerous similar organizations, there are certainly a large number of French Catholics who consider it an integral part of their religious faith to be patriotic but at the same time to eschew what they term " nationalism," that is, jingoism and downright idolatry of the nation. Increasingly, Catholic publicists in France are turning their attention to the menace of extreme nationalism, and the considerable number of books which nowadays they are publishing on the subject will most likely exert a moderating influence on the character and scope of French patriotism in the next generation.[22]

On the other hand, one of the most chauvinist movements in contemporary France, the royalist and nationalist " Action Française," counts many Catholics among its members or supporters. Its doctrines of " practical empiricism," and " integral nationalism," as developed by its leader, Charles Maurras, teach that " order in society, no matter how it is obtained, is more important than individual liberty," that " a nation declines when

---

La Démocratie, 1925), and Robert Cornilleau, *De Waldeck-Rousseau à Poincaré* (Paris, Spes, 1927), pp. 339–346.

[21] See Mgr. Beaupin, *La Ligue des Catholiques français pour la Justice internationale* (Lyons, Chronique Sociale de France, 1926).

[22] Noteworthy in this connection are Maurice Vaussard, *Enquête sur le Nationalisme* (Paris, Spes, 1924); *Le Problème de la Vie internationale, Semaines sociales de France, Le Havre* (Lyons, Chronique Sociale de France, 1926); R. P. Coulet, *L'Église et le Problème internationale* (Paris, Spes, 1923); Mgr. Julien, *L'Évangile nécessaire à l'Ordre international* (Paris, Bloud et Gay, 1927); and the books of Paul Feron-Vrau and Mgr. Gibier, already cited.

it ceases to expand," and that " the reëstablishment of monarchy in France in the restoration of her national greatness will be realized only by force." [23]

The " Action Française " maintains an energetic propaganda through affiliated societies and groups, by publications, lectures, demonstrations, among aristocrats and intellectuals, bourgeois and university-students; its daily newspaper has 40,000 subscribers and a street-sale which occasionally exceeds 150,000. It has catered to Catholics by opposing and denouncing " anticlerical " legislation, and it is estimated that a large percentage of its enrolled members have been Catholics, including many priests. It so happens that Charles Maurras, its outstanding leader, is an agnostic and has expressed anti-Christian opinions in some of his books; and this fact has been seized upon by the Pope as justification for the condemnation which he has recently launched against the " Action Française," forbidding Catholics to belong to it, to participate in its activities, or to read its publications.[24] The French hierarchy have endorsed the papal action, but the " Action Française " as an organization has refused to submit and while some of its Catholic members have left it in deference to ecclesiastical authority a larger number have remained, denouncing what they term the Pope's illegal attempt to interfere in French politics and to check French nationalism. It is clear that some French Catholics put nationalism ahead of loyalty to Church.

3

Protestantism has been in France much less important than Catholicism. During the sixteenth century, it is true, both the Lutheran teachings and the doctrines of Calvin made considerable headway in the country, with nobles and particularly with bour-

[23] See Charles Maurras, *Enquête sur la Monarchie* and *Si le Coup de Force est possible* (Paris, Nouvelle Librairie Nationale, 1925).

[24] The cendemnation was pronounced on December 29, 1926. See *L'Action Française et le Vatican* (Paris, Flammarion, 1927); Maurice Vaussard, *Politique religieuse et " Action Française," Réflexion d'un Catholique* (Paris, Valois, n.d.); Louis Dimier, *Vingt Ans d'Action Française et autres Souvenirs* (Paris, Nouvelle Librairie Nationale, 1926).

geois, but the growth of Protestantism was soon arrested by religious civil wars, by the conversion of King Henry IV, the erstwhile Protestant leader, to Catholicism, and the intolerance of the French State under Louis XIV, culminating in the revocation of the Edict of Nantes, the charter of Protestant liberties, in 1685. Protestants there continued to be in France but they were not formally tolerated and recognized by the State until the time of Napoleon. In 1802, following close upon the conclusion of the Concordat with the Vatican, the French Government legalized the Reformed (Calvinist) Church, and, six years later, the Lutheran Church.

Thenceforth, for about a century, the State, treating Protestantism as on an equal footing with Catholicism, paid the salaries of Protestant ministers as it paid those of Catholic priests. At the beginning of this régime of union between the State and the Churches, there were about half a million Protestants in France,[25] and during the "revival" of the first half of the nineteenth century their number increased.

The Separation Act of 1905, aimed primarily at the Catholic Church, was applied also to the Protestant Churches. These, like the Catholic Church, were deprived of financial aid from the State; they were prohibited from holding property not strictly necessary for the maintenance of worship; their finances were subjected to governmental control; and, in general, they were reduced to the position of merely tolerated voluntary religious associations. At first the Protestant Churches suffered from the change, but gradually they have been able to adapt themselves to the new régime.[26]

Protestants in France, as elsewhere, are divided into several sects. The main body of the Calvinists, the largest sect, has been split, since the Separation Act, into "conservative" and "liberal" wings. The former, the "Union of Evangelical Re-

---

[25] Census of 1802.

[26] See Charles Bost, *Histoire des Protestants de France en 35 Leçons pour les Écoles* (Neuilly, Editions de la Cause, n.d.); and L. S. Houghton, *Handbook of French and Belgian Protestantism* (New York, Federal Council of the Churches, 1919).

formed Churches" ("Union des Églises Reformées Évangeliques"), remains faithful to orthodox Calvinist principles: its 381 parishes are organized into local, regional, and national groups under the jurisdiction of presbyteries.[27] The latter, the "Union of Reformed Churches of France" ("Union des Églises Reformées de France") adopted in 1907 a liberal, that is, a modernist, declaration of faith and established an independent rival organization for its 164 parishes.[28] Besides these two major organizations, the Calvinists have forty parishes in Alsace-Lorraine, where, it should be remembered, the union of State and Churches still exists and all Protestant Churches, like the Catholic Church, are subsidized by the State; a Union of Free Evangelical Churches, dating from the "revival" in the first half of the nineteenth century and now embracing 49 parishes;[29] and some sixty stations of the Central Society, a home missionary organization founded in 1847.

Protestantism, other than Calvinism, is represented in France. The Lutherans have an ecclesiastical organization with 261 parishes, of which 196 are in Alsace-Lorraine.[30] The Baptists have 29 churches.[31] The Methodists (Wesleyans) have 23 churches.[32] And there are 31 independent Protestant churches, the majority of these having been organized by the MacAll Home Missionary Society.[33] Partially to offset the disadvantages of multiple sectarianism, French Protestants created in 1905 a joint advisory

[27] The creed of the Evangelical Reformed Church is that of the Official Synod of 1872, modified by the Synods of Orléans and Reims in 1906. See *Recueil Officiel des Actes du Synode général* (Cahors, Coneslant). The headquarters of the Church are at 47 rue de Clichy, Paris; and its official organ is *Le Christianisme au XXᵉ Siècle* (weekly).

[28] See *Almanach des Églises Reformées* (Paris, Librairie Protestante) and *Annuaire Protestant* (Paris, Fischbacher). The headquarters of the Reformed Church are at 47 rue de Clichy, Paris; and its official organ is the weekly *Évangile et Liberté*.

[29] Headquarters: 47 rue de Clichy, Paris. Organ: *L'Église Libre* (weekly).

[30] Headquarters: 37 due de Petrograd, Paris. Organ: *Le Témoinage* (weekly).

[31] Headquarters: 48 rue de Lille, Paris.

[32] Headquarters: Methodist Episcopal, 89A Boulevard Haussmann, Paris; Wesleyan, 4 rue Roquépine, Paris.

[33] Headquarters: 1 rue Pierre Levé, Paris.

" Protestant Federation of France," which maintains central headquarters and holds periodic congresses.[34]

Altogether, it is estimated that nominal French Protestants now number about 900,000, located chiefly in outlying provinces, particularly of the south, where the earlier intolerances of the French State were not entirely effective.[35] There can be no doubt as to the national patriotism of these French Protestants. Although they may not share in all the national traditions which their Catholic compatriots cherish, they are, as a rule, staunch supporters of the democratic republican state régime of the nineteenth and twentieth centuries which has enacted so much " anti-clerical " legislation against the Catholic Church. This means that they are natural champions of state schools against private (Catholic) schools and of most of the other agencies of national propaganda which the State has created and directs. Belonging, too, as most of them do, to the middle class, they play a rôle in national economics, as well as in republican politics, out of proportion to their actual numbers.

Protestant propaganda in France, like that of the Catholics, is primarily religious, but incidentally patriotic and national. Its methods are likewise similar, except that it employs few schools of its own and puts great emphasis on the distribution of Bibles. French Protestants maintain propagandist societies, such as " The Cause " (" La Cause ") and " Faith and Life " (" Foi et Vie "),[36] which publish tracts and books and train workers. French Protestants also conduct several philanthropic and charitable institutions and disseminate social doctrines in an important review, Le Christianisme Social. For boys and young men they support two organizations, " L'Alliance Nationale des Unions Chrétiennes de Jeunes Gens " (Y. M. C. A.) and " Les Éclaireurs Unionistes de France " (Boy Scouts). In the foreign-mission field, too, they are active. The Society of Evan-

---

[34] The headquarters are at 47 rue de Clichy, Paris. See Annuaire Protestant (Paris, Fischbacher).

[35] For the geographical distribution of French Protestantism, see Carte de la France Protestante (Paris, Fischbacher, 1923).

[36] Headquarters of La Cause are at 69 rue Perronet, Neuilly, and of Foi et Vie at 85 avenue d'Orléans, Paris. The latter publishes a regular review, Foi et Vie.

gelical Missions ("La Société des Missions Évangéliques ")[37] represents united efforts of French Calvinists, Lutherans, and Methodists: it publishes a monthly magazine and expends about a million francs a year for the support of Protestant missionaries in the French colonies.

French Protestants are patriots and in propagating their religion they are prone to propagate their patriotism, but it cannot be said of them, any more than of French Catholics, that they are necessarily extreme nationalists. In 1907 the Protestant Federation sent a message to the Second Peace Conference at the Hague, expressing its "respectful sympathy and its ardent hope for the near and definitive triumph of international arbitration and peace." From then until 1914 the Protestant Churches in France observed annually a "Peace Sunday," a practice which they have revived since the war. The official Calvinist hymnal contains but two songs of patriotic implication.[38]

During the war French Protestants proved themselves zealously patriotic. Their Federation established a "French Protestant Committee for Propaganda Abroad," which published and distributed a mass of partisan writings with a view to swaying public opinion in neutral Protestant countries.[39] And at the conclusion of the war the General Synod of the Calvinists solemnly "glorified God to Whom they are indebted for this marvellous deliverance."[40]

Since 1919 two divergent tendencies of patriotic sentiment have been manifest among French Protestants. One is the tendency to be nationalist to the extent of ignoring or criticising internationalism: this tendency is represented by the foremost Protestant statesman in France, M. Édouard Soulier,[41] and by

---

[37] Headquarters: 102 Boulevard Arago, Paris.

[38] *Psaumes et Cantiques, Recueil adopté par le Synode Général Officieux des Églises Reformées de France* (Paris, Berger-Levrault, 1895), pp. 224–225.

[39] See *Bulletin Protestant Français*, January, 1927. See also L. S. Houghton, *Handbook of French and Belgian Protestantism* (New York, Federal Council of the Churches, 1919).

[40] *Recueil officiel des Actes du Synode Général*, pp. 318–319.

[41] President Doumergue comes of a Protestant family, but he is not a practising Christian.

the weekly Protestant paper, *La Vie Nouvelle*. The other is the tendency to reconcile French patriotism with internationalism, a tendency exemplified by a notable variety of peace-societies and peace-movements and stimulated doubtless by the fact that French Protestants, being a religious minority in their own country, are inclined to seek the friendship and understanding of Protestants in England and America, and even in Germany. It must be borne constantly in mind, however, that these same French Protestants are trained in the national schools and national army of their own country and that, as a minority, they are likely to be peculiarly sensitive to any aspersion on their patriotism or to any insinuation that they are not supremely loyal to the French nation.

4

From very ancient times there have been Jews in France. King Philip IV in 1306 decreed their expulsion from the country, but in the seventeenth century when Alsace was annexed to France a number of Jews were re-incorporated in the kingdom, and to this number were added in modern times some Portuguese and Spanish Jews of the Sephardic branch [42] who had settled in southern France as Christian converts but who reverted to their ancestral religion. Until the Great Revolution the Jews in France were a nation within a nation, separated from their French compatriots by barriers of law, custom, and prejudice.

The rise of rationalism and skepticism in France in the eighteenth century among both Christians and Jews tended to break down the barriers of prejudice, and during the Revolution the Jews, by decree of September 28, 1791, were granted the same civil rights as were enjoyed by other French citizens. In 1806

---

[42] The "Sephardim" are those Jews who for centuries have been subjected to Romance (Latin) culture. They are distinguished from the "Askenazim," who come from Northern and Eastern Europe and who speak Yiddish. The best general history of the Jews is Heinrich Graetz, *Geschichte der Juden von den ältesten Zeiten bis auf die Gegenwart* (1848), latest edition 1900–1909, 11 vols. A briefer history is Max L. Margolis and Alexander Marx, *A History of the Jewish People* (Philadelphia, The Jewish Publication Society of America, 1927).

Napoleon convoked a body of Jewish "notables" to seek their
advice on the regulation of relations between Judaism and the
State. When they were asked whether Jews loved France and
thought of her as their fatherland, they answered "Aye, even
unto death." In 1831 the Liberal Monarchy of Louis Philippe
formally recognized Judaism as a religion on an equal footing
with Catholicism and Protestantism, and thenceforth until the
Separation Act of 1905, each succeeding Government paid the
salaries of Jewish rabbis as it paid those of Catholic priests and
Protestant pastors.

It is estimated that there are now about 165,000 Jews in
France and about 85,000 in Algeria. Of the total number in
France, the majority (probably 100,000, of whom a third have
immigrated from foreign countries since the War) live at Paris,
and a half of the remainder reside in Alsace.[43]

With the exception of the post-war immigrants, the French
Jews are pretty largely Gallicized. Their families have long
lived under French law and their roots are firmly planted in
French soil. They have obtained from the French Revolution
not only formal emancipation but full civil and political rights
and an actual position of social equality with all other Frenchmen. In their gratitude for these benefits they have been throughout the nineteenth and twentieth centuries loyal adherents to the
revolutionary tradition and particularly to that brand of French
patriotism and nationalism which is usually denominated Jacobin.
Especially under the Third Republic they have participated in
politics and have held offices out of proportion to their numerical
importance, coöperating, as a rule, with "anti-clerical" Radicals.
As Radicals and "anti-clericals" they have been zealous supporters of the public educational system from kindergarten to
university, and their French patriotism has been confirmed by
their training in French schools and in the French army. Nowadays the mass of French Jews are distinguishable from other

[43] For statistics, see J. Kreppel, *Juden und Judentum von Heute* (Leipsic,
Amathea Verlag, 1925), p. 342; *L'Univers Israëlite*, Feb. 4, 1927, pp. 688 *et seq.*,
and Sept. 30, 1927, pp. 41–43. For a general survey of contemporary French
Judaism, see Joseph Bonsiven, "Bulletin du Judaïsme français," *Les Études*,
Sept. 5 and 20, 1927.

French patriots only by religion, and even their religion is organized nationally.

The majority of French Jews, for religious purposes, are organized into "associations of worship," as provided by the Separation Act of 1905, and these associations are united to form a national Central Consistory. The Consistory, under a Grand Rabbi, maintains a seminary for the training of rabbis [44] and fosters a propagandist periodical, the weekly *Univers Israëlite;* in strictly religious matters, it steers a middle course between liberalism and conservatism.

At the extreme right are smaller groups of orthodox, conservative Jews,[45] who for the most part have settled in France since the war and belong to the Askenazim. These Jews employ Yiddish, and even German, as well as French; they cling to the national, as well as religious, traditions of Judaism, and as yet represent an exception to the general rule that Jews in France are thoroughly Gallicized. Among these groups of conservative Jews should be reckoned some of the Jews in Alsace.

At the extreme left is an active group of "liberals," whose aim is to "harmonize more completely the external forms of worship with social conditions and modern thought." This group possesses an independent organization [46] and puts special emphasis on the compatibility of French Judaism with French patriotism.

French Judaism has propagandist agencies analogous to those of other religions in the country. There are young people's so-

[44] L'École Rabbinique, 8 rue Vanquelin, Paris. The headquarters of the Central Consistory are at 44 rue de la Victoire, Paris.

[45] Particularly the "Israelite Community of Strict Observance" (La Communauté Israëlite de la Stricte Observance), with headquarters at 10 rue Cadet, Paris, and with an official organ, *Archives Israëlites;* and the "Community of Traditional Israelite Worship" (La Communauté du Culte Israëlite Traditionnel), headquarters at 31 rue Théry, Paris. The Jews of Alsace publish a conservative organ at Strassbourg, chiefly in German, *La Tribune Juive.*

[46] The "Liberal Israelite Union" (L'Union Libérale Israëlite), founded in 1907, with headquarters at 24 rue Copernic, Paris, and with a monthly organ, *Le Rayon.* Its most popular orator is Aimé Pallière, a convert from Catholicism. See his book, *Le Sanctuaire inconnu, ma Conversion au Judaïsme* (Paris, Rieder, n.d.), and the periodical edited by him, *Foi et Reveil.*

cieties,[47] a missionary society [48] "to work for the emancipation and social progress of Israelites, to aid those Jews who suffer because they are Jews, and to encourage all publications serving the same ends," several charitable societies and foundations, and several literary associations and reviews.

More important for our present purposes are the efforts now being put forth by many French Jews to "make" Frenchmen of the minority of their co-religionists who have recently immigrated into the country and settled in Paris. To coördinate their efforts they have established in 1926 a special organization, "The Jewish French Welcome" ("L'Accueil Français Israélite"), which by means of visits, lectures, tracts, and classes, seeks to teach newcomers the French language and French ideals and to prepare them for naturalization as French citizens. A special prayer for France has been inserted in the Jewish prayer-books in use in the country.[49]

French Jews have never convinced all their fellow-countrymen of their supreme loyalty to France. Anti-Semitism, based at least in part on a suspicion that Jews are "internationalists" if not downright "aliens" and that as such they are always potential traitors to the "Christian" countries in which they reside, has flourished in France as elsewhere, and during the Dreyfus trials, at the close of the nineteenth century, it reached sensational dimensions. It is still exploited by the "Action Française" and by some "clericals" and finds expression in a number of contemporary books and articles,[50] but it is distinctly less now

[47] "Chema Israël," founded by the Central Consistory in 1920, with headquarters at 44 rue de la Victoire, Paris, with a publication, *Bulletin de Chema Israël*, with a Parisian membership of 1,500 and with ten provincial branches; and "L'Union Universelle de la Jeunesse Juive," founded by Aimé Pallière in 1923, with headquarters at 22 Boulevard Saint-Denis, Paris, and with a publication, *Chalom*.

[48] The French branch of the "Universal Israëlite Alliance" (Alliance Israëlite Universelle), founded in 1860, with headquarters at 45 rue La Bruyère, Paris. It maintains 116 schools in the Near East and uses the French language for the instruction of their 35,000 pupils. See Maurice Leven, *Cinquante Ans d'Histoire, L'Alliance Israëlite Universelle*, 2 vols. (Paris, Alcan, 1911–1920).

[49] *Rituel de Prières journalières* (Paris, Durlacher, 1924), p. 162.

[50] See, for example, Roger Lambelin, *L'Impérialisme d'Israël* (Paris, Grasset, 1924), and its bibliography, pp. 303–306.

than thirty years ago. The assimilation of Judaism to French nationalism has been too patently demonstrated by the patriotic activity of French Jews during and since the war to permit any reasonable Frenchman, except for the most partisan purposes, to accuse his Jewish compatriots of lack of devotion to France. It is true that there are a number of " Zionists " in France,[51] but these hold that one may be a good Zionist and at the same time a patriotic Frenchman, just as one may be a Breton, a Basque, an Alsatian, or a Fleming, and yet a perfectly good Frenchman. The chief support which Zionism has received from French Jews has been financial, and this largely from Baron Edmond de Rothschild, who has given some fifty million francs toward the purchase of land in Palestine and founded the Palestinian Jewish Colonization Association in order to interest other wealthy Jews in his projects and to carry on the work after his death. Only 105 Jews have actually left France, however, to settle in the Zion of Palestine.[52] The mass of French Jews are too closely interwoven as woof in the warp of French national life to be dislocated by an appeal that is purely sentimental and quite novel. Palestine is merely an ancient memory; France is a present and future fact.

5

Freemasonry is, of course, not a religion in quite the sense that Judaism, Protestantism, and Catholicism are religions. It is not " supernatural " and it is not exclusive. Many Jews and many Protestants are Freemasons. But it does propagate a philosophy of life which the Catholic Church has condemned, and Catholics, therefore, may not be Freemasons. This means that in a traditionally Catholic country, such as France, Freemasonry naturally assumes a sectarian significance; it becomes a rallying point for " anti-clericals;" and, being a secret organiza-

[51] Among French Zionists are Fleg, Spire, Pallière, Fernand Corcos, etc. See Fernand Corcos, *Israël sur la Terre biblique* and *À travers la Palestine juive* (Paris, Jouve). A French Zionist review, *Palestine*, was founded in 1927 and appears monthly.

[52] E. Eberlin, *Les Juifs d'Aujourd'hui* (Paris, Rieder, 1927), p. 81.

tion, it may exert a disproportionately great influence. There can be no doubt that in contemporary France the Masonic lodges belong to the general category of national agencies of propaganda which include the Christian churches and Jewish synagogues.

Freemasonry originated in Great Britain early in the eighteenth century; its first constitutions and rituals were compiled by Protestant clergymen influenced by contemporaneous concepts of reason and Deism, of natural law and humanitarianism. In other words, it was shaped by *philosophes* of the eighteenth century and soon found lodgment wherever the philosophy of "the enlightenment" was highly esteemed. Nowhere was this philosophy more highly esteemed than in France; and here Freemasonry entered from Britain in 1732 and soon found numerous influential followers among the nobility and especially among the bourgeoisie.[53]

A very considerable number of the Jacobin leaders of the French Revolution were Masons, who tended to identify the principles of the Revolution with the tenets of Freemasonry, and *vice versa,* with the result that to French Freemasonry of the nineteenth and twentieth centuries Revolutionary Jacobinism has been a continuous tradition and an impelling force. French Freemasons feel peculiarly that they are the expounders and defenders of "liberty, equality, and fraternity;" they are ardent protagonists of democracy and republicanism; they exalt *étatisme;* and they are patriotic, and nationalist, in the Jacobin way. In their continuous efforts to curb the influence and restrict the rights of the Catholic Church, they have emphasized the "anti-clerical" tradition of the Great Revolution and many of them have become not only anti-Catholic but atheist.[54] This fact has militated against the maintenance of most cordial relations between Freemasons in France and those in foreign

[53] See Albert Lantoine, *Histoire de la Franc-Maçonnerie française* (Paris, E. Nourry, 1925), and *La Franc-Maçonnerie* (Paris, Grand Orient, n.d.).

[54] The chief Masonic body in France, the Grand Orient, repudiated in 1877 one of the "landmarks" of international Freemasonry, that belief in God is a prerequisite to membership. Thereafter the Grand Lodges of Great Britain and the United States broke off "friendly relations" with the Grand Orient. See Adrien Juvanon, *Vers la Lumière* (Paris, Imprimerie Centrale de la Bourse, n.d.).

countries, and by rendering French Freemasonry peculiar in this respect has contributed indirectly to making it more national in character and conduct.

It is estimated that there are now about sixty thousand Freemasons in France and about twenty-eight thousand in the French colonies.[55] These figures, however, are hardly comparable with those cited earlier of Jews, Protestants, and Catholics, for whereas the statistics of the latter include women and children, the Freemasons are all adult men. Besides, the proportion of educated and well-to-do men, and therefore of men influential in politics and economics, is undoubtedly greater among the Freemasons than among any of the strictly religious bodies in France.

French Freemasonry does not possess, however, a single centralized organization. Ever since a schism in 1772 there have been rival " obediences," quarreling with each other about many details, as well as acting in unison on certain matters of general principle. On one hand is the " Grand Orient " ("Le Grand Orient "), with a French membership of 44,000, following faithfully the so-called " French rite." On the other hand is the " Grand Lodge " ("La Grande Loge "), with a membership of 13,000, adhering to the Scottish rite. In addition are two minor Masonic " obediences " of more recent origin: the " International Mixed Masonic Order of Human Right " ("L'Ordre Maçonnique Mixte Internationale, Le Droit Humain "); and the " Mixed Grand Lodge " ("La Grande Loge Mixte ") which counts only a hundred members.[56]

All the Masonic bodies carry on a good deal of propaganda in various ways.[57] Each local lodge holds stated meetings at which lectures are delivered to the brethren and discussion is encouraged. Annual conventions of the several " obediences " are held, at which general business is transacted and resolutions

[55] Dr. Hugo Schmidt, *Kalender für Freimauers, Statistisches Jahrbuch für 1927, 66 Jahrgang* (Leipsic, Bruno Zechel, 1926), p. 254.

[56] Headquarters of Le Grand Orient are at 16 rue Cadet, Paris; of La Grande Loge, at 8 rue Puteaux, Paris; and of L'Ordre Maçonnique Mixte Internationale, at 5 rue Jules Breton, Paris.

[57] See Gaston Martin, *De l'Éducation Maçonnique* (Paris, Grand Orient, 1926).

are adopted. The Grand Orient publishes a semi-official organ, *L'Acacia*. And individual Masons who occupy important positions in the Government or in newspapers are likely to express in speech or writing opinions which they derive from Freemasonry. It is frequently said by French opponents of Masonry that such Radical newspapers as *Le Quotidien* and *Le Soir* and such Radical societies as " La Ligue des Droits de l'Homme," " La Ligue de l'Enseignement," and " L'Union des Jeunesses Républicaines " are more or less official agencies of Masonic propaganda. It is true that many of the directors of these societies and newspapers are Masons, but their connection with organized Freemasonry is personal, rather than official, and much the same can be said of many school-teachers and other state functionaries under the contemporary Republican régime.

Despite formal declarations that French Freemasonry is not concerned with politics and will not take sides in partisan disputes,[58] the institution, collectively and individually, being by tradition Jacobin, is now solidly Radical, and both the Grand Lodge and the Grand Orient make a practice of adopting resolutions at their annual conventions in favor of the position taken, in debatable political questions, by the Radical and Radical Socialist Parties. Conventions of both bodies, for example, have condemned the resumption of diplomatic relations by the French Government with the Vatican.[59] The Grand Orient at its Convention (" Convent ") of 1923 demanded the rigid enforcement of the laws against religious congregations and the speedy application of all " anti-clerical " legislation to Alsace-Lorraine, declared in favor of according state functionaries the right to organize trade-unions, and urged the thorough " Gallicization " of the French

[58] Chapter I of the Constitution of the Grand Lodge (1907) affirms that ' Freemasonry should not be subject to any sect or take the part of any school. It holds itself aloof from all discussions with a view to offering to all friends of Truth a common ground of understanding and fraternal union." Article I of the Constitution of the Grand Orient (1892) declares that the lodges " must prohibit any debate on acts of the civil authority and any Masonic action in the struggles of political parties."

[59] *Convent, Grand Orient, 1923*, pp. 80–81; *Bulletin Officiel de la Grande Loge de France*, 1920, p. 33.

colonies. The Grand Lodge at its Convention of 1922 called for the enforcement of all lay (" anti-clerical ") laws.

French Freemasonry is predominantly bourgeois, and Frenchmen of the extreme Left, as well as those of the Right, do not like it. The International Congress of the Communists in 1922 condemned it and instructed the directing committee of the French Communist Party "to break off all connection with Freemasonry before January 1, 1923." [60]

French Freemasonry is certainly patriotic. "It prescribes," says the Constitution of the Grand Lodge, "to all its members as *citizens* and as *Masons* that they submit themselves to the legislation of the country where they have the means of free assembly and that they be ready for any sacrifice which the fatherland may demand." And the Grand Orient publishes similar admonitions. Yet, French Freemasonry also stresses the individual's duty to humanity, and the Frenchman's to international comity. As the Grand Lodge has said: " Defend your country because it is she who makes you happy and who embraces all the ties and all the beings dear to your heart; but do not forget humanity and its rights." [61]

In 1898 a French lodge refused an applicant for membership simply because he was a German; and when another lodge offered to initiate him, the Grand Lodge inhibited it. From 1871 to 1908 the Grand Orient printed on a page of its Annual, within a frame of deep mourning, the names of the seven lodges of Alsace-Lorraine which had been removed from its jurisdiction by the German victory of 1870. When the war broke out, the Grand Orient addressed a letter of fervent patriotic devotion to the Government, and the Grand Lodge, "surprised by the declaration of war at a time when it was studying ways and means to a Franco-German rapprochement, abolished the lodge ' Goethe,' which was composed of Germans living in Paris, and confiscated its secretary's records, its archives, and its library." [62]

[60] *L'Humanité,* December 19, 1922. In Italy, it may be remarked, the Grand Council of the Fascisti took similar action on February 14, 1923.
[61] Cited in Albert Lantoine, *Hiram couronné d'Épines* (Paris, Nourry, 1926), Vol. II, p. 499.
[62] *Ibid.,* p. 312.

After the war, when the Masons of neutral countries attempted to call an international congress at Rome, the French declared that they would not attend unless the Germans should perform a public act of contrition, a declaration that doomed the congress to failure.

Nevertheless French Freemasons within the last years have been active in propaganda in behalf of the League of Nations and a closer and better understanding between France and Germany, and Conventions of the Grand Orient and of the Grand Lodge have pledged their support to these causes. Indeed, the international propaganda of French Masons is now so conspicuous that their foes have been redoubling the charges of antipatriotism against them.[63] It is safe to predict, however, that in future crises, as in those of the past, the French State can count upon the enthusiastic national loyalty of French Freemasons, as upon that of French Jews, French Protestants, and French Catholics.

[63] See, for example, A. G. Michel, *La Dictature de la Franc-Maçonnerie sur la France* (Paris, Spes, 1924).

CHAPTER VI

THE PRESS: NEWSPAPERS AND MAGAZINES

I

EVERY French child receives a national training for several years in the educational system of the French State. Every French young man is given a supplementary national training for a period in the army or navy of the French State. Many Frenchmen undergo some measure of national training through membership in semi-private, semi-public religious organizations which are tolerated by the French State and which teach loyalty to the French State. Every Frenchman, man, woman, and child, comes into fairly frequent contact with some official or functionary of the centralized national French State.

But all such training is occasional or temporary, or it affects at any given time only a portion of the entire French nation. What reënforces most substantially the national endeavors of school, army, church, and civil service, and fuses them together and conveys them into the consciousness of every Frenchman and every Frenchwoman throughout life is the French press. Everybody in France is literate; and everybody from childhood to old age reads some French newspaper or magazine. The press in France, as elsewhere, has developed enormously during the nineteenth and twentieth centuries, partly because the rapid growth of popular literacy has created a rapidly growing market for it, and partly because the swift advancement of the industrial arts has greatly stimulated its supply. And the press, catering to an ever wider public, has tended to stress whatever most interests the largest number of readers. This means that the French press naturally emphasizes what is French, and thereby becomes a constant and ubiquitous maker of Frenchmen.

Even the most casual observer of French life must be impressed by the great quantity and variety of periodical matter which is consumed by the public. The heavily laden news-stands at every railway-station, the frequency of "kiosks" and little shops selling books, magazines, and newspapers wherever people pass, whether along broad avenues like the Grands Boulevards of Paris or the Cannebière of Marseilles or in the village square of a half-deserted "hole" in the provinces, are so many visible evidences of the outstanding importance of the press in contemporary France. Or, let the traveler thread his way from carriage to carriage of any railway-train within the national borders, and he will remark the profusion of dailies, weeklies, and even reviews read by the humblest third-class passengers as well as the bourgeois occupants of the more comfortable compartments, and so varied is the assortment of literature that he will assume the existence of a periodical peculiarly adapted to the tastes of man, woman, or child of any social status or degree of intelligence.

As to the exact number of periodical publications actually in circulation, there is no official or semi-official computation obtainable. The very nature of periodical literature, the ephemeral character of the units to be counted, the seasonal demands and political cycles, the thousand variables affecting the vitality of a publication from day to day, make it obviously impossible to compile exact statistics. There is in France, however, an unofficial annual guide to, and list of, periodicals French and foreign, the *Annuaire de la Presse Française et Étrangère*, which, in its 1927 edition, devotes more than fifteen hundred pages to a classified treatment of the French press (compared with 350 pages for the rest of the world) and lists in its index no less than 5,000 titles of dailies, weeklies, and other periodicals (short of annuals) which are assumed to be functioning in France and the French colonies at the end of 1926. From the classified subject-lists in the body of the Annual has been compiled a table (Table VII) showing the number of periodicals of various sorts published at Paris and in the provinces. It will be noted that the table enumerates a total of 3,693 such periodicals. To this figure must be added 2,964 titles of periodicals listed in the body of the Annual as "provincial" but not otherwise classified, or a grand total of 6,657 separate listings of French periodicals. Comparing this figure with the 5,000 individual titles in the index, it is apparent that in at least 1,657 instances the same periodical has been classed in the body of the Annual under more than one heading. Besides, in using the data of the Annual, two special cautions should be borne in mind: first, that many (possibly a third) of the titles are nothing but names, that the publication has ceased to exist while the title endures as the legal property and exclusive right of its owner; and second, that some of the different titles represent variant editions of one and the same daily or weekly.

TABLE VII

FRENCH PERIODICALS CLASSIFIED BY SUBJECTS
PARIS AND PROVINCES

(*Annuaire de la Presse, 1927*)

SUBJECT	NUMBER PUBLISHED	
	IN PARIS	IN THE PROVINCES
Administration	53	6
Agriculture	90	129
Architecture	21	2
Arrondissement journals	37	—
Bibliography	26	—
Catholic periodicals	79	35
Chambers of Commerce and Professional syndicates	105	19
Colonies	52	5
Commerce	81	25
Construction	10	—
Chemical Industries	21	—
Children's magazines	17	—
Diplomacy	10	—
Education	67	5
Electricity	49	11
English and American press	31	—
Fashion	140	—
Financial	211	19
Fine Arts	28	—
Foreign press (exclusive of English-American)	56	—
Furniture	7	—
Geography, History, etc.	12	12

TABLE VII (*Cont.*)

SUBJECT	NUMBER PUBLISHED	
	IN PARIS	IN THE PROVINCES
Hotels and Travel..........................	32	23
Humorous and Satirical....................	32	7
Illustrated magazines......................	59	18
Insurance................................	36	1
Jewish periodicals.........................	1	—
Jurisprudence.............................	96	14
Legal advertisements......................	24	47
Literature and Philology..................	53	—
Lumber trade.............................	18	—
Matrimony...............................	7	—
Medicine.................................	181	23
Metallurgy...............................	24	3
Military (including Veterans')..............	52	24
Mining..................................	12	1
Music...................................	29	—
Navigation...............................	23	5
Paper and binding trades..................	8	—
Paris papers issued by provincial groups......	30	—
Parisian and regional newspapers...........	252	—
Petroleum................................	8	—
Pharmacy................................	11	5
Philanthropy.............................	28	—
Photography and Cinema..................	37	—
Political Economy and Social Sciences.......	60	10
Posts, Telephones and Telegraphs...........	11	—
Press....................................	13	—
Professional journals......................	62	13
Protestant periodicals.....................	18	—
Public works.............................	29	6
Publicity................................	8	—
Railways.................................	22	—
Reviews (literary and political).............	143	27
Science..................................	76	—
Society..................................	7	18
Spiritualism and Occult Sciences...........	7	—
Sports...................................	172	—
Stamp-collecting.........................	5	2
Statistics................................	6	—
Stenography..............................	18	6
Textiles..................................	9	7
Theatres.................................	21	12
Trade papers, miscellaneous................	174	2
Typography..............................	19	—
Women's magazines.......................	15	—
TOTALS.................................	3151	542

Statistics furnished by the French Government are even less satisfactory. The Ministry of the Interior, which, in conjunction with the Ministry of Justice, exercises whatever control the State imposes upon the press, is unable to throw light on the subject, beyond furnishing the following figures: in 1926 the Ministry of the Interior received at its " Dépôt Légal " 478,724 separate issues of periodicals published in France, of which 132,436 were published in Paris and 346,288 in the provinces.[1] Every day including Sunday an average of 1,311 separate issues of dailies, weeklies, and other periodicals was received by the " Dépôt."

Whether we estimate the quantity of publications from the *Annuaire de la Presse* or from government sources, therefore, we are convinced of the vast supply of material which looms up before the student who would observe the formation of public opinion and national psychology in France by means of the printed word. It would be impossible to give equal attention to each of the five thousand publications listed in the *Annuaire;* but the fact that such a large number does exist is in itself an interesting commentary on the social and economic life of the French people.

The part which the press has played in the history of France, especially during and since the Great Revolution, is too well known to be discussed here;[2] it is sufficient for our purpose if we recognize at the outset the traditional aptitude of the French for expressing themselves, as groups or as individuals, through the medium of journalism. It is, however, only within comparatively recent years — since, let us say, 1880 — that the French press has turned its major attention from the dissemination of political propaganda, its chief *raison d'être* during the troubled century preceding the establishment of the Third and relatively stable Republic, to the vending of news and general information. Impartial presentation of news is still the exception; editorial opinion finds its way into practically every type of periodical.

---

[1] Figures furnished by M. Porcher, Dépôt Légal, Bibliothèque Nationale.

[2] See A. de Chambure, *À Travers la Presse* (Paris, 1914), for a survey of the press in France from the earliest times to 1914.

While there may be several versions of a given event, the essential facts, however distorted, must be the same; the number of interpretations, on the other hand, is limited only by the number of groups of like-minded persons who are willing to read them. Differences in opinion, in other words, make not only horse-races but many adventures in journalism. And it is a far less costly sport in France to run a paper than to run a horse. A facile pen, a few hours of spare time, a subscription list of a hundred or more names of friends, admirers, and enemies, an astounding title, and a cheap printer — and any Frenchman who has editorial or political aspirations may follow in the footsteps of Camille Desmoulins, Louis Blanc, or Henri Rochefort. In spite of the important economic changes which have affected the nation, post-war France still remains a land of small-scale producers, small workshops, small tradesmen, and small papers. It is estimated that not more than twenty per cent of the five thousand periodicals published in France may be considered first-class business enterprises, requiring corporate management, large investment of capital, and a staff of full-time collaborators. Of the remaining eighty per cent, the majority are managed, financed, edited and often entirely written by the same person, who may or may not be engaged at the same time in a more lucrative enterprise.

Closely allied to the question of cheap production is low selling-price, a prime economic factor in the stimulation of popular demand and abundant supply. The daily newspaper which cost one sou in 1914 costs five sous to-day, and the prices of other periodicals have advanced in like proportion. The movement of general retail commodity prices has been the pace-maker, but has always kept ahead of the prices of periodical literature. Instead of advancing the price, the proprietor of a journal has preferred to hold his public by selling his paper at the same price despite increased costs of production, while recouping his losses by decreasing the size of the issue, eliminating expensive features, and reducing his editorial staff or getting cheaper contributors. Compared with the prices of other articles in 1927, the cost of periodicals is low, ranging from ten centimes for two different children's magazines to twenty-five francs for an elaborate fashion journal. Most daily newspapers, in Paris and the provinces, are twenty-five centimes, with the exception of *L'Humanité, Le Figaro,* and *Le Quotidien,* which are thirty centimes, and *Le Temps,* which is forty centimes. Weeklies cost seventy-five centimes or one franc; the average cost of fortnightlies is two francs fifty centimes, and monthlies four francs fifty centimes.

If there is such a creature as the " average Frenchman," what are his preferences among the cheap and plentiful assortment of periodicals? Thanks to the fact that the Librairie Hachette of Paris has a virtual monopoly of furnishing periodicals to the railway-stations and news-dealers throughout France, we can determine what the public buys. On the order list of the " Messageries de Journaux " of the Librairie Hachette are 423 titles of publications, which may be bought presumably anywhere in France. Of these 423, the investigator learned from the Librairie Hachette, there are fifty-eight " best-sellers " — weeklies, fortnightlies, and monthlies bought regularly by a large clientèle. An analysis of the best-selling list gives us the following division of subject-matter: fifteen fashion and women's journals; twelve humorous papers (including " Gallic " wit); ten literary reviews and magazines; ten political and satirical periodicals; five magazines of popular science and radio; three " movie-magazines "; and three sporting journals. It would be extremely helpful, in assigning the place of these varied publications in the life of the French people, to know actual circulation figures. Unfortunately there is no law in France which requires the publication or compilation of certified data on circulation. Such information is jealously guarded by each publisher with almost the same secrecy that surrounds his bank balance. The recent organization of an " Office de Justification de Tirages " in Paris, for registering the circulation of periodicals, is an indication that certain publishers have learned that such publicity is not a danger but an asset. At the present time, however, only a very small number of publishers of weeklies and regional dailies have joined the association. Of all weeklies, *L'Illustration* has probably the largest circulation (154,706 in 1926), with *Candide* and *Les Nouvelles Littéraires* following in the 100,000 class. Fortnightlies and monthlies depend on subscription lists for the bulk of their sales and are unwilling to divulge circulation figures.

Apart from the factor of large circulation, we must consider as having an effective part in the formation of a national psychology those publications which are representative of the significant political, social, or religious groups in France. In many cases their circulation is small, but the personality of the editors, the distinctive stand taken on national problems, and the cohesion and force of the readers give such publications an influence far beyond that which may be indicated by the number of copies issued.

With such considerations in mind, a selection of 108 weeklies, fortnightlies, and monthlies has been made for purposes of special study. They are listed in Appendix C to this volume (pages 409–430), and their significance in the molding of French national consciousness will be discussed presently in this chapter.

2

Without minimizing the importance of weeklies and reviews in developing the state of mind we call " French," we must, however, precede our discussion of them by the immediate study of the greatest force of all in the creation of public opinion — the daily newspapers. The French daily press is divided into two distinct groups, one comprising the dailies of Paris, at present (January 1928) thirty-four in number, and the other the provincial papers, of which there are 241 in the entire country. (See Table VIII.) In other words, it would appear that the three million Parisians, who are about one-fourteenth of the entire population of France, read about one-seventh of the dailies published in the country, that is, that the Parisian reads two papers to the provincial's one. We should remember, however, that Paris journals are to be purchased all over France, and that the " Big Five " of Paris, *Le Petit Parisien, Le Journal, Le Matin, Le Petit Journal,* and *L'Écho de Paris,* have special news deliveries and large subscription lists in the provinces.

Of the thirty-four newspapers which were published in Paris

in January 1928,[3] we find ten which attain a circulation of 200,-
000 or more, and which in consequence would be important as
powerful organs of national influence, regardless of any other
characteristics. While it is impossible to obtain certified circula-
tion-figures for the reasons already noted, the approximate circulation of these ten is a matter of common knowledge in the world
of journalism and publicity. First we have the " Big Five "
morning papers: *Le Petit Parisien*, with a circulation of 1,700,000,
conceded to be the largest of any daily newspaper in the world; [4]
Le Journal, 1,000,000; *Le Matin*, 800,000; *Le Petit Journal*, 600,-
000; and *L'Écho de Paris*, 200,000. Outside of this group, which
was formed as a " consortium " for the joint exploitation of advertising space through the Agence Havas, and for other mutual
interests not made public,[5] we have *L'Intransigeant*, with an
evening circulation of 450,000; *Excelsior* (owned by *Le Petit
Parisien*), 250,000; *L'Humanité*, organ of the Communist Party,
200,000; *Le Quotidien*, organ of the Radical groups, 200,000;
and the Royalist *Action Française*, which sporadically mounts to
the 200,000 mark.

Taking the " Big Five " morning dailies as representative of
the journals which specialize in giving news of the entire world,
we find little, on first sight, that distinguishes one from the other.
Each covers from six to eight large news-sheets, contains a liberal
assortment of photographs and cartoons on the front page (an
average of ten separate illustrations), and follows practically the
same make-up — front-page editorial and feature articles, flashy
headlines, vivid and popular presentation of news; each publishes
regular features of interest to women, children, sportsmen, and
other groups; each has vast and imposing editorial offices, a corps
of special writers, and elaborate foreign news organizations. On
closer study, certain individual characteristics appear (which have
been noted in the detailed description in Appendix D) and we

---

3 For titles and detailed description, see Appendix D, pp. 431–459.

4 The New York *Daily News*, next in circulation, had a certified issue of 1,224,-
243 daily average in 1928 (from sworn statement made for Audit Bureau of Circulations as reported by *American Newspaper Annual and Directory*, Philadelphia,
1929).

5 See Billy and Piot, *Le Monde des Journaux* (Paris, Crès, 1924), p. 148.

learn that each of the " Big Five " has traditions, methods, specialties, and types of readers which distinguish it from the others. The most salient distinction is that which sets apart *L'Écho de Paris* from the other four as the one great journal of information which is at the same time a leading organ of political propaganda. *Le Petit Parisien, Le Journal, Le Matin,* and *Le Petit Journal* steer a middle course between conservative and radical tendencies, and are recognized as the semi-official organs through which the existing Government, whatever its political complexion, tells the public what it wants it to know about domestic and foreign affairs of state. But *L'Écho de Paris* is openly and emphatically conservative, takes the offensive against the Left, and conducts active campaigns for those political groups which support the " nationalist " aims of France, especially the wider diffusion of French culture, the greater development of colonial resources, a stronger foreign policy, and a more powerful military organization. Similarly *L'Écho de Paris* is a champion of the Catholic Church, whereas the other four are careful to treat all cults impartially, and thus not to give offense to any group. While all five vie with each other in giving front-page space and prominence to great national celebrations and patriotic movements, *L'Écho de Paris* surpasses the others in the intensity of its expressed devotion to the fatherland and in the irresistible eloquence of such patriotic leaders as the Count de Mun and Maurice Barrès in the past and Gabriel Hanotaux, Louis Madelin, and General de Castelnau to-day. Since the war it has been the prime mover and perhaps the original inspiration of such great national manifestations as the Festival of Saint Jeanne, and the burial of the Unknown Soldier.

One evening paper, *L'Intransigeant,* should really be classed among the " great journals of information," although it lacks the attractive format and expensive features which lend color to the " Big Five." It concentrates on the presentation of news of the late morning and afternoon, which is rapidly assembled for hasty reading.

With the exception of the politically significant *Écho de Paris,* the great dailies which we have named exercise their influence on the French people by means of that indirect and impersonal suggestion which penetrates the more successfully when its operation is unperceived. The directors choose to remain anonymous and take pains to keep their personalities out of the public eye: the members of the Dupuy family, owners of *Le Petit Parisien*, prominent figures in politics, rarely address the public in signed editorials; M. Louis Loucheur keeps well in the background of his *Petit Journal;* the name of M. Bunau-Varilla, director of *Le Matin,* never obtrudes in his own columns. None the less the public thinks and feels to considerable degree as the man or corporation invisibly directing a great journal wills. By the choice of news and illustrations, by the delaying or speeding up of despatches, by the emphasis placed on one event and the slurring of another, by an infinite number of subtle journalistic touches which are far more potent than direct editorial comment, those who control the French popular press have played with the destinies not only of France but of the world. " This seat is worth three thrones," is M. Bunau-Varilla's famous description of his administrative chair in the office of *Le Matin.* And indeed it is impossible to overestimate the power of those who govern the great dailies when we look back on the history of the Third Republic, and note how they have sown seeds of hatred for one country and stimulated friendship for another; fomented some political crises and deliberately stifled others; exploited incidents like Fashoda and Agadir; made heroes or fools of public persons as means to definite ends, causing the French, for example, to worship Woodrow Wilson in 1917–1918 and to scoff at him in 1919; destroyed confidence in the financial stability of France, and then restored it.

In combating the far-reaching and occult influence of the few great impersonal newspapers, the numerous political and personal journals of Paris are fighting a battle against the most modern press with the weapons and tactics of French journalistic tradition of the nineteenth century. Fifteen of the thirty-four newspapers of Paris are *par excellence* organs of political groups. Of the five which express the opinions of the Right, the most reactionary as well as the largest in circulation is *L'Action*

Française, which expounds many doctrines too extreme for the others — *L'Avenir,* Millerand's organ; *La Liberté; La Presse;* and Hervé's *La Victoire.* The extreme Left concentrates its ammunition in one important organ of the Communist Party, *L'Humanité,* read by 200,000 workers of Bolshevist sympathies. Between these outposts of Right and Left we have nine papers which represent nuances in Left opinion from the pale pink of *L'Homme Libre* to the Socialist red of *Le Populaire.* Le *Quotidien,* the largest of the radical papers, takes a middle position as the strongest supporter of the whole Left bloc. *L'Ère Nouvelle* and *L'Œuvre* are less widely read, but are dynamic forces in the Radical camp; *Le Peuple* is the spokesman of organized labor, the General Confederation of Labor (C. G. T.); *Le Rappel, Le Soir,* and *La Volonté* are the least significant and most volatile of the Left press.

In viewing the line-up of political papers from Left to Right we are impressed by the youth of the majority. Only five were founded before the twentieth century (*La Presse,* 1833; *Le Soir,* 1864; *La Liberté,* 1865; *Le Rappel,* 1869; and *L'Œuvre,* as a weekly, 1893). Three survive from pre-war years (*L'Action Française,* 1908; *L'Humanité,* 1904; and *L'Homme Libre,* 1913). The remaining seven were established during and after the war (*La Victoire,* 1914; *L'Avenir* and *Le Populaire,* 1918; *L'Ère Nouvelle,* 1919; *Le Peuple,* 1921; *Le Quotidien,* 1923; and *La Volonté,* 1925). The ephemeral character of the French political press is evident from the fact that of the thirty-two predominantly political dailies which were flourishing in Paris in 1914, twenty had ceased to exist in 1923. Of the twelve which were still alive in that year, only seven survived in 1927. Such are the "vital statistics" of political journals — high birth-rate, high death-rate, low expectation of life. All of the "great journals," on the other hand, date from the last century (*Le Petit Journal,* 1863; *Le Petit Parisien,* 1876; *L'Intransigeant,* 1880; *Le Matin* and *L'Écho de Paris,* 1884; and *Le Journal,* 1892). Paradoxically enough, the long-established journals of large circulation are constantly evolving newer and more subtle methods for swaying public sentiment, while the majority of the political journals, carrying on the traditions of the pamphleteers of the Revolution and Empire, fill their pages with long controversial editorials, articles of political propaganda, discussion of personalities, and appeals for funds. With the exception of *L'Œuvre, Le Soir,* and *Le Quotidien,* the journals of " opinion " neglect items of ordinary news interest or use them as grist for the political mill. They are generally small four-page sheets, with few illustrations or advertisements, but always with a large section reviewing the editorial comments of the other journals with appropriate retorts.

While the great daily screens its director or editor from the public eye, the political journal owes its existence and fortune, good or bad, to the personality of its chief. Thus a Frenchman can hardly think of the title of one of these papers without immediately linking with it the name and presence of its editor, and even the peculiarities of his literary style. The following associations are self-evident: *L'Action Française* — Léon Daudet and Charles Maurras; *L'Avenir* — Alexandre Millerand; *L'Homme Libre* — during the war, Clemenceau, now Eugène Lautier; *L'Humanité* — Marcel Cachin; *Le Peuple* — Léon Jouhaux; *Le Populaire* — Léon Blum; *La Presse* — André Payer; *Le Quotidien* — Pierre Bertrand; *Le Rappel* — Edmond du Mesnil; *La Victoire* — Gustave Hervé; *L'Œuvre* — Gustave Téry; *La Volonté* — Albert Dubarry and Joseph Caillaux. The phrases and signatures of these men stamp their respective papers with a distinctive trade-mark; and to the man-in-the-street, more interested in people than theories, the constant grappling of the editors is the greatest charm and most diverting quality of the political press.

Not only do the journals of the Right abound in patriotic, even nationalist, utterances (see detailed analysis in Appendix D), but it should be noted that in the majority of the organs of the Left may be found striking expressions of pride in national achievement, colonial administration and development, sentimental editorials on patriotic manifestations, and occasional ridicule and depreciation of foreign institutions and culture. In short, no sharp dividing line may be drawn between Left and

Right on the general principle of national patriotism. Even the Communist *L'Humanité* occasionally forgets its allegiance to the Third International so far as to exhort the French never to submit to the invasion of foreign capitalists, the inference being that it is better for the proletariat of France to be exploited by capitalists of their own country.

The same finely shaded distinctions which separate the states- man from the demagogue set apart from the journals of " opin- ion " already noted a group of four newspapers deeply concerned with the foreign and domestic politics of France. Like venerable solons who enhance their prestige by holding themselves aloof from the tumult and shouting of the political arena, *Le Journal des Débats* (founded in 1789, the oldest daily newspaper in France), *Le Figaro* (1826), *Le Temps* (1861), and to a lesser degree *Le Gaulois* (1865) carry the authority and dignity of their years on every page. They are the patricians of the press, reflecting those qualities of French civilization which French- men regard as their special contribution to modern culture: elegance and purity of style, well-balanced judgment, and deli- cately tempered wit. Their comparatively small circle of read- ers includes the aristocracy of France, whether measured by birth, wealth, or brains, and, notably in the case of *Le Temps* and *Le Figaro*, of the entire world. Each of these journals caters to the tastes and traditions of a specialized clientèle: the appeal of *Le Gaulois* is not that of *Le Figaro*, both read by the *monde des salons*; *Le Journal des Débats* and *Le Temps*, although concerned with the same political, literary, and scientific de- velopments, are not substitutes for each other. To enter into the subtle but fundamental differences which separate one from the other as distinctly as all four detach themselves from the press as a whole would require a social study far beyond the scope of this chapter.

Confining ourselves to the factor of " nationalism," we may note a few gradations in patriotic fervor. While they are all identified with the " spirit of France," *Le Journal des Débats* is the least interested in patriotic manifestations, is more alarmed by the alleged Bolshevist peril in France than by the hostile movements of border enemies, and sometimes makes judgments on foreign policy which have another inspiration than the Quai d'Orsay. *Le Temps,* on the other hand, is rather more ostentatiously patriotic, opens its front-page columns regularly to erudite patriots like the late Ernest Lavisse, and regards itself as the ambassador of French culture to the foreign hinterland; economic considerations, however, play a larger part than sentiment in its careful study of France's colonial resources. In the personality of the late Marquis Robert de Flers, aristocrat, Academician, dramatist, literary critic, and editor-in-chief of *Le Figaro,* we may observe the same versatility and charm which give that paper its significance as an organ of pro-French propaganda. Its traditions are those of the sparkling but impractical wits of the eighteenth-century salons, adapted more or less successfully to the materialism of present-day democracy. *Le Gaulois,* in contrast, has never reconciled itself to the Republic, and the France which it defends or exalts with intense zeal is that of the Royalists.[5a]

Whatever the fundamental differences, all four display the same outward signs of gravity, restraint, and disdain for modern journalistic devices. There are no photographs, cartoons, or striking headlines to catch the public eye; the fonts of type and arrangement of material have not changed in generations: characteristics which appeal to the well-ordered mind of the conservative Frenchmen. All his life he may open *Le Temps,* for instance, with the assurance of finding in its time-honored place the commentary of the same type of journalist, viewing the changing world from the same vantage-point, expressing himself with the same scholarly precision and urbanity, tinged with the same prejudices and preferences which were shared with the same enjoyment by the reader's grandfather. It is by this daily communion with the sacred institutions and traditions of the past that Frenchmen confirm and strengthen their faith in the fatherland.

There remain to be discussed a number of Paris dailies which

[5a] Since these lines were written, *Le Gaulois* has been bought by, and merged with, *Le Figaro.*

are composed and edited for the needs of special groups of readers. Since they have been examined in detail in Appendix D, we shall do little more than name them here: *Comœdia,* journal of the seven lively arts as well as the more conservative modes of self-expression; *La Croix,* the leading Catholic newspaper of France and a powerful organ of political and social influence; *Excelsior,* a family paper imitating the English and American illustrated dailies; *L'Information,* for investors and speculators; *La Journée Industrielle,* designed for the business and industrial world; *Le Petit Bleu,* specializing in Paris gossip and municipal scandal. When we add to this list *Paris-Matinal,* established in 1927 and fighting for its life, and two afternoon papers, *Paris-Midi* and *Paris-Soir,* we have completed our rapid survey of the metropolitan press.

3

The French newspaper press, like its paternal Gaul, may be divided into three parts: the first and most important, the daily press of Paris, has been discussed; but two other parts, which are of great importance to the student of public opinion in France, remain to be considered, the regional dailies and the local journals of the thirty-eight million French who do not live in Paris. A glance at Table VIII will give some idea of the number of daily newspapers, weeklies (including semi-weeklies, etc.), and other periodicals which originate and circulate in the provinces.

At the outset we must separate from the 241 daily newspapers of provincial France that influential portion of the press which is called " regional," embracing dailies of large cities which issue for circulation in outlying towns or départements special editions containing local news furnished by private correspondents, as well as news items and articles of interest to all. Thirty-one of the best known regional dailies of France have been analyzed in some detail in Appendix E, and two of them, *La Dépêche de Toulouse* and *Le Nouvelliste de Lyon,* have been given special attention as typical respectively of radical and conservative tendencies in regional journalism.[6] Most of the

[6] See pp. 460–470 below.

TABLE VIII

PROVINCIAL PUBLICATIONS BY DÉPARTEMENTS

(Source: *Annuaire de la Presse, 1927*)

DÉPARTEMENTS	DAILIES	WEEKLIES [8]	OTHERS [9]	TOTAL
1. Ain	1	20	11	32
2. Aisne	—	23	7	30
3. Allier	5	22	12	39
4. Alpes (Basses-)	—	9	2	11
5. Alpes (Hautes-)	—	7	7	14
6. Alpes-Maritimes	6	38	29	73
7. Ardèche	—	18	13	31
8. Ardennes	2	11	9	22
9. Ariège	—	9	8	17
10. Aube	4	4	4	12
11. Aude	1	10	8	19
12. Aveyron	1	10	6	17
13. Bouches-du-Rhône	10	51	49	110
14. Calvados	2	34	12	48
15. Cantal	1	12	8	21
16. Charente	3	12	4	19
17. Charente-Inférieure	—	30	14	44
18. Cher	2	8	6	16
19. Corrèze	1	4	2	7
20. Corse	4	3	5	12
21. Côte-d'Or	2	14	25	41
22. Côtes-du-Nord	—	16	3	19
23. Creuse	—	5	—	5
24. Dordogne	3	13	11	27
25. Doubs	3	10	14	27
26. Drôme	2	8	4	14
27. Eure	—	39	15	54
28. Eure-et-Loir	1	12	6	19
29. Finistère	1	16	22	39
30. Gard	2	11	13	26
31. Garonne (Haute-)	4	17	26	47
32. Gers	—	13	6	19
33. Gironde	3	36	44	83
34. Hérault	8	23	19	50
35. Ille-et-Vilaine	3	22	9	34
36. Indre	1	11	7	19
37. Indre-et-Loire	2	12	8	22
38. Isère	4	15	14	33
39. Jura	—	16	5	21
40. Landes	—	8	3	11
41. Loir-et-Cher	1	12	9	22
42. Loire	5	22	19	46
43. Loire (Haute-)	2	8	1	11
44. Loire-Inférieure	4	32	23	59
45. Loiret	3	14	7	24

[8] Includes publications issued twice and three times a week.
[9] Periodicals appearing less frequently than once a week.

TABLE VIII (*Cont.*)

Départements	Dailies	Weeklies [8]	Others [9]	Total
46. Lot	—	8	5	13
47. Lot-et-Garonne	1	13	5	19
48. Lozère	—	3	2	5
49. Maine-et-Loire	5	22	13	40
50. Manche	1	27	6	34
51. Marne	7	5	6	18
52. Marne (Haute-)	2	22	7	31
53. Mayenne	1	19	12	32
54. Meurthe-et-Moselle	3	31	36	70
55. Meuse	—	10	5	15
56. Morbihan	1	10	2	13
57. Moselle	12	5	3	20
58. Nièvre	2	15	4	21
59. Nord	15	68	88	171
60. Oise	1	17	5	23
61. Orne	—	41	5	46
62. Pas-de-Calais	8	25	11	44
63. Puy-de-Dôme	3	15	12	30
64. Pyrénées (Basses-)	6	15	14	35
65. Pyrénées (Hautes-)	2	9	3	14
66. Pyrénées-Orientales	1	7	10	18
67. Rhin (Bas-)	15	37	48	90
68. Rhin (Haut-)	14	9	10	33
69. Rhône	10	24	89	133
70. Saône (Haute-)	—	9	6	15
71. Saône-et-Loire	3	36	10	49
72. Sarthe	2	24	3	29
73. Savoie	—	15	13	28
74. Savoie (Haute-)	—	15	5	20
75. Seine (Suburbs of Paris)	—	31	21	52
76. Seine-Inférieure	7	44	33	84
77. Seine-et-Marne	1	17	3	21
78. Seine-et-Oise	—	35	20	55
79. Sèvres (Deux-)	1	14	10	25
80. Somme	3	22	9	34
81. Tarn	—	18	7	25
82. Tarn-et-Garonne	—	6	3	9
83. Territoire de Belfort	1	3	4	8
84. Var	3	11	14	28
85. Vaucluse	1	14	11	26
86. Vendée	2	13	4	19
87. Vienne	2	10	9	21
88. Vienne (Haute-)	3	11	12	26
89. Vosges	3	12	19	34
90. Yonne	2	12	8	22
Totals	241	1569	1154	2964

" great regionals " have organizations, technical equipment, and advertising importance which place them on a par with any Paris newspaper outside of the first six. Eleven have circulations which reach or surpass the 200,000 mark: *La Petite Gironde* and *Le Petit Marseillais*, each 300,000; *Le Progrès de Lyon*, 250,000; *L'Écho du Nord* (Lille) and *Le Nouvelliste de Lyon*, each 225,000; *La Dépêche de Toulouse*, 217,000; *La France de Bordeaux, Le Lyon Républicain, Le Petit Provençal, L'Ouest-Éclair,* and *La Tribune Républicaine* (St. Étienne), between 200,000 and 210,000.

The growth of the powerful regional papers has been at the direct expense of the Paris dailies. In the days before the war, when the French public was less interested in the press for its news items than as a vehicle for the opinions of its political leaders, the newspapers of Paris had no serious competition. The provincial readers cared little whether the news was twenty-four or forty-eight hours old, as long as they could follow the controversies of party chiefs, whose activities centered in Paris. But when an increasing number of Paris newspapers, following the improvement in the mechanics of news transmission and the quickened pace of post-war events, transferred their emphasis from opinion to information, they developed in the provinces as well as in Paris the taste for rapid news that was to destroy the marketability of day-old Paris journals. To-day all the " great regionals " are united by private wires to their own Paris offices or special correspondents, and receive and transmit world news as rapidly as any big Paris daily. The front page of an early morning newspaper of Marseilles contains the same news in the same detail as that of the early morning newspaper of Paris. When the Paris papers arrive in provincial cities as speedily as express trains permit, they are bought and read primarily for the Parisian "*je ne sais quoi,*" the charm which the life and spirit of the metropolis continues to exert in the provinces.

Small local journals as well as the big Paris papers suffer from the competition of the " great regionals." In the special edition designed for his obscure département the provincial reader finds " home-town " news gathered and edited by a local correspondent. By subscribing to one regional paper he has news of the world and of his next-door neighbor, both reported with the same speed and completeness. The growth of the regional press may prove to be eventually an important factor in bringing about some measure of political and social decentralization of France and as such perhaps a moderating influence on French nationalism.[7]

As we might suppose, every regional daily is "patriotic," but the character and degree of its "nationalism" is determined by the political and religious opinions of the constituency which it serves. Those dailies in départements which are predominantly conservative in politics and in which the Catholic Church has the greatest social and intellectual influence give a good deal of attention to patriotic ceremonies and national defense. Of the thirty-one "great regionals," twenty-two are conservative in this sense, and six of them, *La Petite Gironde, Le Petit Marseillais, La Phare de la Loire, Le Nouvelliste de Lyon, L'Éclaireur de Nice,* and *L'Express du Midi,* are imbued with an ostentatiously patriotic spirit. On the other hand, not a single regional daily of the nine which favor the policies of the Left is really international in outlook, if we measure such "internationalism" by the standards of the Paris *Humanité:* they too are "nationalist," though their "nationalism" is more of the Jacobin variety. The cities which have important Left dailies are those which have large industrial populations and which belong to départements represented in the Chamber almost exclusively by Socialist or Radical Socialist deputies: Marseilles, Lyons, and Bordeaux, in order named the largest cities in France after Paris; St. Étienne and Nantes, fifth and sixth in size; Toulouse and Reims.

In spite of the serious competition of the "great regionals" in the small towns and rural communities, the local news-sheets — dailies and journals issued once, twice, or three times a week — have not yet been crowded out of the provincial press. The encroachment of the out-of-town dailies has made rural journalism far less profitable and has induced many editors of local dailies to economize by issuing their small sheets only every other

[7] For political regionalism, see Chapter XI.

day or twice or once a week. About two hundred small provincial dailies survive, appearing in all but twenty-three départements, while every département in France has three or more local weeklies (including publications which come out twice or three times a week). In 1927 there were 1,569 local journals, comprising more than half of the publications originating in provincial France, with an average of seventeen to each département. (See Table VIII.) These papers, having an average circulation of 5,000 to 6,000 readers, support themselves for the most part independently of subscriptions: first, by printing legal notices and other advertising matter, and second, and far more important, by accepting subsidies of local political aspirants, officeholders, or groups of voters. Many journals are in fact owned and operated at a financial loss by local party leaders who find it extremely profitable to influence public sentiment in communities where the intrigues and campaigns of the commune and arrondissement are of more immediate concern to the voter than national political problems. Leaving to the regional and Parisian dailies the expensive publication of general news, the local sheet is frankly an organ of editorial opinion. National party leaders recognize that the voting strength of rural France is largely controlled by the editors of these obscure sheets and have always made special efforts to gain their support. There is no speedier method of realizing one's political ambitions in provincial France than to become the proprietor or editor — or both — of a local journal. Many French political figures have made their first public appearance in the columns of some modest country weekly.

Although representing all shades of Left and Right opinion, the editors of small provincial sheets are generally too much occupied in attacking or defending local personalities and issues to give any great emphasis to national aims and utterances. Nevertheless, their absorption in politics tends to render them most loyal to the idea of the State and most interested in the Government: they are almost uniformly patriotic. On the other hand, many of these journals often introduce a feature against which French national patriots periodically inveigh — the publication of a column, sometimes an entire page, of the journal in the peasant *patois* or provincial language — Basque, Breton, Alsatian, Corsican, etc. — and the use of this space by leaders of such linguistic groups for propaganda in favor of a more intensified sub-national consciousness.[10]

4

We have now surveyed that portion of the French press which gives the public its news. There remain to be considered the weekly, fortnightly, and monthly publications which provide the French with additional entertainment, instruction, inspiration, or excitement. All of the significant weeklies and reviews are issued in Paris; although the *Annuaire de la Presse* for 1927 lists 1,154 titles of periodicals (exclusive of dailies and weeklies) which are published in the provinces, almost all of them represent parochial bulletins, trade and professional journals, tourist propaganda and other local reviews of small regional circulation, hardly relevant to our present study. Out of the thousands of periodicals published in Paris and read everywhere in France, we have chosen 108 weeklies and reviews for special examination.[11] Of this number, one appears twice a week; sixty-five are weeklies; one appears three times a month; seventeen are fortnightlies; and twenty-four are monthlies.

In the weeklies, which constitute the major portion of the periodical press, French journalism finds its most characteristic expression. There are five main groups of weeklies: of the sixty-five reviewed in Appendix C, thirty are organs of political propaganda; thirteen are devoted to political satire and social scandal; ten are illustrated family journals or comparatively impartial reviews; seven are humorous magazines or papers, featuring "Gallic" wit; and five are literary and artistic reviews. We have not considered in this grouping several very popular types of weekly which the Librairie Hachette places high in the list

10 See Chapter XI, pp. 292–317, below.
11 See Appendix C: "Select list of French periodicals which are important because of their wide circulation or because they are representative of significant political, social, or religious forces in France."

of its best-sellers [12] — the fashion journals, radio and popular science papers, " movie " weeklies, and sporting journals.

Publishing a weekly is perhaps the most effective and relatively the cheapest type of propaganda at the disposal of a Frenchman. From the years of preparation for the French Revolution to the present day, pamphleteering has been a favorite weapon of political and social warfare. The advantages to the publisher are many as compared with the production of a daily paper — news may be picked up from second-hand sources, yet is not too stale for interpretation and comment; it is unnecessary to employ a staff of salaried collaborators, since articles may be written and copy edited in the spare time of the editor and his friends; general running expenses are of course greatly reduced. It is a common practice for a political daily to husband its dwindling resources by turning itself into a weekly, and *vice versa*, for a weekly, on the acquisition of new funds or the approach of an electoral battle, to blossom forth as a daily. The format in most cases remains the same. Of the sixty-five weeklies under consideration, thirty-nine are printed on news-sheets as contrasted with twenty-six which are issued on heavier stock and bound in pamphlet form. Practically all of these weeklies of newspaper format are organs of political propaganda. The transitory character of the weekly press is worthy of note, especially in the case of the journals which appear on news-sheets: of the thirty-nine in our list, only six have survived from the nineteenth century; five were founded between 1901 and 1914; five, during the war; and twenty-three since 1918 (of which thirteen date from 1923 to 1926). Of the twenty-six pamphlet weeklies, on the other hand, nine were founded in the nineteenth century; four, between 1901 and 1914; two, during the war; and eleven, since 1918 (of which four date from that year). Grouping news-sheets and pamphlets, we sum up for the sixty-five weeklies: fifteen, founded in the nineteenth century; nine, between 1901 and 1914; seven, during the war; and thirty-four, from 1918 to 1927.

The periodicals which are significant from the standpoint of

[12] See p. 130, above.

patriotic and national emphasis have been indicated in Appendix
C. With few exceptions they are weeklies. On the other hand,
the periodicals which have been designated as being critical of
nationalism or predominantly international include many more
monthlies and fortnightlies than weeklies. From this evidence we
may infer that the national patriotic element in France displays
greater energy and has larger funds at its disposal for propaganda. Most periodicals, however, do not easily lend themselves
to arbitrary classification on the subject of national patriotism:
of the 108 examined, the investigator was able to select only
thirty which stress continuously and consistently either national
or international aims: fourteen of these are representative of as
many shades of nationalist thought, from the extreme doctrines
of *L'Action Française Agricole* to the utopian program of *La
Démocratie Nouvelle.* Among the sixteen which actively oppose what they term " nationalism " and " militarism," we find
the widely read satirical and humorous news-weekly, *Le Canard
Enchainé,* the sensational *Grand Guignol,* five publications of
various groups of the extreme Left (Communists and Socialist-
Communists), and an international weekly, *Pax.* Strikingly
similar methods of propaganda are used by both camps: political
cartoons, sensational revelations, satirical editorials, attacks on
persons, and appeals for moral and financial support. In spite
of the natural interest of the French in any vigorous expression
of extremist policy, Left or Right, the most successful publications from the standpoint of circulation and prestige are those
which steer a middle course, flinging ridicule on both sides. A
sprightly magazine such as *Aux Écoutes, Cyrano,* or *L'Opinion,*
to name a few of the political reviews which let the quips fall
where they may, is the Frenchman's intellectual *apéritif,* and none
such has any unpatriotic ingredient.

When we turn to the fortnightlies and monthlies, we find the
following types predominating: first, in number and in importance,
the dignified reviews of literature, politics, and the fine arts,
leavened by new fiction, drama, and poetry from the pens of
Academicians, present and future, and designed for that limited public familiarly called " high-brow." Foreign affairs

and achievements in the liberal arts are treated, in general, with sympathetic interest and appreciation, while there are very few issues of any French review which do not contain contributions of foreigners. A favorite topic is the discussion of the psychological and social background of other peoples, and the inevitable comparison of French with foreign standards of morality — rarely to the disparagement of the former.

Next in numerical importance are the journals of political propaganda. Monthly political publications differ in several respects from the weeklies of the same political complexion; they are as a rule more devoted to dogma than action, more concerned with theory than practical problems. These are the organs of the intellectual leaders of each party, which the masses rarely have time or inclination to read.

The third type of publication imitates the American and English popular magazine. There are still comparatively few of these ventures in tabloid literature, as few publishers in France can afford to invest in glossy paper, elaborate illustrations, and other expensive features. *Je Sais Tout*, the popular scientific magazine, and *Lectures Pour Tous* are the outstanding names among the publications patterned after foreign models, and they compare most favorably with English and American magazines of entertainment. Since their success depends on large circulation and advertisements, such magazines are careful to avoid controversial subjects. It is always safe to play up national achievements, which are pictured and described with enthusiasm.

Our survey of the French press would not be complete without some reference to the daily *Journal Officiel de la République Française*, edited, published, and sold by the Government, with an average circulation of 30,000 copies. Founded in 1869, the *Journal Officiel* became the official organ of the Republic by the decree of November 5, 1870, issued by the Government of National Defense, providing that all laws, to become effective must be published therein, and were, unless otherwise provided to be in force one full day after such publication. It is printed on news-sheets somewhat larger than our *Congressional Record* and is issued in three separate editions: (1) the Edition of Laws and Decrees, containing the official "*lois, décrets, arrêtés, circulaires,*" and the non-official "*avis, communications, information et annonces,*" such as announcements of civil-service examinations, bank statements, etc.; (2) the Edition of Parliamentary Debates, containing the complete report of proceedings in the Senate and Chamber of Deputies, and the written questions to ministers with their written replies; (3) the Complete Edition of the *Journal Officiel,* comprising not only the two editions described above but also all other parliamentary and administrative documents published as "*annexes*" to them, and an annual index. Since 1884 the *Journal Officiel* has published a separate edition for communes. The *Journal Officiel* is under the direction of the Ministry of the Interior, and employs a large staff and its own office-building and printing-plant. In 1927 the total amount expended by the Government for the support of the *Journal Officiel* was 9,057,708 francs; while no figures on receipts from sales and subscriptions are available for the same period, it is safe to assume that such receipts, as in previous years, were substantially below expenditures.

5

The long and diversified series of newspapers, pamphlets, and magazines just reviewed is what the public sees of the French press. But our study is incomplete unless we look behind the scenes to learn who pulls the strings which animate the performers at the daily puppet-show. The owners and directors, the journalists, the Government, the great news agencies, and the propagandist organizations — these are the main forces which direct the French press of to-day and shape public opinion of to-morrow.

More suspicion falls on the owners and directors of newspapers than on any other of the occult influences which are constantly accused of "enslaving" the press. In the first place, there are so few directors of powerful dailies who are themselves journalists that it is easy to believe that adventurers and financiers have acquired newspapers for purposes best known to themselves. Of course there are a few notable exceptions of dyed-in-the-wool newspaper-men who have risen to proprietorship through sheer literary and executive ability, such as Léon Bailby of *L'Intransigeant* and Gustave Téry of *L'Œuvre*. As a rule, however, newspapers are headed by business-men who have no journalistic pretensions or taste for personal publicity, as we have seen in discussing the editorial policies of the dailies of large circulation.[13] It takes courage for a captain of industry such as M. François Coty to ignore the rule by enblazoning his name as prominently on the front page of his *Figaro* as on his perfume bottles and powder-boxes, and although five years have passed since his journalistic début, he is still a butt for columnists and *chansonniers*.

It goes without saying in France that nobody invests in a newspaper purely for direct financial gain. While in many cases, the owner, through his business acumen, is able to realize some profits on his journalistic investment, he could almost certainly obtain larger profits from the same investment in other enterprises, and there are instances where the financial return from a newspaper is so negligible that it obviously plays no part in the undertaking. It is asserted that Louis Loucheur, for example, owns *Le Petit Journal,* not because it is a money-making proposition, about which there are serious doubts, but because of his other interests. That the wealthy business-man invests in journalism is attributable to the indirect benefits which he expects to derive therefrom. In general, the owner, no matter how anonymous, makes the pages of his journal a mirror for his personal preferences and animosities, an echo of his political opinions, a step-ladder for his dramatic or literary protegés. And being a man of affairs, he is bound to have certain economic interests and objectives which are served by, and give a bias to, his news-sheet.

Without having any official capacity, the director of a journal is nevertheless an outstanding figure in governmental and national circles. Everyone, from the President down, is anxious to avoid trouble with him, and if possible to curry favor. Foreign embassies extend to him special courtesies, if not, as often

13 See p. 134, above.

alleged, substantial subsidies. Great corporations and trusts, especially the banks, railways, and metallurgical interests, negotiate for his eloquence or his silence, whichever the situation demands.[14] In short, the proprietor of a sucessful journal enjoys a sense of personal power and absolutism approaching that of an unlimited monarch, yet possible only in a democracy. He is apt to think of himself as an embodiment, so-to-say, of the nation, and to extol the nation as he would extol himself.

To acknowledge that the press is ruled by a nationally minded autocracy is one thing, to name the actual incumbents of the invisible thrones is another and far more difficult matter. In the United States all publications enjoying second-class mailing privileges are compelled by law to print in their pages at stated times a notice giving the names of their executive officers, stockholders, and bondholders. No similar legal obligation exists in France, where only the name of the salaried manager (*gérant*) must be declared. It is practically impossible for an outsider or even for the journalists themselves to know what persons or interests are financing the holding-corporation or nominal chief of a given French publication. The scandals which arose from this situation, especially just before and during the war, need not be retold here. The publication of secret documents, the confessions of spies and all the other evidence of the free use of Imperial Russian and German gold in the French press, the trial of Charles Humbert of *Le Journal* and the fate of the editors of *Le Journal des Ardennes* and *Le Bonnet Rouge* have left the French public with no illusions about the sanctity of the Fourth Estate. Gossip and rumor are constantly at work evolving sensational exposés of new venality and startling disclosures of the "real" lords of the French press. Especially in the stress of financial and political crises during the fall of 1925 and the summer of 1926, accusations were plentiful in the journals of the Left. Sir Basil Zaharoff, the Greek ammunition king, and M. Horace Finaly, head of the *Banque de Paris et des Pays-Bas*, were most frequently denounced as conspiring, by their manipulation of several newspapers, to undermine con-

---

14 For a case in point, see Appendix D, *Le Quotidien*, pp. 451–452, below.

fidence in the financial stability of France in order to profit from the inevitable débâcle. The latter was charged with supporting all types of journal — *Le Petit Bleu, Le Radical, Le Rappel, La Victoire, L'Éclair, Paris-Soir, La Liberté, La Journée Industrielle, L'Œuvre, Le Journal,* as well as several important regional papers. At the same time the Conservative press declared that *L'Humanité* and other Communist publications were subsidized by Bolshevist agents.[15]

Another path by which secret funds may find their way into the coffers of unscrupulous editors is through the sale of financial publicity. It is customary, even in the more reputable French journals, for investment-houses and stock-companies to solicit new business not only in the advertising columns but also in the financial articles and notices written or edited by a supposedly impartial economist. A timely reference to the good prospects or large earnings of a particular enterprise, inserted as news, gives no indication that it appears in accordance with a paid contract for publicity and is therefore especially effective in inducing new investments. Other speculative undertakings find it more to their advantage to pay for receiving no publicity at all — in other words, the editor obtains " hush-money," sometimes unsolicited, more often extorted.[16]

The dangers to which a subsidized press exposes the nation are thoroughly understood and vividly described by French publicists. André Billy and Jean Piot, both, incidentally, members of the editorial staff of *L'Œuvre,* itself under fire, sound a warning:

[15] The accusations of one group of Frenchmen against the venality of the press of another group serves a nationalist end, for the accusations usually involve a charge of " internationalism " or " lack of patriotism," if not of downright " treason " to the fatherland, and such a charge is presented as most incriminating.

[16] The prosecution of the directors of *La Gazette du Franc,* the sensational failure of which ruined thousands of small French investors in the fall of 1928, revealed a combination of three forms of journalistic venality. First, the promoters of the speculative enterprise published their own weekly, *La Gazette du Franc,* and financial news-service, *Interpresse,* ostensibly as patriotic propaganda for the rehabilitation of the franc; second, they paid for favorable publicity in the financial columns of *Le Quotidien* and other journals; and third, they alleged that they were obliged to pay M. Georges Anquetil, editor of *La Rumeur,* a fixed sum monthly to avert threatened exposure of their insolvency.

If a day should come when a little group of very rich men will have secured control of all the important journals of a nation, freedom of the press will have ceased to exist. That liberty will not have been brutally strangled, as by a dictator, but despatched by an anaesthetic. Its death will be more peaceful, but none the less certain. And the catastrophe will be all the greater because, with no official announcement of the end of that freedom, many people will not suspect it and be the more easily deceived . . . On that day, the Press, daughter of Democracy, will have killed her mother.[17]

The directors of large papers, as we have seen, prefer the substantial advantages of occult power to noisy but less effective public triumphs. But for the directors of the smaller political journals, the realization, by self-advertisement, of personal and political ambitions is the main objective. A list of directors of journals whose efforts to keep in the public eye have been rewarded by high political office or party leadership includes such men as Clemenceau, Millerand, Caillaux, Maurice and Albert Sarraut, Alexandre Israel, Eugène Lautier, Théodore Steeg, and Alexandre Varenne. The dramatic political come-back staged by Clemenceau in 1917 is said to have been in large part a result of his success as a newspaper director. In 1913 he founded L'Homme Libre, which the outbreak of the war soon made the stronghold of the opposition to the Governments of Viviani, Briand, and Painlevé. " For three years," as Léopold Marcellin explains, " he conversed with France on all questions which might evoke alarm or enthusiasm. And that is why, in the hour of need, his name rose spontaneously to everyone's lips." [18] Not only Clemenceau's own paper paved the way for his premiership, but the sympathy which he had won from other newspaper directors was a decisive element in his victory. Marcel Sembat, the Socialist leader, wrote at the time:

Several directors of important newspapers of Paris have played a leading rôle in the preparation for the Clemenceau Cabinet. This is very curious, rather novel, and most natural. It is well known that on several occasions various premiers have called together a group of directors of newspapers for the purpose of giving them certain instruc-

---

[17] Billy and Piot, Le Monde des Journaux (Paris, 1924), p. 230.
[18] Cited by André Billy in La Guerre des Journaux (Paris, 1919), p. 193.

tions. This procedure works perfectly when the premier has self-confidence and a mastery of the situation. If not, it happens that those whom he expected to command turn about and dictate to him.[19]

The close relations maintained between the press and the national Government may be one explanation of the prestige and respect which the French public accords to the journalist and also of the generally patriotic, even nationalist, efforts of French journalism. In France, as in few other countries, journalism is a profession entitled to the same honors and endowed with the same responsibilities as those of the more ancient professions of teaching, law, medicine, and the sciences. " Journalism leads to everything," is an axiom which is constantly cited to explain why during the last century so many of the notables of the arts, sciences, and literature, as well as lawyers and politicians, have made their public débuts or enhanced their reputations through journalism. " The greatest school of our statesmen and men of letters," is the characterization of the profession by M. de Chambure,[20] who lists at length the members of the French Academy and the Institute who are active collaborators on journals and reviews.

The art of journalism is evidently one which does not demand exclusive application or constant practice on the part of its devotees. Unlike the sword, the journalist's pen does not grow rusty in its sheath, but may be drawn out after years of inactivity, its point sharper and more sensitive than ever before. " Statesmen, parliamentary orators, important actors on the great political stage — playing the leading rôles in the drama — at a given moment in their fighting careers, take up again and wield with burning passion the journalist's pen, which is worth all the powers in the world." [21]

The career of M. Poincaré is a typical as well as celebrated example. For twenty years he was a regular contributor to the Lyon Républicain and the Dépêche de Toulouse and to various political and literary reviews in Paris. When, as President of

[19] Ibid., p. 192.
[20] Op. cit., p. 431.
[21] Jules Claretie, quoted by A. de Chambure, op. cit., p. 433.

the Republic, he looked back over his life in the newspaper world, he told the members of the press of Paris (at their banquet on March 17, 1913) that he would always remain a journalist, since, "However free the bar and the tribune, they perhaps do not always offer a means of self-expression as far reaching, as varied, and as easy as the newspaper." He made good his words as soon as his term of office was ended by taking up his journalist's pen, with marked effect, in *Le Temps* and *Le Matin*, dropping it only while Premier from 1922 to 1924 and again since the summer of 1926.

As a preparation for a parliamentary career in France, journalistic experience is second only to the law. An examination of the professional background of the members of the Senate and Chamber in 1924 showed that of 314 senators, 61 (or 20 per cent) had newspaper connections, as directors, editors, or contributors; of 584 deputies, 123 (or 21 per cent) were connected with the press. In a list of the most prominent members of both houses, including ministers and *ministrables* (ministerial "timber"), compiled by Louis Damon,[22] 73 out of 219 leading parliamentarians (or 33 per cent) were journalists or ex-journalists. It has always been recognized in every country that legislators are recruited in greater numbers from the legal professions than from any other group. While this is true of France, it is interesting to note that 26 per cent of the senators are lawyers, only 6 per cent more than are journalists; and 24 per cent of the deputies, or only 3 per cent more than are journalists. When we study the careers of the leading members in M. Damon's compilation, we find that exactly the same percentage (33 per cent) holds for the lawyers and for the journalists, while many of those who are listed as members of the legal profession only have also had experience as journalists.

It is characteristic of the French to admire leaders who not only are orators but can express themselves forcefully and eloquently in print; just as a glance at the parliamentary debates will show that the most popular senators and deputies are those who declaim frequently and at length, so a survey of the

[22] *Nos Parlementaires* and *Ministres . . . et Ministrables* (Paris, 1925).

content of newspapers and periodicals will show the efforts of politicians to make a favorable literary impression on their constituents. As the journalistic output of a public man increases, in like proportion is he deemed more worthy of confidence. Commenting on Clemenceau's victory in 1917, Marcellin observes, "Journalism is the school of national sentiment for public men. A politician rises to the level of his mission according to his collaboration on newspapers. The more ' copy ' a Senator produces, the more pledges he gives of his sincerity and integrity." [23] The same principle, however illogical it may be proved, holds for other popular idols; generals, admirals, scientists, university and church dignitaries, novelists, and dramatists take the public into their confidence by means of press articles and become national figures.

6

With justifiable pride, the French, comparing their journals with those of other countries, point out that the average literary quality of the French press is considerably higher than the average elsewhere. The fundamental reason for this superiority, admitted by foreigners as well as by Frenchmen, is not hard to discover. The journalists themselves, from the special correspondent down to the humblest reporter, bring to their profession that deep-seated respect for purity of style and syntax which is the result of years of training in the secondary schools. A foreigner who examines, no matter how superficially, the curricula of French educational institutions, cannot fail to be impressed by the overwhelming importance given to the art of writing good French, whether the preparation is for the baccalaureate in philosophy (liberal arts) or in the exact sciences. There is hardly a journalist who has not received training for one of the professions, especially teaching. Graduates of the École Normale Supérieure, the highest governmental institution of learning in France, are found as frequently in the newspaper world as in the faculties of universities or in scientific laboratories. " Our editorial rooms are full of ' normaliens,' " declare the au-

23 Quoted by André Billy in *La Guerre des Journaux.*

thors of *Le Monde des Journaux;* "from the point of view of rhetoric, that's not a bad background."[24] It is not strange, therefore, to find every-day problems discussed in French newspapers with a style and erudition worthy of more permanent form. The literary world and the newspaper world are almost one — the young reporter of to-day is the laureate of the Prix Goncourt of to-morrow, and many successful novelists continue to take regular assignments from the newspapers to which they owe their introduction to the public. The national patriotism voiced in the French press is usually beautifully voiced, and consequently carries weight with the intellectual as well as with the man-in-the-street.

Especially since the war, the journalist has been driven to feverish activity not only by literary or political ambition, but through economic necessity. The salary paid to a reporter by a single paper is so low that even by padding his expense account to the limit of plausibility, he cannot live comfortably. Hence it is tacitly assumed that he will carry, in addition to his regular work, a number of part-time jobs: he may write a daily humorous column for one paper, review books for a weekly, act as political correspondent for a foreign journal, or even become a theatrical press-agent. Many provincial papers pay so little to their Paris correspondents that in order to live, these must furnish copy to four or five journals in various parts of the country. Nor will the same write-up be suitable for each; a parliamentary report, for instance, must be edited to appeal to the political and economic preferences of the region for which it is intended; a Right victory in the Chamber would have to be emphasized for a journal like *Le Réveil du Nord* and minimized for *Le Progrès de Lyon,* and yet the same contributor might be in the employ of both dailies. The one thing about which the harassed journalistic chameleon can be constant is the stressing of national interests and national patriotism.

The difficulty of making adequate financial provision for declining years is perhaps the chief reason for the existence of numerous associations of journalists in France. Probably no

[24] *Op. cit.,* p. 223.

profession in France is so thoroughly organized for the protection of its material (and ethical) interests as that of journalism. In Paris there exist, according to the 1927 *Annuaire de la Presse*, no less than 106 associations of French journalists and seven groups of foreign press representatives, while forty-seven associations function in the provinces. Practically all of these " syndicates " are mutual benefit associations, giving free medical care and paying old-age pensions from funds which have been contributed partly by the members and partly by the governmental " Loterie de la Presse." In general the amount paid by each group is so small that in order to draw a sufficient income a journalist must affiliate himself with four or five.

The " Syndicat des Journalistes," founded May 1, 1918, is the largest and most important of all these associations in that it does not merely pay benefits, but actively defends the professional interests of its membership of over 1,000. It has drawn up a code of journalistic ethics, which it enforces by its own Council of Discipline; it has attempted to regulate conditions of labor for journalists on the same principles as those followed successfully by trade unions; in 1919 it obtained a minimum salary agreement from newspaper directors and was responsible for the passage of the law of July 25, 1925, requiring one day of rest in seven for journalists, hailed as the first legislative conquest of organized journalism.

Among the other influential associations we may list the " Association Syndicale Professionnelle des Journalistes Républicains," founded in 1881, the oldest of all groups, with 450 members and an imposing list of officers, including Poincaré, Millerand, Klotz, and other political figures; the " Association des Journalistes Parisiens," with a membership of 375, headed by Louis Barthou, Minister of Justice; the " Association et Syndicat de la Presse Républicaine Départementale," uniting 450 provincial journalists; the " Association de la Presse Monarchique et Catholique des Départements," with 275 representatives of the conservative provincial press; and the " Association Générale des Nouvellistes Parisiens," with 375 members.

In addition to the associations which admit journalists of all categories, there are in Paris certain organizations of specialists, resembling the medieval craft gilds: for those who report trials in the Palais de Justice, there is the " Association Confraternelle et Mutuelle de la Presse Judiciare Parisienne," dating from 1885; police-court reporters belong to the " Association des Informateurs Judiciaires Parisiens "; news from the " Parquet," office of the public prosecuting attorney, is furnished by members of the " Association des Informateurs Parisiens "; reporters covering the ministries are united in the " Association des Journalistes-Informateurs des Ministères "; sporting-news writers belong to the " Association des Journalistes Sportifs "; for those who write on financial and economic topics there is the " Association de la Presse Économique et Financière "; theatrical news is supplied by members of the " Association Professionnelle des Courrieristes de Théatre des Quotidiens de Paris "; dramatic and musical critics are organized into the " Association Professionnelle et Mutuelle de la Critique Dramatique et Musicale." Similarly there are separate associations of literary critics, movie critics, parliamentary reporters, writers of religious news, racing news, municipal news, fishing and hunting news, and so on. The necessity for so many protective bodies is explained by the fact that were it not for their influence, the large news agencies, like that of Havas or Fournier, to which we shall have occasion presently to refer, would be able to supply the Paris papers with the same news items which they furnish to the provincial press, saving each paper the expense of maintaining a staff member for each department. Agreements between the large agencies and the organizations of specialists bind the agencies not to encroach on the field of such news in Paris, with the result that the positions of the special reporters are secure.

The patronage of newspaper associations by the officials of the Republic is still another important link which binds the press to the State. Municipal authorities have also coöperated with journalists by contributing to their treasuries and obtaining concessions from the city. In the near future the journalists of Paris are to have their new club-house, " La Maison des Journalistes," which is to be built on land donated by the city of Paris in the *quartier du Croissant,* " newspaper row."

In view of the cordial relations which exist between the State and the press, it is not surprising to find decorations of the Legion of Honor frequently in the lapels of journalists. For " distinguished services to their country " in 1926–1927, ninety-seven journalists were admitted to the Legion of Honor with the rank of *chevalier,* forty-one were promoted to the grade of *Officier,* and eleven were made *commandeurs.*

7

The centralized national French State has final authority over the press; and under every régime, from the old monarchy, through the Revolution, and on into the period of the Third Republic, the French press has been subjected to close governmental surveillance and severe restrictions. By virtue of the law of July 19, 1881, passed after the decisive defeat of the Royalist element which had governed during the first eight years of the Third Republic, the press found itself relieved of the two heaviest burdens of state regulation — the necessity of obtaining permission from the Government before a new publication might be issued, and the requirement of financial surety against seditious propaganda. Since then, the press has enjoyed, at least in times of peace, comparative freedom from direct state control. But the State still supervises the press.

The present law requires the registration of newspapers and periodicals with the Public Prosecutor (Procureur de la République) or his local representatives, who must receive from each new publication a statement of its title, printer, and the name and address of its manager. The latter, who is held personally responsible if the publication is prosecuted for violations of the law, must be of French birth, of legal age, and in full possession of his civic rights (i.e. have committed no offense or crime punishable in part by deprivation of such rights). Four copies of every issue, signed by the manager, are forwarded to the Government at the moment of publication: two copies are deposited with the Public Prosecutor for examination in respect of infraction of the law, and two are deposited at the Ministry of the Interior, if published in the département of the Seine, otherwise at the prefecture or nearest administrative office (*sous-préfecture* or *mairie*) for preservation in the National Library. The name of the manager must be printed at the bottom of every issue. In giving the Courts of Assize instead of the ordinary police courts jurisdiction over the majority of cases in which the press is liable to prosecution, the law of 1881 has allowed greater opportunities for defense against arbitrary repression.

The law of 1881, moreover, improved the status of foreign journals in France. Previous to its passage the Minister of the Interior might arbitrarily forbid the circulation of any foreign paper a single copy of which contained an offensive article or statement. While the Minister of the Interior still retains the power of prohibiting the circulation of a single number of a foreign journal or any publication printed in France in a foreign language,[25] the journal itself cannot be banned from the country without a vote of the whole council of ministers duly convened.

As a result of serious anarchist disturbances in the early nineties, culminating in the assassination of President Carnot, additional limitations were placed on the freedom of the press by a law which was passed on July 28, 1894. The police courts were to judge and sentence those responsible for publications which, for the purpose of anarchist propaganda, incited one or more persons to theft, arson, murder, pillage, or other crimes or " appealed to the armed forces of land or sea with the intent to deter them from performing their military duty and from obeying the commands of their officers for the enforcement of military laws and regulations and the defense of the republican Constitution." [26] Under the provisions of this law the Government has been enabled to take action against journals of extreme anti-governmental tendencies — whether or not actually " anarchist " — as, for example, the recent condemnation of the manager of *L'Humanité* for publishing articles inciting revolt in

---

25 For recent exercise of this power, see pp. 282, 285–286, below.
26 *Cf.* Dalloz, *Code de la Presse* (Paris, Librairie Dalloz, 1912), p. 313.

the army, and of the managers of certain " autonomist " organs in Alsace.[27]

On the whole, the surveillance of the French press in time of peace by the Public Prosecutor or his local representatives in behalf of the Ministry of Justice is far from rigorous. With the exception of the political journals of the extreme Left and those of autonomist sympathy in Alsace, which are examined with some care for their seditious tendencies, French journals are permitted a latitude in choice of subject matter, in vehemence of language, and in use of personalities [28] which might be construed in other countries as punishable by law.

In sharp contrast to the liberties enjoyed by the press under normal conditions, the restrictions of war-time censorship imposed by France have been marked by noteworthy severity. With a vigilance that never relaxed from the outbreak of hostilities to the conclusion of the peace negotiations, the Government took measures to protect the morale of the country as one of the great sources of fighting strength. The French mobilized on August 1, 1914; on August 2 all the départements of France and Algeria were declared in a state of siege, during which, under a law of 1849, military authorities might prohibit publications and meetings calculated to incite or maintain disorder. This extreme method of repression, used effectively after the Revolution of 1848, was difficult to apply to a press which had been in possession of comparative freedom since the law of 1881; the Government therefore secured the passage, on August 4, 1914, of a law which became operative the next day to " prevent press indiscretions in war-time " and which restricted the application of the law of 1849. The law of August 5, 1914, prohibited, under penalty of fine and imprisonment, the publication of any information or article concerning military or diplomatic operations which might aid the enemy or exercise an unfavorable influence on the spirit of the army or the civilian

[27] See below, pp. 285–286.

[28] A person named has the " droit de réponse," i.e. the offending journal must publish his reply within three days of its receipt, in the same place and in the same size of type as the original article.

population. No information on military movements might be published other than that communicated by the Government or army authorities. Theoretically, the press might print what it chose and take the risk of being punished for an indiscretion; in practice, however, the Government looked to it that nothing should be published without its previous permission. On the evening of August 4, after the voting of the law on press indiscretions, a government communiqué was addressed to directors of daily and periodical publications expressing the hope that it would not be obliged to resort to the drastic methods provided by law and announcing that " the Government counts on the patriotic good will of the press of all shades of opinion, in Paris and in the provinces, not to publish, regarding the war, a single item of information whatever its source, its origin or its nature, without its being previously approved by the Press Bureau, which has been established since yesterday at the Ministry of War." [29] In this informal manner, without any legal enactment or ministerial decree, was established the régime of " preventive censorship " which was to rule the world of the press by an " amicable agreement."

At the outset, many newspapers hailed the semi-official control as a protection against incurring the displeasure of the Government by publishing unauthorized material. It soon became apparent, however, that the courteous " invitation " of the Government was in reality a command; the Press Bureau considered itself empowered to require newspapers to submit proofs of each number as soon as the issue was composed, and offending passages were deleted, sometimes leaving whole columns blank. If a publication defied the orders of the censor — frequently conveyed by an anonymous telephone call — sanctions were used: for the first offense, a " warning "; for repeated disregard of orders or a graver offense, the paper might be suspended for a varying period; suppression was the final penalty. Both suspension and suppression required an edict of the Minister of War.

[29] *Cf.* account of French censorship by Pierre Renouvin in *The Forms of War Government in France* (New Haven, Yale University Press, published for the Carnegie Endowment for International Peace, 1927), pp. 39–51.

Having provided for military and diplomatic censorship, the Government found that a political censorship was also necessary to " maintain the country in a favorable frame of mind " so that public confidence might not be disturbed by the constant criticism of government executives so prevalent in time of peace. A circular of September 22, 1914, gave the prefects authority to censor statements on internal politics. In February 1915 the prefect surrendered this function to a civilian representative whom he appointed to sit on the local military censorship committee, thus permitting the Government to disclaim the existence of a separate " political censorship " of unpleasant connotation. As M. Malvy, Minister of the Interior, declared in reply to a written question of a deputy on April 15, 1915,[30] " There exists only a military censorship . . . applied not exclusively to military and diplomatic questions, but also to articles containing violent attacks on the Parliament and the Government and to those calculated to disturb public opinion from the standpoint of national defense."

" The Government escaped the control of public opinion, stifled criticism, and shaped the mind of the nation," is M. Renouvin's summing-up of the rôle of censorship in France during the War. " But in doing so, it undertook a grave responsibility. By spreading optimism, it might in the long run weaken the public sense of the difficulties still to be overcome. By an economy of official truth, it ran the risk of creating a kind of apathy in the country. It was a question of degree, it will be said. But the Government of France appears to have gone very far in its anxiety to spare the nation from too vivid flashes of the truth." [31]

Almost from the start friction arose between the press and the bureau of censorship. On September 29, 1914, Clemenceau's paper, L'Homme Libre, was suspended for eight days for printing

[30] Cf. Renouvin, op. cit., p. 44.

[31] Ibid. The French Government has not yet seen fit to allow the public to examine the archives of the " Bureau de la Presse," so that the full account of the proceedings of that organization, " one of the most troublesome subjects in the history of the war government and administration of France," remains for a future historian.

an editorial in defiance of the Press Bureau's veto. Clemenceau's retort was to publish the paper the next day under a significant title, *L'Homme Enchainé*, and to carry on a war against political censorship until his return to power in 1917. The mistakes and inconsistencies of the Press Bureau were the subject of vigorous protests in the Chamber of Deputies. Articles were arbitrarily deleted, yet the headings which might alarm the public were allowed to remain; often news which the morning papers were forbidden to print was passed by the censors of the evening papers. Censorship operated more severely in Paris than in the provinces, where special commissions could apply orders according to their judgment. Thus an item prohibited in *Le Petit Parisien* might appear unmolested in *La Liberté du Sud-Ouest* or *Le Journal de Rouen*. One of the most frequent complaints was that the censors discriminated habitually against certain newspapers which were forbidden to publish a piece of news permitted to appear elsewhere. Ministers and legislators of the Government majority were protected from personal attacks in the press; certain topics, such as the " aims of the war " or the terms upon which the peace treaty would be drawn, were taboo.

Throughout the successive ministries of Briand, Ribot, and Painlevé there were formal protests by the " Syndicat de la Presse " and other press organizations. There were hearings on the severity of the censorship before the Committee on Civil and Criminal Legislation of the Chamber of Deputies, there were interpellations of the Government; but all attempts to modify the procedure of the Press Bureau were in vain. In 1916 new regulations made the working of the censorship more formidable than ever; the editor of a suspended newspaper was prohibited from publishing another under a different name, and articles which had been censored were not permitted to be sent privately in the mails — a practice which Clemenceau and other prominent journalists had followed in order to bring their suppressed editorials to the attention of deputies and senators.

When Clemenceau became Premier on November 16, 1917, the enemies of political censorship had won a hard-fought triumph. While the censorship was to continue on diplomatic and military intelligence and " pacifist " articles, personal opinions were to be respected, he declared. " The right of insulting members of the Government must be made inviolable," he wrote in a note to the press on January 8, 1918. After the signing of the Armistice, however, Clemenceau did not regard the cessation of hostilities as an occasion for the abolition of the Press Bureau. The French press found itself powerless to publish any information on the peace negotiations other than that communicated by the Government, while foreign newspapers, especially the British, containing articles and interviews on forbidden topics, circulated freely in France. Vehement protests by both the Conservative and Radical journals were unheeded while the censors watched over public opinion during the Conference and the discussion of the Treaty of Versailles by the French Parliament. On October 3, 1919, the Treaty was ratified, and on October 12 the state of siege was abolished and with it the Press Bureau. The press had been subjected to direct governmental control for five years and two months, eleven months of which had seen no fighting.

8

In time of peace the Government has three main channels of direct control over the press: first, as we have already noted, through the formal surveillance of all publications by the Ministry of Justice and the Ministry of the Interior; second, through the press departments in each ministry and under-secretariat; and third, through the secret payment of subsidies to various journals.

Daily contact with the press is an important function of each ministerial department. It is the duty of one of the secretaries to read whatever the newspapers and periodicals have to say on the activities of the minister, his staff, and his department, and to keep the minister informed of relevant news items, editorials, or gossip. Each ministry has its own publicity bureau which furnishes " official " information on the achievements and program of the administration, gives out press statements of the minister or his spokesman, and provides facilities for interviews between the minister and assembled press representatives. The amount of importance which the press department assumes in various ministries is of course determined by the type of portfolio: the Ministry of Agriculture or Pensions, for example, pays relatively little attention to its press connection in comparison with the Ministry of Foreign Affairs or of Colonies. At the Quai d'Orsay the organization of the press bureau is necessarily most elaborate: a large staff reads and files foreign as well as French journals and periodicals, while official communiqués for the press on diplomatic negotiations are prepared by experts in the art of shaping national opinion.

The matter of governmental subsidies to the press, from its very nature, cannot be discussed except with vagueness and delicacy. The provision of " secret funds " in each national budget for use at the discretion of the premier and other members of the Cabinet is considered, by Radicals and Conservatives alike, essential to the smooth working of the French governmental machine. As M. Pams, senator and former member of several Radical ministries, has remarked, " secret funds are the necessary basis for reciprocal good-will." In the budget of the premier and of each minister there is a margin allowed for expenditures for which the minister is accountable only in a confidential report to the premier. The destination of these sums, often asserted to run into millions of francs, is the subject of continual speculation and rumor. Certain political and patriotic organizations at home and abroad are said to benefit from the private patronage of the Government; bureaus of espionage, secret missions, and *agents provocateurs* are alleged to be supported by such funds; and it is universally admitted that a goodly portion finds its way into the coffers of the press in France and elsewhere. The sudden prosperity of *Le Quotidien,* partisan of the " Cartel des Gauches," soon after the Left victory of May 1924 was ascribed to secret subsidies by the new Government. It is a recognized principle of political strategy for a ministry not only to aid friendly journals but also to silence annoying criticism in the press of the opposition by the judicious use of " hush-money," and seasoned journalists declare that many political papers are founded simply to place their directors on the Government's private payroll. Earlier in this study the high birth- and death-rate of political newspapers and weeklies has been noted; what relationship, if any, exists between " vital statistics " and secret funds can only be conjectured.

The directors, the journalists, and the Government have influenced the press from its earliest history. In more recent years French journalism has been profoundly affected by a constantly increasing force — the great news-agencies. All of the leading countries of the world have been similarly affected by the rise of large organizations which have a virtual monopoly over the reception and transmission of international news dispatches, whether by telephone, telegraph, cable, or radio. For the United States, there is the service of the Associated Press; for London, Reuter; for Rome, Stéfani; for Berlin, Wolf; for Madrid, Fabra; and for Switzerland, the Basle Agency. In France the most powerful news organization is the *Agence Havas,* which grew from a little office for the translation of foreign papers founded in Paris by M. Havas in 1835, to a corporation to-day capitalized at 50,000,000 francs and equally important for its news-service and as an agency for advertising and publicity.

Aside from the transmission of news and advertising, the news-agencies occupy a distinctive place in French journalism as syndicates for the supplying of all types of feature articles, special departments, fiction, and illustrations to publications, mainly in the provinces, which cannot afford to run such features independently. In 1927 there were fifty-eight active organizations in Paris which served provincial papers with news information, financial quotations, and various features. Among the most prominent may be listed: *Actualités,* headed by Senators Henry Bérenger and Paul Bluysen, which syndicates every month forty articles on political subjects signed by well known Radical and Radical-Socialist deputies and senators; *Agence Fournier,* which ranks next to the *Agence Havas* in political and financial information; *Agence Technique de la Presse,* specializing in parliamentary and financial items; *Agence Économique et Financière,* headed by the economist Yves-Guyot, furnishing international financial quotations and analyses; *Actualité Illustré*, syndicating news photographs; *L'Agriculture Nationale et Coloniale*, supplying to country papers all matter of interest to farmers — crop reports, market news, veterinary advice — and assuming full charge of the agricultural page of dailies and weeklies; *Paris Télégrammes*, financial news; *L'Information*, connected with the Paris newspaper of that title, specializing in commercial and industrial dispatches; *Radio*, one of the largest and most progressive agencies; *Agence Télégraphique Universelle*, political, economic, and financial news; *La Presse-Associée*, a co-operative organization of French and foreign journalists, furnishing to subscribers a daily news service, a weekly political bulletin of conservative tendencies, short stories, serial novels, Aunt Rosalie's column for women's interests, and publishing a German edition for the press of Alsace, Germany, Switzerland, Poland, and the Balkans.

By subscribing to a news-agency, the owner of a small provincial news-sheet, single-handed, may compose his paper, from editorial to advertisements, with the aid of scissors and paste and a few local news items. The task of assembling, editing, and commenting on the news of the day, the writing of special feature columns and the selection of jokes and fiction has been performed by the agency in Paris, where three shifts of editors and copy-writers work eight hours each for a twenty-four hour day. An editor is assigned to a geographical division of the country; for the various subscribers from that region he must prepare copy adapted to the political nuance and to the religious and social views of each. Often he is in the employ of rival journals in the same district, which necessitates a facile shifting in point of view. Only national patriotism may be seen steadily and purveyed constantly.

The tendency of the large news syndicates to supplant independent journalism has alarmed the profession. Various organizations of journalists, as we have seen, have succeeded in preventing the syndicates from furnishing to the press of Paris certain types of news covered by special reporters, such as municipal events, court cases, meetings of learned societies, and parliamentary debates. But with the exception of less than two score of important regional dailies which are able to maintain Paris headquarters and large editorial staffs, the press of provincial and colonial France is increasingly dependent on the services of the great national agencies.

Recognizing a powerful and impersonal ally in the large news syndicates, the Government has made a practice of using them as intermediaries in its relations with public opinion of France and with foreign governments. If a political or diplomatic move is learned prematurely by the independent press, a denial of the affair published by the *Agence Havas* or *Fournier* is often equivalent to an official disclaimer. On the other hand the first intimation of a new project or change in governmental policy is generally made in guarded terms through the communiqué of an agency: by watching the reaction of the press and the public the Government knows whether to expect approval or criticism when the measure is officially announced.

There remains for mention, in our survey of the influences which shape public opinion through the French press, the rôle of propagandist societies. The editor of a newspaper in the United States, for instance, finds in each day's mail a great quantity of prepared " copy " — generally well written and devised to interest the average reader — which he is invited to use in his editorial or news columns without indicating the source of his material if he does not care to do so. Such reading matter is the product of highly paid " specialists in public relations " who are employed by propagandist societies to further the interests of political or economic groups, to serve particular patriotic ends, or to agitate in favor of this or that principle or program. In the United States, at any rate, experience has indicated that such indirect propaganda is profitable. When we examine the situation in France, first evidence seems to point to similar activity. Elsewhere in this volume are described the numerous propagandist organizations which flourish in France.[32] With very few exceptions, however, their methods of obtaining publicity through the printed word offer a vivid contrast to those

[32] Chapter VIII.

employed in the United States. An indirect appeal for popular sympathy is considered less effective than an open campaign: the French public will swallow propaganda without the sugar-coating of impersonality required in America. Hence each French organization publishes its own news-bulletin, issues numerous brochures and pamphlets under its own auspices, and advertises its principles at critical moments on flaming posters and placards. When " copy " is furnished to the great dailies, the propagandist organization is careful to demand and receive public credit for its contribution. Even if a propagandist article or editorial bears simply the name of its author, his affiliations are so well known as to make it unnecessary to name the groups for which he speaks.

Altogether, it may be concluded that the French press, generally speaking, is closely identified with national interests, that it is harmoniously articulated with the national State, and that, whether or not it directly inculcates " nationalism," it constitutes a continuous and most potent force in " making Frenchmen " and inspiring them with supreme loyalty to France.

CHAPTER VII

RADIO AND CINEMA

I

SUPPLEMENTAL nowadays to the press are novel agencies of publicity — the radio and the cinema — which, actually or potentially, are also agencies of popular training in national patriotism. The press itself is relatively old; it dates from the invention of printing in the fifteenth century; and, although it has been enormously developed and expanded by the revolutionary improvement of the industrial arts in the nineteenth century, it existed and evolved many of its traditions prior to the age of socialism and *étatisme*. One result has been that almost universally in national states, including France, the press has been treated mainly as a private enterprise and has not been directly owned or controlled, except in time of national crisis, such as the Great War, by the Government. On the whole, it has certainly sponsored and stimulated national patriotism, but it has done so less because it is the official mouthpiece of a centralized national Government than because it naturally caters to an ever widening circle of readers whose training as national patriots has already been carried far by national schools, by a national army, and by innumerable other forces inherent in a modern national environment.

The radio and the cinema, on the other hand, are very recent inventions; they depend upon the latest scientific advances and they appear in France, for example, only after the Third Republic has been firmly established and has acquired the habit of utilizing all manner of institutions and movements in its own service. It is not surprising, therefore, that the French State of to-day, still reluctant to restrict the freedom of the press, should seek to control, if not to own and monopolize, both the cinema and the radio. These institutions, being new, have not had much to do in the past, as the press has had, with the inculcation of national patriotism. Consequently they do not stand on an equal footing with such agencies as have already been discussed in this book — the civil service, the educational system, the army and navy, the churches, the press. But it is recognized that potentially they are important agencies for the future. And for this reason, and also because of the interesting policy which the French State is adopting in respect of them, it seems desirable to devote some attention to the status of radio and cinema in France.

2

Although French scientists have been among the first to discover and extend the possibilities of wireless telegraphy and telephony, France has been outdistanced in the practical application of radio-broadcasting by Germany, Great Britain, Sweden, and the United States. There are in France fifteen broadcasting stations in actual operation and three new stations projected, and approximately 1,000,000 receiving sets; in Germany there are twenty-three broadcasting stations now operating and 1,635,000 homes equipped with receiving sets; in Great Britain there are twenty-two broadcasting stations and 2,200,000 receiving sets; Sweden has twenty broadcasting stations, and Spain has fourteen stations in actual operation and three to be opened in the near future. Thus, France, with a population of about 40,000,000, finds herself with fewer broadcasting facilities than Sweden, with a population of 6,000,000, and only slightly ahead of Spain, with a population of 21,000,000. In all Europe there are 178 broadcasting stations (141 now operating and 37 projected);[1] while in the United States there are 685 broadcasting stations and 6,535,000 receiving sets.[2]

[1] Figures as of July 1, 1927. Cf. La Radio, No. 17, July, 1927, p. 147, and La Journée Industrielle, June 25, 1927. See Table IX.

[2] Cf. U. S. Department of Commerce, Radio Service Bulletins. The American figures are of November 1, 1927.

Paris is the center of French broadcasting. The Government operates the high-powered Eiffel Tower station and the station of the École Supérieure des Postes et Télégraphes of lesser range, while private initiative controls the powerful station of *Le Petit Parisien;* " Radio-Paris," owned by the French Radio Corporation; and two smaller stations heard occasionally, " Radio-Vitus " and " Radio-L.L." In the provinces the best known stations are those under the control of the government Department of Posts and Telegraphs at Marseilles, Toulouse, Bordeaux, Lyons, and Grenoble. Other stations in operation are located at Mont-de-Marsan (Landes), Toulouse, Lyons, and Agen (Lot-et-Garonne). Wave-lengths have been assigned to stations at Angers (Maine-et-Loire), Bourges, and Caen, while some sporadic broadcasting in the past has been heard from stations at Issy-les-Moulineaux (near Paris), Pic-du-Midi (in the Pyrenees), St. Étienne, Strasbourg, Rennes, Lille, and Montpellier. (See accompanying map.)

Paris is not an ideal city for radio-reception on account of its situation in the center of a great plain; the humidity in the atmosphere in the western and central regions of France is a further obstacle to clear audition. Despite the assigning of specific wave-lengths to European stations, there are times when it is almost impossible to prevent interference, and the air becomes a veritable chaos. Most of the receiving-sets sold in France are designed to meet the demand for an inexpensive equipment which will pick up local stations. Of the million radio-sets said to be in operation in France, a very small proportion provide the selectivity, long range, and clear reception of the average medium-priced radio-set in America. Under such unfavorable conditions, it is not difficult to understand why radio-broadcasting in France has not made the progress which has been attained in America, Germany, and Great Britain. Conditions in the provinces vary with the geographical advantages of the region: Marseilles, Limoges, Nantes, and Reims are among the cities least endowed with favorable factors in radio-reception; Lyons, Strasbourg, Nancy, Lille, Nice, and Toulouse enjoy the best geographical and atmospheric conditions.

FRENCH RADIO BROADCASTING
STATIONS   JULY 1927

TABLE IX

RADIO BROADCASTING STATIONS IN EUROPE

(July, 1927)[3]

Country	No. of Stations Operating	No. of Stations Projected
Albania........................		1
Austria........................	5	2
Belgium.......................	2	4
Bulgaria.......................		1
City of Danzig..................	1	
Czechoslovakia.................	4	1
Denmark.......................	1	
Esthonia.......................	1	
Finland........................	8	1
France.........................	15	3
Germany.......................	23	1
Great Britain...................	22	
Greece.........................		1
Hungary.......................	1	
Iceland........................	1	
Italy..........................	4	4
Latvia.........................	1	
Lithuania......................		1
Luxembourg....................		1
Netherlands....................	1	
Norway........................	6	7
Poland.........................	2	1
Portugal.......................		2
Rumania.......................	1	1
Russia.........................	4	1
Spain..........................	14	3
Sweden........................	20	
Switzerland....................	2	
Yugoslavia.....................	2	1
Total.........................	141	37

The use of radio-broadcasting as a form of advertising for the development and retention of the good-will of the consuming public has not yet taken root in France. To be sure, the great newspaper, *Le Petit Parisien,* owns one of the most powerful stations in France, and takes every opportunity thereby to secure readers for its publications; and various other newspapers sponsor programs from time to time or provide news items to

[3] Compiled from list, "Répartition des Fréquences des Stations de Radiodiffusion," *La Radio,* No. 17, July, 1927, p. 147.

be broadcast. But aside from advertising by the press, the commercial and industrial world has ignored the possibilities of radio-publicity. As a direct consequence the programs furnished gratis by the Government or private companies leave something to be desired from the point of view of variety of entertainment, quality of the performers, and duration of broadcasting. Only a few French stations begin their programs early in the afternoon and continue without silent periods until midnight; the majority are " on the air " merely for three or four hours in the evening, while some stations broadcast every other night or even less frequently.

The Paris stations provide the best entertainment and are heard all over France, their programs being often the only ones printed regularly in the provincial papers. The Government has the coöperation of the Institut Radiophonique de la Sorbonne and the Université Populaire in its programs from the Eiffel Tower and the P.T.T. stations; for several hours each day lecturers discuss current topics of interest; a fifteen-minute review of books or speech in English is a daily feature; and advice is given on the care of the home, children, and other topics which appeal to women. The musical programs, which furnish the greater portion of the entertainment on all stations, public or private, are generally orchestral. " Jazz " forms a small part of the French entertainment, the most popular programs being a combination of classical numbers (without discrimination as to nationality of the composer) and French semi-classical music, selections from light operas, and sentimental ballads. Certain important official functions, such as meetings of commemoration, and eulogies of the dead, etc., by leading political figures, are broadcast especially by government stations. On the whole, however, it cannot be said that either the publicly or privately owned stations have as yet availed themselves of the opportunities for national or other propaganda afforded by radio-broadcasting.

Granted favorable atmospheric conditions, it is within the power of all except the very simplest and cheapest of radio-receiving sets in France to pick up other European stations — chiefly those in England, Switzerland, Germany, Austria, Spain, and Italy. Nearly all the French daily newspapers publish the programs of certain foreign stations which may be heard successfully by the radio-amateurs of the region. In a survey of the radio programs published by the newspapers of the fifteen largest provincial cities, Lyons led in the number of foreign stations represented — stations of six foreign countries were within reach, including three English, two Swiss, two German, one Belgian, one Spanish, and one Italian; Strasbourg reported stations from five foreign countries — two English, two Swiss, two German, one Austrian, and one Czechoslovak; Nancy listed stations in five foreign countries — one English, one German, one Austrian, three Italian, one Swiss; and Nice could hear programs from stations in five foreign countries — two English, three Italian, three German, three Spanish, and one Austrian. That the radio may become a force in promoting international understanding and good-will is a theoretical possibility; at present its effectiveness is limited by the lack of an international broadcasting language, and by the interference of local stations which may be in operation during the greater part of the period when foreign stations are broadcasting.

In view of the serious conflicts between stations using ether waves of similar length and in view of the recognized importance of broadcasting in the development of national public opinion, the French Government has decided on a policy of national ownership and operation of radios in France. A decree of December 28, 1926, instituted an inter-ministerial commission on radio-diffusion, which has assumed supervision of all broadcasting activities. Small stations owned by amateurs for scientific purposes are subject to nominal control only, but all other broadcasting stations are to become the property of the State on January 1, 1933. Under government control these stations will present programs to which the " vital forces " of the nation will be invited to contribute — associations or groups of authors, composers, and artists, the press, great organizations, universities, and other factors in national life. The State will provide the technical facilities; the talent will be furnished by its patriotic public-spirited citizens. Until 1933, private initiative will be permitted to build and operate stations which will revert to state ownership in that year. It was decreed that before December 31, 1927, concessions should be given for the installation and exploitation of three national stations by national groups, and eighteen regional stations by groups representing private regional interests such as chambers of commerce, agricultural organizations, etc. When the inter-ministerial commission met on December 29, 1927, to consider the assignment of these stations, it was able to give concessions to two regional stations only: Paris and Toulouse. As for the sixteen regional stations remaining, no decision could be reached because of the evident lack of competition for the privilege to be bestowed and the poor documentation submitted by the applicants for such concessions.[4] The decree had provided that all regional stations not assigned by January 1, 1928, would revert automatically to the State: i.e. that no stations in France other than those established by the State itself would be allowed to operate. Under the circumstances, a new delay in assigning regional posts was deemed advisable.

The inter-ministerial commission which is charged with the broad powers described above is headed by the Minister of Commerce, and is composed of fifty-four members, representing the leading national and private enterprises. There are four sub-commissions, dealing with intellectual expansion, technical problems, administrative questions, and juridical matters. It is not to be supposed that the members of the commission are unanimously in favor of rigid governmental control: included in the number are some partisans of private initiative — broadcasters, writers, journalists, engineers, parliamentarians.

The strongest objector to the impending state monopoly of radio broadcasting is the " Syndicat Professionel des Industries Radio-électriques," which asserts that from the point of view of technical and administrative achievements the only hope of development lies in private initiative. As an example of the relative incapacity of the State, it cites the state-owned telephone system, which has resulted in the almost complete paralysis of

4 *Le Temps,* December 30, 1927.

French invention and manufacture of apparatus, forcing the purchase of material from the United States. From the literary and artistic world come protests that the law which insures the liberty of the press should be equally applicable to radio-broadcasting. The expression of ideas through the latest medium provided by science should be unrestricted, or else the Government will violate "the most sacred rights of the individual." [5] It is indeed a difficult matter to censor the air. As the opponents of state control declare, "The State could, if it wished, prevent its nationals from hearing free and spontaneous French voices, but it can never prevent them from hearing foreign stations. After all, the universality of radio-diffusion, its ignorance of frontiers, its practically unlimited reach, make the conception of a state radio-system ridiculous." [6]   .

To such arguments the partisans of government control reply that there is room for only about twenty wave-lengths for broadcasting in France, and that these must be used for the service of the entire nation. Private enterprises should not be allowed to divide up the national patrimony of the air among themselves; the State alone should use radio-broadcasting to inform, educate, and protect its people. The national weather bureau should supply forecasts to farmers and the Ministry of Agriculture should provide them with market reports and advice; education by means of radio should be a state function and form part of the national school system. Each ministry should watch over the broadcasting programs with the same vigilance that it exercises over the press. The Ministry of Foreign Affairs, for instance, should prevent the dissemination of false or untimely news or undiplomatic commentaries which may misrepresent French sentiment when picked up in other countries or sow discord among nations. And there are many who believe that radio-broadcasting offers an unequalled opportunity to create and maintain pro-French sympathies in foreign lands.

Instead of imposing a burden on French taxpayers for the

[5] Louis Dausset, "Le Statut de la T.S.F. en France," *Revue Politique et Parlementaire,* Vol. CXXXII, July 10, 1927, pp. 18–26.

[6] *La Journée Industrielle,* June 25, 1927.

upkeep of national radio-diffusion, the stations operated by the Government are expected by supporters of the new decree to produce some revenue. It is proposed to rent the services of the station for commercial advertising, following the methods of radio-publicity in the United States. Whether French advertisers can be persuaded to expend the large sums necessary for providing regular entertainment over the air with uncertain prospects of a return on the capital invested, remains to be discovered. Up to the present time, they have not interested themselves in the project of advertising by air, and opponents of the Government's ambitious enterprise declare that economic and industrial conditions as well as the psychology of selling in France do not adapt themselves to American practices.

Unless the decree of December 28, 1926, is abrogated by another administration, France in 1933 will be in full control of a great instrument for the formation of public opinion and national psychology. The effects of the state monopoly of the air-waves will be observed with intense interest.

3

The cinema in France to-day is primarily a foreign institution. Unlike the press, the radio, and the theatre, which are essentially French in that they follow French traditions and standards of taste, employ mainly French talent under French direction and are designed primarily for the French people, the motion-picture world is predominantly alien. Five-sixths of the time the Frenchman spends in a cinema he is under the influence of a foreign production, conceived and executed by persons whose environment, manner of living, and even physical appearance are strange to him. Especially since the war France has been invaded peacefully but none the less sweepingly by the film interests of other nations and particularly by the United States, farthest away and most difficult to understand of all countries which provide motion-pictures for the French. From every point of view — social, economic, artistic, and political — French patriots have denounced the present condition of the cinema in

France as being hostile to national interests. A review of the situation which has existed for nearly a decade and of the recent efforts of the leaders of the French motion-picture industry and the French Government to control the foreign invasion throws many interesting lights on the problem of national psychology.

From seven to ten per cent of the population of France patronize the motion-picture theatres regularly.[7] Compared with the number of cinema patrons in other countries, especially the English-speaking, this proportion seems unusually low, and is partly explained by the fact that the poor man in France enjoys many other inexpensive distractions, such as cafés, café-concerts, circuses, fairs, races, popular-priced theatres, and community opera houses, while in America and England the cinema is often the only form of amusement within the average wage-earner's reach. Then, too, about half of the population of France is agricultural, living at some distance from a motion-picture theatre and unable to support the cinema regularly with its patronage. In certain classes of French society, moreover, especially in the provinces, the " movies " have not yet won the stamp of respectability and are scorned as haunts of the vulgar and impious. A great many of the patrons of the cinema in America are young girls and boys who attend shows as often as they please without being accompanied by a parent; in France such freedom is unknown, in all save the very lowest social stratum, and no respectable young girl would be permitted to visit a cinema unchaperoned.

In December, 1927, there were 3,994 motion-picture theatres in France, as compared with 4,293 in Germany, 3,300 in Great Britain, and 25,000 in the United States.[8] These theatres are scattered rather evenly throughout France, with perhaps a larger proportion in the south. An inquiry made in January, 1927, showed that the city having the greatest seating capacity in relation to the population was Toulon, with 93 seats per thousand persons.[9] The proportion in the other cities was as follows:

7 Cf. La Cinématographie Française, No. 449, June 11, 1927, p. 16.
8 New York Times, December 23, 1927.
9 Cf. La Cinématographie Française, No. 427, January 8, 1927, p. 6.

St. Étienne, 87; Bordeaux, 82; Marseilles, 80; Lille, 77; Nancy, 72; Roubaix, 69; Reims, 62; Nice, 61; Rouen, 49; Toulouse, 48; Nantes, 47; Paris, 45; Le Havre, 44; Strasbourg, 42; Mulhouse, 38; and Lyons, 35. The high ratio in Toulon may be due to the demand for cheap amusement by the military and naval population as well as by the workers in the arsenal. In general the industrial cities are prepared for a large attendance at cinemas, though Lyons at the bottom of the list is a notable exception. The comparatively low percentage of seats in Paris may be explained by the competition offered by numerous other popular entertainments. Among the smaller towns, Lourdes, famed for its shrine which draws pilgrims from all Europe, heads the list by providing 3,000 seats for cinema patrons; the native population of Lourdes is 9,000.

It is claimed that 75 per cent of the better class of motion-picture theatres are owned or controlled by American film interests,[10] who thus insure an outlet for American films and at the same time reduce the market for films of French manufacture. During 1927, French public sentiment was strongly opposed to the acquisition of the Gaumont theatres by the American firm of Metro-Goldwyn-Mayer, the Marivaux Theatre in Paris by the United Artists, and the Paramount Company's conversion of the old Théatre Vaudeville on the Grands Boulevards into one of the largest and most modern cinemas in Europe. The introduction, by the last named, of American systems of rapid ticket-selling, presentation of free theatre programs, and abolition of the custom of tipping the ushers, was hailed as nothing short of sacrilege.

The average motion-picture entertainment in France is at least an hour longer than that in America. Except in a few of the largest houses in Paris which present one feature film for a run of several weeks or months, the program consists of two multiple-reel films and several short-reel subjects — a news weekly, a slapstick comedy, an educational film or travelogue, and often an episode in a serial thriller. Programs are changed usually once a week. It is customary to give only two performances daily, in

10 *New York Times*, December 19, 1927.

the afternoon and evening, with sometimes three shows on Sundays and holidays. The continuous performance is practically unknown. The price of admission varies with the district, the " exclusiveness " of the featured film, the time of the performance, and the location of the seat. But even on the Grands Boulevards the highest price is normally eighty cents, and elsewhere tickets cost from eight to twenty cents. These rates may be cut in half on week-days by the use of a cut-price coupon, which the thrifty obtain as premiums by trading regularly at certain shops in the neighborhood.

The feature film — and there are usually two on every cinema program — is the substance of the entertainment. Up to the present time the French production of feature films has been submerged by foreign importations. Only ten per cent of the multiple-reel pictures shown in France from 1924 to 1927 were of French origin. Necessity has forced the French exhibitor to be cosmopolitan, and the French public has become accustomed to a varied succession of productions — American, German, Italian, Danish, Austrian, English, Swedish, Spanish, Russian, and Hindu. In spite of the international aspect of the French cinema program, however, statistics show that American film interests have enjoyed almost undisputed possession of the field. The following table [11] indicates the preponderance of American feature films in France as compared with films from all other nations:

TABLE X

FEATURE FILMS SHOWN IN FRANCE 1924–1927

ORIGIN	1924		1925		1926		1927	
France........	68	10% of total	73	10% of total	55	10% of total	74	13% of total
United States..	589	85% " "	577	82% " "	444	79% " "	368	63% " "
Germany.....	20	3% " "	29	4% " "	33	6% " "	90	16% " "
Italy.........	9	1% " "	13	2% " "	14	2% " "	14	2% " "
Russia........	1		0		1		10	2% " "
Other countries	6	1% " "	12	2% " "	18	3% " "	25	4% " "
Total feature films shown.	693		704		565		581	

11 Compiled from statistics published annually in *La Cinématographie Française.*

Before discussing other tendencies shown in Table X, we may point out some of the reasons for the success of American films in France. First of all, the American producers suffered no ill effects from the World War, which crippled the film industries of most of their European competitors. Second, American pictures, although more lavishly produced, cost the exhibitor less than European pictures. Since the cost of producing a motion-picture negative must be amortized by the rental charges on the positives, it follows that large-scale distribution lowers the rental charge of each positive. When an American picture is shown in France, it has usually been exhibited throughout the United States and has already more than repaid its producers. European pictures, on the other hand, have so limited a market that the relatively few positives cannot be rented as cheaply as an American film. This factor alone would seem decisive in inducing French exhibitors to choose American features. Third, the majority of the first-class motion-picture houses in France are owned or controlled by American film interests, which discriminate as far as expediency permits in favor of their own productions. A picture which has been shown in the better theatres, moreover, acquires a certain prestige which the smaller cinemas are anxious to capitalize. Fourth, certain kinds of American films and many American "stars" are extremely popular in France. Perhaps the most preferred are the Wild West films, combining all the familiar elements of rugged scenery, horseback pursuit, spectacular battles with Indians, and hair-raising adventure into a distinctively American contribution which European producers would find it difficult, if not impossible, to imitate. American slapstick comedies, centered around the personality of a "star" like Charlie Chaplin (dear to the French as "Charlot"), Harold Lloyd, Buster Keaton, or Larry Semon (nicknamed "Zigoto" in France), have little European competition. Domestic comedies, depicting American home life as a rapid succession of farcical complications happily solved in the final fade-out, interest French spectators. The screen actors and actresses of America, thanks to American publicity experts and their own charms, are as well known and admired in France as at home. The personal appearance of an American "*vedette*" in France is a signal for cheering crowds, and front-page prominence is given to Hollywood scandals in the French press.

During 1926 and 1927, French imports of American feature films steadily decreased. While 85 per cent of all feature pictures shown in 1924 were of American origin, the proportion dropped to 63 per cent in 1927 — a loss of 22 per cent in three years. The rise of anti-American sentiment as a result of the war-debt negotiations and the mounting of the dollar at the expense of the franc were held to be important factors in reducing the number of American films exhibited. In 1926 and 1927 the showing of several American films which seemed to reflect on French military honor was accompanied by protests in the press and near-riots in certain theatres. *Beau Geste,* an American film purporting to depict life in the French Foreign Legion, was banned by the censors,[12] while *The Big Parade,* showing episodes in the life of an American soldier at the French front, excited the displeasure of the French because of the inference that the Americans had won the war single-handed.

Until the turning of the tide of public opinion against the United States, the French had considered it better policy to import films from America than to give business to their continental rivals in film production. As the Americans fell from favor, European animosities seem to have been subdued, and a corresponding increase of imports from other countries was observable in 1926 and 1927. Especially noteworthy were the gains made by the Germans, who furnished 90 pictures to France in 1927, three times as many as in the previous year. The production of French feature films, which had been practically stationary in 1924, 1925, and 1926, rose only from 10 to 13 per cent of the total number exhibited in 1927. In other words, the German film interests, not the French, profited most by the decrease in American films marketed in France.

Obviously, those who have an artistic or financial interest in the French motion-picture industry have reason to be dissatis-

[12] It was forbidden in Germany also, at the request of the French Ambassador. *Cf. La Cinématographie Française.*

fied with its weak position at home and abroad. If we compare the development of the industry in France with that in Germany, we may be able to understand more readily the debility of the former and the vigor of the latter. With national pride, the French recall that the film industry was born in Paris in the laboratory of the Lumière brothers, in the early nineties. When the Germans first exhibited motion-pictures in 1896-1897, they used French apparatus and French films. As the new art made a place for itself in Europe and America, French films, notably those bearing the famous insignia of Pathé Frères and Gaumont, enjoyed undisputed prestige and popularity. The effect of the war on the French motion-picture industry was suffocating, if not lethal; its effect on the German industry, on the contrary, was stimulating. In France there were no longer enough French pictures produced to supply demands at home, not to speak of foreign markets, and American films found an appreciative public. Meanwhile Germany, forced by the Allies' blockade to do without foreign films, saw an opportunity to develop home production. By the end of the war the industry had made such progress that it was able to supply not only the German theatres but also in large part those of Austria, Switzerland, Poland, and Scandinavia. A powerful organization of German exhibitors and producers, the " Reichsverband," formed with the coöperation of the Government in 1917, was of material assistance in placing the industry on a firm foundation.

After the Armistice, the French producers began their efforts at reconstruction. The situation was far from attractive to investors of new capital. There were projects for the increased taxation of theatres which would discourage the opening of new cinemas and consequently limit the market for films. The public, moreover, had acquired a taste for American feature films and an affection for Charlot, Mary Pickford, Douglas Fairbanks, and Jackie Coogan. The French motion-picture business, before the war a full-fledged industry, found itself reduced to a shadow of its former self, disorganized, without sufficient capital for reconstruction, an infant industry in need of government protection.

For the German producers, the period of inflation following

the Armistice was an incentive to continued expansion. The public was pleasure-mad; motion-picture palaces multiplied; the falling mark prevented the importation of foreign films on a large scale and at the same time encouraged exports. With the stabilization of the mark, the German film industry came upon harder times; the period 1924–1925 saw a number of companies forced to suspend production and an influx of American pictures. Again the Germans found strength in union. In order to combat the menace of American competition and increased tax burdens, a new executive body, the " Spitzenorganisation," comprising not only producers and exhibitors, but all allied branches of film manufacture, technicians, artists, and press representatives, set up a government lobby. It secured in June 1926 a reduction by a third of the taxes on the various branches of the industry. And among its other achievements may be listed the reduction of export taxes, the increased credit facilities granted to producers, and the organization of huge national expositions. But the most radical change in the status of the cinema in Germany is due to the pressure of the organization on the Government which resulted in 1925 in the restriction on the importation of foreign feature films. For every German picture produced, not more than one foreign film may be imported. While certain modifications made the quota less drastic in the first years of its operations, its stimulating effect on home production is already noticeable. A comparison of the situation in France and Germany in 1926 emphasizes the progress of German production: [13]

TABLE XI

1926

FRANCE		GERMANY	
Films produced in France	55	Films produced in Germany	202
American films shown in France	444	American films shown in Germany	229
European films shown in France	66	European films shown in Germany	84
Total feature films exhibited in France	565	Total feature films exhibited in Germany	515

[13] Marcel Colin, " La Situation du Marché Français," in *La Cinématographie Française*, No. 438, March 26, 1927, p. 25.

In quality as well as quantity, the film industry of Germany has outdistanced that of France. The originality of their scenarios, the pictorial and dramatic technique of their directors, and the development of a number of " stars " of the first magnitude have made German productions the only rivals which America needs to consider seriously in the European market. Many important German feature films have recently secured the much coveted entry into American theatres — the height of the European producer's financial ambition.

The healthy progress of the German cinema since the war has served to make the French more acutely conscious of the inadequacy of their own production. Who is responsible for a situation which for a number of years French producers, by propaganda half economic and half patriotic, have declared to be a national disgrace? In the press and on the platform they have blamed the public, the critics, the exhibitors, and the Government. The public, they assert, is unpatriotic enough to be indifferent to the nationality of the films shown, requiring only that they be entertaining. The critics are accused of partiality to foreign films and of pouncing too severely on the blemishes in French productions. The owners of motion-picture theatres have placed profit before " fatherland " in their choice of programs. They have neglected French offerings for cheaply-rented sure-fire successes of American or German origin. The Government, according to the producers, has been guilty on two counts: first, it has imposed such high taxes on motion-picture theatres that the industry cannot expand; and second, it has made no attempt (until 1928) to protect the French industry from foreign competitors.

The growth of anti-American sentiment in 1926 and 1927 aided French producers in their efforts to arouse public opinion to demand protection for their national film interests. American films were declared to have a stultifying effect on the populace and to be designed for the masses in the United States of a mentality far below that of the average French spectator. The " Syndicat des Directeurs de Cinémas " in November, 1927, passed a resolution deploring the Gallophobe practices of foreign films, and especially those of America, "which represent the French as an immoral people, the Frenchman as a villain, the Frenchwoman as a 'vamp,' the French Foreign Legion as a group of fugitives from justice, and the French soldier as lacking in discipline." French churchmen joined in the patriotic protest and declared that American social customs, as depicted in their films, were a menace to the morality of the French.

The fact that American audiences are not attracted by French photoplays is the sharpest thorn of all in the side of French producers, since America, with its 25,000 theatres, offers a greater opportunity for realizing large profits than the entire European market. In the fall of 1927 a group of French producers sent a delegation to America to sell several feature films, but the mission was not a success. Replying to the assertion of the French press and producers that only the unfair discrimination of American exhibitors prevents the French from entering the American market, the Americans contend that French films do not please the American public, and they give specific instances.

4

After two years of agitation against the conditions which were stifling the national film industry, the French producers were finally able to obtain the coöperation of the French State. As a result of the pressure of the " Chambre Syndicale de la Cinématographie," headed by M. Louis Aubert, owner of the largest film interests in France, and M. Jean Sapène, honorary president and official spokesman for the producers, in 1927 the Minister of Public Instruction and the Fine Arts, M. Édouard Herriot, appointed a plenary commission to investigate the situation and to recommend appropriate legislation. The main problem before the Herriot Commission was to devise a method of control which would limit the number of foreign films shown in France and at the same time induce the film interests of foreign countries, particularly the United States, to buy more French pictures. On February 19, 1928, the secrecy which had veiled the deliberations of the Commission was broken by the publication in the *Journal Officiel* [14] of a decree approved by the Council of Ministers establishing the status of the cinema as a " protected national institution."

Full control over the licensing of all French and foreign films for exhibition in France is vested in a permanent commission of thirty-two members named by the Minister of Public Instruction and acting under his supervision. The personnel of the commission is fixed as follows: the Director-General of the governmental Department of the Fine Arts, who is the presiding officer; one of the sub-directors of the Department; three representatives of the Ministry of Public Instruction; four of the Ministry of the Interior; one each of the Ministries of Agriculture, Foreign Affairs, Colonies, Justice, Commerce, War, and Navy; two delegates from the French producers; two from the French scenario writers; two from the French motion-picture theatre proprietors; two from the French motion-picture actors; and eight members chosen at large. In other words, sixteen of the thirty-two members are state officials, and eight others, in practice, are chosen by them.

The decree of February 19, 1928, imposed a special restriction on foreign films by declaring that " every foreign film for which a visa is desired must be shown in the exact and undeleted version which was exhibited in the country of its origin, with the exact and undeleted titles and sub-titles of the original version, for which a certified translation into French must be supplied." Formerly pictures were specially edited for French spectators before they were reviewed by the board of censorship. Under the new ruling a picture like *The Big Parade*, which in its original form contained many features which might offend French sensibilities, would have little chance of being approved, since the Commission, according to article 6 of the decree, " must take into consideration all national interests involved, and especially the conservation of national morals and traditions." In order to limit the number of foreign pictures licensed, it is thus possible to exclude any film which portrays the villain or " vamp "

[14] *Cf. Journal Officiel*, February 19, 1928, p. 2076.

as of French nationality or which shows Paris as a city of lax moral standards.

Additional regulations published by the Cinema Control Commission on March 17 were even more drastic. The number of foreign-made feature films to be admitted to France and her colonies from March 1, 1928, to September 30, 1929, was fixed at 500. Films produced in France were placed in two categories: (1) first-class films, made entirely by a French company, the authors, technical and scenic directors and their assistants, as well as camera men, being of French nationality. The scenic equipment and decorations must have been manufactured exclusively in France and the films photographed on French territory. While the leading rôles may include some by foreign artists, the proportion of these artists must not exceed 25 per cent, unless by special authorization of the Commission. (2) Second-class films, subject to the same regulations except that only 50 per cent of the personnel contributing to their manufacture must be of French nationality. Only manufacturers who have produced films of the first class are entitled to produce films of the second, and only at the rate of one film of the second class for every two films of the first class. For every film of the first class sold abroad, the French manufacturer is to receive a license enabling him to import and exploit in France seven foreign feature films. The sale abroad of a film of the second class would entitle a producer to 50 per cent of the rights granted to first class films. Moreover, seven " world visas " were to be allotted as follows: for every French film bought by an American company, four American films would be admitted to France; for a German purchase, two; and for a British, one. Besides, the Commission was empowered to refuse or revoke censorship licenses of any person, producer, distributor, or society which produces, distributes, or exploits anywhere abroad films which are regarded as reflecting unfavorably upon France. Under this clause, a company which produced a film such as *Beau Geste,* reflecting on the French Foreign Legion, *even if exhibited only in the United States,* would be barred from showing any other films, however innocuous, in France.

The proposed regulations were received by American producers with undisguised indignation. In view of the fact that the American film interests would find themselves obliged to buy more than half of all the French pictures made each year in order to obtain the necessary number of government visas for American pictures, at a cost of between $800,000 and $1,000,000 — an amount approximately equal to the net profit made by American producers annually in France — it was declared advisable to boycott the French market altogether. On March 24 Mr. Will H. Hays, President of the Motion Picture Producers and Distributors of America, sailed for Paris, with the avowed purpose of negotiating with the French Cinema Commission. The need for a firm stand by American producers was urged in consideration of the principle involved. If France were successful in forcing Americans to purchase her films, a number of other European countries might do likewise.

Apparently in deference to the storm of protest which the proposed regulations had aroused not only in America but among the proprietors of motion-picture theatres in France, the French Government on March 28 decided to defer final adoption of the restrictions, and there ensued parallel debates in the French press and discussions between Mr. Hays and M. Herriot. Editorials in the French press were divided in their attitude. The vehemently patriotic papers, such as *L'Intransigeant,* while greatly concerned over the possibility of unemployment for French workers, resented the American attitude as an attempt to force the hand of the French, and called the threatened boycott " bad, unpopular, and tactless." *Le Soir,* of the Left, was typical of the working-class point of view, and voiced its indignation against the governmental decree which it claimed was designed to impose upon the French public the worst films of French manufacture:

For there is no denying that the French motion picture industry is the worst of all from the viewpoint of scenario writing as well as from that of technique, and that is merely because influence over it is wielded by half a dozen financiers, capitalists, and industrialists. The new statute is absolutely against the general interests of the public and even violates the right of free thought, since it wishes to monopolize the cinema industry and place it at the service of reactionaries, exactly as has been done with the radio. The truth is that the new statute will be to the interest exclusively of a certain group who, menaced by their stupidity, are facing danger or ruin because of the excellence of American and German productions. We have pointed out before that the result of the statute will be to close American movie houses in France and throw more than 8,000 employees out of work. Such a scandal is intolerable. However injurious to the interests threatened, powerful as they may be, this new movie statute should be abolished immediately, and with it this shameful censorship which dishonors us.

At length, after rather stormy discussions, the French Government and its Cinema Commission effected a compromise with Mr. Hays, and accordingly modified the earlier regulations affecting American films. The four-to-one quota was abandoned. Instead, every company, whether French or foreign, which produces a film in France, is thereby entitled to seven licenses for the importation of as many foreign pictures into France; and two additional licenses, making not more than nine altogether, are to be granted to a foreign company which buys a French film and exhibits it in recognized foreign film-producing nations.

There are now three methods by which American film interests may obtain the privilege of doing business in France: first, by producing films in France, in which event each production will be entitled to seven import licenses; second, by purchasing French productions, without the obligation of showing them outside of France, for which seven licenses will be granted, and two additional permits if the picture is shown by the purchaser in other large countries; and third, by purchasing import licenses from French producers, who will receive from the Government seven for every film they make. Thus it will be possible for Americans to comply with all the new regulations and provide themselves with the necesary import licenses without buying a single picture produced by a bona-fide French company.

Finally, as a gesture of good-will, the French Cinema Commission has made less drastic the ruling which expelled from the French market any foreign company showing anywhere a film derogatory to the French people. Such a company will now be permitted to continue selling films in France until its supply of licenses is exhausted, after which the right is reserved by the Commission to refuse to issue further permits to the offending company. Thus the American film interests were able to reduce the formidable decrees of the French Cinema Commission to a series of relatively mild regulations, which, it is true, will weave a mesh of official red-tape about the film industry in France but erect no insurmountable difficulties in the way of foreign imports.[15]

Has the French film industry gained materially by its attempt to place itself under the protection of the national Government? This question cannot be answered until the statistics of the production and importation of films are available in the years to come. In any event, students of nationalism have had an opportunity to observe the development of a movement fostered by a combination of patriotic sentiment and financial ambition, and to note at least the temporary fate of such a movement under the pressure of foreign economic strategy.

There can be no doubt, however, that the French State is determined, in conjunction with French patriots generally, to render the French cinema more truly national and to develop it as a means of training for French citizenship. Nor can there be any reasonable doubt that American or other foreign producers, in view of the recent flare-up of French patriotism and the resulting danger to their own financial interests, will be increasingly careful to respect French susceptibilities and to make the pictures which they exploit in France more and more French. The cinema, like the radio, is likely to become in France an agency of the first importance in making patriotic Frenchmen.

[15] In September 1928, French interests renewed their agitation for more drastic import restrictions, obtaining unanimous approval of a four-to-one quota by the Cinema Commission on May 27, 1929. American producers united to defeat the measure by boycotting the French market, discharging thousands of employees and creating a " cinema famine," while the American State Department negotiated with the French Government. A settlement, effected September 24, 1929, continued the seven-to-one quota to October 1, 1931.

CHAPTER VIII

NATIONAL SOCIETIES

I

THE "right of association" is one of the basic personal liberties in contemporary France: proclaimed in principle by the French Revolutionaries in 1789, its present exercise is regulated and conditioned by an act of 1884. Any group or number of Frenchmen may legally form an " association " for political, social, cultural or philanthropical purposes simply by filing a statement of aims and a copy of by-laws with the central Government, and the Government is bound to tolerate all such associations unless they be adjudged " subversive." [1]

Frenchmen, being human, are socially minded; and they have taken advantage of the favorable legislation of the Third Republic to constitute a multiplicity of private associations and societies for almost every conceivable human activity — economic, professional, political, athletic, eleemosynary. Most such societies are not avowedly or intentionally nationalist or even patriotic. But certain categories of them, at least indirectly, serve national ends and coöperate with the State, the educational system, the army and navy, and the press in " making " Frenchmen and fashioning a French national psychology. To these categories we shall address ourselves here.

To a first category may be assigned a host of economic and professional associations which exist in France, as elsewhere, to bring together in social relationship persons of like interests or like technical training and to represent and advance their individual efforts by means of corporate action. Perusal of the

---

[1] And unless they be " religious congregations." The formation and toleration of religious congregations have been rigorously restricted by a law of 1901. See above, p. 99.

volume by Professors Ogburn and Jaffé on *The Economic Development of Post-War France* [2] suggests a vast number of associations of manufacturers, farmers, buyers, and sellers. A reading of the volume by Professor Saposs and Dr. Evans on *The Labor Movement in Post-War France* [3] reveals likewise a vast number of trade unions and coöperative societies. In other chapters of the present book some attention has been given, moreover, to still another vast number of professional organizations of teachers, journalists, army-officers, and clergymen. And if to these numbers be added the host of organizations for other professional men — lawyers, physicians, dentists, engineers, architects, painters, sculptors, musicians, littérateurs, chemists, physicists, biologists, philosophers, psychologists, economists, sociologists, historians, etc., etc. — some conception may be had of the variety and multiplicity of economic and professional societies in France.

These societies are concerned only incidentally with the purposeful propaganda of patriotism, but their national rôle should not therefore be slighted. In almost every case they are organized nationally. Metallurgical manufacturers, for example, are federated in a single " Comité des Forges "; coal industrialists, in a " Comité Central des Houillères de France "; owners of mechanical engineering plants, in a " Fédération des Syndicats de la Construction Mécanique, Électrique et Métallique de France "; manufacturers of cotton goods, in a " Syndicat Général de l'Industrie Cotonnière," and of artificial silk, in a " Société Nationale de la Viscose." Similarly, workingmen adhere in large numbers to a " Confédération Générale du Travail," and there are national unions of the local societies of physicians and lawyers, artists and scientists. In almost every trade or profession, local groups are federated in a national organization, with national headquarters, national officials, an annual national congress, and a varying amount of national publication; and in every such instance the national viewpoint is naturally emphasized.

With the national State, moreover, almost every economic or professional society is in more or less constant contact. It

[2] Volume III of this series (New York, Columbia University Press, 1929).
[3] Volume IV of this series.

receives its authorization to exist from the State. It functions in accordance with the laws of the State. It represents to the State the united efforts of an important segment of the State's citizenry. It usually watches with the utmost solicitude any action of the State, legislative or administrative, which may jeopardize the interests of the society's constituency. It sometimes labors actively in press and on rostrum, in the lobbies of Parliament and in electoral campaigns throughout the country, to uphold and advance the economic interests of the group it represents. Frequently it numbers among its active members state dignitaries and functionaries — ministers, deputies, senators, prefects, heads of bureaus and boards. In certain cases its activity has aided in the establishment of a coöperating or coördinating special ministry in the state cabinet; such ministries, for example, as those of Commerce and Labor.

A professional or economic association, of national scope, with national organization, and in close practical relationship with the national State, is bound to think of itself as being the champion not only of a particular group within France but also of national French interests in respect of the world outside. Associations of French manufacturers and French farmers in agitating for, and securing, national tariff protection have sought primarily to serve their respective economic interests, but in so doing they have made eloquent use of the argument that French manufacturing and French farming, for the greater glory of France, must be safeguarded against foreign competition. Likewise, both the General Confederation of Labor and the more specialized professional organizations have customarily enveloped their particular and sometimes selfish demands in the broad mantle of national charity. No implication is here intended that any professional or economic association in France is dishonest or dissimulating or that its public propaganda lacks sincerity and candor. Rather, the frank, full, and free use of national arguments in behalf of partial objects is still another, and very significant, evidence of the fact that the directors of economic and professional associations in France are nationally minded, that they have been imbued from infancy, in home, in school, in army, in daily reading and conversation, with the conviction that they are part and parcel, in person and in interests, of the France whose well-being it is their greatest care to assure. This state of mind they bring to their several national societies, and in these societies it is confirmed and from them it permeates in devious ways but normally in intensified form to the various social classes of the French population.

2

A second category of national societies consists of political organizations which sponsor particular political programs and participate in national elections. It has previously been pointed out that French politics are not based on a hard-and-fast two-party system but rather that the political " groups " in the Chamber of Deputies and in the Senate are numerous and in perpetual flux. Nevertheless, back of the fluid groups in the Parliament are a considerable number of relatively solid political associations. These associations differ widely among themselves, not only as to program, but also as to size, strength, and permanence. The Socialists, the Communists, and the Royalist " Action Française " have well-knit national organizations, with local branches and sizable dues-paying memberships. The Radicals and " Radicaux-Socialistes " also maintain a national organization, though it is in the nature rather of a loose federation than of a disciplined unit. Loosest and most subject to change are the organizations of the Moderates. All these political associations hold conventions, adopt resolutions, support publications, and in other ways engage in a good deal of popular propaganda. All of them command the allegiance of a certain number of deputies and senators, and most of them have members in cabinets. All, with the possible exception of the Communists, are patriotic, though the brand of patriotism may vary from the Jacobinism of the Radicals to the Traditionalism of the Royalists. Each insists that the national interests of France will be served best and most usefully by its own electoral triumph and by popular adoption of its own program. One usually calls another by hard names, but all (except possibly the Communists) vie with one another in boasting, at election-times and constantly between elections, of the great patriotic work they have done or will do for the greater glory of the fatherland. Professional politicians, who guide and dominate these political associations, use them as sounding-boards for the transmission to the public of their own traditionally oratorical praises of patriotism.

Every convention of every political association (except that of the Communists and ordinarily that of the Socialists) is addressed by patriotic speakers and clothes its resolutions in patriotic garb. Political associations of Radical or " Radical-Socialiste " complexion are no exception to this rule, though they are likely to couple the expression of their patriotism with avowed humanitarianism and internationalism. Political associations representing shades of opinion more moderate and to the Right are apt to be more single-minded and less restrained in voicing patriotism and even nationalism. To these latter organizations we may profitably devote some special attention, though it should be remembered that political associations of the Centre and of the Right enjoy no monopoly of patriotism or of the agencies of its propaganda: Radicals and Socialists are also very patriotic, in their way, and it is political organizations of the Left which have most zealously and persistently developed the modern State, the educational system, and the army as means of inspiring all Frenchmen with supreme loyalty to the fatherland.

Perhaps the most influential of the national political societies of the Centre and the Right is the " Republican Federation of France " (" Fédération Républicaine de France " [4]), which was founded in 1903 to combat Radical policies of " anti-clerical " and alleged " pacifist " character. Under the leadership of Louis Marin, a member of Parliament and a conspicuous figure in the coalition Poincaré Ministry, it has been extraordinarily active in preaching patriotism. The Federation scored

[4] Headquarters, 36 rue de Varenne, Paris. Officers: President, Louis Marin; Vice-Presidents, G. Bonnefous, Chassaigne-Goyon, François-Marsal, Manuel Fourcade, Hervey, General Hirschauer, Édouard Soulier; Secretary, Jean Guiter. Organ: La Nation (weekly, founded 1925).

many successes in the general election of 1919 and became the core of the " Bloc National " which controlled the Government during the ensuing four years. It suffered reverses in the election of 1924, but again strengthened its position in the election of 1928. Specifically, the Federation urged the occupation and opposed the later evacuation of the Ruhr; it condemned the debt-settlements with Great Britain and the United States; it has been critical of the League of Nations and hostile to Franco-German reconciliation. As M. Marin said in the Chamber of Deputies in 1926: " You have admitted Germany to the League of Nations. You have given her a privileged place. Now you will see what she will do with the League, what authority she will take, what intrigues she will start. You will see if you will not soon regret that you allowed her to enter so soon. In what concerns the victors of war, Germany from a moral point of view has wiped out three-quarters of the past. How could she have dreamed of winning the peace in such a fashion? She has won it by the Pact of Locarno." [5]

The " Democratic and Social Republican Party " (" Parti Républicain Démocratique et Social " [6]) has been, since 1920, the name of an organization founded in 1901 by Adolphe Carnot as the " Democratic Republican Alliance " in an effort to unite the Republicans of the Left Centre. It was a member of the " Bloc National " from 1920 to 1924, and is differentiated from the " Republican Federation " only by a tradition of very mild " anti-clericalism." The platform of the party in respect of foreign affairs has been set forth in 1927 in the following words: " A policy worthy of France's past and faithful to her democratic traditions, without imperialist tendencies, but safeguarding the *rights of France* in the world, the *security of the frontier* and of her colonial empire, and the strict execution of the Dawes Plan; a realization of peace, founded on the *respect for treaties* and guaranteed by a disarmament of Germany, by respect for pacts

---

[5] February 27 and March 1, 1926.

[6] Headquarters: 17 rue de la Rochefoucauld, Paris. Officers: Honorary President, Jonnart; President, Antony Ratier; Secretary, A. Mamelet. Organ: *La République Démocratique* (weekly).

of security, by the development of the *League of Nations,* and by a social and vigilant organization of national defense; fidelity to the tradition of France as *protector of small nations;* an energetic resistance to the increase of revolutionary internationalism and to the propaganda of the Soviets."

The " National Republican League " (" Ligue Républicaine Nationale " [7]) was founded after the general election of 1924, by a juncture of elements in the several defeated groups which had constituted the " Bloc National," in order to carry on a more unified and effective campaign than any single group could wage. Alexandre Millerand, who in his earlier days had been a Socialist but had later become a Nationalist and who was forced out of the Presidency of the Republic by the Radicals in 1924, was the League's first president and retained this position until his defeat in the senatorial election of 1927. The League has opposed the early evacuation of the Rhineland and the payment of the American debt and has demanded that the Franco-German frontier be fortified regardless of expense and that in all things the French Government follow a strictly patriotic and national policy. The League holds political rallies, maintains a press-service for five hundred newspapers, and forms local branches. Certain Parisian newspapers, notably *Le Temps, L'Écho de Paris, L'Avenir, La Victoire,* and *La Liberté,* nicely reflect the spirit of the League.

The " Action Française " [8] is at once the outstanding royalist and the most vehemently nationalist political association in France. It has grown out of a committee formed in 1898 of extreme Conservatives and anti-Dreyfusards. It began the publication of the *Action Française* as a weekly in 1899 and as a daily

[7] Headquarters: 47 Avenue d'Iéna, Paris. Officers: President, André Maginot; Board of Directors (among others), François-Marsal, François-Poncet, Louis Marin, Jusserand; Secretary, Seignette.

[8] Headquarters: 14 rue de Rome, Paris. Officers: Honorary President, Duc de Guise (pretender to the French throne); Directors, Léon Daudet, Charles Maurras, Jacques Bainville, Bernard de Vesins, René Benjamin, Maurice Pujo. Organs: *L'Action Française* (daily), *L'Action Française Agricole* (weekly), *L'Étudiant Français* (semi-weekly), *Le National* (weekly, published in German at Strasbourg), *La Voix Nationale* (weekly), *La Revue Universelle* (monthly), *Almanach de l'Action Française* (annual), *Cours et Conference d'Action Française* (quarterly).

in 1908. It became definitely royalist in 1901 under the influence of its prominent intellectual leader, Charles Maurras. The central organization supports a number of dependent propagandist societies, as well as publications, for city and countryside, for students and professional men; the interesting "Camelots du Roi" are a body of young men who police the meetings and lead the street demonstrations of the Action Française. The doctrine of the association is summarized in three formulae: integral nationalism, practical empiricism, and the forceful blow. "Integral nationalism" means that "a national policy should be pursued, involving the multiplication and strengthening of institutions which benefit the greatest possible number of living organisms by maintaining national integrity and furthering the growth of national power (for a nation declines when it ceases to progress)."[9] By "practical empiricism" is meant the teaching that "order in society, no matter how it is obtained, is more important than the liberty of the individual."[10] Concerning "the forceful blow," Charles Maurras has written: "The Action Française has always declared that the substitution of the Monarchy for the Republic (a condition necessary for the salvation of the country) will probably not be realized (unless extraordinary things come to pass) by the ballot. The Action Française has always said that the existing Government will probably be overthrown, like most preceding Governments, by force. The Action Française has always said that the preparation and organization of the needful *coup de force*, as well as the creation and diffusion of a state of mind which would assure success to the use of force, are essential and necessary elements of its program."[11]

The Action Française is militantly nationalist. Its tirades against Germany and its criticisms of the League of Nations are incessant. It preaches the necessity not alone of adequate French "defense" and "security" but also of forceful French expansion in Europe and in colonial domain. It opposes French evacua-

[9] Charles Maurras, *Enquête sur la Monarchie* (Paris, Nouvelle Librairie Nationale, 1925), pp. 18–19.

[10] *Ibid.*, p. 12.

[11] Charles Maurras, *Si le Coup de Force est possible* (Paris, Nouvelle Librairie Nationale, 1925), p. 583.

tion of the Rhineland and scoffs at the Pact of Locarno. It scents treason and ferrets out pro-German conspirators and sympathizers in Alsace-Lorraine. It perpetually accuses the Republican Government of France of cowardice if not treason, and has latterly directed especially venomous attacks against a fancied "pacifist" and anti-French alliance of the Pope with M. Aristide Briand, the French Foreign Minister.

The popular influence of the Action Française is difficult to estimate. Its direct influence on French politics is certainly slight: not a single professed member of the organization now occupies a seat in the French Parliament, and only one (Léon Daudet) occupied such a seat from 1919 to 1924. Indirectly, however, its influence is considerable. Not only have young persons, particularly university students, been attracted to it in increasing numbers, but many of its nationalist activities and "campaigns" have been welcomed and praised in newspapers and by politicians who profess abhorrence of its royalist principles. Even certain journals and statesmen of the Radical Left, whose Jacobinism is seemingly antithetical to the Traditionalism of the Action Française, have found it convenient to their own "anti-clericalism" to broadcast the latter's assaults on the alleged pro-German, anti-French bias of the Papacy; and Republican papers of the Centre and Right frequently cite with approval nationalist utterances of the *Action Française*. On the other hand, the organization has suffered internal schisms as well as external setbacks. Two of its prominent leaders, Louis Dimier and Georges Valois, have left it as a result of domestic dissensions, the former in 1920 and the latter in 1925. On August 27, 1926, Cardinal Andrieu, Archbishop of Bordeaux, publicly condemned many of its teachings and counselled Catholics to withdraw from it, and his action was formally approved and endorsed by Pope Pius XI on September 7, 1926; on December 29, 1926, the Pope went farther, forbidding faithful French Catholics to belong to the Action Française or habitually to read its literature, and almost the entire hierarchy of the Catholic Church in France, by a circular letter of March 10, 1927, recorded their support of the Papal position, while emphasizing its moral, rather than political, implications and reiterating their own patriotism and their own ardent devotion to France.

Another and much smaller political association of the extreme nationalist Right is " Fascism " (" Le Faisceau " [12]), which was founded in 1925, in conscious imitation of the Italian example, by Georges Valois, who had formerly been a member of the Action Française. It scorns all royalist pretensions and demands simply the dictatorship of the most able. The dictator of the future, it asserts, will be put in power by the patriotic spirit of war-veterans, and, through the coöperation of the great intellectual, moral, and spiritual elements of the nation, will realize the grandeur of France. " In Europe, where she has the victor's privilege, France will raise her sword as a standard around which her people will rally in order to establish a new European and Christian fraternity and to remind those nations who are daughters of Rome that it is their mission to unite for the protection of the frontiers of the ' Empire ' whose limits none of them has forgotten and in which human virtues are honored, cruelty is repressed, and reason reigns as the mark of divine power."

Still another small political society is the " Federation of Republican Renovators " (" Fédération des Républicains Rénovateurs " [13]), founded and directed after the war by J. Corréard, a former employee of the Ministry of Finance and commonly known under the pseudonym of Probus. It labors for a " better " and " greater " France and advocates a reformation of French

[12] Headquarters: 20 rue d'Aguesseau, Paris. Officers: President, Georges Valois; Vice-President, Jacques Arthuys; Delegate of Propaganda, Philippe Barrès; Delegate-at-Large, André d'Humières; Administrator, Serge André. Organ: *Le Nouveau Siècle* (weekly). See also the following books by Georges Valois, all published by the Nouvelle Librairie Nationale, Paris: *La Révolution Nationale* (1924); *La Politique de la Victoire* (1925); *L'Économie Nouvelle* (1924); *L'État, les Finances et la Monnaie* (1925).

[13] Headquarters: 8 rue de Richelieu, Paris. Organs: *La France Vivante* (weekly), *France et Monde* (quarterly). " Probus " has published several books: *La Plus Grande France* (1916), *Construire* (1917), *L'Organisation de la Démocratie* (1918), *La Constitution Syndicale de la France* (1919), *Rénovation* (1919), *Des Finances modernes pour Vivre* (1920), *Nos Petits Hommes d'État* (1925).

government and administration in the direction of democratic simplification. It emphasizes the nation but is not chauvinist.

3

The two categories of national societies which have been described — that of economic and professional associations and that of political organizations — naturally tend, in most instances, to stress the nation and, at least incidentally, to propagate national patriotism. But their primary purpose is to champion the special interests, professional, economic, or political, of particular groups of Frenchmen; and by acting in competition and sometimes in bitter rivalry with one another they tend also to emphasize within France economic differences, intellectual divergencies, and social cleavages, which may militate against any absolute national solidarity. In other words, they are simultaneously nationalist and anti-nationalist.

Cutting across both categories and embracing Frenchmen of diverse professions and politics, however, is a third category of national societies — the so-called patriotic societies — whose paramount accomplishment, as well as aim, is the inculcation of national patriotism. There are many of these in contemporary France, and they differ widely in the means and methods by which they achieve their common end. Of the several kinds of French patriotic societies consideration should be given to a few outstanding examples.

In a sense, the French Academy may be conceived of as a patriotic society in intimate relationship with the French State. It was established by statesmen in the seventeenth century, and down to the present time its " forty immortals " have been subsidized by the State both personally and for the great work they have collectively done in preserving the purity of the French language and promoting the prestige of French literature. Latterly, Academicians have been of the " Right " and " Left," " clerical " and " anti-clerical," Republican and even Royalist, but almost invariably they have been supremely devoted to the fatherland. When a new member is received into the august assembly, he delivers a lengthy eulogy of his deceased predecessor, and a designated Academician responds with an equally extended eulogy of the new member; both eulogies normally glow with national patriotism as well as scintillate with wit: they are listened to by a crowded audience, are printed in full in such newspapers as *Le Temps* and *Le Journal des Débats,* and are commented upon by almost the entire French press; they carry far. The Academy awards a great variety of prizes and pensions, and patriotic pronouncements are rarely absent from such awards. The Academy represents at home and abroad the dignity of French letters and learning; with all its authority and force it explains to the French people, for example, how superior the French language is to any other as the medium of international intercourse.

Another patriotic society in the closest relationship with the French State is the famous " Legion of Honor." [14] The Legion was created by decree of Napoleon Bonaparte on May 19, 1802. The Republican Constitution of 1799 had stipulated (art. 87) for the award of special national distinction to "warriors who render the Republic distinguished service in action;" but the decree of 1802 extended membership in the Legion not only to such warriors but also to persons who should render the State distinguished service in the civil administration, in the diplomatic corps, in science and art, etc. The decree obligated all members of the Legion to swear on their honor "to dedicate themselves to the service of the Republic, to the preservation of her territorial integrity, to the defense of her government, her laws and her property, and to employ every means to prevent the reëstablishment of the feudal system, and of its titles and honors, in order to ensure the maintenance of liberty and equality." This oath was abolished in 1870, and in other respects the Legion has undergone numerous changes of detail during the century and a quarter of its existence. Always, however, its predominant spirit has been that of special service and devotion to France.

The members of the Legion of Honor are named by the

[14] Headquarters: 1 rue Solferino, Paris. Grand Chancellor: General Dubail. See J. Durieux and A. Vovard, *Les Décorations françaises* (Paris, Chiron, 1922).

national Government, and during the Great War no limit was put on the number. At the present time an annual quota is allotted to each Ministry, and a certain additional number of appointments may be made by the Cabinet as a whole on special occasions. Each Ministry fills its quota, in accordance with its own rules, from persons who have performed important national service in a particular field: the Minister of Commerce, for instance, nominates business men; the Minister of Foreign Affairs designates diplomats and foreigners; the Minister of War names soldiers, etc. In 1922 the membership of the Legion was estimated at 142,000 of which number 22,000 were foreigners; 4,934 new members were appointed in 1922; 7,289 in 1923; 6,007 in 1924; 6,712 in 1925; and 5,453 in 1926.[15] The members are divided into five grades: Chevalier (Knight), Officer, Commander, Grand Officer, and Grand Cross; and promotion in grade is, of course, an honor additional to that of original appointment. The nominal head of the Legion, with the title of Grand Master, is ex-officio the President of the Republic. The actual head, with the title of Grand Chancellor, is always a military or naval officer, and he is assisted by a Council of Ten and by a staff of permanent officials and employees.

The Legion of Honor comprises many men who occupy positions of considerable influence in France and abroad: they are given the honor of membership in it because they have shown devotion to France; and normally their devotion to France is confirmed and strengthened by the honor of membership in the Legion. Foreign members are likely to be centres of pro-French sentiment abroad, and the Frenchman who wears the ceremonial badge of the Legion — the star with the motto " *Honneur et Patrie* " (Honor and Fatherland) — or its little red ribbon on the lapel of his coat is a marked national patriot. The Legion has funds of its own and receives subventions from the State.[16] It maintains beautiful headquarters, close to the Chamber of

---

[15] Figures furnished by the " Bureau de Statistique " of the Legion of Honor. See also J. Durieux and A. Vovard, *op. cit.*, p. 19.

[16] Members of the Legion in active military or naval service receive special annual stipends from the State, as follows: Chevaliers, 250 francs; Officers, 500; Commanders, 1,000; Grand Officers, 2,000; Grand Crosses, 3,000.

Deputies and the Ministry of Foreign Affairs, on the banks of the Seine, and is creating a Museum for the relics of its glorious past. It supports three schools (Saint-Denis, Ecouen, and Les Loges) for daughters of its French members.

4

Of the private patriotic societies (as distinct from the governmental Legion of Honor and French Academy), the most famous perhaps is the " League of Patriots " ("Ligue des Patriotes "[17]), founded in 1882 through the strenuous inspiriting influence of Paul Déroulède. Déroulède sketched its program as follows:

> There are three things which I particularly recommend as propaganda for you: to develop everywhere and in everything the particular spirit which makes one love the nation with passion; to develop the military spirit, which makes one serve the nation patiently and valiantly; and to develop the national spirit, which is the exact and reasoned knowledge of the interests and needs of the whole nation and which should not be sacrificed to internal particularistic enterprises or to foreign humanitarian endeavors. Let us concentrate, let us rally, let us aid each other. Be Frenchmen, good Frenchmen, nothing but Frenchmen.[18]

The first patriotic rally of the League (in 1882) was presided over by Félix Faure, subsequently President of the Republic, and was addressed by Déroulède and by Henry Martin, the historian. Gambetta speedily joined it, and his example was followed by Victor Hugo, Sadi-Carnot, Massenet, and a large number of less famous Frenchmen in all parts of the country. The League was active in propaganda and politics: it preached a war of revenge against Germany and the forceful recovery of Alsace-Lorraine; it championed the alliance of France with Russia; it supported Boulanger and opposed Dreyfus. In 1914 it

[17] Headquarters: 11 rue Montyon, Paris. Officers: President, General de Castelnau; General Director, General de Pouydraguin; General Delegate, Marcel Hobert; Secretary, Jean Bourgoin. Motto: " Qui vive? France. Quand même." Organ: *Le Drapeau* (weekly).

[18] Georges Poignant, *La Ligue des Patriotes* (Paris, Ligue des Patriotes, 1923), p. 11. See also J. and J. Tharaud, *La Vie et la Mort de Déroulède* (Paris, Plon, 1925).

claimed to have an active membership of 200,000 and as many more sympathizers.

During the Great War, the League of Patriots, under the leadership of Maurice Barrès, sought to sustain the morale of the soldiers at the front and the civilians at home. It was Barrès who suggested the *croix de guerre* as a special decoration for personal bravery. The League established an information service for soldiers in Paris; supplied those at the front with sweaters, etc.; organized French girls as "Sowers of Courage" for the combating of pessimism and defeatism; and created still another special organization, "The Village Conference" ("La Conférence au Village"), which by means of lectures, motion-pictures, and tracts, opposed anti-war propaganda in the country-side. The League denounced Caillaux and Malvy as "traitors," and demanded a "victorious" peace.

After the war, the League of Patriots at its general assembly in 1920 adopted the following statement of aims:

Defense of our national ideal and the expansion of French influence: *Outside of France:* Through (1) execution of the Treaty of Versailles, essential guarantee of the peace of the world; (2) development of our Rhenish policy; (3) maintenance of our alliances; (4) moral and economic radiation of France. *Inside of France:* Through (5) harmonious reintegration of Alsace and Lorraine with the French fatherland; (6) reconstruction of the devastated regions; (7) maintenance of the union among all classes and all citizens, propaganda of and instruction in the ideas of French fraternity; (8) organization of defense against the constant plot of the Germans to Bolshevize France; (9) development and coördination of the organization of patriotic, military, and athletic education; (10) worship of the glories of the fatherland and of the heroes who have given us the victory of right.

The League has been, and is, severely critical of Germany. It insistently demanded the occupation of the Ruhr and has opposed French withdrawal from the Rhineland. It has supported the alliance with Poland and the Little Entente. It has opposed the Mellon-Bérenger and the Caillaux-Churchill debt agreements, and has ridiculed the Pact of Locarno. For its propaganda it utilizes a newspaper of its own — "The Flag" (*Le Drapeau*) —

and supplies material to *L'Écho de Paris*. It also organizes large meetings in Paris and holds other meetings of its local groups. It conducts an annual pilgrimage to the statue of Jeanne d'Arc in Paris. In May 1921, it took advantage of the Napoleonic centenary to pay nationalistic homage to French military glory. After the death of Barrès in 1923, General de Castelnau became President of the League. Alexandre Millerand was made Honorary President in 1924. The League's membership is considerably less now than in 1914, attributable in part to the secession of many younger members.

Most of the young men who have been lost to the League of Patriots since the war have not been lost to ultra-patriotic propaganda, for they have left the older organization to form a new and even more energetic patriotic society, the " Patriotic Youth " ("Les Jeunesses Patriotes"[19]). This owes its origin to an emotional reaction of " nationalist " young Frenchmen against the spectacle of thousands of young Socialist Frenchmen escorting the remains of Jean Jaurès, in November 1924, to the Panthéon for national burial. The actual program of the Patriotic Youth is similar to that of the League of Patriots. It demands the sacrifice of the individual for the good of the nation. " If it is necessary to die, death unto me. But, O my France, may you live! " It assails the Pact of Locarno and condemns any *rapprochement* with Germany. It demands the repudiation of the American debt. It insists that France must seek security, not through the League of Nations, but by a grand alliance with Latin and Slavic peoples.

The " Patriotic League of French Women " ("Ligue Patriotique des Françaises"[20]) was founded by patriotic Catholic Frenchwomen about 1903 to combat anti-clerical tendencies of the Government and to defend Catholicism as a basic national tradition. This League has conducted patriotic, as well as Catholic, propaganda by means of a widely disseminated organiza-

[19] Headquarters: 10 rue Cardinal Mercier, Paris. Director: Pierre Taittinger. Organ: *Le National* (weekly).

[20] Headquarters: 368 rue Saint-Honoré, Paris. Officers (1927): President, Vicomtesse de Vilard; Vice-Presidents, Mme. Delacourt and Marquise de Juigné; Secretary, Mlle. Frossard. Patroness: Saint Jeanne d'Arc. Organ: *L'Écho* (monthly).

tion, meetings, speeches, and publications. It boasts of reaching some 600,000 French women and 33,000 French girls. In its official organ such patriotic statements as the following are not uncommon: " Devotion to the nation should be the same as devotion to the family, for the nation is really only a large social family." [21]

It is a criminal dream, a practical danger, to wish to sacrifice the life of the national family to a sentiment of solidarity surpassing natural frontiers or to wish to extend one's love to what is far away, thereby hating what is near at hand . . . The modern enemy of the Nation is humanitarianism, idolatry of humanity, which deifies the individual, conferring upon him all rights and freeing him from all duties . . . Our League ought to defend equally all these: Morality, Family, Religion, Nation.[22]

The " French League " (" Ligue Française " [23]) was founded in March 1914 by Ernest Lavisse and General Pau and now claims to have a membership of 50,000. It solicits the coöperation of all Frenchmen who place love of country and service to the nation above political parties. It has favored a more intensive exploitation of the French colonies, has elaborated a program for the construction of model tenements in large cities, has devoted much attention to the problem of France's stationary population, and, in particular, has been (and is) quite hostile to Germany. In a pamphlet distributed by the League and entitled *Where Do the Moral Responsibilities of the Great War Rest?* (1925), the following opinions are voiced:

The Germanic peoples remain attached to their former governments, to their deceit and their crimes. They maintain the innocence of the Central Powers. They have not delivered the guilty and they have not judged them . . . They flee from the duty of paying reparations. *The method of lies continues to be used. Its use has never ceased* . . . Their school textbooks teach what is universally recognized as false; for example, the fable of Germany's being attacked by

21 *L'Écho*, June 1924.
22 *L'Écho*, July 1924.
23 Headquarters: 237 Boulevard Saint-Germain, Paris. Officers: Honorary President, General Pau; President, M. Alapetite; Secretary, Guy de Traverssy. Organ: *Le Temps Présent* (five times a year).

France. And thus the younger generation are learning that their nation was innocent, that might is right, and that they must stand firm against the conquerors of their fathers. That is an abominable crime, worthy to crown all others. But one should be just. One should recognize that in Germany it is neither easy nor prudent to tell the truth. Powerful societies, which employ every conceivable means of intimidation, even murder, silence anyone who would speak the truth.

The " Federation of National Leagues " (" Fédération des Ligues Nationales "[24]), formed in 1916 in order to unite all the French patriotic societies in common propaganda against Germany, held a general congress at the Sorbonne in Paris in February and March 1919, which was attended by representatives of 170 constituent organizations and which adopted the following peace-proposals: return of Alsace-Lorraine to France; payment of full reparations by Germany; expulsion of Germany from the left bank of the Rhine; German disarmament; an Allied protectorate of the Rhineland; creation of Poland, Czechoslovakia, Yugoslavia, and a greater Rumania; refusal to treat with a united Germany, but only with individual German states; refusal to return the German colonies; post-war measures against German industry, etc. Similar congresses were held in 1920, 1922, and 1923, urging French military support of separatist movements in the Rhineland and in Bavaria, exclusive right of France to Cilicia, Palestine, and Syria, the maintenance and extension of French alliances, energetic action against Bolshevism, etc. After 1923 the Federation gradually lost its hold on the constituent societies and has now ceased to function actively.

Somewhat similar to the " Federation " is the " Union of Great French Associations for National Development " (" Union des Grandes Associations Françaises pour l'Essor National "[25]), which was founded in February 1917 and during the ensuing two years held weekly conferences for the consideration of ways and means of combating German propaganda. Since 1919 the

[24] Headquarters: 102 Boulevard des Batignolles, Paris. President: A. S. du Mesnil-Thoret. See A. S. du Mesnil-Thoret, " Le Mouvement anti-Allemand en France," *Réforme Sociale*, December 1926.

[25] Headquarters: 96 Boulevard Raspail, Paris. Officers: President, Paul Appell; Secretary, L. Armbruster.

activity of the Union has greatly decreased. Many of its original members have fallen away and its funds have been much reduced. Its most important service now is that of a clearing house for such societies as wish to broadcast patriotic programs by radio.

Another war-time patriotic society which is now far less active than formerly is the "Civic League" ("Ligue Civique" [26]) founded in 1917 by the late Ernest Denis, professor at the Sorbonne, and other intellectuals in order to combat defeatism. Each member is required to endorse a statement of principles, including the following: "Duty to France and devotion to national interests is an intangible dogma, above all international hopes and dreams, . . . for when internationalists try to get rid of the idea of the nation they become the worst seeds of disintegration, decadence, distress, and death."

A newer and much more important patriotic society is the "French Recovery" ("Redressement Français" [27]), founded in 1926 and having a membership of 50,000. It

appeals to all men of good faith and good-will, whatever their party, religion, or social class, who think that a common, open, and energetic effort should be made to surmount present difficulties and put France on a higher economic, political, and moral plane. More especially it issues a call to all the great associations which unite the healthy forces of the Nation: first, to associations of war-veterans whose members have proved by their sacrifice their devotion to the national cause; second, to intellectual and university groups whose duty it is to maintain the high standards of French thought; third, to the organizations of producers and artisans who collaborate so usefully for the public welfare and for social and economic peace; fourth, to syndicates of employers, workers, and farmers, whose most immediate interests do not allow them to be indifferent to anything which concerns the grandeur and expansion of the country; fifth, to scientific, artistic, and athletic societies and associations; and finally, to all citizens who are interested in the future of the Nation and are worried about our present danger.

[26] Headquarters: 16 rue de Condé, Paris. Officers: President, Maurice Lailler; Vice-President, M. Bethélemy; Secretary, Hubert Bourgin. Organ: *Bulletin* (irregular).

[27] Headquarters: 28 rue de Madrid, Paris. Officers: President, Ernest Mercier; Secretary, M. Grandclement. Organ: *Le Redressement Français* (fortnightly).

The Society preaches the coöperation, rather than the conflict, of classes, and advocates a number of economic and political reforms. It favors colonial development, proposes that the " French debt to America be linked with German reparations," and, while demanding that the conditions of the Treaty of Versailles be fulfilled, advocates a Franco-German *entente*.

There is also the " Michelet Committee " (" Comité Michelet " [28]), formed in 1914 and named after the great French protagonist of patriotic history. Its purpose, as stated in its by-laws, is " to put to work all the energies of national sentiment, . . . to forward by means of history the education of the French democracy, to contribute in this way to the maintenance of a spirit of concord among all the French, to develop in the minds of the masses, by means of lectures and publications, a knowledge of the great interests of the country, and to establish more cordial relations with other nations, such relations being based on the study and cult of history." The Committee conducts its propaganda chiefly among school teachers, supplying them with patriotic information about current events. It urges international coöperation, but is distrustful of Germany's sincerity, opposes the payment of the interallied debts, and champions the development and expansion of the French colonial empire.

The " French Hearth " (" Foyer Français " [29]) was established in 1924 in order to hasten the national assimilation of foreign workingmen in France. It provides free legal advice regarding naturalization and offers free courses of instruction in the French language. In one of its tracts it states that some twenty such courses " are given in public school buildings by professors who can directly instill in foreign students a love of our fatherland."

[28] Headquarters: 3 Avenue Mirabeau, Versailles. Officers: President, Édouard Driault; Secretary, E. Cintract. Organ: *Bulletin Michelet* (monthly).

[29] Headquarters: 18 rue du Banquier, Paris. Officers: President, Paul Painlevé; Vice-Presidents, André Honnorat, R. A. Olchansky, etc.; General Secretary, René Lisbonne; Secretary, Paul Raphael; Director, Gabriel Voitoux. Organ: *Le Compte-Rendu* (annual).

5

Two important patriotic societies devote themselves particularly to the problem of France's stationary population. The older is the " National Alliance for Increasing the French Population " (" Alliance Nationale pour l'Accroissement de la Population Française " [30]), founded in 1896, and basing its activity on the following principles: " France is in danger. Depopulation condemns her to ruin and to new invasions if her birth rate does not increase rapidly. It is every man's duty to contribute to the perpetuation of his nation exactly as it is his duty to contribute to her defense. Everyone without children ought to aid those with large families. French citizens who have four or more children have a right to the respect and gratitude of their fellow citizens; the State ought to recompense them on every occasion and in the most liberal manner." The younger society is the " National Federation of Associations of Large Families " (" Fédération Nationale des Associations de Familles Nombreuses " [31]), formed in 1921 and now embracing a hundred branch associations with a total membership of 300,000 families of at least three children each. These societies publish elaborate statistical data and direct a vast amount of propaganda toward the securing of legislation favorable to large families, such as reduction of railway fares and military service, bonuses to mothers, prizes for additional children, family suffrage (one family, one vote), etc. Both societies coöperate in holding annually a " National Congress of Births."

Several patriotic societies specialize in colonial propaganda. There is the " French Colonial Union " (" Union Coloniale Française " [32]): founded in 1893, it is not only the oldest but also

[30] Headquarters: 26 rue du 4 Septembre, Paris. Officers: President, P. Lefebvre-Dibon; Director, General Borie. Organ: *Revue de l'Alliance Nationale* (monthly).

[31] Headquarters: 24 rue du Mont-Thabor, Paris. Officers: Honorary President, Alexandre Millerand; General Delegate, Félix Vieuille. Each of the federated associations has an organ of its own.

[32] Headquarters: 17 rue d'Anjou, Paris. Officers: President, François-Marsal; General Secretary, C. A. LeNeveu. Organ: *Le Bulletin de l'Union Coloniale.*

the strongest of French colonial societies; at first it urged the acquisition of new colonies, but latterly it has stressed a more vigorous exploitation of lands already occupied; it has counted among its members such leaders as Jules Ferry and Marshals Lyautey and Galliéni. There is also the " French Colonial and Maritime League " ("Ligue Maritime et Coloniale Française "[33]), founded in 1899 to arouse the interest and pride of the French people in their navy and overseas empire: it advocates the acquisition of new colonies, the enlargement and development of colonies already acquired, the expansion of the merchant marine in order to render France independent of foreign carriers, and the establishment of French markets for colonial products; it claims to have a membership of 600,000. There is likewise the " Bugeaud Committee (" Comité Bugeaud "[34]), founded since the war for the purpose of encouraging French citizens, especially French peasants, to settle in North Africa and to hasten the Gallicizing of the natives. There is finally the " French Association of Friends of Palestine " ("Association Française des Amis de la Palestine "[35]), formed in 1923 and insistent that " Palestine is a national irredenta of France." The patriotic spirit which all these colonial societies represent may be fairly illustrated by a brief quotation from a publication of the Colonial and Maritime League:

To confirm our pride, we must have before us a map contrasting in different colors French possessions in 1921 with those in 1870. We shall then see at a glance our old colonies of the former period: Algeria, a trans-Mediterranean extension of France; Senegal; Gabun; Reunion; the French Antilles and Guiana; constituting then almost the whole block of our colonial empire. What a gigantic task has since been accomplished! All North Africa has become French. All West Africa is ours, even to the centre of the Dark Continent, from Morocco far

[33] Headquarters: 30 Boulevard des Capucines, Paris. Officers: President, Charles Chaumet; Director, Maurice Roudet-Saint. Organ: *Mer et Colonies* (monthly).

[34] Headquarters: 26 rue de Grammont, Paris. Director: J. Saurin. Organ: *Bulletin du Comité Bugeaud.*

[35] Headquarters: 26 rue de Grammont, Paris. Officers: President, E. Godefroy; Secretary, Roger de Gontant-Biron. Organ: *Correspondance de l'Association Française des Amis de la Palestine.*

into the southern hemisphere where our Congo holds an immense reserve of future wealth. In Indo-China the miserable little colony of Cochin-China of 1865 has become a magnificent Asiatic empire, whose geographical expansion is halted by the frontiers of China but whose power really reaches to the very heart of the ancient Yellow Empire through the province of Yunan which is under our influence. Besides, to us belongs Madagascar, admirable jewel of the Indian Ocean, whose exploitation, as its population grows, will be a new factor in our economic strength. All that is an immense and marvelous achievement, without precedent in history, wrought by our fatherland in the brief space of a few decades — a mere second in the life of a nation.[36]

Another organization, the " Dupleix Committee " ("Comité Dupleix "[37]), founded in 1894 and named after the great French empire-builder in India, did much for many years to stimulate popular interest in colonial matters and to encourage Frenchmen to settle in the colonies. Since the war, the Committee has considerably widened the scope of its endeavors; while it continues to favor a vigorous colonial policy, it combats pacifism, denounces the proposed debt-settlements, and demands the suppression of German influences in Alsace, the annexation of the Saar to France, and the separation of the Rhineland from Germany. It holds monthly luncheons, which are addressed by prominent patriots, and issues tracts, brochures, and a monthly bulletin.

Several patriotic societies, emerging during or soon after the Great War, devote themselves almost exclusively to anti-German propaganda. Among them, for example, is the " Remember League " ("Ligue Souvenez-Vous "[38]), founded in 1916 "to perpetuate in France and throughout the world the remembrance of the crimes committed by the Germans during the war and to prevent the recurrence of similar events." It has given lectures and published innumerable tracts and pamphlets. It has distributed hundreds of thousands of copies of a book entitled *Their Crimes*. A poster which it has widely displayed shows a Ger-

[36] *Mer et Colonies,* December 1922, p. 2.

[37] Headquarters: 26 rue de Grammont, Paris. Officers: President, Gabriel Bonvalot; Secretary, J. Donteville. Organ: *La France de Demain* (monthly).

[38] Headquarters: 7 rue Royer-Collard, Paris. Officers: President, Louis Marin; Secretary, H. Rousseau. Organ: *Ligue Souvenez-Vous* (bi-monthly).

man soldier with a torch in one hand and a dagger in the other, and alongside of him the same German as a post-war salesman of German goods in France: it bears the inscription, " Remember! this Boche who has killed, burned, and pillaged, and this travelling salesman who offers you his wares and who would again settle among you, are one and the same person — don't ever forget! " Then, too, there are the " Committee of the Left Bank of the Rhine " (" Comité de la Rive Gauche du Rhin " [39]), the " ' Halt ' League of Franco-Rhenish Friendship " (" ' Halte ' Ligue d'Amitié Franco-Rhénane " [40]), and the " Franco-Rhenish Friendship Society " (" Les Amitiés Franco-Rhénanes "), — all agitating in behalf of the strengthening of France and weakening of Germany through the creation of an autonomous Rhineland in close alliance with France. The first and second are now less active than formerly, and the third in 1926 enlarged its scope and changed its name to the " Union for France " (" Union pour la France " [41]): its main purpose now is to inculcate nationalist ideas in promising young men and to train them in the technique of nationalist propaganda, particularly in journalism and public speaking.

Special mention should be made of three patriotic societies whose single function is to honor the soldier-dead of France. One is the " French Memorial Society " (" Souvenir Français " [42]), founded in 1887 for the purpose of venerating those who had fallen for France on the field of battle and of marking and caring for their graves, a purpose admirably stated by Alexandre Millerand at one of its meetings in these words:

The French Memorial Society! What a magnificent promise is conveyed in its title! An organization which takes advantage of every

[39] Headquarters: 26 rue de Grammont, Paris. Officers: President, J. L. Bonnet; Secretary, A. S. Mesnil-Thoret. Organ: L'Indépendance Rhénane (quarterly).

[40] Headquarters: 6 rue Chaptal, Paris. Officers: President, M. Dontenville; Secretary, Mme. Dutreb. Organ: La Garde au Rhin (quarterly).

[41] Headquarters: 3 rue des Prêtres-Saint-Séverin, Paris. Officers: President, General d'Arman de Pouydraguin; Director, P. L. Guinchard. Organ: Journal de France (fortnightly), formerly Le Rhin.

[42] Headquarters: 229 rue du Faubourg Saint-Honoré, Paris. Officers: President, General Ferré; Secretary, Military Intendant Deverre. Organ: Le Souvenir Français (monthly).

opportunity to set before the eyes of the French people France's glorious and heroic past; which does not permit the effacement of those sublime hours when the children of France, transcending their own powers and oblivious of their personal welfare, have given themselves unreservedly to the nation: such is the mission you have undertaken, and there is nothing nobler or more useful.

Another similar society is the " General Federation of the Fathers and Mothers Whose Sons died for France " (" Fédération Générale des Pères et Mères des Morts pour la France " [43]), founded in 1920 and intended to " establish a worship of the heroes so that the memory of their sacrifice may be perpetuated in history "; this society is only mildly nationalist; it has labored to secure additional pension-grants from the State and has taken a decided stand against war. The third society, of like character, is the " Flame under the Arch of Triumph " (" Flamme sous l'Arc de Triomphe " [44]), founded in 1920 to maintain the cult of the Unknown Soldier.

6

French war-veterans themselves have constituted since the Great War a whole special category of patriotic societies.[45] Until 1927, however, there existed no central confederation of even the majority of such societies, although two important publications catered to all the veterans: (1) the *Almanach du Combattant*,[46] an annual directory of veterans' organizations, containing much nationalist and anti-German propaganda; and (2) the *Journal des Mutilés et Reformés*,[47] a widely circulated weekly, whose chief concern is the securing of material state-aid for veterans. The latter publishes occasional patriotic articles, but is not militantly nationalist. The former, on the other hand, is replete with

[43] Headquarters: 9 rue Dulong, Paris. Officers: President, Paul Lecourtier; Director, André Neau. Organ: *Journal des Pères et Mères des Morts pour la France* (monthly).

[44] Headquarters: 100 rue Réaumur, Paris. President: General Gouraud, Military Governor.

[45] See *Revue des Vivants*, March 1927.

[46] Office: 3 Place de la Sorbonne, Paris.

[47] Office: 20 rue de la Chaussée d'Antin, Paris.

anti-German cartoons and with such comments as the following: "A German asks 'Why does the *Almanach* perpetuate the terrible hate which separated Frenchmen and Germans before the war? Why call us Boche? Why believe that the two nations will never, never, never be able to meet except on the field of battle?' Why? The history of the two nations supplies the answer, particularly the history of the Great War."[48]

Of the actual societies of French war-veterans, the number is legion. There are independent societies for particular regions of the country, for particular branches of the service, for particular divisions or corps, for particular shades of political opinion, and for particular professions and occupations.[49] More general societies include the " National Union of Combatants " ("Union Nationale des Combattants "[50]), the "National Union of the Wounded and Crippled" ("Union Nationale des Mutilés et Reformés "[51]), the "General Association of Maimed War Veterans" ("Association Générale des Mutilés de la Guerre "[52]), the " National Association of Comrades of Combat " ("Association Nationale des Camarades de Combat "[53]), the " Federal Union of French Associations " ("Union Fédérale des Associations Françaises "[54]), the " Society of Reserve Officers of France "

---

[48] *Almanach du Combattant*, 1926, p. 137.

[49] For example, the "National Federation of Mobilized Commercial and Business Men " ("Fédération Nationale des Commercants et Industriels Mobilisés "). Headquarters, 10 rue de Rome, Paris. Officers: President, Jean Desveaux; Secretary, Paul Veluard. Organ: *Le Journal des C. I. M.*

[50] Headquarters: 13 rue Lafayette, Paris. Officers: Honorary President, Humbert Isaac; President, Henry Rossignol; Secretary, A. Calleau. Organ: *La Voix du Combattant* (weekly).

[51] Headquarters: 15 rue Molière, Paris. Officers: President, Henri Chatenet; Vice-President, Dr. Odinot; Secretary, Jacques Teutsch. Organ: *U. N. M. R.* (weekly).

[52] Headquarters: 85 bis, rue du Faubourg Saint-Honoré, Paris. Hospital: 54 Boulevard de la Saussaye, Neuilly-sur-Seine. Officers: President, Jean Thébaud; Secretary, Edmond Bloch. Organs: *Bulletin de l'Association Générale des Mutilés de la Guerre* (monthly), and *Revue des Vivants* (monthly).

[53] Headquarters: 8 rue Nouvelle, Paris. Officers: President, M. Chauvin; Secretary, M. Prugnard. Organ: *L'Écho du Combattant*.

[54] Headquarters: 16 rue de l'Abbaye, Paris. President: Maurice Randoux. Organ: *La France Mutilée*.

("Société des Officiers de Complément de France " [55]), the " National Union of Reserve Officers " (" Union Nationale des Officiers de Reserve " [56]), the " Union of the Wounded in the Face — the ' Broken Mugs ' " (" Union des Blessés de la Face — Les Gueules Cassées " [57]), the " National Federation of Former Prisoners of War " (" Fédération National des Anciens Prisonniers de Guerre " [58]), etc., etc. All these societies, it goes without saying, are patriotic, but they differ considerably in the intensity of their nationalist utterances, and it must not be assumed that every individual member agrees with every statement in the official organ of the veteran's association to which he belongs. Most of the official organs of the societies named are strenuously national in content and emphasis, and many of them are naturally quite anti-German. The attitude of probably the large majority of officers and propagandists of the veterans' associations is that of M. André Maginot, a prominent statesman since the war and himself the president of an influential veterans' society, the " National Federation of French Associations of the Wounded " (" Fédération Nationale des Associations Françaises de Mutilés " [59]): " I think that if the governments appear for political reasons to have forgotten the past, the memory of which would be an obstacle to an attempted *rapprochement* between Germany and ourselves, it cannot be the same with the veterans of this country, from whom no one can expect such an easy amnesia of the crimes of those who were the aggressors." [60]

On the other hand, one at least of the above listed general organizations, the " Federal Union of French Associations," has been a staunch supporter of the League of Nations and has not

[55] Headquarters: 26 Galerie Montpensier, Paris. Officers: President, Robert Monnier; Secretary, M. Bère. Organ: *L'Horizon* (monthly).

[56] Headquarters: 17 Avenue de l'Opéra, Paris. Officers: President, André Lefèvre; Secretary, Léonce Lefèvre. Organ: *L'Officier de Complément* (monthly).

[57] Headquarters: 38 Boulevard de Strasbourg, Paris. Officers: President, M. Picot; Secretary, B. Jourdain. Organ: *Les Gueules Cassées*.

[58] Headquarters: 10 rue de Rome, Paris. Officers: President, Jean Desbous; Secretary, Jean Valvey.

[59] Headquarters: 23 rue de Bourgogne, Paris. Officers: President, André Maginot; Secretary, Edmond Mathure. Organ: *Bulletin*.

[60] *Revue des Vivants,* March 1927, p. 281.

missed an opportunity to advocate a rapid *rapprochement* with Germany. It should be remembered, moreover, that there are associations of Communist and Socialist and other " radical " war-veterans in France, and that these flavor their patriotism with a good deal of internationalism of one sort or another. Besides, French veterans have been especially active and interested in the creation (in 1920) and functioning of the " Interallied Federation of Veterans " (" Fédération Interalliée des Anciens Combattants " [61]) — commonly called, from its French initials, the FIDAC — which is distinctly international in word and deed. " The Fidac affirms," its President wrote in 1926, " that if the peoples who were allied and associated during the war now will sincerely to remain united no power will dare to attack them. To avoid war for a long time will perhaps prevent its return for all time. Doubtless during the years of peace, provided only that progress is not a phantom, humanity should succeed in the definite creation of strong and respected courts of justice capable of imposing their arbitration on the nations.[62]

In November 1927, after protracted negotiations, a congress of some six hundred delegates, representing most of the French veterans' associations, was held at Versailles and a central coördinating federation was effected. This " Confederation " — the " Estates General of Wounded France " (" États Généraux de la France Meurtrie "), as the newspapers of the time described it — excludes Communist and certain other " subversive " associations from membership but otherwise eschews political and economic differences among Frenchmen and affirms " the necessity of making prevail above special interests the interests of the country, of making prevail above purely political questions the social and economic questions, and of guaranteeing peace through respect for treaties." [63]

61 Headquarters: 96 rue de l'Université, Paris.   Officers: President, George R. Grosfield; Secretary, Roger Marie d'Avigneau.

62 *Almanach du Combattant*, 1926, p. 311.

63 *Le Matin*, November 13, 1927, pp. 1–2.

7

Another group of French patriotic societies is concerned with the propagation of a favorable opinion of France and her national culture among foreigners, whether sojourning in France or remaining in their own countries.[64] The best known of these societies is the " French Alliance " (" Alliance Française " [65]), founded in 1883 and pursuing the following aims:

(1) In our colonies and protectorates — to teach our language and to make the natives love it as the surest way of conquering their hearts; to facilitate social and commercial intercourse; and by pacific means to spread overseas the French race which increases so slowly on the Continent; and (2) elsewhere, to enter into relations with groups of Frenchmen in foreign lands in order to maintain among them a cult of the national language and similarly with friends of French language and literature even if they are different in race, nationality, or religion, in order to strengthen the ties of literary and moral sympathy which unite ·France with other people; and to support, whether in the Orient or in barbarous countries, French missionaries of various religions who engage in the teaching of the French language.

The Alliance is very active in France and abroad. It conducts courses of instruction for foreigners in Paris. It directs schools, clubs, and lecture-courses in foreign countries. It subsidizes French schools abroad. It distributes French books widely and sends French lecturers on extended speaking tours. It operates in close relationship with the Ministry of Foreign Affairs. In 1925 it had five hundred affiliated committees in different parts of the world and spent about four million francs on French schools and libraries abroad.

The " Catholic Committee of French Friendships Abroad " (" Comité Catholique des Amités Françaises à l'Étranger " [66]),

[64] See Firmin Roz, *Comment faire connaître la France à l'Étranger* (Paris, Plon, 1922).

[65] Headquarters: 101 Boulevard Raspail, Paris. Officers: Honorary President, Raymond Poincaré; President, Paul Doumer; Secretary, Paul Labbé. Organ: *Revue de l'Alliance Française* (quarterly).

[66] Headquarters: 3 rue Garancière, Paris. Officers: Director, Mgr. Baudrillart; Secretary, Mgr. Beaupin. Organs: *L'Almanach Catholique Français* (annual) and *Les Amitiés Catholiques Françaises* (monthly).

founded in 1915, "aims to defend the reputation of France in foreign Catholic circles, to learn about foreign Catholics, and to interest French Catholics in Catholic movements abroad." During the war, it sent to foreign countries six million French books and pamphlets and numerous French lecturers. Since the war it has continued this work and has supplemented it by the distribution of an *Almanach* and a review and the establishment of a press service whose articles reach two hundred publications each week. Besides, it awards annually some thirty scholarships to foreign students to enable them to study in France.

The " French Idea Abroad " ("Idée Française à l'Étranger " [67]), was established in 1915 to conduct pro-French propaganda in neutral countries. It conducted a special press service from Copenhagen for the Scandinavian nations, and another from Berne for Switzerland, Czechoslovakia, Poland, etc. Since the war its activity has greatly lessened but it maintains correspondents in most foreign countries, supplies ocean liners with patriotic French literature, presents French books to libraries abroad, and supports a few foreign study-clubs.

The " French Union " ("Union Française " [68]), founded in 1916, " is composed of intellectual, financial, agricultural, and commercial leaders of France devoted to French propaganda in foreign lands." The Union has a review of its own and, in addition, subsidizes *La Revue Bleu* and *La Revue Scientifique*. It also publishes many pamphlets, including some with such titles as " German Barbarism " and " Moral Lessons of the War."

The " Committee of the French Entente " ("Comité de l'Entente Française " [69]) was formed in 1917 for the purpose of studying foreign problems and presenting the results in patriotic form to the French Government and people. Information

[67] Headquarters: 11 Place de la Bourse, Paris. Officers: President, Georges Leygues; Secretary, Alpie Jean-Bernard. Officers of Ladies' Auxiliary: President, Mme. Paul Deschanel; Secretary, Mme. Piat. Organ: *Bulletin de l'Idée Française à l'Étranger*.

[68] Headquarters: 286 Boulevard Saint-Germain, Paris. Officers: President, Joseph Noulens; Secretary, Paul Gaultier. Organ: *La France Nouvelle* (monthly).

[69] Headquarters: 11 bis, Impasse de la Visitation, Paris. Officers: President, Philippe d'Estailleur-Chanteraine; Secretary, F. X. Lalan-Keraly.

is obtained by study-groups and by visits to foreign countries, and is communicated to the French press and often directly to the Government.

The " French Welcome " ("La Bienvenue Française "[70]), established in 1920, aims "to encourage our allies and foreign friends to come to France either individually or in groups as representatives of great associations in their respective native lands, and to show them our country in a true light which is the best way of making them love her." In reality, this society is a permanent reception-committee which supplies much useful information to foreign visitors and does much to make pleasant their stay in France.

Two special organizations may be mentioned in this connection, as illustrative of a large number of patriotic French societies which seek to stimulate pro-French sentiment in particular foreign countries. The one is the " Friends of Poland " ("Amis de la Pologne "[71]), which since its formation in 1919 has sponsored lectures, study-clubs, and publications on Polish culture in France and on French culture in Poland; it supplies the French press with semi-weekly news articles. The other is the " France-America Committee " ("Comité France-Amérique "[72]), established in 1909, which performs similar service in respect of America, especially of Latin America.

8

Still another category of French patriotic societies comprises certain organizations which foster athletics.[73] There is, for example, the " Union of Societies of Physical Education and of

[70] Headquarters: 19 rue du Four, Paris. Officers: President, Marshal Foch; Vice-Presidents, François Arago, Prince Roland Bonaparte, H. Cachard, Baron Éd. de Rothschild, etc.; Secretary, Mme. Boas de Jouvenel.

[71] Headquarters: 16 rue Abbé-de-l'Epée, Paris. Officers: President, Louis Marin; Secretary, Mme. Rosa Bailly. Organ; Les Amis de la Pologne (monthly).

[72] Headquarters: 9 Avenue Victor Emmanuel, Paris. Officers: President, Gabriel Hanotaux; Director, Gabriel Louis-Jaray. Organs: France-Amérique (monthly), and L'Amérique Latine (weekly).

[73] See Miroir des Sports: Almanach 1928, 6th year (Paris, Miroir des Sports 1928); and Philippe Tissié, L'Education physique rationelle: la Méthode, les Maîtres les Programmes (Paris, Alcan, 1922).

Preparation for Military Service " (" Union des Sociétés d'Éducation Physique et de Préparation au Service Militaire " [74]), founded in 1885, and now claiming the affiliation of 2,000 societies and a total membership of 341,000. It has built a stadium, a swimming school, and a flying field. It holds an annual national competition in the Gardens of the Tuileries. It conducts a good deal of propaganda in behalf not only of physical and military training but also of patriotic education in the schools and an increased birth rate in France. The President of the Union, in an address on December 12, 1922, said: " What gives our stadium its peculiar character is the rifle range beside the play-field. The proximity of field and range expresses better than any speech the care taken by us to prepare for an uncertain future." The official organ, appealing to its youthful readers in November 1926, proclaimed: " You are full of the spirit of the young Athenian who said: ' I shall not let my country perish, I shall defend her in union with the rest or even quite alone.' "

There is, also, the " Union of Gymnastic Societies " (" Union des Sociétés de Gymnastique " [75]), formed in 1871 and now embracing 1,764 societies with a membership of half a million. " Intensify the training of the youth! " is now its motto, and its patriotic spirit may be judged from the following typical quotation (January 1927) from its official organ: " Believe me, Gymnasts, your rôle is of essential importance . . . As President Raymond Poincaré has said, you are professors of physical and moral energy. To your posts, then, Gymnasts! Make people realize the truth of Gambetta's words, ' When a citizen is born in France, he is born a soldier.' "

There is, likewise, the " National Federation of Societies for Physical Education " (" Fédération Nationale des Sociétes d'Éducation Physique " [76]), whose object may be gathered from a state-

[74] Headquarters: 23 rue de la Sourdière, Paris. Officers: President, Adolphe Chéron; Secretary, Jacques Maine. Organ: *Le Soldat de Demain* (monthly; still employs the Revolutionary calendar).

[75] Headquarters: 8 rue Reignier, Bordeaux. Officers: President, Charles Cazalet; Secretary, J. Pancol. Organ: *Le Gymnaste* (fortnightly).

[76] Headquarters: 16 rue de Grammont, Paris. Officers: President, Lucien Lattès; Secretary, Lucien Danziger. Organ: *Vers l'Armée* (monthly).

ment in its official publication: " All the Unions or Federations seek but a single end — to exalt the patriotism of the youth and to make the youth strong and vigorous and prepared, as was necessary during the last war, to render to the fatherland immediate service. We have always been proud and we always shall be proud of the results we have obtained."

The " Boy Scouts " [77] in France, too, though international in affiliations and by no means " nationalist," are taught patriotism. The requirements for the " tenderfoot " class of scouts include the following: " One must be able to recite briefly the principal periods of French history. One must know the origin of the French flag and our duties to it. One must be able to hum correctly and to sing without accompaniment three stanzas of the national anthem." [78]

The associations mentioned in the present chapter do not exhaust the list of French national societies. They do not include, for instance, the numerous organizations which have an international complexion. [79] In fact, they include only relatively few of the multitudinous associations which, directly or indirectly, conduct patriotic propaganda. They are enough perhaps to indicate the important part which national societies perform in the " making " of Frenchmen.

[77] The majority of the Boy Scouts in France belong to a Catholic organization, " Scouts de France," founded in 1920 [Headquarters: 51 rue Saint Didier, Paris. Director, General Guyot de Salins. Organs: *Le Scout de France* (monthly) and *Le Chef* (monthly)]. Some 7,000 belong to a Protestant organization, " Éclaireurs Unionistes de France," founded in 1912 [Headquarters, 94 rue Saint Lazare, Paris. Director, Pasteur Laroche. Organ: *Le Lien* (monthly)]. And some 4,000 belong to a third " neutral " organization, " Éclaireurs de France," founded in 1911 [Headquarters: 6 rue Saulnier, Paris. Director, M. Berthier. Organ: *Le Chef* (monthly)]. The two latter organizations publish jointly still another organ: *Le Journal des Éclaireurs* (fortnightly).

[78] *Pour Devenir Scout de France* (Paris, Scouts de France, 1925), p. 11.

[79] Some of these will be discussed in Chapter XII.

CHAPTER IX

SYMBOLS AND CEREMONIES

I

INHABITANTS of France are made into nationally conscious Frenchmen in many ways. They are subjected to national influences and training by the national State, by a national educational system, by a national army or navy, by national churches, by a national press, and by national societies. They are also subjected throughout life to the frequent contemplation of solemn rites and memorials which have been nationally evolved and which provide a kind of emotionally suggestive stage-setting for the more or less reasonable action of the other agencies of French nation-making.

The French, it has already been remarked,[1] are, like other Latin peoples, much given to ceremonial formalism, and it is quite natural that they, who have been almost first among the peoples of the world in preaching and practicing national unity and solidarity, should be easily first in attending their national conduct with studied form and ceremony. They possess, moreover, a rich heritage of historic buildings and monuments, as well as a copious harvest of traditional usages and customs, which can conveniently be made to serve as symbols of national life. These symbols, especially when surrounded by solemn rite and public ceremony, have done much to quicken national consciousness among Frenchmen.

"La France" itself is a symbol — a dream-ideal. It is a phrase impressed on the minds of all manner of Frenchmen and often expressed by them with mystical, almost religious, connotations. It becomes to them a personification, an incarnation of the country and its people, its past and its future, a veritable

---

[1] See above, p. 33.

woman, sometimes gay, sometimes sad, now resembling Jeanne d'Arc, now with the Phrygian cap of revolutionary Jacobinism, now with the sword of vengeance or the ploughshare of peace and plenty, but always lovely. " La France," by the pens of French littérateurs and the brushes and chisels of French artists, is represented to their compatriots as " la belle France " and " la douce France."

" La Patrie " is another symbol of the same sort, another charming lady. If " La France " is sometimes depicted as an impulsive girl, the image of " La Patrie " is always that of the tender and solicitious mother. Both are a bit other-worldly, but both, like the pagan deities of ancient Greece and Rome, are subject to some measure of human suffering and ambition: they lament, they plead, they direct.

Besides, there are certain phrases and catchwords which most French Governments since the Great Revolution have inscribed on public buildings here and there all over the country and which patriotic individuals have repeated ostentatiously in books and newspapers. Such are " Liberté, Egalité, Fraternité," and " République Française " or its mystical abbreviation " R. F.," akin to the " S. P. Q. R." of ancient republican Rome or modern Fascist Italy. These words, these initials, have acquired, through conspicuous and constant advertising, the value of shibboleths, the significance of national symbols.

There is, too, the Gallic cock, the strutting crowing bird which for some time has been popularly recognized as a national emblem, and as such has commanded national respect. To the cock, the State has accorded worth and dignity by imaging it on the more valuable gold coins of the nation. Indeed, the State's coinage, the State's paper money, and the State's postage stamps have been made to serve as couriers, throughout the length and breadth of France, of a considerable variety of national emblems: not only the Gallic cock, but " La France " or " La Patrie," " République Française " or " R. F.," and also pictures of national heroes. All are calculated to stir the patriotic emotions of the users.

Most impressive and most dignified of national symbols is

the French flag, the tricolor. National flags, as distinct from royal standards, are very modern inventions; France shares with the United States the honor of having been first among the nations of the world to create and employ a strictly national flag, and this creation dates only from the Revolution at the close of the eighteenth century. Not all Frenchmen during the last century have cherished with the same ardor the national tricolor; some royalists — the so-called reactionaries — have actually despised it and have sought to replace it with the lilied white flag of the Bourbon monarchy; on the other hand, a few communists have latterly preferred the blood-red flag of international Socialism. But the Government of the Third Republic has kept the red-white-and-blue tricolor flying before the eyes of all Frenchmen, and to the vast majority of Frenchmen of the present day this tricolor is the symbol par excellence of France, of the fatherland, of French development and French destiny. It floats every day over all public buildings, and on holidays it is in evidence everywhere. It is carried in parades and waves over public ceremonies. Around it has grown up a special national cult, taught in school and in army and navy, and almost unanimously observed throughout the country. Popular literature pays glowing tributes to the flag; text-books give detailed instruction about personal behavior toward it. From a popular catechism for military training,[2] we select a few questions and answers for purpose of illustration:

Q. What is the flag?
A. The flag is the emblem of the fatherland — wherever ours floats, it represents France.
Q. What does the flag of the regiment represent?
A. The flag of the regiment is not only the emblem of the fatherland, but it recalls the high feats of arms of the regiment and honors the memory of those who have died for the country.
Q. What must an isolated soldier do when passing a flag?
A. He stops, faces it, and salutes it. If he is armed, he presents arms.
Q. What honors are due the flag from an armed troop?
A. The troop present arms.

[2] Commandant J. Chanal, *Questionnaire pour l'Instruction et l'Éducation militaire du Soldat* (Paris, Librairie Militaire Berger-Levrault, 1927).

Q. When you return to your own homes, should you continue to salute the flag?
A. Yes, every good Frenchman should uncover when the flag passes by.

2

France, as a separate and independent nation, has had a relatively long history; and a goodly number of her historical productions in the realm of architecture, literature, and music have been so long or so generally sensed and prized by Frenchmen as to constitute in the present age of sharpening national consciousness so many objects whose perception by French minds can and does supply a symbolic setting to French patriotism.   The majestic palace of Louis XIV at Versailles, with its vast park, its myriad groves and fountains and statues, is at once a national monument and a sort of national shrine.   Here are halls and chambers hung with more or less fanciful paintings of the long line of French battles.   Here is the historic Hall of Mirrors in which many a peace treaty has been signed.   Here is the stately chamber to which repair from Paris the Republican Senate and Chamber of Deputies to amend the Constitution or to elect with fitting solemnity the President of the Republic.   Hither flock on Sundays and national holidays great swarms of Parisians and other Frenchmen, as well as foreign tourists, to observe and enjoy the palace and park which now belong to the nation and exalt it.

But Versailles is only one of the architectural symbols of the French nation.   There are the palaces of Saint-Germain, of Fontainebleau, of the Louvre, of Malmaison; there are the châteaux of the Valois kings in the valley of the Loire.   Most of these are national museums, treasure-houses of French achievement in the past, generators of French pride in the present and the future.   A large number of the historic palaces of France are still used for government business: the Palais Bourbon houses the Chamber of Deputies and provides a sumptuous residence for its president; the Luxembourg houses the Senate and affords magnificent quarters for its presiding officer; the Élysée is the seat of the President of the Republic, and the regal hunting lodge at Rambouillet is likewise his.   The Ministry of Finance occupies part of the huge palace of the Louvre; the Ministry of Foreign Affairs, part of the Palais Bourbon; and most of the other ministries perform their special services in buildings which long ago acquired a national glamour and around which have accumulated a mass of national traditions.

Less striking in most instances, but far more numerous, are the public buildings, both new and old, which accommodate the subordinate agencies of the centralized national Government: the school buildings, the barracks, the town halls, the post offices. These exist in profusion in Paris and throughout the provinces. They fly the tricolor; they are inscribed with the formula "Liberté, Égalité, Fraternité" and with the initials "R. F."; they are themselves myriad mute symbols of the ceaseless ubiquitous activity of the French national State.

The architectural background of contemporary national psychology in France is not restricted to state buildings. It includes also a vast deal of ecclesiastical architecture — medieval cathedrals, magnificent basilicas, sequestrated abbeys and convents, and historic chapels and parish-churches. These, too, are treated as national monuments; repairs to them are made at public expense by Governments that are "anti-clerical" as well as by Governments that are "clerical"; and, as a sort of revenge, they greet the passers-by not only with the Christian emblem of the cross but also with the national formula of "Liberté, Égalité, Fraternité." And nowadays, at any rate, every cathedral and every parish-church enshrines a tablet to the memory of "those who have died for the fatherland."

French literature also, in its long and glorious progress, has fashioned many a phrase, many a form, many an idea, which, impressed by constant repetition on the minds of the generality of Frenchmen, have become conventional notes of national character. Tales of medieval romance, aphorisms of Montaigne, classical formalisms of Racine and phrases of Corneille, droll rôles of Molière and Beaumarchais, fables of La Fontaine, eloquences of Bossuet, chatty letters of Mme. de Sévigné, have combined with more modern verses and tales of Victor Hugo, poems of Alfred de Musset and Charles Baudelaire, philosophizings of

Adolphe Taine and Ernest Renan, criticisms of Sainte-Beuve, epic histories of Michelet, novels of Flaubert, short stories of de Maupassant, and the whole human comedy of Balzac, to make up a rich and varied garden of literary flowers, tended with consummate care by innumerable Frenchmen and supplying the gardeners with beautiful symbolic blossoms of national fragrance.

Contemporary Frenchmen, under the fostering care of the French Academy and the Ministry of Public Instruction, are familiarized almost from infancy at home, in school, by the press, and by public address, with a large body of classical French literature, literature which abounds in national themes, in military themes, in themes of devotion to the fatherland and respect for its usages. No modern nation has gone so far as France in maintaining state-theatres and state-actors for the performance at popular prices of classical French plays; no people go in larger numbers or follow the play more closely than do the Parisians in attendance upon the Comédie Française or the Odéon. In national temples, as it were, they are saturated with national traditions.

Music is likely to be the most universal of the arts, but in France it has been put to peculiarly national use. The State supports opera-houses as it maintains play-houses, and at the Opéra and the Opéra Comique in Paris all operas, no matter what may have been the nationality and language of their composers, are sung in French. French composers, a Gounod, a Bizet, a Saint-Saens, a Massenet, have frequently drawn their operatic themes from foreign sources, from Germany or Spain, from ancient Judaea or Egypt, but they have so transformed them by the media of French language and French conventions as to Gallicize them pretty effectually. At any rate, the French auditors think of them as works of French genius and, in addition, receive as " French " the compositions of many a foreigner, Meyerbeer, Flotow, Rossini, Chopin, even Wagner in his early manner.

From national orchestras and national singers, as well as national opera-houses, Frenchmen acquire an ear for national music. Public concerts in the great Trocadéro at Paris, or out of doors in the gardens of the Tuileries or in the open square of provincial town-halls, are frequent, and the selections most appreciated are those written by native composers or dealing with national themes. Military bands and military music are likewise common, and have reached a high development in France: their importance as national symbols needs not to be stressed.

And there is the national anthem, the stirring strains and feverish words of the *Marseillaise*. Of all national anthems, it is the most emotionally moving. Composed at Strasbourg by Rouget de Lisle in the darkest days of the great Revolution, it has been played and sung by all the generations of the last hundred and thirty years so solemnly, so ceremoniously, that to contemporary Frenchmen it signifies less the perfervid expression of revolutionary Jacobinism than the outpouring of an eternal French soul. As a sacred national symbol, the Marseillaise ranks with the tricolor. The military catechism from which we have already quoted some questions and answers, treats of the national anthem in the section devoted to " Honors to the Flag ":

Q. Should one salute when the National Anthem is played?
A. Yes, one should salute if one assists at a ceremony in the course of which the *Marseillaise* is played. The attitude of salute is kept until the moment when the music ceases.

3

Architecture and the attendant plastic and pictorial arts have been especially employed in the erection and embellishment of national monuments and national memorials, to the solemn dedication of which and to the recurring ceremonial celebrations in which, national literature and national music have made appropriate contributions. The Panthéon is an outstanding example. Begun in the reign of King Louis XV as a massive Christian basilica to enshrine the remains of Saint Genevieve, the patroness of Paris, it was hardly completed when the anti-Christian Revolutionaries seized it and consecrated it to the memory of the national heroes of French Jacobinism. Alternately Christian church and national shrine during most of the nineteenth century, as the struggle between " clericals " and " anti-clericals " turned to the advantage of the former or to that of the latter, it finally, under the Third Republic, has fallen entirely to national, non-Christian uses, though still retaining, as part of its "national" trappings, many reminders of its Christian past. The cross still surmounts it; the exquisite paintings of scenes from the life of Saint Genevieve by Puvis de Chavannes still adorn its walls; there is place for the high altar and there are niches for images of the saints. But on all sides are statues and groups of statuary commemorating Voltaire and the Philosophes, the generals and soldiers of the Revolutionary armies, Victor Hugo, Gambetta, Émile Zola, and Jean Jaurès. And it may be that the curious juxtaposition of "anti-clerical" national heroes in a "clerical" national framework is a most fitting symbol of the fusion of dissident Frenchmen into national unity and solidarity.

The Invalides on the banks of the Seine is a similar monument. Erected by Louis XIV as a hospice for old soldiers and embellished with an impressive chapel in honor of Saint Louis and decorated with historic battle-flags and other trophies of victorious foreign wars, it is now most famous as the final burial place of Napoleon Bonaparte, at once the product of the Revolution and the self-made man, who has thus realized his ultimate ambition of "resting on the banks of the Seine among the French people whom he so dearly loved."

Almost outranking nowadays both Invalides and Panthéon, as a national shrine, is the colossal Arc de Triomphe in Paris. It was built to commemorate the triumphs of the first Napoleon, but it now arches the grave of the "Unknown Soldier," the anonymous symbolic representative of the millions of Frenchmen who on the field of honor gave their lives for the fatherland during the last Great War.

Outside of these essentially national shrines in Paris are a considerable number of like shrines in the provinces. There are, it may be recalled, historic palaces and châteaux and cathedrals which are deemed to be "national" in association and interest. There are, also, particular memorials marking spots hallowed by the birth, deeds, or death of some national hero or heroine, the memorials of Jeanne d'Arc at Rouen for example. There are, most sacred of all, the sites of certain epic national battles, especially of the World War, and the inseparable cemeteries for the soldiers who fell fighting. The battlefields are duly placarded; the graves bear a forest of little whitewashed crosses, each with the simple inscription in black letters, "*Mort pour la Patrie*" ("Dead for the Fatherland"); and great progress has been made since the war in the construction of massive permanent temples or other striking memorials to solemnize the national glory and the national sacrifice. One such memorial is the Chapel of the Marne, erected, under the patronage of Marshal Foch and the Cardinal Archbishop of Reims, at the spot "where God, through the genius of our generals and the bravery of our soldiers and the Allies, manifested his protection of us at a decisive moment," and dedicated to "Christ who loves the French, to His divine Mother, and to the Saints who protect France." Another, the memorial of Hartmannsvillerkopf, consisting of a national cemetery and a national altar on the once wooded mountain of Hartmann near Mulhouse overlooking the plain of southern Alsace, commemorates the tremendous effort put forth by France to recover her lost provinces. A third such monument is the Chapel of Notre-Dame de Lorette, under the patronage of the Bishop of Arras, in honor of the men who were killed during the World War on the Arras front. A fourth, to the Armies of the East, is at Marseilles, and symbolizes, as its parliamentary champion told the Chamber of Deputies in 1922, "the great tombstone of all of our heroes who died for the fatherland in the East and whose families are unable to go out there and weep on their graves."

Last and most impressive is the Ossuary of Douaumont, completed in 1927 under the patronage of Marshal Pétain and the Bishop of Verdun, and consecrated to the 400,000 unidentified French and Allied soldiers who fell on the battlefield of Verdun during the four years of warfare. The monument comprises fifty-two sepulchres containing the bones of the dead gathered from as many sectors of the historic battlefield, and, in addition, a Catholic chapel, a Protestant oratory, and Jewish and Moslem memorials. Surmounting the monument is a huge bell which was tolled first in Paris under the Arc de Triomphe during the ceremony of purifying the Unknown Soldier's tomb after it had been defiled by a Communist in the summer of 1927.

But, after all, the average Frenchman beholds a great monumental war-memorial or visits a great national shrine only occasionally. What perhaps shapes his national consciousness more continuously and more certainly is his everyday encountering of minor homely memorials in his own habitat. For wherever in his own country the average Frenchmen may be, in city, town, or rural village, he is in the presence of national symbols. These may be state buildings or public parks or statues or the very names of streets. Every provincial town and every large village has a town hall, a municipal library, and a school-house, all flying the tricolor, as well as a public square and a church located on its most important thoroughfare. The town halls of the older and wealthier settlements are usually adorned with statues representing sometimes justice, wisdom, virtue, or industry, and frequently " France " or " La Patrie," and almost always some national French hero or some local notability who performed signal service to the nation. For the most part, however, the smaller villages are devoid of statuary (with the exception of religious statues on the church or a " Calvary " on the outskirts of the village and, since the Great War, of a memorial to the local " dead for the fatherland " occupying a central position in the village), but each of them possesses a village-fountain which, though in poorer hamlets it resembles a pump more than a fountain, is so typical of rural France as to have acquired the nature and value of a national symbol. The relative absence of patriotic statuary in the villages is compensated for, however, as its frequent presence in larger towns and cities is supplemented by, the universal French practice of naming numerous streets in honor of patriotic heroes and events.

Whether walking or riding in a French town, one finds it difficult to avoid a Boulevard, an Avenue, a Rue, or a Place bearing the name of La République, Alsace-Lorraine, Jeanne d'Arc, Colbert, Carnot, Hoche, Austerlitz, Jena, Solferino, Gambetta, Victor Hugo, Thiers, Foch, Verdun, or Pasteur. It is not only statesmen and warriors and battles that are so honored, but also

French scientists and French artists and even distinguished foreigners who have aided or praised France; indeed, anyone or anything that serves the cause of national history or redounds to the national credit. Nor is this honoring of national heroes restricted to any sectarian list: Danton Street may lie next to Jeanne d'Arc Street; the Avenue Jean Jaurès may lead out of the Place Maurice Barrès; and a whole congeries of medieval lanes named in honor of Christian saints of French national significance may be bounded by modern boulevards designated by events of the Revolution or by date of the proclamation of the Third Republic.

4

If small villages lack statuary, Paris and the chief provincial cities are filled to overflowing with symbolic plastic art — statues of La France, La Patrie, La République, La Liberté; statues, such as those in the Place de la Concorde in Paris, commemorating the great cities of France; statues made of captured foreign cannon; statues of a vast galaxy of patriotic soldiers, statesmen, jurists, scholars, poets, novelists, historians, scientists, engineers, clergymen, philanthropists. There are busts and equestrian figures and allegorical groups. Probably the proportion of them which are in good taste and of excellent craftsmanship, real works of art, is considerably larger than that in any other country; and most of them are avowedly national and patriotic.

To the patriotic public sculpture, already profuse in France before the Great War, has been added since the war an almost unbelievable quantity. A good deal of the new is not inherently French; it is the natural outcome of patriotic desire on the part of foreign peoples — British, Americans, etc. — to commemorate the valorous fighting and glorious death of their respective fellow countrymen on French soil; and it finds expression in tablets and markers, as well as in some very grandiose statues and monuments, to the memory of individual soldiers, regiments, divisions, branches of the military service, and whole armies. Among such outstanding American monuments in France, for example, are the "doughboy" statue by Gertrude Payne Whitney, at the port of Saint-Nazaire; the eagle-topped shaft of the First Division at Buzancy; the memorial of the Third Division at Château-Thierry; that of the Twenty-eighth Division at Varenne; that in honor of Missouri soldiers at the little town of Cheppy in the Argonne; etc., etc. But the French themselves have reared thousands of sculptured memorials to their own war-dead during the past ten years.

The spirit which has actuated the rearing of these innumerable war-memorials was beautifully expressed, while the war was still in progress, by several prominent French littérateurs and artists, notably by J. A. Ajalbert, the director of the tapestry works at Beauvais, and by Edmond Rostand, the distinguished dramatist. M. Ajalbert wrote in 1916:

I wish for an ineffaceable commemoration of the victims of the war . . . It is in full daylight, in the wind and the sun under which they were born, under which they lived, and under which they fought, that our dead of yesterday, of to-day, and of to-morrow must again find life. Let their pictures be handed down through the ages, haunting posterity which is inclined to forgetfulness. Let our descendants during their hours of toil and pleasure be forced to remember them. Let the shepherd, leading his flock to graze in the fields, stop to spell out the names of those who were the flower of the land, the names which he will find engraved on the chapel porch, on the fountain of the village green, and in the market square. Let the moss of our river banks repeat to the roadside Calvary and to the port jetty the names of the men who went to the front never to return. Let the townsman who mounts the steps of a playhouse give thought to his compatriot whose death surpassed in actual fact the horror and the beauty of any stage fiction.[3]

In similar vein wrote M. Rostand:

The most obscure soldier dying must know that his name will be written upon a wall in a conspicuous place where the eyes of the thoughtful will search for it and the eyes of the dreamer will light upon it. Thus all the dead will be assured of life, for one dies only where one's name is forgotten; and all the living will be assured of animation by the spirit of the dead, for the soul is embodied in the name and when Psyche is invoked a butterfly comes. I should like — I have often wished — to have the names of the dead heroes engraved

[3] *Éveil*, June 12, 1916.

upon the walls of the houses in which they lived. This would be the simplest and most logical means of dispersing over the surface of the earth an immense litany of short " remembers." Our houses, which are now signed by those who built them, would thus be countersigned by those who saved them from destruction, and the architect would reserve for the name of the rescuer the best place. Then would insignificant stuccoes shine forth while marble palaces devoid of inscription would look less proud . . . And if there be any heroes who were born under the starry sky and who never slept under a roof, who went to meet death in order to safeguard the roofs of others, let the names of such be put upon the most magnificent of palaces. " They died for us." [4]

The French, it must be said, are less disposed than some other nations to sacrifice their artistic sense to patriotic fervor. Even during the highly emotional strain of the Great War, many a French voice was raised in protest against ugly memorials.

" Since 1870," wrote Urbain Gohier, " monuments commemorating our defeat have littered public thoroughfares; it is to be feared that sculpture will rage furiously after our victory." " For the sake of France's dead, a law should be passed," wrote Marcel Boulenger, " prescribing that all the hideous monuments and scandalously ridiculous statues, by means of which unfortunate sculptors attempt to perpetuate the beautiful memory of our heroes, be thrown into the river, or, if preferred, be placed in a single town delivered over to this dreadful purpose." [5]

Hardly was the war ended, however, when the State itself responded handsomely to the undoubted popular demand for sculptured memorials of the million and a half Frenchmen who had been killed in the gigantic struggle. A law of October 25, 1919, directed every town to erect a memorial and promised subsidies from the state Treasury " to towns in proportion to the effort and the sacrifices that the latter will make for the purpose of glorifying the Heroes who died for the Nation." In accordance with this law, the State granted 3,000,000 francs in 1921; 5,300,000 in 1922; 2,100,000 in 1923; 2,100,000 in 1924: a total, for four years, of twelve and a half million francs. As the sum given by the State was usually a fifth of that raised by

[4] *Comment glorifier les Morts pour la Patrie?* (Paris, Cres, 1917).
[5] Joseph Dasonville, *Pour relever les Ruines* (Paris, Perrin, 1919).

the town, the cost of war-monuments erected by the communes up to the end of 1924 may roughly be estimated at sixty-two and a half million francs.

Multitudes of war-memorials have been put up in France since the war. So numerous, indeed, are they that it is impossible to secure reliable statistics. There are at least 38,000 official communal memorials, the cost of which has been defrayed partly by local taxation, partly by popular subscription, and partly by state subvention.[6] Besides, almost every church in France has a tablet, if not a more pretentious memorial, to its communicants who "died for the fatherland"; and similar markers are very frequent in schools, clubs, and industrial establishments.

A few of the war-memorials are militantly nationalist. Such, for example, is the statue "Paris 1914–1918" in the Place du Carrousel of the Tuileries Gardens, representing a woman grasping a large sword, her head raised in haughty defiance and facing toward Berlin. Such, too, is the monument designed by M. Réal del Sarte on instructions of General Gouraud, which stands on the site of the battle of the Navarin Farm and shows three French soldiers charging in the direction of Germany. These, it must be said, are exceptional. It is only in the case of a few monuments, made during or immediately after the war, when feeling ran very high, that vindictive hostility is expressed.

A sample of the various kinds of war monument is conveniently provided by the random post-card collection made by the War Museum at Vincennes between 1917 and 1925. Of the 205 post-cards in the collection, ninety-five represent obelisks, cenotaphs, or other simple geometrical figures; sixty display a soldier in uniform and with gun; twenty-one depict Gallic cocks; eleven show a soldier with a woman symbolizing peace, love, or victory; eleven represent statues of victory; three, crucifixes; one, a mausoleum; one, a statue of grief; one, an allegorical

---

[6] In the département of Finistère, for example, 263 monuments of this kind have been erected at an expense of 2,894,598 francs, of which 1,402,569 francs have been raised by popular subscription and 1,361,747 by local taxation, and the remaining 130,282 francs have been received from the State.

group with the inscription " *N'oubliez Pas* " (" Do not forget ");
and one, " The Soldier of France and the Grateful Fatherland."

The war-monuments erected since 1925 are more consciously
and purposefully pacific. The return to normal daily life is por-
trayed and the horror of warfare is stressed. A very beautiful
example of the newer tendency is the monument to the dead at
Compiègne: the sculptor, M. Réal del Sarte, employs the symbol
of wheat growing over the dead hero's grave, with the survivors
giving thanks before it while bewailing their dead and attempt-
ing to face anew the problems of life. This theme has particularly appealed to French Socialists, who have utilized it in one
way or another for the considerable number of war-memorials
which they have erected in communes whose local government
they dominate. The war-monument at Lille, of Socialist inspiration, is in the manner of a triptych: the first section suggests the
flight of the inhabitants of Lille before the enemy's invading
troops; the central panel represents the horror of war; and the
third depicts, not the joyful reëntry of the eventual victors, but the
sad return of the inhabitants into their free but ruined city.
Mention should be made, likewise, of the monument which a
Communist local government erected in the cemetery at Levallois-
Péret, a suburb of Paris, in 1927: it represents a soldier breaking his rifle across his knee. Although the Communists insisted
that this monument was truly patriotic and pointed out that
it had been designed and executed by a veteran of the Great
War, it shocked profoundly a large section of the French population, which for the most part supported the nationalist Action
Française in a violent, though ineffective, demonstration against
the " unpatriotic " character of the monument.

Inscriptions constitute a whole category of war-memorials.
Many have been made at the direction of the State or of local
authority to commemorate some deed of French valor. Many
more have been made on the initiative of private groups or patriotic societies to mark some outrage by the enemy. Thus, in
Paris, inscriptions call the attention of passers-by to number 58
rue des Marais and to number 89 rue Pelleport where fell the last
bombs thrown from German airships; to spots on the Quai de

Seine and Boulevard Ney, where fell the first and last shells fired from distant German cannon; and to the church of Saint Gervais, the maternity ward of the Port Royal Hospital, and the cemetery of Père Lachaise, " the places where crimes committed by the enemy's artillery most revolted public opinion." [7] A characteristic example of the wording of a certain kind of these inscriptions is that on the Town Hall of Senlis: " On September 2, 1914, Place de l'Hotel de Ville, at 3 P.M. the Germans of Von Kluck seized the mayor of Senlis, Eugène Odent, aged 59, and after a day of torture shot him in the evening in the forest of Chainant. Six unfortunate workmen were taken as hostages and were murdered with him: Emile Aubert, aged 52, tanner; Jean-Stanislas Barbier, aged 66, carter; Auguste Cottran, aged 17, plunger; Pierre Dewart, cultivator; Jean-Baptiste Pommier, aged 67, day-laborer; Arthur Rigault, aged 61, stone mason."

5

Quite a different kind of national symbol is presented to the eye of the sojourner on French soil by the badges of state officials, by the distinctive uniforms of army, navy, and police, and by the ribboned decorations of war-veterans and members of the Legion of Honor. As one notes on many Frenchmen in all parts of the country the insignia of the Legion or of the Medaille Militaire or of the Croix de Guerre, one learns to perceive a national brotherhood of patriotic heroes.[8] And the presence everywhere of soldier and sailor uniforms not only adds color to solemn public ceremonies but also testifies impressively to the solidarity and strength of the French nation.

Around all the material symbols of national patriotism have grown up a great variety of forms and rites and ceremonies. The holding of general elections at stated intervals is not especially ceremonial, but it is, after all, a symbolic national observance. The occasional election of a President of the Republic in the Palace of Louis XIV, with the antecedent ride of the senators

[7] *Guide Bleu* (Paris, Hachette, 1925).
[8] See J. Durieux and A. Vovard, *Les Décorations françaises: Manuel pratique des Titulants et des Postulants* (Paris, Chiron, 1922).

and deputies out to Versailles and with their ensuing return, with the newly elected President, to Paris, is a bit more ceremonious and arouses much national interest. The reception of a new member into the French Academy is attended with dignified formalism and is reported in detail in numerous newspapers for the edification of the entire nation. The tours of the President, of a Minister, of a Marshal, or of some other high state dignitary, into the provinces, for the purpose of laying a cornerstone or dedicating a public building or monument or presiding over a patriotic demonstration, are frequent and are marked usually by the wearing of uniforms, the parading of soldiers, the flying of the tricolor, the singing of the national anthem, the making of set speeches, the shouting of " Vive la France." A few days later, in motion picture theatres throughout the country, the news-reel reproduces the event, accompanied by patriotic music and usually the cheers of the audience. And, of course, the patriotic press does its best to convey to absent Frenchmen by means of the printed page some of the emotion which is supposed to have been experienced by Frenchmen who could fortunately be present.

To cite but one of innumerable examples, the *Journal de l'Est* of Strasbourg devoted most of its issue of September 26, 1927, to a glowing account of the state visit of the Prime Minister, M. Poincaré, to towns in the Alsatian département of Haut-Rhin. The account is headed on the first page with bold black-faced type: " In Haut-Rhin Beautiful Hours of French Union. At Saint-Amarin, at Guebwiller, at Thann and at Mulhouse M. R. Poincaré has praised the sacrifices of the combattants. The President of the Council was accompanied by M. André Tardieu, Minister of Public Works, and by M. Painlevé, Minister of War. The ceremony at Guebwiller was of moving and serene grandeur. That at Mulhouse has magnificently associated the whole population unanimously." The introductory paragraphs glowingly summarize the events and conclude with these words concerning the fête at Mulhouse.

The crowd there played a great rôle. But what was most remarkable about this crowd was not its composure, however exceptional. It was its perfect diversity. For such a fête, however, no parties, no castes, no shades of difference. A single heart! A single soul! The audience, massed around the head of the Government and around the mayor of Mulhouse, was indeed that of France, that which does not traffic in its devotion to the national ideal. It suffices to say that thus was given a magnificent crown to a great day of civic union. We have the right to congratulate ourselves and to felicitate all the artisans of these days of union.

There follow special write-ups of the several fêtes and verbatim reports of the speeches. Of the fête at Mulhouse it is stated:

An immense crowd — twenty or twenty-five thousand, perhaps more — is massed on the long esplanade of the Boulevard de la Porte Haute — the whole city is represented — notables and commoners, employers and workers, bourgeois and proletarians, firemen and soldiers, old men and boy scouts, gymnasts and choristers, veterans of the war and parents of war-victims, such is the astonishing mosaic of this civic fête. All this crowd, surrounded by a moving but respectful cohort of onlookers — they are an army! — circles the masterly monument chiselled by Réal del Sarte and designed by MM. Doll and Schulé, architects. About the monument sixty flags of as many societies form a colorful and solemn hedge. . . . When M. Poincaré appears, an immense shout is raised, and, in a city the majority of whose inhabitants are Socialists, it is the whole people unanimously who acclaim joyously and with a sort of veneration the man who incarnates French authority. Then the President reviews the troops, the firemen, and the societies on parade, and deposits a floral bouquet to the memory of the 2,200 dead of Mulhouse. Then M. Max Dollfus takes his place at the tribune beside the monument and delivers an admirable discourse. . . . On its conclusion, M. Wicky, Socialist Mayor of Mulhouse, whose popularity is great with all groups by reason both of the dignity of his bearing and of the sincerity of his attachment to France, pronounces in French a short address. Then, speaking from his place, the head of the Government reads in a strong voice, twice broken for a second, however, by interior emotion, a solid discourse, clear as a page of history and eloquent as a citation. . . . The peroration of M. Poincaré is greeted with loud cheering which, it seems, will never end. M. Bouché-Leclerq, sub-prefect, conducts the President of the Council, M. Painlevé, and members of Parliament, to the terrace of the monument, where they review a procession of striking size: veterans of 1870, wearers of Military Medals, old veterans, members of the Legion of Honor, wounded soldiers, war-widows, war-orphans, etc.

How can we relate here the length and majesty of this procession, with its veterans, some strong and some weak, with widows whose mourning garb passes slowly, with the children who march with short steps, two by two, holding each other's hands . . . ? Then the societies of civilians: 50 different societies each consisting of an imposing number of participants. The gymnasts and especially the members of the " Proscribed by Germany " Society are greeted with cheers of popular affection. The President of the Council bows a long time as the latter pass by. . . . The fanfare of the chasseurs, which has timed the faultless march of the troops, the music of the firemen, and three civil bands have supplied entertaining selections for this wonderful parade.

It is now 4:45 P.M. The President takes his train at 5:02. He signals to his attendants to call his carriage. The parade ends in enthusiasm, and, at the instant the President gets into his auto, the crowd breaks the cordons and makes a furious demonstration all around the presidential carriage. At the railway station the cheers redouble. . . . And by the time these lines appear in print, M. Poincaré will be at Nancy, where to-day at 3:00 P.M. he will deliver a discourse at the opening of the General Council of the Meuse. . . .

Many patriotic rites are associated with the national army. Perhaps the one which possesses the greatest popular appeal is the formal presentation of the colors to each year's class of youthful conscripts. The presentation is made in different ways at different times, but it is always an emotional spectacle. *Le Petit Journal* of February 22, 1915, describes, for instance, such a spectacle in that dark year of warfare:

M. Albert Sarraut, Minister of Public Instruction, took yesterday the occasion to congratulate, in the name of the Government, the young men full of patriotic zeal who are collegians to-day and soldiers to-morrow. They are the students from the great schools and lycées of the classes of 1916 and 1917 who are following the course of the Federation of Societies of Military Preparation. In the Garden of the Tuileries amid the grey forest of lightly besnowed trees, since nine o'clock in the morning, these young battalions have been ranged, armed to the foot, along the great central alley, at the ends of which and facing each other are two triumphal arches, symbolical respectively of past centuries and of the future. . . . The group of official personages is not slow to assemble at the gilded stand opening on the Place de la Concorde: M. Sarraut; M. Liard, vice-rector of the University of Paris; M. Saint-Germain, vice-president of the Senate; M. Lemarchand, representing the city of Paris; etc. The parade begins. In perfect order, while the bugles and drums of the Republican Guard keep time, the future soldiers march before the Minister who salutes the flag of these battalions the appearance of which is splendid. Then, after various exercises by sections, the Minister, M. Sarraut, to whom M. Lattès, president of the Federation, presents his "men," delivers a speech, emphasizing the words, "You were the springtime of the University; you will be the pride of the Fatherland," and, after remarking upon the glory recalled by the Arc de Triomphe, "heavy with accumulated victories and the glory of the future surpassing in brilliance the sunbeams of Marathon, Poitiers, Bouvines, and Valmy," he concludes: "To have been a ray of this sun, a gleam of this glory, a spark of this splendor, is the happy lot of each of you. There is nothing nobler. It summarizes and magnifies all the beauty of life. This is why, ye young men who go out to your destiny, those who were your masters or your elders salute you with tenderness, with pride, with respect. Vive la France!"

There are patriotic fêtes in connection with the national schools. There are ceremonial dedications of innumerable national monuments and memorials. There are official and unofficial rites appropriate to recurring anniversaries of national heroes and celebrities. There are pompous national obsequies. There are frequent patriotic services and observances in church, synagogue, and lodge. There are the gala festivities of State and nation on the fourteenth of July — military parades and reviews, profusion of flags and bunting and fireworks, band concerts, patriotic speeches, popular dancing on the streets and in the public squares. There are similar demonstrations, though in a minor key, on the eleventh of November.

About the Tomb of the Unknown Soldier, under the Arc de Triomphe in Paris, has developed since the Great War a patriotic cult of perpetual adoration. Over the tomb is kept burning a mystical flame; and hither repair every evening at dusk a special delegation of patriots, who, with a gleaming sword expressly constructed and consecrated for the purpose, turn up the flame so that it may shine more brightly during the night. A minute of patriotic silence follows the ceremony of turning up the flame. To the Tomb and its sacred fire repair also, on occasion, all manner of distinguished foreign visitors, kings and queens, presidents, ambassadors, generals, and admirals — as well as a host of French war-veterans with their parents, sisters, brothers, wives: speeches are made; wreaths and floral emblems are deposited. Once, in the summer of 1927, a disorderly group of Communists extinguished the flame and profaned the Tomb. The next day the myriad patriotic societies of the capital rallied as a man in defense of the shrine and the cult: they performed a great and spectacular service of expiation; under the broad folds of the national flag and to the stirring strains of the national anthem, they solemnly consecrated the rekindled flame.

6

Some part of the patriotic ritual is in almost constant use. It may be daily and brief as at the Tomb of the Unknown Soldier or in salutes to the flag. Or it may be occasional and more elaborate, as on the occasion of the dedication of a monument. Of the numberless patriotic rites of the latter type which might be described, we have arbitrarily selected two examples to illustrate the propagandist character of national symbols and ceremonies.

The first example is the annual celebration at the national war-monument of Notre-Dame de Lorette, as reported in the official *Bulletin*, in 1923.[9] The report opens with a general statement:

The tradition is created and will live. Once more the innumerable caravan of the pilgrims of the Memorial has climbed the hill of Notre-Dame de Lorette to render grave, thoughtful, and moving homage anew to the great dead who under thousands and thousands of little crosses sleep their glorious sleep. The ceremony has been more imposing than ever. The presence of a great chieftain, one of the conquerors of Artois, Marshal Fayolle; the unanimous attendance of all the civil and military authorities; the prestige and the amiable and captivating grace of Mgr. Julien, Bishop of Arras; the activity of the Committee of Lorette and in particular the devotion of its eager and distinguished secretary, M. Choplain: all have given to this fête an incomparable brilliance. . . .

At 10:15, Marshal Fayolle alights from the express; he is accompanied by his son, a naval engineer attached to the Ministry of

[9] The celebration was held in 1923 on September 16. The report is from the *Bulletin du Souvenir*, organ of the Comité de Lorette (Arras, Abel Barbier), October 15, 1923.

Marine, and by Captain Bernard, his officer of ordnance. He is received on the platform of the railway station by Mgr. Julien, General Hoerter, M. Bertin Ledoux, secretary-general of the prefecture, M. Maréchal, the vicar-general of the diocese, M. Sens, president of the Academy of Arras, Colonel Duperray, commandant of the garrison, and several other personages. When the procession leaves the station, the crowd cheers Marshal Fayolle and the Commercial Band plays the *Marseillaise.*

At 10:30 a special service is conducted in the Protestant temple by the pastor, M. Honorat Taquet, formerly an army chaplain, who preaches a sermon in elevated language on national unity and concord. Mass is celebrated in the Catholic cathedral by the Abbé Carrel, former chaplain of the 119th Infantry, in the presence of many dignitaries, including Mgr. Julien, Marshal Fayolle, M. Lefebvre du Preÿ, Deputy and former Minister, General Hoerter, etc. Luncheon follows, presided over by the Marshal and at which patriotic speeches are made by the Bishop and representative of the Prefect. The principal ceremonies, however, are at Lorette in the afternoon. These open with an address of welcome by the Mayor and the response of the Marshal. Follows a parade of soldiers, war-veterans, patriotic societies, gymnasts. While all these various groups are massed together in a specially reserved space, the flags are ranged before the reviewing stand, and an actress of the Comédie Française, Mme. de Chauveron, recites with consummate art a magnificent patriotic poem by M. Léon Bocquet, beginning

> " C'est ici qu'ils ont fait le don de leur jeunesse,
> Pour que l'antique honneur du pays soit sauvé
> Et que du crepuscule appesanti renaisse
> Un clair matin. Moissons de Lorette, ' *Salve.*'

> " Qu'une grave ferveur pieusement s'incline
> Vers le sol; c'est ici qu'ils sont tombés, laissant
> Fleurir sur les ronciers de fer et la colline
> La rose merveilleuse et pourpre de leur sang.

> " Mais nul ne se lamente au tréfonds de l'abîme
> Une aube de clarté rayonne des tombeaux,
> Le vent de France est doux sur la plus haute cime,
> Comme un souffle d'enfant sur le feu des flambeaux."

Next the Abbé Boulet, former army chaplain, pronounces a " vibrant and luminous discourse to the glory of the heroes of Lorette, a ' palladium of Right.' " And Marshal Fayolle delivers the final address. A solemn visit of the dignitaries to the ossuary and the rendition of a sacred cantata, composed for the occasion by Dr. Poiteau, "the bard of Artois," complete "this cult of the martyrs of our victory."

The other illustration, with which we would close this chapter, is "the moving ceremony at the Panthéon to the writers who have died for France." The account of it in *Le Temps* of October 15, 1927, begins:

Under the vaulting of the Panthéon, the moving apotheosis of the writers who died for the Fatherland has taken place with a solemnity in which the entire nation shares. The President of the Republic presides, surrounded by the members of the Government, by representatives of literary associations, and by the diplomatic corps. The presidents, directors, or delegates of the academies and literary associations deposit in silence upon the tribune their written homages. These tributes are enclosed by M. Thierry Sandre, President of the Association of Writer-Veterans, in a bronze tube enveloped with a flag and are then sealed by M. Doumergue in the wall bearing the 560 names of the heroes inscribed henceforth in the Panthéon. The principal address is made by M. Édouard Herriot, Minister of Public Instruction and Fine Arts, who says in part: ". . . . The inscription of these names on a wall of our Panthéon has for us a symbolic value. These dead were knights of the spirit. In them is concentrated what France has defended in the course of this last war, which ought to have been, according to their wish, only the bloody prelude to a decisive peace. In this conflict which represented, for intelligence, the latest of barbarian invasions, a new irruption into an old seat of light and culture, they protected the rights of quality, the gentleness of manners, the supremacy of intellect, the human treasure of liberty, of knowledge, and of goodness. If Force should occupy all visible space, it would have no title against Thought, mistress of Time; that is, at any rate, the doctrine of France. Thanks to them, this doctrine survives. From our fields of battle a vast light streams up toward heaven; from within distant nations, it is seen; there have been hours when one might ask if it was the firing of a funeral pile or the flame of an altar. It was indeed the flame of an altar; by the sacrifice of the victims, it still gives light, brighter than ever. . . . The true tomb of the dead is the heart of the living. Let us read again the works of these writers dead for the country; let us know how to make them a part of our reunions, of our educational programmes. . . . Greater than we, stronger than we, more enduring than we, more tender also, it is maternal France which will guard, here, their memory as that of precious and beloved children."

CHAPTER X

THE MAKING OF FRENCHMEN IN ALSACE–LORRAINE

I

ALL the agencies which have given form and content to French national psychology — patriotic ceremonies and symbols, patriotic societies, the press, the churches, the national army, the national educational system, the national State itself — have dwelt a good deal, at one time or another, in one way or another, upon Alsace-Lorraine. From 1871 to 1914 they made Frenchmen feel acutely that two historic French provinces had been unjustly and outrageously torn by force from the fatherland and annexed to Germany, the hereditary foe. From 1914 to 1918 they set forth clearly and singly the recovery of the lost provinces as the goal of French suffering and sacrifice in the Great War. And since the conclusion of the war in 1918, they have hailed the actual recovery of the provinces not only as a vindication of abstract justice but also as a reunification of the French nation, a pledge of an eternal future of national solidarity. Alsace and Lorraine are not simply names of geographical districts on the northeastern frontier of France. They are, for contemporary Frenchmen, sacred symbols of national unity; and as such the contribution they have made to the arousing and sustaining of national patriotism throughout France can hardly be exaggerated.

But, granted that Alsace-Lorraine has helped to "make" Frenchmen in other parts of France, are the inhabitants of Alsace-Lorraine real Frenchmen themselves? And what has France done since the war to "make" patriotic Frenchmen in Alsace-Lorraine? These questions cannot be answered categorically. They require — and merit — no little elucidation.

If nationality is determined chiefly by language, then the majority of the inhabitants of Alsace-Lorraine would seem to be German, rather than French. We have, it is true, no thoroughly reliable statistics. The latest available statistics (1928) are those compiled by the Germans in their census of 1910. At that time there were reported to be 1,874,014 inhabitants of Alsace-Lorraine, of whom 1,634,260, or 87.2 per cent, claimed German as their mother tongue; 204,262, or 10.9 per cent, claimed French; 3,395, or .2 per cent, French and German; 27,434, or 1.5 per cent, Italian; and 4,663, or .2 per cent, some other language. It was indicated that the percentage of the inhabitants claiming French as their mother tongue was 6.1 in Upper Alsace, 3.8 in Lower Alsace, and 22.3 in Lorraine (Moselle), that for the most part the French-speaking population was concentrated in certain border towns, and that, even in the supposedly French city of Metz, it comprised only 24.9 per cent of the total.[1] Though these percentages may have been seriously minimized in the interest of Germany, it can hardly be doubted that to the majority of the inhabitants of Alsace-Lorraine in 1914, and in 1928 also, German was more familiar than French.

On the other hand, it must be remembered that Alsace and Lorraine had been integral parts of the old French monarchy in the eighteenth century; that they had experienced in common with other French provinces the national quickening of the Great Revolution and had participated in the national achievements of Napoleon Bonaparte. They had shared in all national French developments from 1815 to 1870. Their elected representatives unanimously declared in 1871 that the people of Alsace-Lorraine willed to be French and they protested vehemently against the enforced cession of the provinces from France to Germany.

It is true likewise that after 1871, despite the emigration

---

[1] The German census of 1910 has been severely criticized in respect of its linguistic statistics for Alsace-Lorraine. Doubtless, a very considerable number of the inhabitants who stated in reply to questioning by officials of the German Government that German was their " mother tongue " could also speak French; and it is possible that had they been asked the same question by officials of the French Government they could and would have replied that their " mother tongue " was French. However widespread bilingualism may have been — and on this point the statistics do not inform us — it must be conceded, nevertheless, that a large majority of the inhabitants of Alsace-Lorraine in 1910 spoke German.

of many pro-French Alsatians to France and the immigration of a considerable number of ardently patriotic Germans, despite the most strenuous attempts of the German Government to " Germanize " the conquered provinces, and despite the undoubted lessening, with the lapse of time, of antipathy to Germany on the part of an increasing number of natives, there remained widespread throughout Alsace-Lorraine a sentimental regard for the " old fatherland," which was France.   This fact, in conjunction with the general distaste for Hohenzollern militarism and the special grievances and privations of the war-period from 1914 to 1918, explains why the French armies that occupied the provinces in November 1918 were popularly hailed as deliverers.[2]

When, very early in the war, a French army made a brief incursion into Alsace and penetrated as far as the town of Thann, Marshal (then General) Joffre, the generalissimo of the French armed forces, declared solemnly and a bit rhetorically: " Your return is definitive.   You are French forever.   France brings to you, with the liberties for which she has always stood, a respect for your liberties, for your traditions, for your convictions, for your customs.   I am France.   You are Alsace.   I bring you the kiss of France." [3]

And when, at the close of the war, French armies, amid the plaudits of the populace, were in possession of Alsace-Lorraine, and it was a question of translating Marshal Joffre's rhetoric into political and social action, very great practical difficulties were encountered — difficulties which have perplexed the French Government and disturbed Alsace-Lorraine from 1918 to the present day.   For, not only did a majority of the Alsatians and Lorrainers speak a " foreign " language, but many of their other usages had developed differently from those of France during the forty-seven years of separation.

France, during these years of separation, had continued and intensified her policy of governmental centralization, while Alsace-

---

[2] See newspapers for November 22–25, 1918.

[3] Published in the *Bulletin des Armées de la République*, December 2, 1914; republished in Defensor, *Elsass-Lothringen im Kampfe um seine religiosen Einrichtungen 1924–1926* (Schwerdorff, Lothringen-Volksbund, 1926), p. 17.

Lorraine was part of a federal Empire which accorded its constituent parts a certain amount of legislative and administrative autonomy. France, moreover, had separated the Churches from the State, reduced them to the position of voluntary private societies and adopted stringent " anti-clerical " measures which had weakened, temporarily at least, the Catholic Church in France. In Alsace-Lorraine, on the other hand, the arrangements between Church and State which had obtained in France in 1871 remained in force throughout the whole period of German domination: the Concordat of Napoleon I with the Pope was still law, and with it the other measures by which the State recognized and financially supported Protestant churches and Jewish synagogues as well; and the " Kulturkampf " in Germany, unlike the " anti-clerical " legislation in France, had served politically to solidify Catholics, including those in Alsace-Lorraine, in defense of their special rights and privileges. Besides, France, in centralizing her public educational system, had " secularized " it, that is, banished clergymen and religious instruction from it, while Alsace-Lorraine, retaining her own local school-system, kept it on a confessional basis.

Then, too, the long subjection of the inhabitants of Alsace-Lorraine to German law had operated to habituate them to numerous practices and customs which were at variance with those under French law. For instance, in Alsace-Lorraine a notary public had the right to open an office at will, while in France he had to await an official appointment. Again, a druggist in Alsace-Lorraine had to obtain a license from the Government, while in France he had only to consult his own pleasure. In Alsace-Lorraine, professors of medicine might choose freely their own internes; in France, a strict examination regulated the choice. In France there was a state monopoly of tobacco with inferior products; in Alsace-Lorraine, where no such monopoly existed, the citizens were accustomed to good cigars. These differences and hundreds of others complicated the re-assimilation of Alsace-Lorraine by the French national State.

2

From the outset it was recognized by many patriotic Frenchmen that Alsace-Lorraine was entitled to exceptional treatment and should not be deprived of a certain amount of " regionalism," that is, of peculiar local patriotism. At the same time, it was claimed by equally patriotic Frenchmen that the recovered provinces would not be truly and thoroughly French until their inhabitants should bear the same relationship to the French State, French language, French schools, French law, as did the citizens of the other French lands. In other words, there has been a conflict in France between the forces of national tradition and the patriotic wish to make easy and natural the return of Alsace-Lorraine, just as in Alsace-Lorraine there has been a conflict between the desire to be French and the determination to retain and defend local differences. Here, in a nutshell, is the present situation of the problem. It is a question of French nationalism versus Alsatian localism, and it perplexes France as it troubles Alsace-Lorraine. It has many angles.

First is the question of government, bureaucracy, and law. The French tradition and practice in these matters, as we have seen, are of rigid centralization, and they were the tradition and practice of Alsace-Lorraine from the Revolution to 1871. But as unwilling members of the German Empire after 1871, the provinces demanded and obtained organs of local self-government, which in time they came to cherish.

In 1874, Alsace-Lorraine was granted by Germany a provincial chambre (*Landesausschuss*).[4] Although its members were elected indirectly and its powers were at first only consultative, it gradually became a sort of regional parliament able to make local laws for the provinces and to vote an annual budget, with the sole check that its action might be vetoed by the Imperial Parliament at Berlin.[5] In this Imperial Parliament Alsace-Lorraine was represented by fifteen democratically elected deputies.[6] After a long struggle for more autonomy a new constitu-

4 Imperial Decree of October 29, 1874.
5 Laws of March 2, 1877, and July 4, 1879.
6 Law of June 25, 1873.

tion was granted, May 31, 1911, which provided for a *Landtag*. It was composed of two houses, the lower being elected by universal suffrage every five years, and the upper house being composed of members ex-officio (representatives of the leading religious bodies, of the leading cities, of the Council of Agriculture, etc.), and an equal number of members appointed by the Emperor on the recommendation of the *Bundesrat*. The *Landtag* had the right to make laws with the consent of the Emperor.[7]

Upon the return of Alsace-Lorraine to the French fold the question of autonomy immediately appeared. Dr. Ricklin, one of the leading political figures in Alsace, convoked the *Landtag* on November 12, 1918 at Strasbourg in order to present the French with regionalism as a *fait accompli*. The conquerors, however, ignored Dr. Ricklin and dissolved the *Landtag*.

The new régime which the French set up was of a temporary nature.[8] The civil administration was placed in the hands of the Prime Minister (M. Clemenceau), who in turn delegated much of the work to an Under-Secretary of State, M. Maringer, a man who had passed many years of service in the French civil administration. A commissioner was appointed for each of the former French départements — Lower Rhine, Upper Rhine, and Moselle. The commissioner at Strasbourg was given the title of High Commissioner, but the commissioners in Metz and Colmar were not his subordinates, each being directly responsible to the Under-Secretary of State. The latter in turn was aided by a consultative body, the Superior Council, composed of governmental appointees.[9] In addition, a General Service for Alsace-Lorraine was created, composed of a delegate from each ministry at Paris. Its function was to " centralize the administrative action which the Commissioners of the Republic exercise in the

---

[7] See Fritz Bronner, *Die Autonomiebestrebungen der elsass-lothringischen Landesausschusses 1885–1911* (Frankfurt a. M., Wissenschaftlisches Institut des Elsass-Lothringes im Reich, 1928).

[8] See Georges Delahache, *Les Débuts de l'Administration française en Alsace et en Lorraine* (Paris, Hachette, 1921).

[9] J. P. Niboyet, *Répertoire pratique de Droit et de Jurisprudence d'Alsace et Lorraine* (Paris, Sirey, 1925–1927), Vol. II, p. 738.

territory of Lorraine, Upper Rhine, and Lower Rhine. . . ." [10]
and finally there was an Office of Legislative Studies, a consultative body of a more technical nature than the Superior Council.[11]

In 1919 the three temporary commissionerships were superseded by the creation of a " Commissariat Général " with far reaching powers; [12] and to the new office were appointed in turn M. Millerand (1919–1921) and M. Alapetite (1921–1924). Under their auspices, the policy of governmental centralization was steadily pursued. The three départements, into which Alsace-Lorraine had been divided prior to 1871, were restored and organized along the same lines as the other French départements. The provincial budget, which under German rule had been submitted to the *Landtag* for approval, was fused with the French national budget.[13]   Most of the local services were gradually brought under the authority of the French ministries at Paris. The service of the railways for Alsace-Lorraine was joined to the Ministry of Public Works; [14] the provincial department of justice, to the Ministry of Justice; [15] the regulation of mines, to the Ministry of Public Works; [16] the administration of posts, telegraphs, and telephones, to the Ministry of Public Works; [17] etc.   Moreover, a good deal of French legislation was introduced: penal legislation,[18] the greater part of French private law,[19] the forestry code, the commerce code, etc.   Only the municipalities and communes preserved some measure of local autonomy.

The " Commissariat Général," with its " Superior Council," kept the form, if not the substance, of provincial autonomy.   But even this form was abolished after the general French elections of 1924 had put in power M. Herriot and the Radicals, who were particularly bent on centralization.   The new régime, according

[10] Decree of November 26, 1918.
[11] Decree of December 31, 1918.
[12] Decree of March 21, 1919.
[13] Law of December 31, 1921.
[14] Decree of November 30, 1920.
[15] Decree of July 4, 1921, and law of August 4, 1924.
[16] Decree of February 25, 1922.
[17] Decree of March 30, 1922.
[18] Decree of November 25, 1919.
[19] Laws of May 31 and June 1, 1924.

to the law of July 24, 1925, provided for a bureaucratic "Direction Générale des Services d'Alsace et de Lorraine" which was directly dependent upon the Prime Minister and had offices at Strasbourg and Paris. Its office at Strasbourg was to administer the civil services which had not already been attached to the several central ministries — the schools, the churches, social insurance, and local personnel and pensions. The office at Paris was charged with the making of investigations, with the control and centralization of all business transacted by the services at Strasbourg, and with the duty of acting as a liaison between the several French ministries and the services which they respectively directed in Alsace-Lorraine.

Under German rule, the administrative functionaries and civil servants — the bureaucracy — of Alsace-Lorraine had largely been natives of the provinces and had enjoyed special rights and privileges. For example, such a person could be appointed, discharged, or transferred only in accordance with strict civil service rules; he was paid quarterly and in advance; if he died, his heirs were entitled to his salary for the quarter; he was guaranteed an annual vacation, indemnity for special expenses incurred by him, and a good pension on retirement; he benefited from the German system of social insurance; and he advanced automatically in service by right of seniority.

With the French occupation of the provinces came a great influx of French functionaries who in many cases supplanted natives in important positions. For instance, while in 1918 twenty-two of the inspectors of primary schools were natives of Alsace-Lorraine and only three were Germans, in 1919 twenty were French and only five were natives.[20] The newcomers, though remaining under French law, which was less favorable to the civil service than the German law still in force in Alsace-Lorraine, were accorded larger salaries than the native functionaries.[21] Naturally this seeming discrimination was distasteful to many natives; and what was merely distasteful to them was

20 *Revue Scolaire*, Jan. 10, 1927, p. 2.
21 It has been estimated by M. Rossé, President of the "Fédération des Fonctionnaires," that the salaries averaged thirty per cent higher.

turned into strenuous opposition, when a decree of April 16, 1920, seeking to bring Alsace-Lorraine into closer union with the rest of France, abridged the special privileges of the local functionaries. The local state employees of the Upper Rhine, including the teachers, and those of the Lower Rhine, exclusive of the teachers, promptly went on strike for three days: telephone, telegraph, and postal services stopped. For three years the struggle continued with varying intensity. Some appeasement was offered by the law of July 22, 1923, which allowed local functionaries to choose whether they would remain in a " local category " and retain certain local privileges, or join a " general category " and work under the same conditions as obtained for the French civil service; the law increased the salaries of Alsatian functionaries in the " local category " by eight per cent and of those in the " general category " by sixteen per cent, it being explained that the cost of living was higher in Alsace-Lorraine than in France. Even this law did not entirely satisfy the local functionaries. They still thought that they were discriminated against and they pointed out that the slight increase in nominal salary fell far short of the actual loss they incurred through the depreciation of the French currency.

It has also been difficult to unify the tax-system of Alsace-Lorraine with that of France. Under German rule, the cities had been allowed to engage in all sorts of semi-socialistic undertakings — water-works, lighting-systems, transportation, etc. — and to pay for them out of urban loans and taxes, with the result that the tax-rate in German cities was relatively high. French cities had not undergone the same evolution. In France, in accordance with the national tradition of centralization, the State itself performed many of the functions which in Alsace-Lorraine the several cities performed, and the State distributed the expense by national taxation throughout the country. Alsace-Lorraine, upon its surrender to France, was subjected to the same national tax-rate as was in force in the other French départements, but its urban communities continued to pay especially heavy local taxes. The result was that the total tax-rate in the recovered provinces was higher than in the rest of France.

The French Government, intent upon making Alsace-Lorraine an integral part of the fatherland, has been confronted since November 1918 with the problem of citizenship in the recovered provinces. Between 1871 and 1918 a considerable number of Germans had settled there more or less permanently; [22] and these were likely to be quite hostile to France. Besides, a certain number of native Alsatians had developed special loyalty to Germany in the course of time, and these were not enthusiastic over the prospect of a change of citizenship. Soon after the Armistice, the French military authorities set up so-called " culling commissions " (" commissions de triage ") in order to weed out the most anti-French inhabitants of the provinces. These commissions acted secretly and no record of their proceedings is available. It has been estimated, however, that, directly or indirectly as a result of their activity, the number of persons who emigrated from Alsace-Lorraine to Germany between the date of the Armistice and the end of 1920 amounted to 80,000.

Various means were provided by which remaining inhabitants of the recovered provinces might become French citizens. Individuals who had lost their French nationality by the Treaty of Frankfurt (1871) and who never voluntarily acquired another nationality, descendants of these individuals, and persons with no nationality or of an unknown nationality, automatically became French citizens with full rights, without the necessity of option. Individuals who came within the following categories were allowed to claim French nationality: persons who had a male or female French ancestor and who had lost their French nationality by the Treaty of Frankfurt; persons who had voluntarily acquired the nationality of a third state after 1871; foreigners who had acquired the Alsatian-Lorraine nationality prior to August 3, 1914; Germans who had been residents of Alsace-Lorraine prior to July 15, 1870; Germans, born or residing in Alsace-Lorraine, who had served in the Allied armies during the Great War; persons who had been born of foreign parents in

---

[22] The census of 1910 showed that 80.2 per cent of the population were of native birth; 15.7 per cent were born in Germany outside of Alsace-Lorraine; and 4.1 per cent were born in other countries.

Alsace-Lorraine prior to May 10, 1871, and their descendants; and husbands of wives who had the right to become French citizens. These individuals were required to make their claims in the year beginning January 15, 1921. As soon as they were admitted to French citizenship they were to be granted all the political, public, and private rights of Frenchmen.[23]

Germans who did not fall in any of the foregoing classes might be naturalized within three years of the date of their application, provided that they had continued to reside in Alsace-Lorraine after November 11, 1918, and that they had not begun their residence there after August 3, 1914. From the end of 1921 to the end of 1924, 11,829 Germans made the necessary application. During the same period, 1,947 applications were granted, distributed geographically as follows: 103 in Lower Alsace, 495 in Upper Alsace, and 1,349 in Moselle. At the beginning of 1925 only 548 applications had been definitely rejected.[24]

The French Government sought to " make " Frenchmen of the Alsatians and Lorrainers not only by the expulsion of the most ardently pro-German among them and by the extension of French citizenship and French centralized administration to those who remained, but also by removing visual reminders of the German régime and renewing the memory of the more distant French past. To this end the French were assisted by the return, soon after the Great War, of several prominent families that had left the provinces after 1870 and that, from a long sojourn in France, had become thoroughly accustomed to French laws, French customs, and the French language. These families had a good deal of prestige with the natives, as well as with the French Government, and they supplied several of the most active and determined supporters of the new régime, such as General Hirschauer and Guy de Wendel in the Moselle, General Bourgeois in the Upper Rhine, and Comte de Leusse in the Lower Rhine. It was but natural in the first flush of emotional en-

---

[23] Treaty of Versailles, Annex, par. 1 and 2. *Cf.* J. P. Niboyet, *Répertoire Pratique de Droit et de Jurisprudence d'Alsace et Lorraine* (Paris, Sirey, 1925), Vol. II, pp. 325–327.

[24] J. P. Niboyet, *op. cit., Supplément pour l'Année 1925*, p. 78.

thusiasm over the return of Alsace-Lorraine to France and the return of French exiles to their ancestral homes, that the natives should elect such men to represent them in the French Parliament and that, in turn, such men should sponsor the speedy assimilation of the recovered provinces to the rest of France.

To this end, also, the French Government encouraged and welcomed the prompt transformation of national symbols from German to French. The provincials who had been used to the Imperial German flag now beheld everywhere the republican tricolor of revolutionary France. The people that had listened to *Die Wacht am Rhein* and *Deutschland über Alles* now heard on all possible occasions the *Marseillaise* and were daily reminded that it had been composed in their own city of Strasbourg. The names of many streets were changed almost over night. In Strasbourg, for example, the Kaiserplatz became the Place de la République, Manteuffelstrasse became the Rue du Maréchal Foch, Mannheimerstrasse became the Rue de Verdun, and Neue Strasse was rechristened the Rue du 22 Novembre (the date of the entry of the French troops into Strasbourg). Almost all shop-signs were changed into French; the language in the municipal theatres became French, and for the most part French dramas and French operas were played.

French patriotic societies entered the field and conducted a vast amount of propaganda. " Popular Courses " ("Les Cours Populaires ") in the nature of patriotic extension teaching were founded to spread among the natives a knowledge of the French language and a love for France. They were very important during the early years of the French régime, but latterly their work has gradually been absorbed by the public schools. "La Conférence au Village " [25] also performed signal service by sending French lecturers to country villages and sometimes providing them with moving-picture machines in order better to set forth the glories of the fatherland. " Le Livre Français en Alsace-Lorraine " took upon itself the task of distributing French literature; from 1919 to 1926 it established 2,050 libraries and donated 127,738 general books, 16,254 textbooks, and 69,000 pamphlets.

[25] See above, p. 210.

The " Alsatian Committee of Information and Studies " (" Le Comité Alsacien d'Études et d'Information "), which included among the members of its governing board the presidents and secretaries of most of the other patriotic societies, is a kind of central clearing-house and devotes particular attention to the reception and guidance of foreign visitors.

3

Not all the newly-made " French " citizens of Alsace-Lorraine have been deeply impressed by the work of the French patriotic societies, by the transformation of symbols, or by the activity of the returning exiles. Not all have been enthusiastically pro-French. Not all have been eager to promote rapid assimilation. A sizable number, from the very outset, while professing their ultimate loyalty to France, have put great emphasis on what they call the " Heimatsrechte " — the home-rights, the local privileges, the exceptional position of Alsace-Lorraine in respect of language, law, education, religion — and have demanded official recognition of some measure of provincial autonomy, what we would call " home rule." As early as 1919 a certain Catholic priest, the Abbé Sigwalt, attempted to create a political party or group to resist the Gallicizing of the provinces. The candidates nominated by this party received only a handful of votes in the general election of that year, and so great was the pressure brought to bear upon the party by pro-French forces that it soon ceased to exist.

In the course of time, however, the movement for the " Heimatsrechte " gathered new strength and new momentum. Gradually the first flush of enthusiasm over the " deliverance " of the provinces faded; the centralizing tendencies of the French Government and bureaucracy became ever more apparent; and ever more vexatious and contentious grew certain problems of assimilation, especially those of language, education, and religion.

What language should be used in the schools? French, or German, or both? The German régime had ordered in 1872 that the German language should be used " in general," but that French should be employed " in classes in which all the children " spoke French " as their mother-tongue " and that the Government might authorize the use of French in classes in which only a portion of the children spoke French. Such authorization had seldom been given, however, prior to 1911, when by the constitutional act, Germany guaranteed to French-speaking people in Alsace-Lorraine the free use of their language within, as well as without, the schools.[26]

The French after 1918 not only reversed the German policy, but profoundly modified it. They prescribed that French should be the sole language of instruction in the schools " in order to unify the spirit and harmonize the affections of the children on both sides of the Vosges." [27] The practical argument advanced was that the children of Alsace-Lorraine could never aspire to positions in the highly centralized French civil service without a mastery of the French language.

The decision to make French the sole language for school-instruction involved serious hardship for both teachers and pupils. At the time of the Armistice, many of the former, who had devoted their lives to educational work, did not speak French; and at once they had to learn French as best they could, even though some of them lived in out-of-the-way hamlets where French had never been spoken. The majority of the pupils could not speak French, either; and with every new class was presented the problem of teaching them what was virtually a foreign language before they could be taught other subjects.

The direct method of teaching French was adopted. It was ordered that from the moment children entered the class-room to the end of the second year of primary education, French and only French should be spoken. Children of five, six, and seven years of age are taught the French words for different objects by simultaneously seeing the thing and hearing its French name. A bird may be pointed out to them, and although they may know it is *ein Vogel* they must learn it is *un oiseau*.

At first there was surprisingly slight popular opposition to the

[26] J. P. Niboyet, *op. cit.*, Vol. II, p. 784.

[27] *Ibid.*, p. 797. The French decree provided that religious instruction should be given in French or German as the teacher might choose.

linguistic revolution in Alsace-Lorraine. Many of the inhabitants were very anxious and eager to learn French. After a time, however, their enthusiasm waned, and many doubts began to multiply about the efficacy of the new system. The children, for their part, usually get a speaking knowledge of French before they reach the end of their period of compulsory education at the age of fourteen. This speaking knowledge, however, does not supplant German. The children rarely speak French during recess-periods, and they normally speak German at home unless, as is seldom the case, their parents speak French. After they leave school they have greater opportunity to speak German than French. The consensus of opinion seems to be that the boys lose a great deal of their French between the time they leave school at fourteen and the time when they enter the army in their early twenties. The military service gives them a chance to speak French again and they get a new smattering of the language. Girls lose their French somewhat less rapidly but hardly less surely. There are, of course, night schools (" enseignement post-scolaire ") which boys and girls may attend, but they are not obligatory and their total effect is not very extensive. The process of forgetting French goes on more rapidly in the country districts than in the urban centres, for the simple reason that there are fewer opportunities to use the language. It is also more rapid among the lower classes, because they are brought less in contact with French culture and language.

From the beginning of the restored French régime the Government recognized that, although French should be the sole language of instruction, German should be taught in the schools, primary as well as secondary, as a needful " foreign " language; and accordingly it has been decreed that three hours a week from the third to the last year of primary education shall be devoted to German.[28] This has produced embarrassing consequences. The time allotted has seemed too much to ardent French patriots and too little to a growing number of Alsatian " home-rulers." Most serious of all, perhaps, is the complication it adds to the

[28] In October 1927 it was decreed that the teaching of German should begin in the second half of the second year of primary education.

already crowded curriculum of the schools of the recovered provinces. These schools must give, on the whole, almost twice as much time to instruction in French as the schools in other parts of France and, in addition, must give every week, what the other French public schools do not give at all, four hours of religious instruction, as well as the three hours of German. Yet the total number of class-room hours is the same for all French schools of like grade, including those of Alsace-Lorraine, and all are expected to prepare students for uniform state examinations. It is obvious that in this respect, at any rate, the recovered provinces are at a distinct disadvantage.

The linguistic problem has been less acute in the secondary schools than in primary education. For a time the Government permitted the use of German in them, and although this privilege was soon withdrawn, the students who attended the secondary schools had already acquired a sufficient command of French to enable them to follow the courses intelligently.

The University of Strasbourg, the only institution of higher learning in Alsace-Lorraine, has undergone a radical transformation. Prior to 1918 it had been a thoroughly German institution, a centre of German culture and German propaganda in the provinces. At its reopening in November 1919 M. Raymond Poincaré, then President of the Republic, declared that its new mission was to be " a great university for the honor and joy of France, a university clearly Alsatian but destined to find in the profound reflections of French thought its principles of life and its forces of radiation." The linguistic problem was treated much the same in the University as in the secondary schools. For a time courses were given in both French and German, but in May 1924 the University was reorganized in conformity with the other French universities and French became the sole language of instruction. In the meantime the personnel of the institution had been almost completely changed, so that there remained in active service in 1924 only two or three instructors who had been connected with it prior to 1918. Most of the new professors were selected at least in part because of marked patriotic devotion to France and were transferred to Strasbourg from other

French universities. In a corresponding effort to purge the student life of the University of German traditions, the French Government dissolved the various German student clubs and fraternities (" Verbindungen ") and confiscated their property, and at the same time fostered the formation of a comprehensive student organization, on French lines — " L'Association Fédérative Générale des Étudiants de Strasbourg." This organization maintains a restaurant, a book-store, a fund for needy students, etc., and, though not at all political, is very influential and strictly pro-French. Mention should also be made of the " Society of the Friends of the University " (" Société des Amis de l'Université de Strasbourg "), founded in 1919 by an ardent French patriot, Dr. Pierre Bucher, and of which M. Poincaré has been president since 1920: it has collected funds for special lectureships and fellowships and for other means of strengthening French influence in the University.

Complicating the educational and linguistic problems and giving rise to still other vexatious problems is the peculiar religious situation in Alsace-Lorraine.[29] As has already been indicated, the Concordat between the Emperor Napoleon and the Pope, which had been abrogated in France in 1905, remained in force in Alsace-Lorraine throughout the period of German rule, with the result that the French Government since 1918 has had to deal with special rights of the Catholic Church in the recovered provinces quite different from those which obtain in the rest of France. Similarly the special rights which had been abolished in the rest of France by the legislation of 1905 still continued in force in Alsace-Lorraine. This meant that the French Government was called upon to do in the two provinces

[29] Religious affiliations of the inhabitants of the provinces were recorded in 1926 as follows:

DÉPARTEMENTS	CATHOLICS	PROTES-TANTS	OTHER CHRIS-TIANS	JEWS	OTHER RELIGIONS	No RELIGION	TOTAL
Lower Rhine......	413,508	190,565	533	13,177	1,389	51,813	670,985
Upper Rhine......	421,715	51,601	950	5,703	712	9,973	490,654
Moselle..........	585,228	30,412	1,112	7,243	2,410	7,056	633,461
Total............	1,420,451	272,578	2,595	26,123	4,511	68,842	1,795,100

what it was forbidden to do in other parts of the country — to nominate bishops, to pay salaries of priests, pastors, and rabbis, and to ensure religious instruction (Catholic, Protestant, or Jewish) in the public schools.

It was but natural that certain French patriots who were bent upon the speedy assimilation of Alsace-Lorraine to France should desire the annulment of exceptional religious rights and the uniform enforcement of French laws respecting religion on both sides of the Vosges, and that Socialists and Radicals who had sponsored the " anti-clerical " legislation in France should be particularly zealous for its extension to Alsace-Lorraine. It was also but natural that the church members in the provinces, including those who were sincerely pro-French in all other respects, should demand the maintenance of the *status quo* in religion, and that the most ardent French patriots of " clerical " leanings should give them encouragement and support.

So long as the " Bloc National " held the political helm in France, from 1919 to 1924, there was no serious difficulty. The Government repeatedly declared its intention to respect the religious privileges and usages of the provinces, and its resumption of diplomatic relations with the Vatican was heralded as a guarantee of its good faith. The only change which it effected was in the personnel of church officials, weeding out those who were pro-German and substituting such as were pro-French. For instance, the two Catholic bishops in the provinces at the time of the Armistice, Mgr. Benzler of Metz and Mgr. Fritzen of Strasbourg, were constrained to resign because of their German proclivities, and in their place the Pope appointed, on the nomination of the French Government, Mgr. Pelt and Mgr. Ruch respectively. Mgr. Pelt was a native of Lorraine who had received most of his schooling in Paris, a retiring man with a reputation as a peacemaker. Mgr. Ruch was more aggressive; a native of Nancy, he had spent most of his life in France, and his service in the French army during the war had earned him the *croix de guerre* and the ribbon of the Legion of Honor; he was both a sturdy champion of the cause of France and a stout defender of the rights of the Church.

The French general elections of May 1924 brought to the premiership of the country M. Édouard Herriot, with the backing of an " anti-clerical " coalition of Radicals and Socialists, and precipitated a kind of *Kulturkampf* in Alsace-Lorraine. The official declaration of the new premier to the effect that the religious situation in the provinces would be altered was met by an immediate protest on the part of twenty-one of the twenty-four provincial senators and deputies and by an appeal of the Bishops of Strasbourg and Metz to their people to organize themselves in defense of their religious rights. Mgr. Ruch instructed the priests in his diocese to conclude every Mass with a special prayer, *contra persecutores Ecclesiae*. Meetings were held in various cities to protest against the impending action. There was one in Colmar, July 6, 1924, with an estimated attendance of 8,000 people; another in Metz, July 13, with 6,000; still another in Mulhouse, on July 13, with 20,000 people, and on the same day another in Strasbourg with 50,000, etc. The " Catholic National Federation " (" Fédération Nationale Catholique "), with General Castelnau at its head, came into existence in order to organize the opposition and to conduct Catholic defense in Alsace-Lorraine as well as in other parts of France.

The first act of the Radical Government was to abolish the French embassy at the Vatican. This of course aroused Catholics throughout France and the cries of opposition came not merely from Alsace.

The second act of the Government, however, was aimed directly at the religious régime in Alsace-Lorraine. As has already been pointed out, religious instruction was given as part of the regular course in the schools of the recovered provinces. And besides, most of the public schools in the provinces were " confessional " schools, that is, there were Catholic schools for Catholic children, Protestant schools for Protestant children, and Jewish schools for Jewish children. There were some exceptions to this general rule, for in certain towns the population was so evenly divided among the various religions that separate " confessional " schools were impracticable. In these towns all the children

went to " inter-confessional " schools,[30] in which they received all
non-religious instruction together from the same teachers but
were taught religion in separate groups by representatives of the
several creeds. Now, on March 6, 1925, M. Herriot telegraphed
the prefects of the three départements of Alsace-Lorraine that
the time had come to extend the inter-confessional schools and to
supplant with them the confessional schools. The religious bodies
affected — the Catholic Church particularly, and the Protestant
Churches to a considerable extent — were furious; they regarded
the instructions of M. Herriot as a first important step toward
the extinction of religious instruction in the schools and the introduction of the French educational system into Alsace-Lorraine.
The question of the establishment of the new inter-confessional
schools immediately arose in Colmar. Mgr. Ruch ordered the
parents in his diocese not to send their children to them, and in
order to show his disapproval he ordered a school strike which
was to last one day in all the towns of his diocese and for three
days in Colmar. And the Bishop was obeyed. In some towns
on the day of the strike the schools were absolutely empty; the
average attendance throughout all Alsace was less than a third
normal.[31] Despite the protest, M. Herriot persevered in his
policy; and only the fall of his ministry, chiefly because of its
financial difficulties, halted, in April, 1925, the religious conflict
in Alsace-Lorraine.

M. Painlevé, who succeeded M. Herriot, was himself a Radical
and naturally in sympathy with his predecessor's religious and
educational policies, but he and the other French premiers who
have followed him to the present day have taken no positive
steps to change the religious *status quo* in Alsace-Lorraine.
Nevertheless, to the ecclesiastical leaders and to their loyal supporters, the example of what M. Herriot started to do is an
abiding menace, a menace which Radicals and Socialists in Alsace-
Lorraine as well as in France at large keep alive in public
speeches, in the public press, and even in Parliament. One of

30 About forty towns had " inter-confessional " schools. The earliest of such
schools had been established at Mulhouse in 1830. Altogether, they constituted
only a very small part of the school-system in Alsace-Lorraine.

31 *Der Elsässer* (Strasbourg), March 14–16, 1925.

the two Socialist deputies of Alsace in the French Parliament, M. Peirotes, Mayor of Strasbourg, presented to the Chamber on May 31, 1927, a bill providing for the complete abrogation of the Concordat, the abolition of religious instruction in the schools, and the restriction of religious orders. The bill was not passed, but it indicated clearly to one kind of French and Alsatian patriot what would happen if another kind of French and Alsatian patriot had its way.

It is impossible to estimate with any precision how much of the contemporary unrest (or *malaise,* as the French call it) in Alsace-Lorraine is attributable to religious conflict. It is certain that the autonomist ideas have been more current in the recovered provinces since 1924 than before, and that nearly all the active opposition to the French régime dates from M. Herriot's attempt to introduce " anti-clerical " legislation. Some Frenchmen say that the religious difficulty has had little to do with the rising resistance on the part of Alsatians and Lorrainers to the Gallicizing of the provinces, and that the true cause is to be found in the beginning about 1925 of influential popular propaganda inspired by Germany and directed from Germany. On the other hand, some Alsatian autonomists contend that only in 1925 did the results and tendencies of the centralizing French régime begin clearly to appear, and that thereafter a growing number of natives perceived the inefficiency of French administration and the danger to local custom and local autonomy in the compulsory teaching of the French language and implanting of French culture.

At any rate it was Catholics in Alsace-Lorraine whose French patriotism could hardly be questioned that made the first widespread determined stand against an attempt of the French Government to " make " Frenchmen of the provincials by abridging, or threatening to abridge, certain local rights. And it is probable that other persons whose French patriotism had been less fervent were encouraged by the stand of pro-French Catholic leaders to become vocal themselves and to dare quite openly to challenge all manner of French intrusion, real or fancied, in the internal affairs of Alsace-Lorraine.

Several Catholic priests, since 1924, have become very critical of things French, if not decidedly hostile to them. Such are the Abbés Fashauer and Haegy of Colmar and the Abbé Valentiny of Metz, all of whom edit autonomist newspapers. The case of Abbé Haegy is celebrated. He was the object of severe attacks by a M. Helsey, a Parisian journalist, who accused him in the columns of Le Journal in January 1927 of being paid by the Germans to conduct anti-French propaganda in Alsace-Lorraine.[32] Abbé Haegy immediately sued M. Helsey and Le Journal for libel. The trial was held at Colmar in April 1927, and attracted much attention. Feeling ran high on both sides. M. Helsey could not prove his charges, and Abbé Haegy could not obtain a judgment. When a deadlock impended, the judge created a sensation by rising to his feet and making a long impassioned plea to the two parties to forget their differences; and the trial ended with cries from both sides of " Vive la France," the singing of the Marseillaise, and the presentation to the Abbé Haegy of a bouquet of flowers of the colors of the French flag, which the priest accepted and then passed on with a few felicitous words to his opponent. The case was ended. Both sides had professed loyalty to France, but everybody knew that Abbé Haegy's loyalty had a different connotation from Le Journal's.

Protestants in Alsace-Lorraine, though not nearly so numerous as Catholics, have been relatively as jealous of local rights, and perhaps more so. Accustomed to the prestige which Protestantism enjoys in Germany, they have been inclined to distrust both a Catholic France and an " anti-clerical " France and to uphold local autonomy as the best guarantee against either. Besides, Alsatian Protestants have been especially disturbed by the linguistic question. The Government expects that the religious instruction in the schools will be given in French, and yet a large number of the Protestant pastors who are supposed to give the instruction, speak only German. Moreover, in Protestant public worship the congregation plays a particularly im-

---

[32] See also Oscar de Férenzy, Les Erreurs et Lacunes d'une Enquête sur la Situation en Alsace (Strasbourg, Société d'Édition de la Basse-Alsace, n. d.).

portant part in singing and responsive reading. If the people use different languages, unseemly confusion is likely to result. At Strasbourg the Protestants have solved this difficulty by holding one service in German and another in French, but such a solution is impracticable in many a smaller community. For one reason or another, a considerable number of Protestant pastors have become actively identified, since 1924, with autonomist or anti-French organizations. Only the Jews, of the major religious bodies in Alsace-Lorraine, seem to have been quite contented under the French régime. Their chief Rabbi, M. Schwartz, came to them after the war with strong French sympathies, and under his leadership they made no protest against the threat of " anticlerical " legislation in 1924. When the manifesto of the autonomist " Heimatbund " was published in 1926, no Jewish name appeared among its signatures. Wherever possible, French has been substituted for German in the synagogues.

4

From 1918 to 1925 the " making " of Frenchmen in Alsace-Lorraine was prosecuted by numerous agencies, official and unofficial, with vigor and much success. During those years there was surprisingly little opposition to the introduction of French administration, French legislation, French language, or French usages. The political groups which commanded the overwhelming majority of suffrages in the recovered provinces were unquestionably loyal and devoted to France. The major group, the " Republican Popular Union " as it was called in Alsace ("Union Populaire Républicaine " or " U. P. R."), or " Liberal Republican Union " as it was styled in Lorraine ("Union Républicaine Libérale "), represented a continuation of a political party which prior to 1918 had been affiliated to the Centre Party of Germany and had been peculiarly critical of the Imperial German Government; it was largely Catholic and markedly democratic, especially strong in the rural districts, and well organized. In the French general elections of 1919 and 1924 it adhered to the " Bloc National," and, although from the first it demanded " re gional autonomy, bilingualism in the schools, courts, and civil service, and the maintenance of the religious *status quo*,"[33] it proudly declared just prior to the election of 1919: "A new period, full of promise, began for Alsace-Lorraine . . . with our return to our beloved Fatherland. The last forty-eight years have not left France unchanged, nor have we ourselves remained the same. One thing alone remains unaltered, our love for France and our trust in her."[34]

With the "U. P. R." was allied in the elections of 1919 and 1924, as a member of the "Bloc National," the "Democratic Party" ("Parti Démocratique"). It comprised industrial and commercial magnates, a large number of Protestant pastors, and many pro-French bourgeois. It asked for the maintenance of the religious *status quo*, the teaching of the German language in the schools, and a certain amount of regional autonomy, but it stressed its devotion to France and made "anti-Bolshevism" the chief plank in its platform.

Against the allied groups in the "Bloc National" were arrayed in the elections of 1919 and 1924 smaller groups of Socialists and Radicals. The alignment, however, was not on any patriotic question. In fact, both the Radical Party and the Socialist Party were, in a sense, more nationalist than their opponents: they championed the rapid assimilation of Alsace-Lorraine by the centralized French State and the abrogation of exceptional provincial legislation.[35] The appeal of the Socialist Party, for example, just prior to the elections of 1919, was at once patriotic, "anti-clerical," anti-militarist, and anti-capitalistic: "Electors of Alsace! The fate of France is in your hands. Our marvellous Fatherland bleeds from many wounds. Big capitalistic bloodsuckers, who have increased the poverty of the people, and the Jesuits, who have abused religion in the most abominable manner for political ends, have united in

---

[33] *Programm und Organisation der Elsässischen Volkspartei* (Strasbourg, 1919).

[34] *Der Elsässer*, November 15, 1919, p. 1.

[35] Except, in the case of the Socialists, the advanced social-legislation of the German régime.

order to get power into their own hands. Capital, Militarism, and the Jesuits intend to crush the people! " [36]

In the elections to the French Chamber in 1919 the U. P. R. N. and the Democratic Party elected their entire coalition-ticket by an absolute majority in each of the three départements of Alsace-Lorraine. In the elections of 1924 the coalition parties of the " Bloc National " gained another victory, though not so decisive. They failed this time to secure an absolute majority of the electorate, and, under the French system of proportional representation, Alsatian Socialists secured two seats, and an Alsatian Communist obtained one seat,[37] out of the total of eighteen allotted to the recovered provinces.

Linguistic and other questions involving the " home rights " of Alsace-Lorraine were not dominating issues in the electoral campaign of 1919 or in that of 1924. After 1924, however, the situation changed, and a breach appeared and gradually widened between French nationalists and Alsatian autonomists. The religious conflict of 1924–1925 was undoubtedly one factor in effecting the change. It was then that Abbé Haegy, one of the most influential journalists and prominent leaders of the " U. P. R.," began to preach in his numerous newspapers [38] the necessity of uniting the Alsatians in defense of their traditional privileges and in demands for regional autonomy. It was then, too, that Abbé Valentiny,[39] similarly conspicuous in the counsels of the corresponding " Liberal Republican Union " of Lorraine, urged like policies upon his people.

[36] *Freie Presse,* November 15, 1919.

[37] Since 1920 there had been in Alsace-Lorraine rival parties of Socialists and Communists. The latter party is sympathetic with Russian Bolshevism.

[38] Abbé Haegy edits a chain of newspapers: three at Colmar — *Der Elsässer Kurier* (daily, in German), *Die Heimat* (weekly, in German, founded in 1920) and *Le Nouvelliste d'Alsace* (daily, in French, founded in 1923); two at Strasbourg — *Der Elsässer* (daily, in German) and *Le Courrier* (daily, in French founded in 1920); and a large number of petty rural sheets, mainly in German, with a combined circulation of 42,000.

[39] Abbé Valentiny, the Lorraine prototype of Abbé Haegy, is editor of a daily in German at Metz, *Die Lothringer Volkszeitung,* with an estimated circulation of 23,000 and also of a weekly at Metz and a score of small rural paper throughout Lorraine.

The fact that the Abbés Haegy and Valentiny were not content to oppose " anti-clerical " French legislation but proceeded to criticize the French régime in general, displeased many pro-French members of their own political group and led to the establishment of two new Catholic papers at Strasbourg, both decidedly nationalist, *La Voix d'Alsace* in French (1925) and *'s Elsass* in German (1926). Besides, two French newspapers at Metz, *Le Lorrain* and *Le Messin,* each with an estimated circulation of 15,000, while ardently Catholic, have combated autonomist agitation.

The divergent tendencies in the Catholic political groups have appeared likewise in the Democratic Party. Here the opponents of assimilation have found a leader and spokesman in M. Charles Altorffer, a Protestant pastor and a deputy, while the pro-French wing of the party conducts its propaganda through a newspaper at Strasbourg, *Le Journal de l'Est,* founded in 1924, very well edited, and analogous in patriotic spirit to *'s Elsass.* Other and older papers of the Democratic Party are inclined to be moderately nationalist — *La France de l'Est* and *Das Mülhauser Tageblatt* of Mulhouse and *Die Neue Zeitung* of Strasbourg.

In 1924 emerged a special group in Alsace, the " National Republican Committee," with a newspaper, *Le Journal d'Alsace et de Lorraine,* and with a strongly nationalist program, demanding " in the first place that the Treaty of Versailles be enforced to the letter and Germany be made to pay " and secondly that " Alsace-Lorraine be assimilated as rapidly and completely as possible by the Fatherland." [40] In 1925 the ultra-patriotic royalist group of the Action Française, having secured a small but noisy following in the recovered provinces, established at Strasbourg a weekly newspaper, *Le National,* German in language but militantly anti-German in content. Youthful members of this group on more than one occasion have employed physical force against members of autonomist organizations,[41] and their

---

[40] *Journal d'Alsace et de Lorraine,* April 29, 1924.
[41] *Die Zukunft,* August 28, 1926.

organ is ever on the alert for real or fancied propaganda emanating from Germany.[42]

On the other hand, a special group in Lorraine, the " Democratic and Republican National Union," championed international peace, the League of Nations, and the Treaties of Locarno, and at the same time advocated zealously the cause of bilingualism and regionalism in Alsace-Lorraine. Its organ, the *Metzer Freie Journal*, has a circulation of about 18,000.

Similar cleavage has appeared among the urban workingmen. The Communists, who seceded from the Socialist Party in 1920 and formed a separate party of their own, have gradually become voluble exponents of cultural and political autonomy. They are especially active in Lorraine, and maintain a newspaper in German, though with the French title of *L'Humanité*, at Strasbourg. The Socialists, on the other hand, have become more and more convinced of the desirability of promoting assimilation, and their newspaper at Strasbourg, *Die Freie Presse*, is almost nationalist in tone.

Only one great newspaper in Alsace-Lorraine has been able to maintain a vestige of impartiality between the conflicting claims of national and regional patriotism. This is *Die Neueste Nachrichten*, with German and French editions at Strasbourg and a German edition at Colmar, and with an estimated total circulation of 110,000. It aims to be simply a journal of information and to present both sides of the patriotic question impartially.

Since 1925, the religious issue has been but one of the bones of contention in Alsace-Lorraine between " assimilators " and " autonomists." Another, and latterly more debated, question is that of language.

Against the prescription of the French Government that the French language should be the sole medium of instruction in the schools of Alsace-Loraine, voices were raised almost from the outset. As early as January 1921, Abbé Müller, dean of the Catholic Faculty of Theology at the University of Strasbourg

---

[42] For instance *L'Action Française* joined with *Le Journal* in the accusations against Abbé Haegy. See its issues of February 16–17, 1927.

and a senator, declared: " It is necessary that in our schools German should be the main dish and that French should come at the end of the meal like a sweet or a dessert." [43] But it was not until after the political and religious events of 1924 that concerted activity was undertaken against the supremacy of French.

In 1925 the " Federation of State Employees and Teachers," the largest organization of its kind in the recovered provinces, took a stand for the parity of German with French. " The mediocre results in German," its official organ stated,[44] " have greatly disquieted the population of the three départements. This is what has begun to be called the Alsatian *malaise*. We think the situation could be remedied by beginning the instruction of German in our bilingual schools in the very first year. We would base the instruction on the German language which the child already speaks. . . . We do not wish to have it said that our schools give a preference to French or to German. We hold to the principle that everything which the child learns to say, read, or write in French he should learn to say, read, and write in German."

In the summer of 1926 the Communists demanded, as part of their political platform, that more German be taught in the schools.

In February 1927 M. Thomas Seltz, a leader of the U. P. R. and deputy of the Upper Rhine, submitted to the French Chamber a report on what he and his associates asserted to be the favoritism shown to French by the school-authorities in Alsace-Lorraine and an accompanying resolution asking for the creation of a special commission to study the situation and recommend reforms. The report emphasized an assertion by Comte de Leusse, mayor of Reischoffen (Lower Rhine) and former deputy, a most patriotic Frenchman, that " in the matter of the schools we have taken the wrong road in districts where the German language is spoken. In the schools of these districts the children learn French fairly well and sometimes very well. But they hardly ever hear French outside the school. At home they con-

[43] *L'Alsace Française,* January 15, 1921.
[44] *Revue Scolaire,* October 25, 1925.

tinue to speak a language which they scarcely know how to read or write." The report went on to propose that children begin their education in German and that French be gradually introduced and stressed " until it be given the more important place in the schools." [45]

The " National Syndicate of Teachers " is on the whole pro-French and in favor of the existing linguistic arrangements. Its leaders insist that the teaching of French is the only way of indoctrinating the children with French sentiments. Nevertheless, M. Klein, secretary of the organization for the Lower Rhine and a native of Alsace, writes: " The teaching of French in the cities is satisfactory, but in many rural communities it encounters obstacles. In single-class schools the teaching of two languages is extremely difficult."

There are, of course, many who ardently favor the existing regulations. The French Government itself is among these. M. Charléty, the Government's educational director in Alsace-Lorraine after 1919, issued on January 31, 1927, new instructions concerning the teaching of the two languages, but made no concessions to German. M. Pfister, who succeeded M. Charléty in 1927, on the latter's transfer to the rectorship of the University of Paris, affirmed that he would never yield on the one point that " French should remain the ' first ' language in the schools." Nor has M. Poincaré changed his earlier attitude on the question. In a speech at Strasbourg on April 21, 1927, he declared that the time devoted to the teaching of French would not be shortened.

It has been said that France has sought to destroy the Alsatian dialect, to prevent children from corresponding with their parents who do not know French and to forbid the giving of religious instruction in German. All that is false, and it is indispensable that it remain false, not only on paper but also in fact. On the other hand, when M. Charléty and I spoke of bilingual schools, some fervent defenders of the French language feared that France would lose its favored status in the educational system and be pushed into second place. This fear is no better founded than the other. Children need to know how to write German

[45] The report and the resolution may be found in the *Bulletin d'Alsace et de Lorraine* (Office d'Information, 12 rue Wimpfeling, Strasbourg), April 10, 1927.

wherever German is spoken by their parents. They need to know it also because they live in a frontier region in which it was spoken even before 1870. But they should know French as well as German, because French is the national language; because it is only through an understanding of French that they can have intercourse with their compatriots, that they can open the doors of the public administration, that they can easily enter into commercial and industrial relations with the rest of the fatherland.[46]

5

The agitation in behalf of special linguistic and religious privileges for Alsace-Lorraine was increasingly coupled, in certain circles, with a growing demand for regional autonomy. In 1925 a group of extremists, led by Dr. Ricklin, a physician of the Upper Rhine, who had had considerable influence in Alsace prior to the Armistice, founded a newspaper, *Die Zukunft*, to conduct propaganda for political and cultural " home rule "; and at about the same time another paper of the same sort, *Die Volkstimme*, began to appear. In the spring of 1926, through the agency of these papers, a propagandist society was launched, the " Home League " (" Heimatbund ").

The manifesto of the Heimatbund, as published on June 8, 1926,[47] was addressed to " all true sons of Alsace-Lorraine." It declared that the Gallicizing of the provinces could no longer be endured and that there must be complete autonomy of Alsace-Lorraine " within the French State," including the creation of a separate legislature and administrative organization such as had been provided by the German law of 1911, with a regional capital at Strasbourg and in national coöperation with the Parliament at Paris. The manifesto insisted that if such political reforms were effected, the religious and educational problems would automatically be solved. Then the manifesto proceeded to make a large number of specific demands: that the German language should be given the place in public life which it deserves, " inasmuch as it is the mother-tongue of the majority of the population "; that the schools should be freed from the central

[46] *L'Alsace Française*, May 14, 1927, p. 339.
[47] Special edition of *Die Zukunft*, June 8, 1926.

administration in Paris and brought under local control; that the railways should be operated by Alsace-Lorraine; that local agriculture, commerce, and industry, especially the wine industry, should be locally protected; that the fiscal system should be reorganized; that the social and municipal legislation should be preserved; and that Alsace-Lorraine be recognized as a region in which " two great cultures exist side by side without the destruction of either." " We do not wish to be a party; we wish only to be an organization which will stimulate the existing parties of the land to abandon policies of delay, weakness, and illusion and to lead with unwavering courage the fight for the home-rights (*Heimatsrechte*) of Alsace-Lorraine." The signatories of the manifesto included persons who had been prominent in the older political groups, Catholic priests, Protestant pastors, publicists, school-teachers, and functionaries.

French patriots immediately assailed the Heimatbund. The French patriotic press was in the forefront of the attack. *L'Action Française* was particularly furious and drew forth counter-attacks in kind from *Die Volkstimme,* one result of the engagement being that the latter paper was fined 48,000 francs in court.[48] The patriotic French press generally maintained that the Heimatbund's program for the autonomy of Alsace-Lorraine within the French State was merely a cloak to conceal the leaders' real desire to return to German rule, and that the whole movement was supported by German gold: naturally neither of these charges was admitted to be true by any official or organ of the Heimatbund. Several large and influential organizations in the recovered provinces, though sympathetic with some of the specific demands in the manifesto of the Heimatbund, expressed disapproval of its " radical " claim of political autonomy. The U. P. R. N., the largest political party in Alsace, on the whole considered the Heimatbund too advanced in its ideas and scorned political coöperation with it.[49] The "Republican Union " of Lorraine ostracized its members,[50] and Mgr. Pelt, Bishop of Metz,

[48] See *Le National,* June 11, 1927.
[49] Letter of M. Brogly, President of the U. P. R. N., in *La France de l'Est,* May 20, 1927.
[50] Resolution of the Party's convention, May 30, 1927.

condemned its policies.[51] Mgr. Ruch, Bishop of Strasbourg, sharply criticized its program, and then, in answer to its charges that he was persecuting priests who adhered to it, he ordered the Catholics in his diocese not to read *Die Zukunft*.[52]

Inasmuch as members of the Heimatbund were not welcomed by the moderate and conservative political groups, it was natural that they should gravitate toward the radically anti-governmental Communist Party. In a by-election at Niederbronn in March 1927, *Die Zukunft* urged its readers to vote for the Communist " home-rule " candidate.[53] The candidate in question failed of election, but the curious coalition in support of him aroused lively apprehensions among French patriots.

In the latter part of 1926 emerged another new political group — the " Alsatian Progressive Party " (" Elsässische Fort-schrittspartei ") — much more moderate than the Heimatbund but quite insistent on regional rights and privileges. Under the leadership of George Wolf, it formulated a program and pre-sented candidates for the senatorial elections of January 1927. The Progressives did not claim, as did the Heimatbund, a politi-cal autonomy for Alsace-Lorraine similar to what the provinces had had under German rule after 1911, but argued, rather, that the actual governmental machinery had been radically altered and that it could be made to harmonize no better with the federal German system than with the centralized French administration. They suggested that the French State inaugurate a policy of decentralization by enlarging the functions of the départements and arrondissements throughout the whole country. Specifically, they demanded that German be used for early instruction in the schools, French being introduced later and gradually; that na-tive functionaries be guaranteed the enjoyment of their traditional privileges and that the policy of appointing Frenchmen to the best positions in the local civil service be reversed; that the re-lations between State and Church be regulated, as hitherto, under the Concordat and that religious instruction be continued

---

[51] Speech on February 23, 1927.
[52] *Der Elsässer*, June 17, 1927. See the issues of *Die Zukunft* for May 1927.
[53] *Die Zukunft*, March 5, 1927.

in the schools; that the French civil code be so amended as to better the position of women; and that an accord be realized between France and Germany.[54] For its propaganda, the Party established a weekly organ, *Das Neue Elsass.* In May 1927 its leader, George Wolf, appealed " to all elements which favor the securing of home-rights " to unite in support of the Progressive program, and although the appeal met with opposition, it attracted a considerable number of moderates and conservatives who would not ally themselves with the Communists or with the Heimatbund.[55]

Still another group was organized to work for the assurance of the " home-rights," or perhaps, as some French Nationalists alleged, for the eventual separation of Alsace-Lorraine from France. This was the " Alsatian Opposition Bloc " (" Elsässischer Oppositionsblock "), led by Claus Zorn von Bulach, who comes from a distinguished family, but whose following is not of the élite of Alsace-Lorraine. As early as 1923 he began to form his party, with demands that the people of Alsace-Lorraine be treated as first-class, rather than second-class Frenchmen; that German be put on an equal footing with French in the schools; that the chief governmental positions be filled by natives; that the municipal and other exceptional legislation be maintained; and that the period of military service be reduced.[56] In the spring of 1927 von Bulach founded a fortnightly, *Die Wahrheit,* which he filled with harsh and vulgar attacks on things French. The publication claimed to have a circulation of 56,000, and although this figure was probably an exaggeration, the sheet was certainly read fairly widely among the working class and by subordinate government employees. Von Bulach was assailed by pro-French Alsatians as well as by all French nationalists. His statement in a law-suit, that he had no more respect for a French court than for a Chinese court inasmuch as the people of Alsace-Lorraine had never been accorded the

[54] George Wolf, *Das Elsässisches Problem* (Strasbourg, Imprimerie Strasbourgeoise, 1926).

[55] *Journal de l'Est,* June 4, 1927.

[56] Claus Zorn von Bulach, *Aus meinem Leben* (Osthausen, Verlag der Elsässen Partei, 1926), pp. 8–9.

right of national self-determination, cost him three months in prison.[57]

6

In different ways the " Alsatian Opposition Bloc " of Zorn von Bulach, with its organ *Die Wahrheit*, and the " Progressives " under Wolf, with their organ *Das Neue Elsass*, and the Heimatbund, with *Die Zukunft* of Dr. Ricklin and *Die Volksstimme*, redoubled their efforts during 1927 to secure popular support for their demands for local autonomy. On September 25, 1927, *Die Zukunft* and *Die Volksstimme* jointly issued a new manifesto, demanding from the French Government a liberal grant of local self-government, the right of full and free use of the German language, the exclusive employment of natives in the civil service, and economic and fiscal autonomy. Following the publication of this manifesto, the leaders of the Heimatbund formally founded a new political party — the " Autonomist Party."

To the growing demands of the Alsatian autonomists, the French Government of M. Poincaré replied on November 12, 1927, with a decree, suppressing *Die Zukunft, Die Volksstimme,* and *Die Wahrheit*. The legal basis for this decree was a thirty-four-year-old law which had been directed against certain anarchistic Italian papers in southern France and which permitted the Government to suppress anti-patriotic newspapers published in a foreign language. The Alsatian autonomists were enraged that such a law should be invoked against their newspapers, which, as they pointed out, were printed in the language of over eighty per cent of the population of the annexed provinces. *Die Zukunft* tried to evade the decree by using the Alsatian dialect instead of High German, but to no avail. The French authorities not only remained firm in the enforcement of the decree, but added to the list of proscribed newspapers the Alsatian Communist weekly, *Die Freiheit* (February 12, 1928), and *Das Neue Elsass*, the organ of the Progressive Party (March 17, 1928).

Deprived of journalistic means of propaganda, the autonomist leaders aired their grievances in a profusion of hot-tempered

[57] *Die Zukunft,* May 7, 1927.

speeches, letters, and pamphlets. And the French Government proceeded promptly to prosecute the " inciters to sedition." Claus Zorn von Bulach was condemned (November 13, 1927) to thirteen months in prison and a fine of 500 francs for having threatened to kill the French Prefect of Strasbourg. By the end of 1927 eighteen autonomists were arrested and put in prison awaiting trial for sedition, and by the end of April 1928 this number was increased to twenty-nine. Among the imprisoned were Dr. Ricklin, the proprietor of *Die Zukunft* and the leader of the " Autonomist Party "; Professor Rossé, president of the Federation of Functionaries; Schall, an editor of *Die Zukunft;* Baumann and Kohler, editors of *Die Wahrheit;* Dr. Roos, former secretary of the Heimatbund; Karl Heil, the Strasbourg correspondent of the German daily *Frankfurter Zeitung;* and Abbé Fashauer, an influential member of the Heimatbund.[58]

The drastic action of the French Government had a profound effect on Alsace-Lorraine, as was evidenced by the general elections of April 1928.[59] Although, in these elections, the votes of the autonomists were divided among rival candidates of the Autonomist, Progressive, and Communist Parties and the regionalist wings of the " U. P. R." and the Democratic Party, enough suffrages were concentrated to elect a large majority of avowed regionalist deputies to the French Chamber. In the three départements of Alsace-Lorraine, only six or seven of the twenty-five deputies now squarely opposed the regionalist movement. In the département of Haut-Rhin, two extreme autonomists who were awaiting trial on a charge of sedition, M. Rossé and Dr. Ricklin, were elected by large majorities; and in the same département M. Brogly, one of the outstanding leaders of the regionalist wing of the " U. P. R.," was easily elected. In the département of Bas-Rhin, M. Camille Dahlet, who had just suc-

[58] Certain outstanding " autonomists " were not arested, such as Abbé Haegy, Senator Abbé Müller, and George Wolf.

[59] A forecast of the general elections was furnished by a minor local election in the town of Hagenau. The French Government had dissolved the town's Council on account of its autonomist proclivities. In the election for a new Council, every seat was won by a fusion of Catholics and Autonomists. See *Der Elsässer,* February 27 and March 5, 1928.

ceeded George Wolf as leader of the Progressive Party, was elected as a " Regionalist "; one of the two Socialists was supplanted by a Communist; and MM. Seltz and Walter, members of the " U. P. R." and outspoken advocates of " home-rights," were elected. In Lorraine (the département of Moselle), two Communists, MM. Béron and Doelbe, were elected and also two regionalist members of more moderate groups, MM. Schumann and Labach. It was generally admitted that the cause of autonomy had scored a signal success in Alsace-Lorraine by the general elections of 1928.

No sooner were the elections over than Alsace-Lorraine was stirred anew by the trial of the imprisoned autonomists. The trial was held at Colmar and lasted four weeks. It was a bitter legal conflict between national and local loyalties, and the most conspicuous regionalists — Abbé Haegy, Abbé Müller, MM. Brogly, Walter, and a score of others — not only gave testimony in defense of the accused but also utilized the occasion to expound their grievances against the nationalist French régime. Ten of the defendants were acquitted, but Dr. Ricklin, Professor Rossé, Abbé Fashauer, and M. Schall were found guilty, on May 24, 1928, of " acting with intent to destroy or change the Government and to incite the citizens and inhabitants to take arms against the authorities," and were sentenced to one year's imprisonment, five years' prohibition on travel in certain parts of the country (interdiction de séjour) and costs.

Another group of autonomists were charged with espionage and were condemned at Strasbourg on June 7 to eight months' imprisonment, five years' interdiction de séjour, and a fine of 300 francs.[60] These, however, were later acquitted on appeal. Still another group, who had fled from France, were tried in absentia and sentenced on June 12 to twenty years' imprisonment.[61]

[60] This group included MM. Kohler and Baumann, former editors of Die Wahrheit. René César Ley, who was one of the accused, but who had escaped arrest, was sentenced to five years' imprisonment, ten years' " interdiction de séjour," and a fine of 5,000 francs.

[61] This group included Dr. Roos, Abbé Schmidlin, MM. Ernst, Pinck, Zadock, and the Protestant Pastor Hirtzel. Dr. Roos has since returned to France to serve his sentence as a " martyr."

These verdicts elicited much criticism. The newspapers of Abbé Haegy protested against them with vigor and vehemence. Popular demonstrations in Colmar in favor of the regionally-minded Deputies Dahlet and Brogly were indications of the excitement throughout the provinces. And politicians besought the authorities at Paris to quiet the storm by according grace to the condemned. To the Ministry of M. Poincaré it seemed timely to display a more conciliatory spirit. President Doumergue formally pardoned Claus Zorn von Bulach at the end of June, Professor Rossé, Abbé Fashauer, and M. Schall on July 12, and Dr. Ricklin on July 23. Despite the fact that they were accordingly released from prison, Dr. Ricklin and Professor Rossé were not allowed to take the seats in the French Chamber to which they had been elected in April.

Upon the release of the prisoners, a mammoth mass meeting was held at Colmar under the joint auspices of the Autonomist, Progressive, and Communist Parties and the Republican Popular Union, and addresses were made by such autonomists as Dr. Ricklin and MM. Brogly, Walter, Dahlet, Schall, and Rossé. Similar meetings were held at Hagenau on July 28 and at Strasbourg on July 31. And the autonomists redoubled their journalistic propaganda. Camille Dahlet founded a new organ for the Progressives, the weekly *Freie Zeitung*. Paul Schall established a new organ for the Autonomist Party, *Die Volkswille*. Baumann, once the chief assistant of Zorn von Bulach, made preparations for the publication of a weekly, *Die Zeit*. Abbé Haegy's papers took a firmer and more open stand for autonomy. The home-rulers in the Republican Popular Union (the " U. P. R.") became much more active and precipitated the secession of the French nationalist wing from the Party.

The local elections to the General Councils of the départements in October 1928 showed a strengthening of regionalist sentiment in Alsace-Lorraine, even since the general elections of April. The results are set forth in the table on the opposite page:

TABLE XII

RESULTS OF THE LOCAL ELECTIONS OF OCTOBER 1928

PARTIES	BAS-RHIN	HAUT-RHIN	LORRAINE	TOTAL
OF REGIONALIST TENDENCIES				
U. P. R. (Regionalist wing).........	6	5		11
U. R. L. (Regionalist wing).........			8	8
Autonomists (*Landespartei*).........	2			2
Independent Autonomists..........	2	3		5
Progressives......................	2			2
Communists......................	1			1
Democrats.......................	1	2		3
Christian Socialists			2	2
Total.......................	14	10	10	34
OF NATIONALIST TENDENCIES				
U. P. R. (Nationalist wing)	3	3		6
U. R. L. (Nationalist wing)........			9	9
Socialists.......................		1		1
Independent Nationalists..........	1			1
Total.......................	4	4	9	17

7

It may be appropriate to our present study to point out that there are three societies in Germany which are active in keeping alive the idea of a German Alsace-Lorraine. In Frankfurt-am-Main there is the " Wissenschaftliches Institut der Elsass-Lothringen im Reich " whose purpose it is to inform Germans and the *émigrés* from Alsace-Lorraine about the two lost provinces. The Institute publishes books, arranges lectures, holds conventions, and maintains a library. It has some 2,856 members. Its propaganda, directed by Professor Dr. Wolfram, is of an intellectual character.[62]

In Berlin the " Verein der Alt-Elsass-Lothringer " carries on a more popular propaganda and one which is impregnated with irredentist ideas. It is directed by Dr. Robert Ernst, with the assistance of Dr. Schwander, a former mayor of Strasbourg. By means of a monthly review, *Elsass-Lothringen Heimatstimmen*,

[62] *Elsass-Lothringisches Jahrbuch* (Berlin, Walter de Gruyter, 1926), Vol. V, pp. 255–262.

it informs the German public about current events in Alsace-Lorraine and particularly about developments which it deems favorable to the German cause.

The third society is " Der Hilfsbund für die Elsass-Lothringen im Reich," with headquarters in Berlin, whose main purpose is to aid the *émigrés* who fled to Germany upon the occupation of Alsace-Lorraine by the French and whose property was confiscated. It is directed by Irwin Gadowski and has about two hundred local branches and 20,000 members. Its official weekly organ, *Elsass-Lothringische Mitteilungen,* is very anti-French and cherishes the hope that Alsace-Lorraine will retain its " German culture " until such time as it becomes again an integral part of Germany.

Just what may be the direct or indirect influence of German propaganda in Alsace-Lorraine, it is impossible to say. Some Frenchmen assert that German propaganda is responsible for all the unrest and *malaise* in the recovered provinces. On the other hand, many Alsatians claim that German propaganda has had nothing to do with the situation. At least it can be said that not a single leader of the most radical autonomist groups — not even von Bulach or Ricklin — has been willing to admit openly that he or his following favors the reincorporation of Alsace-Lorraine with Germany, and it can be wondered at that they exercise such continuous and universal restraint if they are in German pay and have an eye single to Germany.

Whatever may be the secret relations, if any, between ardent German nationalists and a few Alsatian autonomists, there can be no doubt that the attempts of French patriots to make all the inhabitants of the recovered provinces conform to the common standard of French nationalism in language, law, administration, education, and culture, have encountered growing opposition from natives whose ultimate loyalty to France cannot, or should not, be questioned but whose immediate patriotism is local and regional. It seems probable that the French language will be increasingly used in Alsace-Lorraine and that there will be slow but sure progress in the " making " or " remaking " of Frenchmen in the provinces. But it seems probable also that German will not and cannot be obliterated and that so long as the Alsatians are bilingual they will be peculiarly subject to cultural influences from Germany as well as from France. In these circumstances they must remain a little different in their national psychology from Frenchmen in other parts of France.

CHAPTER XI

THE PROPAGATION OF REGIONALISM IN FRANCE

I

THE making of patriotic Frenchmen proceeds apace throughout the territorial extent of France. Education in school, in army and navy, and in church, and activity of the press, of patriotic societies, and of the State itself, tend more and more to diffuse and deepen French national patriotism. It is now certainly a conviction in the minds of the vast majority of the inhabitants of the country that they owe supreme loyalty to the French nation. They are proud of being French.

Lest this central fact be misunderstood or misinterpreted, it is necessary to amplify and stress what has been remarked or hinted at here and there in preceding chapters, that contemporary French nationalism is qualified and tempered by popular propaganda of different, if not conflicting, character. The mass of Frenchmen, in other words, are supremely loyal to France, but the propaganda which makes them so is paralleled by propaganda which teaches them to be loyal to something else — to a locality or region or particularistic tradition, or to " humanity " at large and the cause of internationalism. It thus transpires that most Frenchmen, who are imbued with a common love of the fatherland and a common willingness even to lay down their lives in defense of it, are actuated at the same time, in greater or less degree, by an intricate variety of dissident loyalties, and that throughout France a sort of uniformity in ultimate deed is attended by striking discrepancies in everyday thought and behavior.

The unceasing inculcation of national French patriotism does not make Frenchmen exactly alike. Perhaps it would if there were no influential counter-teachings in France. That there are such teachings, it is the purpose of the present and the succeeding chapter to set forth.

So long as Frenchmen differ among themselves economically and socially, there will be divergent patriotic precepts and different interpretations of common patriotic precepts. Even if the banker, the farmer, the manufacturer, the lawyer, and the trade-unionist are imbued with the same theoretical patriotism, they will be inclined to apply their patriotism in different ways as their several economic and social interests or their particular class-consciousness may dictate. The banker or the manufacturer is likely to believe that the true greatness of his country can best be served by national action which the trade-unionist or the farmer may feel to be terribly injurious to the true welfare of the people and therefore essentially unpatriotic. And, *vice versa*, the farmer or the trade-unionist may advocate a public policy against which the manufacturer and the banker may advance patriotic arguments. Nor is there any necessary alliance of trade-unionist and farmer. Each will tend to view the economic interests of himself and his class as national interests, and the resulting clash of interests strengthens a class-consciousness which is bound to qualify and mitigate extreme national patriotism.

Frenchmen also differ among themselves, and differ profoundly, in intelligence and degree of education and refinement. The patriotism of the product of the Sorbonne has a somewhat different content and influence from the patriotism of the product of the ordinary primary school. The patriotism of a M. Raymond Poincaré, of a M. Ernest Lavisse, or of a M. René Bazin, differs in kind as well as in degree from the patriotism of Jacques Bonhomme, though there are a multitude of Jacques Bonhommes with varying orders of intelligence and with corresponding varieties of patriotic understanding. Highly intelligent Frenchmen — acutely critical Frenchmen (and these may be recruited from the relatively uneducated as well as from university graduates) — are especially prone to differ among themselves in their interpretations of patriotism and patriotic obligations: they supply leaders for such widely disparate movements as Action Française,

International Socialism, Provençal Regionalism, Roman Catholicism, Freemasonry, Radicalism, and Conservatism.

Then, too, there are the traditional differences among Frenchmen in respect of religion. There are Catholic Frenchmen, Protestant Frenchmen, Jewish Frenchmen, " anti-clerical " Frenchmen, irreligious and anti-religious Frenchmen. All are patriotic, after a fashion; and, as we have seen, the various churches, temples, and synagogues, and likewise the Masonic lodges, play an important part in propagating national patriotism among their adherents. Yet the national patriotism which these organizations propagate is conditioned by traditions and teachings peculiar to each. Catholic priest, Protestant pastor, Jewish rabbi, and master of Masonic lodge do not hold up for popular emulation the same national heroes, nor do they put the same interpretation upon French history or picture the same future for the French nation. Indeed, religious difference is the basic explanation of the existence, side by side, of the two most important rival patriotisms in France, that of " anti-clerical Jacobinism " and that of " clerical Traditionalism," whose chronic conflicts extend into the fields of education and politics.

Of the foregoing differences among Frenchmen — religious, intellectual, and economic — enough has been said, perhaps, in earlier chapters to make clear the fact that French national patriotism, though it may inspire at critical times a common emotion throughout the nation, does not and cannot normally produce like-minded citizens or unanimously agreeable state action. Short of vague nationalist sentiments which all entertain but which each expresses in his own way, and short of concerted military endeavor, for which, however, varied and even conflicting reasons are assigned, Frenchmen are almost as concerned with their numerous differences as with their common nationality. There is real bitterness between " clericals " and " anti-clericals," between Republicans and Royalists, between communists and capitalists; such groups flood the country with partisan propaganda, which may embody patriotic appeals but which actually prevents the perfect fruition of single-hearted, single-minded national propaganda. Only in the face of foreign developments which appear dangerous to most of the partisan groups within France, do they subordinate their own particularistic propaganda to a common national purpose and adhere to a " sacred " patriotic union, and then only temporarily and partially.

Among inhabitants of France there is still another difference which for our present purpose has peculiar significance. This difference is often referred to broadly as " regionalism," meaning the local contrasts in popular tradition and usage among the several major " provinces " or " regions " such as Provence, Gascony, Brittany, Normandy, Artois, Corsica, Alsace-Lorraine, which came under the sway of the French State at different times and in different historical circumstances. For, though the French State since the Great Revolution at the end of the eighteenth century has labored steadily and ever more effectually, with the backing of numerous patriots, especially Jacobins, Radicals, and Socialists, to destroy the autonomy and to blot out even the names of the old provinces, a considerable measure of sentimental regional loyalty still survives, and latterly some patriots, notably Conservatives and Royalists, have sought to stimulate it and to reclothe it in political habiliments.

The contemporary " regionalist " movement in France is supported, nominally at least, by the ultra-patriotic Action Française, as a part of their program to restore the old Bourbon monarchy and the traditional institutions of the " old régime," but it receives perhaps more solid and convincing support from a minority of patriotic Republicans who react against the centralizing tendencies of the French Government and maintain that the French State would gain efficiency and arouse greater popular interest and loyalty if it were somewhat decentralized, if, for example, the present small administrative départements were merged in reëstablished larger provinces and these were accorded a liberal amount of local self-government. On the other hand, the advocates of centralization point out that regional self-government would tend to exalt local differences and local pride at the expense of national solidarity and national loyalty.

The problem of regionalism is not simply political. It is cultural, too. Certain " regions " of France embrace populations that still speak a non-French language. Provençal and Basque are spoken in the south; an Italian dialect, in Corsica; Celtic Breton, in the west; Flemish, in the north; and German, in Alsace-Lorraine. In all these places, French is the sole language of instruction in the public schools, and the people know French as well as the local " dialect " or language. The great literature of the whole country, moreover, is in French. And French is the national language of government, business, and trade. But of late there has been a good deal of agitation on the part of a few scholars, littérateurs, and publicists among Provençal Frenchmen, among Corsican Frenchmen, among Breton Frenchmen, and among Flemish Frenchmen, to revivify and extend the use of their respective local languages, to create or revive important literatures in them, and to teach them in the schools. The agitation seems to be increasing, though its direct results are not very obvious and must not be exaggerated. Indirectly, however, it undoubtedly represents the development in France of what may be termed " sub-nationalities," each with " sub-nationalist " leaders and with a program of " sub-nationalism." Together, these " sub-nationalisms " tend to modify and mitigate any single French nationalism.

The contemporary situation in Alsace-Lorraine has already been described in considerable detail in the preceding chapter. It has there been pointed out that most of the Alsatians and Lorrainers have a divided allegiance: on the one hand, they are undoubtedly loyal to France and anxious to be thought of as patriotic Frenchmen; on the other hand, they are certainly loyal to their locality, their " region," and desirous of preserving its distinctive language, institutions, and traditions. In this sense, they constitute a " sub-nationality " of the French State. They are " French," but they are also " German French." That is to say, they use the German, as well as the French, language, and, unlike other French patriots, they regard the preservation of the German language among themselves as the best and surest guarantee of the preservation of their distinctive regional life and culture. They are willing to learn French, but they are unwilling to forget German. And efforts of French nationalists completely to Gallicize the recovered provinces have been attended by the rise of an extremist agitation among Alsatian nationalists (or " sub-nationalists ") in behalf of regional autonomy if not political separation. The mass of Alsatians and Lorrainers are not separatists, or even political autonomists, but they are culturally distinct from other Frenchmen, and this fact gives them a peculiar outlook upon the policies and problems of the French nation. It conditions and qualifies French nationalism directly in Alsace-Lorraine and indirectly throughout France.

Outside of Alsace-Lorraine and the German-speaking population of those provinces, there are several regions of France with French citizens who familiarly employ languages other than French. Of the number of such citizens, no official statistics exist, but a distinguished philologist has estimated that in 1881:

140,000 Frenchmen spoke	Basque;
208,855 " "	Catalan (Provençal);
272,639 " "	Corsican;
1,340,000 " "	Breton;
176,860 " "	Flemish.[1]

Each of these linguistic groups, like the German-speaking group in Alsace-Lorraine, has some measure of internal coherence and cohesion, something which distinguishes its patriotism from that of other Frenchmen. In each the " regionalist " movement has assumed a cultural, as well as a political, complexion, and among all has developed a considerable degree of coöperation. As early as the middle of the nineteenth century, Pierre Joseph Proudhon, the philosophical anarchist, pointed out that all the minority linguistic groups in France should coöperate in order to curb the " tyranny " and " militarism " of state centralization.[2] The Paris Commune of 1871 played perilously with the idea of federal regionalism. And about the beginning of the present century the " French Regionalist Federation " was founded for the pur-

---

[1] Gustav Groeber, *Grundiss der romanischen Philologie* (Strasbourg, Trübner, 1902), Vol. II, p. 570. A linguistic map of France is appended to this volume of Groeber's.

[2] *Du Principe fédératif. Cf.* Nicholas Bourgeois, *Proudhon, le Fédéralisme et la Paix* (Paris, Rivière, 1926).

pose of propagating the advantages of decentralization. For more than twenty-five years, under the auspices of this organization, a handful of men, led by a publicist, Charles-Brun, and including several senators and deputies, have conducted propaganda in favor of administrative decentralization, the coördination of economic regional interests, and the development of distinctive local cultures; they have published a small monthly paper, *L'Action Régionaliste,* have distributed many pamphlets, and have held annual congresses. At a congress in February 1926, the Federation adopted a resolution that " in all educational institutions teachers and professors should use local dialects (languages) in teaching French to children." [3]

The French Regionalist Federation is but one, though the most general and the most active, of the organizations devoted to the twofold task of effecting some decentralization in France and of fostering local languages and traditions in the country. Another and peculiarly interesting organization is the Confederation of Minorities in France, which was founded in September 1927, and which unites the most radical elements of the Breton, Corsican, and Alsatian movements. But, apart from any general or central organization, the leaders of the several " sub-national " movements maintain a fairly close touch with one another; and any public demonstration in behalf of a particular regional movement is likely to be attended by representatives of other similar movements who come either to learn or to inspire. Primarily, however, each " sub-national " movement, each variety of " regionalist " agitation, is local in character and distinct in organization and goal, and we must devote some attention to each in turn.

2

A particularly interesting regionalist movement is the Provençal in southern France. Provençal is a Romanic language which developed originally along the Mediterranean regions of southeastern Gaul and eastern Iberia at about the same time as French was developing in northern Gaul and Castilian in central Iberia, and

---

[3] *Cf. L'Action Régionaliste* for February 1926.

which gave birth to a rich and beautiful medieval literature — the literature of the troubadours of the county of Provence, and the kingdom of Aragon. The language was called Catalan in Aragon; in Gaul it was called *langue d'oc* to distinguish it from the *langue d'oïl* (or French) of the north. In time, the kingdom of Aragon was incorporated with the kingdom of Castile to form the modern Spanish monarchy, and Catalan was treated as a dialect of literary Castilian Spanish. In time, too, Provence and all southern Gaul were conquered by the French kings and became integral parts of France, and French (the *langue d'oïl*) supplanted Provençal (the *langue d'oc*) as the language of trade and culture. In 1539 by the Edict of Villers-Cotterets King Francis I forbade the use of Provençal in the transaction of any governmental business.[4]

Intellectual developments of the eighteenth century awakened among some Frenchmen an interest in the literature of the troubadours and consequently in the language in which their works had been written. Philological research into the old Provençal language was undertaken by François Raynouard, who prepared a grammar and edited a number of the works of the troubadours, and compiled a dictionary, which was published after his death. Then, in the first half of the nineteenth century, the rise of Romanticism served to turn the attention of several distinguished French writers to the local medieval history of southern France. Both Augustin Thierry and François Guizot revived the theory of Boulainvilliers and of the Abbés Mably and Du Bos that there had been two different races, with distinct cultures, in France — the conquering Franks of the north and the conquered Gallo-Romans of the south; both romantic historians agreed that the Albigensian Crusade of the thirteenth century had crushed a civilization which otherwise would have been a great glory to modern France.[5] Jules Michelet, the most popular of the romantic national historians of France, evinced much interest in the history

---

[4] See A. Brun, *Essai historique sur l'Introduction du Français dans les Provinces du Midi* (Paris, Champion, 1924).

[5] See Émile Ripert, *La Renaissance provençale* (Paris, Champion, 1918), and *Le Félibrige* (Paris, Armand Colin, 1924).

of the several provinces, particularly Provence, and complained repeatedly of the undue centralization of the country.[6]

It was not long before such ideas took root in Provence. During the decade of the 1840's, a native, M. Mary-Lafon, popularized them, not in the measured phrases of a *savant* but with the vehemence of a regionalist patriot.[7] At about the same time Jacques Jasmin, a Gascon, essayed the rôle of a modern troubadour and went about through southern France reciting his Provençal verses; and in Provence, Joseph Roumanille attempted to organize societies for the promotion of a cultural and patriotic renaissance.

Roumanille, with the aid of Frédéric Mistral, who was to become the literary leader of the movement, and with five other young Provençal writers, constituted in 1854 an association — " Le Félibrige " — for the avowed general object of preserving to Provence forever " her language, local color, liberty of expression, love of country, and high order of intelligence." The immediate aims of the " Félibres " were to purify and restore Provençal as a literary language by formulating grammatical rules for it, by standardizing its orthography, and by enlarging its vocabulary; then, once the language was fixed, they would seek to secure its general use in southern France for literature, public instruction, and government. The young Félibres went about their self-appointed task with ardor. In 1855 they began the publication of a Provençal almanac, *L'Armana Provençau,* which still appears. In 1876 they enlarged and reformed their organization; a central committee of fifty members was created under a chief director, called " *capoulié* "; the territory of the *langue d'oc* was divided into districts according to dialects, and provision was made for local committees in each; the day after Pentecost was annually to be observed as the Provençal " national " holiday; there was to be a " national " anthem — *La Coupo* (" The Cup "); and every seventh year " national " re-

[6] Similar views were expressed by Claude Fauriel in his *Histoire de la Gaule méridionale sous la Domination des Conquérants germains* (1836).

[7] See his *Histoire politique, réligieuse, et littéraire du Midi de la France* (1841), and his *Tableau historique et littéraire de la Langue parlée dans le Midi de la France* (1842).

unions and fêtes were to be celebrated — the " Grands Jeux Floraux " (" great floral games ").

The outstanding figure in the Provençal movement, as everybody knows, was Frédéric Mistral (1830–1914). As a young law-student, he fell under the influence of Roumanille and decided to devote his life to his native province of Provence, vowing to " increase the love for its race, to help resurrect its old language, and to give prestige to this language by writing poetry in it." His first important work, *Mireio* (*Mireille*), a romantic tale of rural life in Provence, won for him a prize from the French Academy and supplied the theme for an opera by Gounod. Mistral's next important work, *Calendau*, was even more locally patriotic; the story of a beautiful maiden who is to be married against her will to a wealthy nobleman and who is rescued from such a calamity by the youthful Provençal lover (Calendau) is obviously symbolical: the maiden is Provence; the nobleman is France; and Calendau is Mistral himself, or perhaps the Provençal movement. Other patriotic works flowed from Mistral's pen, including *La Countesso* and *La Rèino Jano;* and, in addition, he published in 1886, after twenty years' labor, a Provençal dictionary, *Le Trésor du Félibrige.* Money which he received from the Nobel Prize he used as an endowment for a Provençal museum at Arles (" Museon Arlaten ").

Before Mistral's death in 1914, the Félibrige society was firmly established and was issuing several propagandist periodicals — *Cartabèu de Santo-Estello* (an official annual), *Armana Provençau* (the almanac), and *Lou Félibrige* (a journal, directed by Marius Jouveau and published at Avignon). Mistral, moreover, inspired a notable group of poets, such as Félix Gras (1844–1901), the leader of the second generation of Félibres; Marius Girard; Marius André; and Valère Bernard, the outstanding exponent of the movement in Marseilles. Some of these disciples were more ardent and more politically minded than the master; as early as 1892 a group of them published a manifesto, demanding for Provence a large measure of both cultural and political autonomy and for France as a whole the substitution of federalism for centralization. This proved to be the beginning of a more radical Provençal autonomist movement, which is directed at the present time chiefly by the " Federalist Youth " (" Jeunesse Fédéraliste ").[8]

Provence is the centre of " nationalist " agitation in behalf of the *langue d'oc,* but other districts of southern France have been affected and have contributed something to the resuscitation of allied local dialects and to the demand for local autonomy and federalism. The district around Toulouse supplied Auguste Fourès (1848–1891), who, moved by a study of the medieval Albigensians, stimulated local interest in the *langue d'oc.* At Toulouse, also, the " Académie des Jeux Floraux," which had been created in the fourteenth century to combat the spread of French (*langue d'oïl*) in the south but which in the seventeenth century had been transformed into a propagandist agency of French language and centralizing government, reverted at the end of the nineteenth century to its original purpose and established prizes for works written in Provençal.[9]   In Gascony, Jasmin, one of the inspirers of Mistral, has had a number of disciples, of whom Isidore Salles (1821–1900) is perhaps the best known.   In Périgord, Camille Chabaneau, a professor, and Auguste Chastanet, a publicist, founded a society, " Lou Bournat " (" The Hive "), which fosters Provençal literature.   In the district of Limousin, the Abbé Joseph Roux has published a grammar, a dictionary, and a provincial epic — *La Chanson Lemouzina.* In recent years, echoes of Provençal regionalism have been heard on the Côte d'Azur, in Auvergne, Dauphiné, and in the Pyrenees; since the World War, an " Académie Méditerranéenne " has been founded at Nice.   To-day in every province of southern France some littérateur or publicist, usually a member of the lower bourgeoisie, is busily proclaiming the praises of his local language and his *petite patrie.*

[8] Headquarters: Pavillion Cézanne, Avenue Paul Cézanne, Aix-en-Provence. President: Marcel Provence.   Organ: *Le Feu,* published at Aix-en-Provence by Joseph d'Arband.

[9] Toulouse is likewise the seat of the " Institute of Southern Studies " (" Institut des Études Méridionales "), and of two significant publications — the *Almanach Occitan,* and the *Oc,* an organ of a society for the political federation of the south.

3

In western France — in the old province of Brittany — flourishes another regionalist movement, the Breton movement. Brittany includes, roughly, the present départements of Finistère, Morbihan, Côtes-du-Nord, Ille-et-Vilaine, and Lower Loire, and a population (1921) of 3,074,650. Once upon a time the whole population of this area spoke the Breton language, a Celtic language similar to Welsh and related to the Gaelic of Ireland and Scotland, but with the lapse of time and the incorporation of Brittany with the French State, the French language and French culture made gradual steady inroads, so that nowadays French is used almost exclusively in eastern Brittany and by the middle and upper classes in the whole province, while the use of Breton is confined to the lower classes in the western half of the province (that is, in the départements of Finistère and Morbihan and in the western part of Côtes-du-Nord).

Assimilation of Brittany to France went on unimpeded until the nineteenth century, when Romanticism served to create a Breton literary renaissance. Romantic poets appeared: Hersart de la Villemarqué, author of a " national " epic, *Barzaz-Breiz* (1840; twelfth edition in 1913); Brizeux, whose poetry stirred both Bretons and Provençals; and François Marie Luzel, whose most important production was *Bepred Breizad* (1865). Romantic historians likewise appeared: Pitre-Chevalier, author of a " national " history entitled *La Bretagne ancienne et moderne* (1844), maintaining that Brittany had lived in misery since her union with France; and Arthur de la Borderie, who wrote a *Histoire de Bretagne* and taught that

> Brittany is more than a province; it is a people, a real nation, an unique society. . . . Brittany, our Brittany, has a language, the sacred language of our ancestors. Brittany has a character, a well marked national character. . . . And Brittany has a history and a distinctive poetry. . . .[10]

[10] *Leçon d'ouverture du cours d'histoire de Bretagne professé à la Faculté des Lettres de Rennes de 1890 à 1893.*

Romanticism also furnished Brittany with a quota of philologists. Le Gonidec, early in the nineteenth century, translated the Bible into Breton, thus more or less fixing the literary usage of the language, compiled a dictionary, and wrote a grammar. A little later, the scientific study of Breton was greatly stimulated by the work of a German, Zeuss, who published his *Grammatica Celtica* in 1853. Subsequently, F. Vallée published a popular grammar, *Breton en 40 Leçons,* and scientific researches into Breton philology were undertaken by Professors Loth of the Collège de France, Ernault of the University of Poitiers, and P. Leroux of the University of Rennes.

The romantic renaissance of Breton affected at first only a few scholars and littérateurs, but gradually its message was conveyed to considerable numbers in Brittany by means of propagandist societies. In 1898 the " Breton Regionalist Union " was founded in order " to awaken Breton sentiment and to develop all forms of Breton activity "; it established literary prizes, undertook linguistic studies, organized theatrical troupes, and held an annual congress. Because the Union in its early days forbade the discussion of religious or political questions, a group of Catholic Bretons seceded from it and formed in 1904 a rival propagandist society, " Bleun Brug," with an official organ, *Feiz ha Breiz* (*Faith and Brittany*). Another schism in the Breton Regionalist Union led to the establishment in 1911 of a third society, the " Regionalist Federation of Brittany." In the meantime, a " Gorsedd " of Breton bards had been organized after the Welsh model. Just prior to the World War, moreover, a short-lived Breton Nationalist Party was founded by a few fanatics to work for " home rule " and eventual political independence.

Under the widening influence of patriotic societies, common people in Brittany began to take an interest in things Breton. A Breton national holiday was observed, the twenty-ninth of September, anniversary of the coronation of a Breton king in 845 and of a Breton victory over a French army in 1364. A Breton national flag was unfurled, reminiscent of the American flag. A Breton national anthem was composed and sung — *Bro*

Goz Ma Zadou (*Old Country of My Fathers*) [11] The number of Breton theatrical troupes increased from one in 1898 to 42 in 1907. Even a Pan-Celtic movement emerged: the Romanticist Breton Villemarqué had attended the first Pan-Celtic Congress in 1838 in Wales; a second congress had been held in Brittany in 1867; and Bretons participated in the more frequent and larger later congresses of 1899, 1901, 1904, 1907, and 1911.

The Great War interrupted Breton propaganda. Brittany unquestionably proved her absolute loyalty to France by supplying her full quota of troops to the French army and by suffering the slaughter of a quarter of a million of her sons in the sanguinary conflict with Germany. So soon as the Armistice was signed, however, the Marquis de l'Estourbeillon, President of the Breton Regionalist Union, prepared a letter with a large number of signatures for transmission to the Peace Congress, demanding that the rights of small nations and of national minorities be solemnly guaranteed by treaty. " It is necessary," the letter said, " that every people be accorded the right to remain itself, no matter what its location may be, whether inside or outside large states. The impending treaty of world peace must squarely affirm and proclaim . . . the indefeasible right of each nation freely to speak and teach its language and to have its traditions and beliefs respected, in order to assure for the future its free and legitimate development and the survival of its ideal." [12]

Since the war, Breton patriotic societies have intensified their propaganda. The " Bleun Brag " is perhaps the strongest of these societies: it continues to publish an organ, *Feiz ha Breiz,* to hold annual congresses, and to enlist the support of many of the leading Catholics of Brittany. The Regionalist Federation of Brittany and the Breton Regionalist Union are also still active. The latter now represents the conservative wing of the regionalist movement in Brittany: it preaches devotion to Breton traditions and language, but always in subordination to supreme devotion to

[11] A French translation of the anthem may be found in Camille Le Mercier d'Erm, *Les Hymnes nationaux des Peuples celtiques* (Dinard, À l'Enseigne de l'Hermine, 1920), pp. 63–65.

[12] Marquis de l'Estourbeillon, *Le Droit des Langues et la Liberté des Peuples* (Saint-Brieuc, René Prudhomme, 1919), pp. 9–10.

France. In line with the program of the Union, a special " Defense Committee of Breton Interests " was newly formed in 1920: it now claims the adherence of 124 local societies with a membership of 360,000 Bretons.[13]

Another new patriotic society, far more radical than the " Defense Committee," has arisen in Brittany since the war. It is the " Breton Youth Union," now rechristened the " Breton Autonomist Party." It is a young people's organization, not very important numerically, but zealous and energetic. In addition to the usual pleas for the Breton language and for Breton culture, it demands a large measure of political autonomy for Brittany, and a few of its members have gone so far as to talk rather wildly about the future separation of the province from France. The " Youth Union " publishes a popular weekly (*Breiz Atao*), a literary quarterly (*Givalarn*), and a cheap propagandist sheet (*War Zao*). It urges closer relations with other " Celtic nations " and has contributed to the success of post-war Pan-Celtic congresses, notably that at Quimper in Brittany in 1924.[14]

4

Regionalism likewise exists in Corsica. This Mediterranean island was long associated with the Italian city-state of Genoa, and despite the fact that it has been a part of France for a hundred and sixty years, most of its common people still speak an Italian dialect. To be sure, the middle and upper classes, and the urban population generally, know French, but the knowledge of " Corsican " is widespread.

[13] Headquarters: 17 rue de Châteaudun, Rennes.

[14] See *Les Celtes à Quimper* (Aedon, Bouteloup, 1924). It should also be remarked that the literature of the Breton movement has increased greatly since the war. A press at Dinard (L'Hermine) turns out a good many books on the subject. Among its more recent publications are: C. Danio, *Histoire de notre Bretagne;* Meven Mordien, *Notennou divar-benn ar Gelted koz* (Notes on Celtic History and Civilization); Camille Le Mercier d'Erm, *Les Bardes et Poètes nationaux de la Bretagne Armoricaine, Hymnes nationaux des Peuples celtiques, Les Origines du Nationalisme breton, Le Nationalisme breton et l'Action française;* F. Vallée, *La Langue bretonne en 40 Leçons.*

Inspired by the ubiquitous romantic tendency to cherish local traditions and to transform local dialects into literary languages, and influenced particularly by the efforts of Mistral and his fellow Provençals, a few Corsicans began, at the close of the nineteenth century, to study their local language and to write poems and stories in it. Since the World War the number of Corsican regionalists has considerably increased and their labors have multiplied.

At first the Corsican movement centered in a literary review, *A Tramuntana,* directed by Santu Casanova, who has continued to be the outstanding Corsican leader. Now, however, there are two other reviews: *U Fucone,* the quarterly organ of a literary society, " Salvator Viale," at Bastia; and *L'Annu Corsu,* which prints literary notes and an annual anthology of the writings of Corsican littérateurs. There is now a good deal of other literary activity. Anthologies of Corsican legends have appeared.[15] Corsican folk-songs have been collected and published.[16] A Corsican grammar has been made available.[17] A Corsican " national " history has been written.[18]

Recently the Corsican movement has assumed some political significance. Discontented with the highly centralized French administration and asserting that Corsica had not received an equitable share of national appropriations for local improvements, a group of Corsicans founded the " Corsican Party of Action " (" Partitu Corsu d'Azione ") which has now taken the new name of " Autonomist Corsican Party " (" Partitu Corsu Autonomista "); it demands provincial autonomy.[19] Another and more moderate home-rule group was organized in 1926 by Carula Giovoni, the director of a quarterly politico-literary review at Marseilles, *U Lariciu.* Neither political group has had any noteworthy electoral success.

[15] For example, Jean-Marc Salvadori, *L'Âme corse* (Venaco, 1927).

[16] J. B. Marcaggi, *Chants de la Mort et de la Vendetta* (Ajaccio, Rombaldi, 1927).

[17] A. Bonifacio, *A Prima Grammatichella corsa* (Nice, 2 rue du Lycée, 1927).

[18] J. P. Lucciardi, *Manualettu di Storia di a Corsica* (Bastia, Cordier, 1927).

[19] For the platform of this group, see Mattei-Torre, *Que Veut la Corse* (Ajaccio, A. Muvra, 1927).

Corsican regionalism has ramifications outside of Corsica, especially at Paris and in Italy. Many Corsicans have emigrated to Paris, as laborers or as students, and some of these have sought to stimulate among their compatriots a greater knowledge of, and affection for, Corsica. Notable among such is a brilliant young publicist, Pierre Dominique, who edits at Paris a review entitled *Revue de la Corse*. Many Italians, too, have a sentimental regard for Corsica, and some of them openly assert that the island is truly Italian and must in time be " restored " to the Italian national state. A review, *Archivio Storico di Corsica*, is published in Italy, devoted to Corsican affairs and containing occasionally an article of imperialist or irredentist complexion. On the whole, however, there has been little pro-Italian sentiment in Corsica. What the Corsican leaders have demanded is freedom to use and develop their local language and a moderate amount of provincial home-rule within the French State. Their " little fatherland " is Corsica; their " great fatherland " is France.

5

Then, too, there is a similar regionalist movement among the Flemings in the extreme north of France. French Flanders comprises the arrondissements of Dunkirk, Hazebrouck, and Lille. Although Dutch, or a Dutch dialect known as Flemish, was at one time spoken by people as far south as Douai, French has universally usurped the place of Flemish south of a line drawn from Dunkirk, south of Hazebrouck, to a point on the Belgian frontier north of Armentières. North of this line, Flemish has survived as the spoken language of the lower classes, but it was not until the nineteenth century that voices were raised in praise of it.

In 1853 the " Flemish Committee of France " was organized to champion " the mother-tongue and the fatherland "; and subsequently the quickening Flemish nationalism in Belgium and the Pan-Netherlandish agitation in Holland produced some repercussions in French Flanders.[20]

[20] See the forthcoming volume by S. B. Clough, *History of the Flemish Movement in Belgium*, and also Jan Van de Woestijne, " De Dageraed eener

Since the World War, regionalism has borne considerable fruit in French Flanders. The old Flemish Committee of France has been reorganized under the leadership of Canon Looten of the Catholic Institute of Lille, and has inspired the creation of a new association of Catholic young men, the " Flemish Union of France," which awards prizes for works in Flemish literature, conducts courses in the Flemish language, and holds annual congresses. The Catholic Institute of Lille has inaugurated special courses in Flemish (Netherlandish) language and literature. Various groups of French Flemings have established regionalist magazines, such as *Le Mercure de Flandre*, directed by Valentin Bresle at Lille, *Le Beffroi de Flandre*, a monthly at Dunkirk, and *De Vlaamsche Stemme in Vrankryk*. A certain G. Blachon has recently published a book, *Pourquoi j'aime la Flandre*, which is a scathing denunciation of the centralized French administration in Flanders.

6

In the western Pyrenees, straddling the Franco-Spanish frontier, is located a small nationality which speaks the very old and quite distinctive Basque language. The majority of the Basques live on Spanish soil, and their " regionalism " is more significant for Spain than for France. But expressions of the Basque movement, literary, cultural, and mildly political, originating mainly among the Spanish Basques, exert some influence on the French Basques.

The central agency of the Basque movement is the " Sociedad de Estudios Vascos," founded in 1918 and maintaining headquarters in the Palacio de la Diputación de Guipúzcoa at San Sebastián. The society has held biennial congresses since 1918, and supports numerous publications, including a biennial catalogue, an annual of Basque folklore, a quarterly bulletin, and a pretentious *Revue Internationale des Études Basques* (published

Hergeboote," *Ons Volk* (Antwerp, Jan. 23, 1927); A. Hans, " Onze Stamgenoote in Frankrijk," *Gedenkboek van het Algemeen Nederlandsch Verbond* (Amsterdam, Wereldbibliotheek, 1923); W. J. L. Van Es, *Het Fransche Vlaanderen* (Apeldoorn, Dixson, 1918).

in Spanish, French, and Basque at Paris and San Sebastián). The society also maintains a Basque library at its headquarters and seeks to promote among the Basque people an interest in the local culture; recently it has organized a summer-school for special instruction in Basque grammar, history, folklore, and conversation. The president and first vice-president of the society are Spanish citizens, but the second vice- president, Jean Ybarnégaray, is French and a member of the French Chamber of Deputies.

Among other Basque activities, especially in Spain, mention may be made of the popular propaganda of an offshoot of the Society of Basque Studies, the " Federación de Acción Popular Euskerista," which arranges for popular lectures in the towns and for special instruction in the rural districts. Furthermore, an " Academy of the Basque Language " is now (1929) in its ninth year, and so too is a special Basque review (*Gure Herria*). A Basque grammar by Abbé Iturry was published in 1895; and a Spanish review of Basque culture (*Revista de Cultura Vasca*) is now in its seventh year. In France, there is a *Revue Historique et Archéologique du Béarn et du Pays Basque,* published at Pau, under the editorship of S. Annat, and now in its twelfth year.

7

That the regionalism of Basques, Flemings, Corsicans, Bretons, and Provençals, as well as of Alsatians, is becoming at least more vocal and is causing increasing embarrassment to the centralized French Government, may conveniently be illustrated by the extensive discussion of the subject in the French press in 1925. In that year a group of distinguished Provençal leaders [21] addressed a letter to M. Anatole de Monzie, Minister of Public Instruction in the Herriot Cabinet, pointing out that his immediate predecessors had established twenty-seven chairs of

[21] Including Alfred Jeauroy, professor at the Sorbonne and member of the Institute; Charles-Brun; Joseph Auglade, professor at Toulouse; Marius Jouveau, professor at Aix; Jean Bonnafous, of the " League for the ' Langue d'oc ' in the Schools "; Joseph Loubet, of the " Friends of the ' Langue d'oc ' "; Andrieu Frissant, director of the *Provençal de Paris;* and Gandilhou Gens d'Armes, editor of the *Auvergnat de Paris.*

Provençal language and literature in universities and lycées of southern France and had authorized the teaching of Provençal in secondary schools and normal schools, and petitioning him to permit primary-school teachers to utilize local mother-tongues as media for instruction in French.

M. de Monzie took sharp issue with the Provençal petitioners, and he thought the matter of sufficient importance to publish, on August 14, 1925, a formal Ministerial Circular concerning it:

Since the time when Francis I effected in 1539 the monarchy of letters by ordering that all pieces of justice and administration should be written in French, all our Governments have professed a common and constant doctrine of linguistic unification. " As it is of importance to accustom the peoples of ceded provinces to our manners and usages, there is nothing which can contribute more thereto than the assurance that children learn the French language, in order that they may be as familiar with it as with German and that in the course of time the inhabitants of the provinces may even abandon the use of the latter and at any rate have a preference for French." This policy, defined in a letter of Colbert to his brother, March 12, 1666, has always been ours, not only in respect of the Alsatian population, but also in respect of all French subjects in the interior of the country. Indeed, it was a native of Strasbourg, Arbogast, who inspired the text of 5 Brumaire, Year II, where it is stated: " public instruction is directed so that one of its primary benefits will be that the French language shall become in a short time the family language of all parts of the Republic. In all parts of the Republic instruction should be only in the French language. Neither class in Latin, nor school in dialect: unification through public instruction in French." In spite of the vicissitudes which public instruction experienced under the Directory and the Consulate, the essentials of those Revolutionary prescriptions were reaffirmed in the instructions issued by Napoleon to his prefects and bishops. The investigation of dialects which he carried on from 1806 to 1812 redounded to the advantage of the single official language. The same continuity of linguistic policy has been reaffirmed during the years of Republican secularization: M. Fallières, by a circular of October 30, 1890, and M. Waldeck-Rousseau, by a dispatch of January 26, 1901, prohibited the employment of dialects in sermons and in catechism-lessons. On January 16, 1903, by 339 votes against 185 the Chamber of Deputies approved the action of M. Émile Combes, President of the Council and Minister of Worship, in having renewed those prohibitions — and after a prolonged debate in the course of which the Prime Minister had reaffirmed the continuous and traditional doctrine the history of which I have too rapidly sketched.

I attach my instructions to this doctrine. The lay ideal, any more than the Church of the Concordat, would not know how to harmonize rival tongues with the one French language whose jealous cult can never have enough altars. I may observe, furthermore, that there remain too many illiterates among us to allow us to distract, in favor of the most respectable local or regional tongues, any portion of the effort necessary for the propagation of good French. " He alone is truly French in heart and soul, from head to foot, who knows, speaks, and reads the French language." Until this definition of de Musset is applicable to the totality of adult citizens, instruction in the dialects must be deemed a luxury, and I beg you to believe that our era is scarcely favorable to expenditures for luxury at the cost of collectivity.

Finally, I observe that it is not necessary to practice the local language in order to practice all the duties of regionalism. The real thing is the soil and the history which has formed it. The study of this history is of greater actual importance than the renaissance of dialects under the aegis of a State solicitous of other needs of an imperious nature.

The publication of M. de Monzie's Circular evoked a great debate and much agitation throughout France. A Parisian journalist, Roger Giron, conducted in the pages of *L'Éclair* from September 5 to October 8, 1925, a daily symposium of diverse opinions of a large number of Frenchmen and gave prominence to the protests of representative Regionalists. The Regionalist press as a whole and a goodly number of French newspapers in Provence and Brittany assailed M. de Monzie. Fairly elaborate defenses of local languages and regionalism were published in *Les Nouvelles Littéraires,* in *Comœdia,* and in *Candide.* In the Royalist *Action Française,* MM. Charles Maurras and Léon Daudet acclaimed regionalism and denounced Republican centralization.

Paul Garcin, president of the " League of Federalist Youth," expressed the regret of his organization

that M. de Monzie has taken part in the war against the traditional provincial liberties which have been abridged by almost three centuries of a centralization as shameful as it is now unnecessary. We regret, moreover, that M. de Monzie does not yet perceive that the best means of serving the national interest is to enroot Frenchmen to their soil, to their province, to the things which have made them what they are and what they must be. No one changes the nature of things. No ministerial circular will ever do that. . . .[22]

Marcel Provence, president of the " Federation of French Regionalist Youth," announced that his society was preparing to thwart M. de Monzie by starting elementary classes in the local languages outside the public schools. The beginning would be made in Provence, " but we young regionalists shall go ahead extending these classes to all the districts of France, for all their languages and dialects. Such will be the best response to Anatole, dishonorer of his native Périgord. . . ." [23] Another prominent leader of the same society, L.-A. Pagès, editor-in-chief of *L'Ouest-Éclair*, declared that " if you give to the peasant some reasons and means of remaining attached to his soil — self-respect, culture, the vitalizing of his language — you reënforce his conscious love of the great Fatherland." [24]

A majority of the protesting Regionalists seemed to be Provençals, but the Bretons, though fewer in numbers, were more vehement. Joseph Cadic, a member of the Chamber of Deputies from Morbihan, who wore his Breton costume in the Chamber, denounced M. de Monzie with picturesque vigor and glorified Brittany and the Bretons. " Breton is not a dialect," he said, " it is a great language possessing a grammar and a dictionary and a valuable literature." [25] Eugène Delahaye, director of the *Nouvelliste de Bretagne*, asserted: " Breton is a language which has its history, its rules, its literature, and its poets. If it isn't kept in its greatest purity, Breton will degenerate into a dialect. What a fine victory that would be for a Minister of Public Instruction! M. de Monzie wishes to suppress a language which was glorious, which is beautiful, and which will forever be loved by its faithful." [26] Gustav de Kerguézec, senator and president of the départemental Assembly of Côtes-du-Nord, in his address to the Assembly on September 8, 1925, said:

I would have finished here, gentlemen, with the questions of general order, if I did not exercise the mandate which I have received to protest

---

[22] *L'Éclair*, Sept. 12, 1925.
[23] *Ibid.*, Sept. 24, 1925.
[24] *Ibid.*, Sept. 10, 1925.

[25] *L'Éclair*, Sept. 13, 1925.
[26] *Ibid.*, Sept. 21, 1925.

against the ostracism of which our mother-tongue has just been the object on the part of the Government. . . . The Breton language is to our hearts what the crags and jennets and heather are to our land. . . . Have the love, cult, and practice of the Breton language prevented the heroism of our soldiers? . . . We can say that our province, divided on so many points, will be found united in defense of a patrimony to which it clings, which it will not let be touched, and which it will know how to maintain.[27]

Henry d'Yvignac, secretary for eleven years of the *Breton de Paris* and an extremist among the " national " patriots of Brittany, wrote:

The Bretons are French. Their history shows it, ever since the year 1214 when our Duke led his army in support of Philip Augustus in order to conquer at Bouvines the Germanic coalition, down to the most recent fighting at Dixmude. But they are Bretons also. They entered into the French commonwealth by the Act of Union of 1532. This Act stipulates, for the present and the future, that our customs and institutions are to be respected. . . . Is it known that President Wilson received at Paris in 1919 a friend of mine as head of a Breton delegation, and that this delegation claimed for Brittany the famous " right of national self-determination "? A supportable thesis, but if — if there is a holy and sacred right, it is, for the Breton peasant, who pays the tax of gold and the tax of blood, that of speaking the language of his father and hearing his son speak it. He can, if he pleases, law in hand, *exact* it.[28]

This was going too far for the mildly regionalist editor of *L'Éclair,* who observed, " I was ignorant that in 1919 — one year after the war! — a Breton was to be found who would claim autonomy for his land and would treat of it with the sinister Wilson in the name of national self-determination. This negotiation, if it really occurred, was simply shameful. And I am pained to see M. Henry d'Yvignac qualifying as ' supportable ' such an odious thesis. Treason is not to be ' supported.' "

[27] *Ibid.,* Sept. 9, 1925. The editor comments: " M. Gustave de Kerguézec is as good a Jacobin as M. Anatole de Monzie. The two senators are " Radicaux-Socialistes " and supremely anti-clerical. Their complete disagreement on the question of local languages is an additional proof that politics are absent from this debate."

[28] *Ibid.,* Sept. 23, 1925.

From among the Corsicans, Pierre Dominique spoke out vigorously:

For our present governments, France is one nation, called French, whose members must speak exclusively the language of the Île-de-France. For us (regionalists) France is a state composed of a certain number of nations, and several of these nations, notably the Breton, the Provençal, the Basque, the Catalan, the Flemish, the Alsatian, and the Corsican, have their own languages which they speak quite naturally. . . . I must confess that nationalism seems to me to be naturally warlike. It is not bad that a grouping of human beings should not be too much nationalized. Switzerland, you see, is terribly pacific; it is composed of I don't know how many republics. Every federal grouping is pacific. The more the states of Europe are nationalized, that is, centralized, the less permeable they will be, and therefore the more hostile will they be to one another and the greater will be the risks of war. If war is prevented between France and Germany, it will be Alsace which will have wished to prevent it; between France and Italy, it will be Corsica; etc. Thanks to this girdle of nations, the French State was, and is still, a leaven of peace and organization; it bears the future Europe on its back. . . . The fault is not a minister's, or any one else's, it is the fault of an ideology which hardly any European has as yet gotten rid of.[29]

Several French Flemings contributed to the discussion. One of them, M. Martin-Mamy, founder and general secretary of the " Regionalist Federation of the North," and director of the *Télégramme du Nord*, published in his newspaper a series of articles of the following tenor:

Since regionalism exists, or, rather, since it has regained consciousness of its high national virtue — for, let us repeat, local patriotism constitutes the very living substance of every form of patriotism — it has not ceased to claim in all its congresses the utilization of our local languages in school-instruction. In higher education, that goes without saying, and it is known that already in Brittany and in Provence there are chairs of Celtic and of *Langue d'Oc* the utility of which renders all the more regrettable the absence of a chair of Flemish language and literature in French Flanders. In secondary education it is equally so; but likewise, I should say above all, it is so in our primary education, and that not only from the specifically regionalist point of view but also from the pedagogical standpoint.[30]

[29] *Ibid.*, Sept. 29, 1925. [30] *Ibid.*, Sept. 14, 1925.

A Belgian, M. L. Dumont-Wilden, rushed to the defense of M. de Monzie, and in successive contributions to *L'Éclair* [31] exposed certain disadvantages of bilingualism:

Certainly, [he wrote] regionalism which tends to develop provincial life, which opposes excessive centralization, which would wish to substitute a regional administration in direct relation with the locality for the centralized bureaucracy which we owe to Napoleon, is an excellent thing; but linguistic regionalism, the regionalism which appeals to popular mysticism and which reawakens an obscure racial sentiment in populations that compose the nation, is a very dangerous thing. We have a striking example of it before our eyes in Belgium. Flemish regionalism poisons the whole political life of Belgium; it threatens the unity and even the existence of a nation to which the war gave the baptism of glory and whose independence is indispensable to the peace of Europe. . . . Let one study in the universities of the south the beautiful and noble language to which the genius of Mistral has afforded necessary life; nothing is better; but let none deprive any little Frenchman of the priceless benefit of possessing from the cradle the most perfect intellectual instrument which has been invented by man. It is necessary to have lived in a bilingual country to understand the incomparable advantage which unilingual nations have. A single language is the cement of strong peoples.

Within France, M. de Monzie had a host of champions for his stand against the use of regional languages in the elementary schools. Editorials and articles appeared in *Le Temps, Le Journal des Débats, Le Matin, L'Avenir, Paris-Midi, Excelsior,* and many another newspaper in Paris and in the provinces, praising French and expressing fear lest the renaissance of linguistic regionalism would give rise to demands for political autonomy and eventually perhaps to the disintegration of France. As typical of the opinions and arguments of many such articles, may be reproduced here extracts from a long article contributed to *L'Éclair* [32] by M. Abel Biasse, professor at the Collège of Arles:

M. de Monzie puts on the same plane Flemish, Breton, Basque, Provençal, Corsican, and Alsatian German. Put yourself in his place. He can't make one concession without making six. But in Alsace and perhaps in Flanders, bilingual education would be the fissure through which would penetrate in time, with Germany's aid, political autonomy

[31] *Ibid.,* Sept. 20 and Oct. 7, 1925.   [32] Sept. 8, 1925.

and worse. And M. Mussolini, if he lasts, will find means enough, in spite of the Corsicans, of claiming Corsica on the pretext of Italianism. Maurras or Bainville will say that democratic republics are incapable of decentralization. Let's see. The United States and Switzerland are decentralized democratic republics. In the time of the kings, France, eldest daughter of the Roman Empire, was always fused, assimilated, unified. It is her law, her force, her life. A country remains like itself under no matter what régime, through such radical events as revolutions. England has never assimilated anyone, neither the Irish, nor the French Canadians, nor the Hindus, and her greatly admired empire has been built up, is being built up, and always will be built up by fighting. France assimilates the Canadians like the Provençals, and her empire will remain one and indivisible so long as she does not imitate (as she has foolishly tried since Waldeck-Rousseau to imitate) the English colonial methods. You see that I am a good Jacobin, like Louis XIV when he declared the converted Iroquois French citizens. . . .

One last quotation, from an article by Ernest Prévost, in Gustave Hervé's *La Victoire:*

Don't you find, like me, a certain backward taste for particularism in the eloquent objections of M. de Kerguézec and other regionalist Radicals? Kings, great kings, and ministers of genius have worked so hard to effect French unity! And, at the present hour, we have such great need of union, of absolute union, in order to face internal dangers and external threats! If we haven't always the same sentiments, the same ideas, the same philosophies, the same opinions, the same faith, alas! let us have at least the same language.[33]

[33] Quoted in *L'Éclair,* Sept. 28, 1925.

CHAPTER XII

INTERNATIONAL PROPAGANDA IN FRANCE

I

FRENCHMEN as a rule do not like to be called "nationalists" or to have their patriotism described as "nationalism." "Nationalism" connotes to them a degree of uniformity, intolerance, and chauvinism which, they protest, is alien to the French nationality. They point among themselves to manifold differences of economic, intellectual, political, religious, or regional character. They refer to the cosmopolitan nature of their own great capital city and of French culture in general, and likewise to the toleration, nay the proverbial hospitality, extended by them to their numerous foreign visitors. They assert emphatically that it is and always has been a principle and a practice among them to assume international obligations and to make world-wide humanitarianism an integral part of their own national patriotism.

There is much justification for such an attitude. The "nationalism" of the French people, which is inculcated in them by the numerous agencies that have been indicated in this book, includes a supreme devotion to "France," but does not exclude a high degree of internationalism. Indeed, the propagation of internationalism proceeds in France, like the propagation of localism and regionalism, parallel with the inculcation of national patriotism, with the result that "France" and her "mission" are conceived of differently as this or that Frenchman effects this or that amalgam of national patriotism with regionalism or with internationalism or with both.

In the modern world of economic interdependence of nations, France has her full share of industrial and commercial contacts with foreign countries. Her great bankers and her captains of

" big business " adhere to international cartels,[1] participate in international conferences, and tend to view their special interests as being world-wide rather than narrowly national. Her manufacturers seek foreign, as well as domestic, markets; and her traders, backed by the national Government, go to all parts of the world in quest of favorable exchange of commodities. Her vast and numerous coöperative societies of production and purchase are federated not only nationally but also internationally. And among some of her workingmen a pronounced effort is made to decry the name, if not the substance, of patriotism, and to laud internationalism and even cosmopolitanism. French Socialists are actually quite patriotic, but they pay more than lip service to the Marxian tradition of the brotherhood of the world's workingmen: they participate most actively in the counsels and conclaves of their foreign comrades; and at home they are critics of imperialism, militarism, and jingoism, as they are champions of the League of Nations and of all other agencies which in their opinion will promote international understanding and coöperation. French Communists are more stentorian than French Socialists in protestation of their repugnance to " nationalism " and of their love of internationalism; and their intimate association with Russian Bolshevism and their noisy appeals to class cleavage have elicited from the majority of their compatriots the taunt that they are unpatriotic, that they are foes of French unity. Yet these Communists are patriotic, too, after a fashion. They cannot wholly escape the fact that before becoming Communist they have been " made " Frenchmen.

The " internationalism " of a French Communist is likely to be different from that of a French Socialist, and the " internationalism " of any French workingman from that of a French banker or a member of the Comité des Forges. But whatever it really is at any given time or in any given group, it is communicated from leaders to followers and is propagated by speeches, newspapers, meetings, and special societies. It often

---

[1] For instance, note the agreement between French and German steel corporations, as described by Ogburn and Jaffé, Vol. III of this series, *The Economic Development of Post-War France* (New York, Columbia University Press, 1929).

enters into rivalry with, and sometimes is adopted as a supplement to, the " nationalism " officially sponsored by the State and its various agencies. Different forms of economic internationalism conflict on occasion with one another, but all together in the long run mitigate nationalism.

It is similar with religious internationalism. All the religions to which any large number of Frenchmen adhere have ramifications far beyond French frontiers, and the ordinary French religionist is influenced not only by compatriots but also, though perhaps less consciously, by co-religionists in foreign countries. Most Frenchmen who practice any religion are Roman Catholics, and as such they belong to a universal Christian Church, with an international organization, under a " foreign " Pope, with traditions, teachings, precepts, and usages that transcend all bounds of modern nationality. French Catholics are patriotic; they are told that patriotism is a religious duty and are reminded that Catholicism is a national attribute of France. But some of their priests and bishops are educated at Rome rather than in France; their preachers and publications constantly call their attention to what the Pope says and does; they are never permitted to forget the existence of other Catholic peoples or of Catholic minorities in non-Catholic countries, or of Catholic missions in heathen lands. Many of their leaders attend international Catholic congresses; and the tie of a common religion makes it easier for Catholic Frenchmen to support any attempt of the French Government to strengthen political and economic bonds between France and Poland or Czechoslovakia or Belgium or Spain or even Austria or South Germany.

French Protestants are organized nationally, but in spirit and creed, in tradition and outlook, they are akin to Lutherans of Germany and Scandinavia or to Calvinists of Great Britain, the United States, Holland, Switzerland, and Hungary. They preach the same gospel, sing the same hymns, and participate in the same international movements. They are certainly loyal to France, but, in addition, they entertain a high regard for something outside of France. And the French Jews, likewise;

out of proportion to their numbers, they have supplied their country with advocates of international causes.

The most actively " religious " group among Frenchmen of no professed religion — the most belligerent " anti-clericals " — are the Freemasons, who possess a veritable substitute for religion and one that is international. For Freemasonry is widespread throughout the civilized world, and the French Freemasons have many contacts with their foreign brethren.

French intellectuals — scientists and scholars, professors and teachers, members of the learned professions — are organized, as we have seen,[2] on a national basis. But a national association of French biologists or historians or secondary-school teachers or physicians is usually affiliated with a corresponding international association; and in the deliberations and publications of the latter, representatives of the former share. Science and learning, from the very nature of things, cannot be restricted in our modern age to any one nation. Inventions, discoveries, knowledge, and forms of art flow back and forth over political frontiers and become common property of the whole world's intellectual class. To this common property French intellectuals undoubtedly make some original contributions, but from it they certainly derive much that has originated abroad. They derive it, too, not only through the formal international organizations to which they belong, but also in innumerable indirect ways, such as travel, reading, exchange-professors, exchange-students, etc. It should be remembered that the French school-system in its upper reaches of lycée and university puts considerable emphasis on instruction in foreign languages, especially Latin, German, and English, and thereby enables those Frenchmen who receive a higher education to obtain some first-hand knowledge of foreign culture. It should be borne in mind, likewise, that the French newspapers which cater peculiarly to intellectuals — for example, *Le Temps* and *Le Journal des Débats* — though stridently patriotic, carry a particularly large amount of foreign news. French intellectuals as a class are very patriotic, but their patriotism is tempered by some special understanding and appreciation of

[2] See above, Chap. VIII, pp. 197–198.

the aspirations and achievements of fellow intellectuals in other
countries.

2

Cutting across the intellectual class and the religious and
economic groupings in France are to be found, as has already
been pointed out,[3] two major brands of a French patriotism so
intense and compelling as to be described, at least by a foreigner,
as " nationalism." The one is Jacobin nationalism; and the other
is Traditionalist nationalism. But in different degrees both include a measure of internationalism.

Jacobin nationalists — the Radicals, the Socialists, the " Left "
in general — are determined within France to unify and con-
solidate the national State: they have been for a century the
outstanding advocates of centralization of legislation, administration, and education, and the determined foes of any movement
or institution — such as regionalism or the Catholic Church —
which might conceivably conduce to " divided allegiance." On
the other hand, they have never lost sight of the international
traditions of Revolutionary Jacobinism: the principle of national
self-determination, the fraternity of liberal and democratic
peoples, the cult of humanitarianism, and the identification of
the " mission " of France with the progress of the whole world.

Traditionalist nationalists — the Conservatives, the Royalists,
the " Right " in general — are thought of too often and too in-
discriminately as single-minded devotees of militarism and imperialism, of a forceful policy in foreign affairs and particularly
an unyielding attitude toward Germany; they are thought of,
in other words, as nationalists *par excellence*. As a matter of
fact, such a conception is applicable to only a minority of them,
notably to the very vocal leaders of the Royalist fraction. Most
of the " Right " are as sincere in their devotion to peace and
the rule of law in international relations as are the " Left," and
in their traditional allegiance to the Catholic Church, private
education, and regionalism they actually represent something of
a reaction against internal nationalist excesses.

[3] See above, Chap. I, pp. 7-11.

Neither the Traditionalist nor the Jacobin nationalism of France is necessarily chauvinist, though some French chauvinists there are who seem to be inspired by the one, and others by the other. Both nationalisms reserve a plank in their respective platforms for internationalism and give a few first lessons to their followers as to how these may stand upon it.

No matter how " nationalist " Frenchmen may be, no matter how " nationalist " the French Government would like them to be, the very exigencies of international politics render it practically impossible for the Government or any group to lead to a goal of purely doctrinaire nationalism a whole nation that is famed for its intelligence and common sense. Countless individuals in all classes, and Governments too, whether of the " Right " or of the " Left," realize that France simply cannot live to and for herself alone, that she is dependent on other countries for food, raw materials, markets, and trade, that if she were left unaided to wage war against a hostile coalition her independence and very existence could be destroyed. Every French schoolboy knows that his country is in the midst of the restless, quarrelsome continent of Europe, with frontiers abutting on two great military Powers — Germany and Italy — and with seacoasts open to speedy naval attack by Great Britain. This geographical situation of France and the repeated tragic experiences associated with it have tended to quicken national consciousness and patriotic fervor among the French people and to arouse among them a militant nationalism, but a militant nationalism conditioned in part by an informed realistic attitude toward other countries. To French statesmen and patriots the problem of national security is ever live and paramount; [4] for them, unlike American patriots and statesmen whose land is separated by oceans from other Great Powers, there can be no cessation of effort in facing and dealing with it. National security Frenchmen have sought to ensure by heavy armaments at home, which doubtless have stimulated national spirit, and also by sympathetic understandings and diplomatic alliances abroad, which certainly have involved an international and world-wide orientation.

4 See above, pp. 66–69.

If Frenchmen have been taught to view Germany as the national foe and to fear her as the national menace, they have been led by nationalist teachings which curiously partake of internationalism to look upon other potential victims of Germany — Belgium, Poland, Czechoslovakia, Yugoslavia, Rumania, etc. — as natural friends and allies of themselves. As friends they can, and as allies they must, strive sympathetically to understand and please these countries and their peoples.

Besides, Frenchmen are not unmindful of the aid given them in the critical years from 1914 to 1918 by English-speaking peoples; and though there was considerable nationalist friction at that time and though there have been many nationalist recriminations since, intelligent Frenchmen appreciate the desirability alike for sentimental reasons of the past and for practical reasons of the future, of strengthening the bonds between France and Great Britain, between France and the United States.

During the decade since the signing of the Treaty of Versailles (1919–1929), French support of the League of Nations has grown constantly more popular in extent and more sincere in character, and on the whole Franco-German relations have perceptibly improved. These developments have been made possible not so much because of any overwhelming French devotion to doctrinaire internationalism as because of a growing conviction in the minds of French statesmen [5] and even French nationalists that the future security of the French nation, the best serving of French national interests, must depend increasingly on a new world order and on a reversal of the hereditary relations of France and Germany. But, granted that their purpose has been nationalist and selfish, once the French have embarked on a policy of coöperating with the League of Nations and permitting some measure of rapprochement with Germany, they have exposed themselves to new sources of international influence and have confronted themselves with new needs of international understanding. The Pact of Locarno was dictated to the French by fear, not love, of the Germans, and the Franco-German trade

[5] Foremost among whom is undoubtedly M. Aristide Briand. And his attitude has been rendered fruitful by the fact that a like-minded statesman, Dr. Gustav Stresemann, has guided the German Foreign Office during the same period.

agreement was negotiated for self-interest, but both have had educational effects in the realm of internationalism rather than in that of nationalism. The League of Nations has been utilized by French statesmen to serve nationalist ends, but, on the other hand, words and actions proceeding from representatives of almost the whole world assembled at Geneva have been recounted in the French press and have helped immeasurably to crystallize an international sentiment in France. It will probably be a long time before the traditional French view of absolute, national sovereignty is supplanted by that of a sovereign international League; it will surely be a long time before the inculcation of anti-German feeling by French nationalist agencies gives way to the propagation of pro-German sympathies. But already it can be said that French nationalism has been altered in spirit and in content by post-war international developments.

3

It is not alone the force of external circumstances which spreads international teachings in France. Governmental officials, school-teachers, clergymen, newspapers, cinemas, radios — almost all the agencies of national propaganda within France — contribute something, imperfect and partial though it may be, to the education of Frenchmen about foreign peoples and international affairs. In addition, there are certain French agencies specifically designed to propagate internationalism. Of these, the peace-societies and private international organizations are the most important. They are almost as numerous as the national patriotic societies described in a preceding chapter.[6] Some of the most significant may be reviewed here.

Several organizations are engaged in acquainting Frenchmen with the work of the League of Nations and fortifying French support of the League. Of these, the most influential perhaps is the " French Association for the League of Nations " (" Association Française pour la Société des Nations "[7]), founded in 1918,

---

[6] See Chap. VIII, above.

[7] Headquarters: 3 rue LeGoff, Paris. Officers: President, Paul Appell; General Secretary, J. Prudhommeaux; Administrative Secretary, P. Brossolette.

in order " (1) to appeal to public opinion so that France may play the part she should in the international organization of law; (2) to study in detail political, juridical, economic, and military problems arising between France and foreign countries and the development of higher conceptions of international relations; (3) to collaborate with associations in France and abroad which have similar aims; and (4) to assist the Government in surmounting difficulties which may threaten the realization of such aims." The Association has fifty-four sections, some of which claim local memberships upward of 500. It maintains a lecture-bureau and distributes tracts and pamphlets. For two years it published a bulletin of its own, but since 1926 it has supplied monthly supplements to a well-known magazine, *L'Europe Nouvelle*, edited by Mlle. Weiss.[8]

The " French University Group for the League of Nations " ("Groupement Universitaire Français pour la Société des Nations "[9]) was founded in 1923 for the purpose of conducting pro-League propaganda in school and university. The example of the French group was speedily followed by groups in twenty-two other nations, and in 1924 delegates from the various groups held a conference at Prague and organized the " International University Federation for the League of Nations " with the support of the " International Confederation of Students " which claims a total membership of half a million. The French group, which has twelve branches in Paris and the provinces, arranges for meetings, discussions, and lectures, and publishes tracts and a quarterly bulletin. It conducts courses of study at Geneva every year while the League Assembly is in session.

There is also an association of French veterans of the World War which conducts a good deal of propaganda in behalf of peace and particularly the League of Nations. This association — the " Federal Union of French Associations " (" Union Fédérale des Associations Françaises ") — has already been referred to in the chapter on patriotic societies.[10]

[8] See below, pp. 415–416.

[9] Headquarters: 3 rue LeGoff, Paris. Officers: President, J. H. Adam; General Delegate, Robert Bobin.

[10] See above, pp. 221–222.

Also specially laboring now in support of the League of
Nations is the much older society of " Peace by Law " (" Paix
par le Droit " [11]), founded in 1887, with the purpose " of studying
and popularizing the juridical settlements of international conflicts and of securing the assistance of young men and women
in carrying on this work." This society maintains a monthly
review, *Paix par le Droit,* and a more popular quarterly news-
sheet, *Les Peuples Unis;* and its thirty-one provincial groups hold
frequent peace meetings.

Allied to " Peace by Law " and utilizing its publications for
propaganda among French women, is the " Women's Union for
the League of Nations " (" Union Féminine pour la Société des
Nations " [12]). The Union holds that no political, social, or economic progress is possible so long as there is danger of war and
that against war the best guarantee is the League of Nations. It
pledges itself to accept the decisions of the League's World Court
on all international disputes. The Union also advocates the
political enfranchisement of French women on the ground that
they are especially devoted to international good-will and peace.

Of the international Protestant peace society — the " World
Alliance for International Friendship through the Churches "
(" Alliance Universelle pour l'Amitié Internationale par les
Églises ") — French Protestants maintain one of the twenty-
eight national branches.[13] The French branch publishes a quarterly magazine, *L'Amitié Internationale,* and various separate
tracts. It holds meetings and urges general observance of a
peace-Sunday by the Protestant churches. It approves of the
League of Nations and of disarmament and has taken a stand
against secret diplomacy and against chauvinist instruction in
the schools.

[11] Headquarters: 24 rue Pierre-Curie, Paris. Officers: President, Théodore
Ruyssen; Vice-Presidents, Jacques Dumas, Mme. M. L. Puech; General Secretary,
J. Prudhommeaux; Secretaries, Edmond Dumeril, J. L. Puech.

[12] Headquarters: 24 rue Pierre-Curie, Paris. Officers: President, Mme. M.
L. Puech; Vice-Presidents, Mmes. Brunschvicg, Jézéquel, Malaterre-Sellier; General Secretary, Mme. Thibert.

[13] Headquarters: 3 rue Desrenaudes, Paris. Officers: President, Wilfred
Monod; General Secretary, J. Jézéquel.

French Catholics also maintain a peace society, which is favorable to the League of Nations — the " League of French Catholics for International Justice " (" Ligue des Catholiques Français pour la Justice Internationale " [14]). It was founded in 1921 on the basis of a similar pre-war society. It publishes a quarterly magazine, *Justice et Paix,* and enjoys the approbation of Cardinal Dubois, archbishop of Paris, Cardinal Maurin, archbishop of Lyons, and several other prominent members of the French hierarchy. It inspires the publication of books and pamphlets and the discussion of international problems at the great annual " Social Weeks " of leading French Catholics.[15]

Another Catholic organization — " The Young Republic " (" La Jeune République " [16]) — has latterly been very active in support of international understanding and peace. It is the outgrowth of the famous " Sillon," a society formed under the leadership of Marc Sangnier during the Dreyfus affair in order to unite French Catholics who espoused democracy and the Republic and who opposed the intransigeant attitude of the royalists and extreme nationalists. Condemned by Pope Pius X in 1910 on the ground that it tended to deify political democracy, the " Sillon " disbanded, but in 1912 Marc Sangnier, with the approval of the Pope, resuscitated it with a more moderate programme and under the new name of " La Jeune République." The World War interrupted its attempt to rally French Catholics to the Republic, and after the conclusion of hostilities Marc Sangnier, feeling that its earlier purpose had in fact been largely realized, directed the society more and more toward a campaign for better relations between capital and labor and simultaneously toward a campaign for more intensive international coöperation. In 1921 " The Young Republic " organized the first of its annual international

[14] See Mgr. Beaupin, *La Ligue des Catholiques Français pour la Justice Internationale* (Lyons, Chronique Sociale de France, 1926).

[15] On the " Social Weeks," see above, p. 104. Samples of books inspired by the League are *Le Problème de la Vie internationale* (Lyons, Chronique Sociale de France, 1926), and Maurice Vaussard, *Enquête sur le Nationalisme* (Paris, Spes, 1924).

[16] Headquarters: 34 Boulevard Raspail, Paris. Officers: Director, Marc Sangnier; Editor, Georges Hoog. See above, pp. 102, 107.

peace conferences in order to give pacifists, especially young Catholic pacifists, of the several European nations an opportunity to meet and unite their efforts. Similar conferences have been held successively at Paris, Vienna, Freibourg-im-Breisgau, London, Luxembourg, Bierville (France), and Wurzburg (Germany).

Most of the foregoing organizations and certain others are federated in the " French Federation of Associations for the League of Nations " (" Fédération Française des Associations pour la Société des Nations " [17]), which, in turn, is a constituent member of the " International Union of Associations for the League of Nations " at Brussels. The French Federation maintains a " committee of action," holds public meetings, issues public declarations, and studies international problems. It is composed of delegates from its affiliated societies and seeks above all to coördinate their efforts.

4

The activity of pro-League organizations in France, with the support of the French Government, has been largely instrumental in establishing a very important official agency of the League of Nations in Paris. The League in its early days had set up an International Committee on Intellectual Coöperation " in order to study in a broad way how existing international relations of an intellectual sort might be simplified, clarified, and amplified." The meetings of this Committee were held only occasionally and in the relatively inaccessible city of Geneva; and it soon occurred to its friends and supporters that its work could be rendered immeasurably more effective if it were directed in detail by a

[17] Headquarters: 3 rue LeGoff, Paris. Officers: President (1927), A. Aulard; Secretary, J. Prudhommeaux; Treasurer, Mme. Malaterre-Sellier. Among its affiliated organizations are L'Association Française pour la Société des Nations, Le Groupement Universitaire Français pour la Société des Nations, L'Union Fédérale des Mutilés et Anciens Combattants, L'Association de la Paix par le Droit, L'Union Féminine pour la Société des Nations, Le Comité Français de l'Alliance Universelle de la Paix par les Églises, Le Groupe Français de la Fédération Maçonnique Internationale, La Ligue des Catholiques Français pour la Justice Internationale, Le Comité d'Action Démocratique Internationale (La Jeune République), etc.

permanent international body located in such an intellectual centre as Paris. Accordingly, the French Government offered to provide permanent headquarters in Paris and an annual subsidy of two million francs; the League of Nations and its International Committee on Intellectual Coöperation accepted the offer with gratitude; and in 1926 the resulting " International Institute of Intellectual Coöperation " was founded and housed in the famous old Palais Royal, 2 rue de Montpensier, Paris.

The Institute, under a French Director, but with a broadly international staff, at once organized sub-committees on science, literature, art, education, the rights of intellectual workers, and propaganda, and created a number of " departments," and launched several publications, including the quarterly *International Bulletin of University Relations*, the quarterly *International Bulletin of Scientific Relations*, the quarterly *Mousseion* (a bulletin of museums), and the small *Bulletin of the Information and Reference Section*. The Institute also prepares an *Annual List of Notable Books Published in Different Countries*, and, as an exceptional measure, has edited an *International Handbook of Museums* and a *Handbook to Collections of Photographs of Works of Art*. An important effort is made, moreover, to obtain data concerning the intercourse among universities (exchange of professors, movement of foreign students, courses of study relating to other countries, etc.), concerning fellowships, associations for mutual aid in universities, laws and regulations regarding the equivalent recognition of studies and degrees, the obstacles to the circulation of books, etc. A proposal to keep up to date at the Institute a handbook of the world's libraries is being studied and may be realized. The Institute is also preparing an *International Who's Who*.

One of the most important services which the Institute renders is the furnishing of rooms for offices and conferences of a considerable variety of international societies whose influence for international good-will should not be minimized. In this way the Institute is now serving the International Academy of Comparative Law, the International Committee on Historical Sciences, the International Confederation of Intellectual Workers, the

International Federation of National Associations of Secondary School Teachers, the International Federation of National Associations of Elementary School Teachers, the Liaison Committee of the Major International Associations, the International Federation of Journalists' Trade Unions, the International Committee on the School Cinema and Social Education, the International Union for Synthesis, and the World Stage Society. The assembly rooms of the Institute have proved to be a convenient place for the international congresses of such organizations and have already been used by many of them.

An attempt to coördinate national societies of different countries, so that they may work together on an international basis, has been one of the chief cares of the Institute. The Institute has also created a " Liaison Committee of Major International Associations," which includes representatives of the Young Men's Christian Association, the Young Women's Christian Association, the International Scout Bureau, the International Bureau of Federations of Secondary School Teachers, and many others. A special effort has also been made to promote contacts among teachers and students of international law and international relations throughout the world. To this end the Institute publishes a monthly *Bibliographical Bulletin on International Affairs.*[18]

Besides the International Institute of Intellectual Coöperation, there are several quasi-official international organizations which command the support of the French Government as well as of important segments of the French citizenry. One such is the " Interparliamentary Union " (" Union Interparlementaire "), which was founded in 1888 jointly by the Englishman William R. Cremer and by the Frenchman Frédéric Passy, with the aim of " uniting the members of all parliaments, organized in national groups, in order to realize . . . a reciprocal collaboration among states, a universal league of nations, and a strengthening and a development of the international movement for peace and

---

[18] For more detailed information about the Institute, see *The International Institute of Intellectual Coöperation, 1927,* a 52-page pamphlet, and also *The Work of the International Institute of Intellectual Coöperation during the Year 1926* (Paris, Les Presses Universitaires, 1927).

for world coöperation, . . . and of studying all international problems which may be solved by parliaments." By 1914 the Union had secured the adherence of 3,500 statesmen, representing 26 different national parliaments; it was receiving subsidies from several governments and was holding annual congresses in various national capitals. The World War of 1914–1918 brought the work of the Union to a standstill, but it was revived and resumed soon after the conclusion of peace. The post-war congresses of the Union have been well attended and have been concerned with the study of colonial questions, disarmament, international law, social problems, financial rehabilitation, parliamentary control of foreign affairs, etc.; resolutions voted by the congress are submitted by the several national groups to their respective governments. In 1927 the Union held its annual congress at Paris; 440 members were in attendance. The French group [19] of the Interparliamentary Union consists at present (1928) of 109 senators (34 per cent of the total number) and 133 deputies (23 per cent). The French Government grants the Union an annual subsidy of 45,000 francs.

A somewhat similar organization, though without official governmental backing, is the " French Committee for the European Customs Union " (" Comité Français pour l'Union Douanière Européenne "), founded in 1927.[20] Its object is " to study, aside from all political preoccupation, the commercial, industrial, agricultural, financial, and colonial relationships among the various countries of Europe in order to substitute the specific practice of industrial understandings and customs agreements for the tariff wars which cause the ruin of nations. The only method capable of enriching nations is a gradual and reciprocal reduction of tariffs. This is the final aim of the European Customs Union."

[19] The President of the French group is Fernand Merlin, 6 rue de Seine, Paris; its official publications are *Bulletin Interparlementaire* and *Les Comptes-Rendus des Conférences*. See also *La France et l'Œuvre Interparlementaire: Discours prononcés à la XXIVe Conférence Interparlementaire par Paul Doumer, Fernand Buisson, Raymond Poincaré, Aristide Briand, et Fernand Merlin* (Genève, Payot, 1927).

[20] Headquarters: 8 Place Édouard VII, Paris. Officers: President, Yves Le Trocquer; Vice President, Charles Gide; Delegate, Lucien Coquet. Organ· *L'Europe de Demain.*

The French group counts among its members such men as MM. Le Trocquer, Charles Gide, Henri Lichtenberger, Armand Meggle, J. Prudhommeaux, J. H. Ricard, and Jacques Seydoux. It is affiliated with similar groups at Berlin, Vienna, and Budapest, and has coöperated with them, through an international committee, in presenting its views at various international congresses, notably at the twenty-fourth Conference of the Interparliamentary Union at Paris and the International Economic Conference at Geneva.

In 1927, too, several members of the French Parliament, under the leadership of Émile Borel, deputy and member of the Institute, formed a " French Committee of European Coöperation " (" Comité Français de Coopération Européenne " [21]), which soon enrolled about six hundred men the majority of whom were statesmen, professors, and journalists. The Committee announced its intention of fostering " coöperation among the peoples of Europe in the framework and spirit of the League of Nations." Although it has hardly had time to prove its worth, the Committee plans to conduct international propaganda among both the statesmen and the common people of France, and to study, in collaboration with other societies of like character, " the measures which should be taken in order to create a ' rational ' Europe."

5

An important agency of internationalism, and one particularly interesting to Americans, is the " Carnegie Endowment for International Peace," which some time before the World War established a " European Centre " and located it in Paris. This " European Centre of the Carnegie Endowment for International Peace " (" Centre Européen de la Dotation Carnegie pour la Paix Internationale " [22]) is truly international: it is guided by

[21] Officers: Honorary President, M. Gaston Doumergue, President of the Republic; President, M. Émile Borel; Secretary, M. Rais.

[22] Headquarters: 173 Boulevard Saint-Germain, Paris. Officers: Director, Nicholas Murray Butler; Assistant Director, Earle B. Babcock; President of the European Centre, Paul Appell. Members of the International Committee: France, A. Honnorat, G. Lechartier, H. Lichtenberger; Great Britain, Gilbert Murray, A. G. Gardiner; Belgium, M. Nerincx; Germany, Herren Boon, von Prittwitz-

an international committee and it supervises a vast deal of co-operative work among the internationally minded in all countries of Europe. Its purpose has been indicated by its Director as being " to educate the public of the civilized world, to inform each nation about the character, the history, the interests, the temperament, and the ambitions of others, to try to create a sort of international understanding, to promote intellectual relations by such means as study tours for professors and students, to draw scientists, jurists, and business men closer together, and to see that small nations as well as large nations are represented at international gatherings in order that all may consider themselves equal members of the family of nations." [23]

The very fact that the European Centre of the Carnegie Endowment is located in Paris, makes its activities in France particularly significant. It maintains a valuable library on international relations and a reading-room where the chief current newspapers and periodicals of the world are to be found; it arranges lectures by prominent European statesmen and scholars; it organizes courses on international relations in collaboration with the " Institut des Hautes Études Internationales "; and since January 1927 it has published a quarterly review, L'Esprit International. The contacts which are made between the officers of the Endowment and the officials and leaders of the Government, and the aid accorded to private international projects, are perhaps the most efficacious means by which the Endowment fosters pacific propaganda in France.

In 1927 was organized a French Committee of " Pan-Europa," a movement launched two years earlier by Count R. N. Coudenhove-Kalergi, looking to the establishment of a " United States of Europe." The French Committee [24] was formed with

Gaffron; Austria, Count Mensdorff, Dr. Redlich; Switzerland, M. Fatio; Italy, Count C. Sforza; Greece, N. Politis.

[23] From a speech by Dr. Nicholas Murray Butler in Paris, July 2, 1925.

[24] Headquarters: 11 Place Saint-Michel, Paris. Officers: Honorary President, Aristide Briand; President, Louis Loucheur; Secretary, F. Delaisi. See R. N. Coudenhove-Kalergi, Pan-Europa (Vienna, Pan-Europa Verlag, 1925), published in German, French, English, Japanese, Spanish, etc., and his article, " Völkerbund 1927," in his review Pan-Europa, October 1927.

the understanding that " Pan-Europa " would supplement rather than conflict with the League of Nations, but Count Coudenhove-Kalergi's criticisms of the League of Nations and his seeming alignment of the proposed " United States of Europe " against the British Empire, the United States of America, the Russian Empire, and a " Pan-Asia " and a " Pan-America," have created opposition and dissension within the French Committee.

Another instrument of international propaganda in France is *Pax,* a weekly paper founded at Paris in 1926 as an organ of world news and world peace.[25] It is patronized by such eminent men as Jacques Seydoux, Charles Laurent, and Nicholas Politis. Another and more conservative group of Frenchmen, who have become imbued with a desire for international understanding, after having witnessed the horrors of the World War, are endeavoring, it may be noted, to create and finance a syndicate of pacifist newspapers in the chief countries of Europe.[26]

It is worthy of note, moreover, that there exists a significant " Franco-German Committee of Information and Documentation " (" Comité Franco-Allemand d'Information et de Documentation "[27]). A group of important business men and professors founded this Committee in 1926 at Luxembourg " to overcome those psychological obstacles which impede the satisfactory solution of Franco-German problems." Vital questions in the relations between the two countries are discussed at biennial conferences held alternately in France and in Germany. In the interim between conferences special joint commissions study and report on questions of current interest. Two offices, one at Berlin, directed by a Frenchman, and the other at Paris, directed by a German, arrange for the conferences, furnish documents concerning French and German affairs to members of the Committee and other individuals, maintain libraries of French and German works of reference, and facilitate travel from one country to the

---

[25] Headquarters: 18 rue de Tilsitt, Paris. Director: Paul Girard.

[26] The projected *Nouvel Univers.* Headquarters: 4 rue de la Terrasse, Paris. Directors: MM. de Castelnau and Renauld.

[27] Headquarters of the French Committee: 134 Boulevard Haussmann, Paris. M. Émile Mayrisch of Luxembourg took the initiative in creating the Committee and was its leading figure until his death in 1928.

other. Among the French members of the Committee are Charles Laurent, Duc de Broglie, Henri Chardon, M. Duchemin, Henri Lichtenberger, and André Siegfried. Among its German members are Alfred von Nostitz-Wallwitz, Bruno Bruhn, Prince Hermann zu Hatzfeld-Wildenburg, Felix Deutsch, E. R. Curtius, and Professor Oncken.

One of the oldest of the " peace societies " in France is the French branch of the " International League of Peace and Freedom " (" Ligue Internationale de la Paix et la Liberté "), founded at Geneva in 1867 by Garibaldi. It has to-day in France hardly more than a nominal existence or influence.[28]

Under much the same name, however, is a small but flourishing women's peace society, the French section of the " International Women's League for Peace and Freedom " (" Ligue Internationale des Femmes pour la Paix et la Liberté " [29]), founded at The Hague in 1915. During the peace-negotiations of 1918–1919 this society advanced plans for the League of Nations and on several occasions criticized what were thought to be unjust provisions of the treaties. Since 1919 it has carried on propaganda for international conciliation, for the rights of " self-determination " and of minorities, and for general disarmament. The French section has bitterly opposed the idea of compulsory military service and particularly the Paul-Boncour Army Bill.[30] The League holds biennial congresses and conducts international summer schools. It claims a membership of 50,000 distributed among forty-one nations.

An older and somewhat less radical women's peace society is the " International Council of Women " (" Conseil International des Femmes " [31]), founded in 1888. Its original purpose was to ameliorate the position of women in modern life, and to this end it conducted propaganda in behalf of woman's suffrage and im-

[28] President, Michel Revon, 30 rue de Lille, Paris.

[29] International Headquarters: 12 rue du Vieux-Collège, Geneva; President, Jane Addams. French Headquarters: 20 avenue Victoria, Paris; French Director, Mme. Gabrielle Duchêne. Organ: *Pax International* (monthly).

[30] See above, Chap. III, pp. 67–68.

[31] General Secretary, Mme. Pichon-Landry, 68 rue d'Assas, Paris. President of the French Section, Mme. Avril de Sainte-Croix.

proved living conditions and against white slavery. Since the World War, it has participated actively in peace propaganda, has discussed international relations at its congresses, and has maintained at Geneva a liaison representative with the League of Nations. The French section has distributed pamphlets of the League of Nations in the French schools and has organized summer camps.

6

Reference has repeatedly been made in this book to Jacobinism and to Jacobin " nationalism," to the patriotism of those Frenchmen of the " Left " who cling most tenaciously to the principles of the great French Revolution.[32] These are mainly Radical or " Radical Socialiste " in politics and vigorously " anticlerical "; many of them are Freemasons; and most of them combine with their nationalism a very real internationalism. The internationalism of this kind of Frenchman is best exemplified in a select but very active organization, to which reference has already been made in another connection, the " League of the Rights of Man " (" Ligue des Droits de l'Homme "[33]). This was founded in 1898 in order to defend Captain Alfred Dreyfus from what seemed to the Radicals to be persecution at the hands of French militarists and monarchists (the so-called Nationalists of that time). Although, ever since, the primary object of the League has been to see that no injustice is done to innocent persons, it has always conducted a good deal of pacifist propaganda. Before the World War it advocated disarmament, compulsory arbitration, and an end of imperialism. During the war it supported the French Government but urged the necessity of rendering impossible another such conflict. Upon the conclusion of hostilities, an effort was made to oblige the Allied statesmen to conclude a " just peace," and the League was outspoken in its criticisms of the Treaty of Versailles. Since then, the League has favored " a saner settlement of the reparations question than

[32] See above, pp. 322–323.

[33] Headquarters, 10 rue de l'Université, Paris. Officers: President, Victor Basch; General Secretary, Henri Guernut. Organ: Les Cahiers des Droits de l'Homme.

that attempted," has opposed French occupation of the Ruhr, has condemned the Italian expedition in Corfu and likewise the French warfare in Syria and Morocco, and has denounced chauvinist textbooks in the French schools. On the other hand, it has heartily backed the League of Nations and its pacific activities.

In 1922 the League of the Rights of Man joined with fourteen similar societies existing in as many foreign countries to form an international Federation. The first pronouncement of this Federation concluded with the words: " Inasmuch as war is the most brutal negation of justice and the principal cause of all injustice, crimes, and violences, in internal as well as in external affairs, it is against war that we unite our efforts. Let our cry be ' War on war! Peace through respect for the rights of man!' " The French and German Leagues in the Federation have worked for a *rapprochement* between their two nations: officers of the former have lectured in Germany, and those of the latter, in France. Fernand Buisson, an ex-president of the League, was awarded a Nobel Peace Prize in 1927.[34]

Among Frenchmen of the " Right " flourishes, as has been pointed out, a kind of " Traditional " nationalism, which in the case of many individuals is qualified, like " Jacobin " nationalism, by a distinctive brand of internationalism. Especially is this true of a considerable number of French Catholics.

An important Catholic peace-organization is the " Catholic Union of International Studies " (" Union Catholique d'Études Internationales "[35]), founded in 1920 by French and Swiss Catholics, with headquarters at Fribourg in Switzerland. Its purpose is " to study international problems in the light of Christian principles and to instruct Catholics in the work undertaken by the League of Nations and problems before it." The Union now has constituent groups not only in France and Switzerland but also in Italy, Germany, Austria, Great Britain, Hungary,

---

[34] See Henri Sée, *Histoire de la Ligue des Droits de l'Homme* (Paris, Ligue des Droits de l'Homme, 1927). In addition, for the peace-program of the League, see Émile Kahn, " L'Action de la Ligue pour la Paix," *Les Cahiers des Droits de l'Homme*, November 25, 1925.

[35] International Secretary, M. l'Abbé Gremand, Collège Saint-Michel, Fribourg. Headquarters of the French Group: 3 rue Garancière, Paris.

Poland, Spain, Czechoslovakia, and Yugoslavia, and individual adherents in other countries. It is primarily an organization of intellectuals for the scholarly study of the relationship of international developments to Catholic Christianity, and it conducts its study mainly by means of international commissions on (1) intellectual coöperation, (2) humanitarian matters, such as regulation of traffic in drugs and prohibition of white slavery, (3) defense of Catholic minorities, and (4) doctrinal and juridical matters. Reports of these commissions are made in detail and are discussed at the Union's annual congresses. From time to time the Union presents its views and findings to the appropriate officials or agencies of the League of Nations. The French section comprises a hundred intellectuals, including George Goyau of the French Academy, Le Fur, and Mgr. Beaupin.[36]

Other international organizations to which numbers of French Catholics belong are: " International Catholic Association of Works of Protection for Young Girls ";[37] " Catholic International League ";[38] " Society of Religious Studies ";[39] " Apostolic League of Nations ";[40] " International Office of Catholic Scouts ";[41] " Pax Romana," international secretariat of associations of Catholic students;[42] "Christian Trade Union International ";[43] " Institute of Christian International Law ";[44]

---

[36] See Mgr. Beaupin, " Les Problèmes du Jour: les Idées directrices de l'Union Catholique d'Études Internationales," *Chronique Sociale de France*, November 1926, pp. 782-793. The French Section is closely allied, through its officers and activities, with the League of French Catholics for International Justice, mentioned above, p. ooo.

[37] Headquarters: 24 Grand'Rue, Fribourg, Switzerland.

[38] French Director: M. Pierre J.-A. Muffang, 14 bis avenue Galois, Bourg-la-Reine (Seine).

[39] French Section: 34 rue du Bac, Paris.

[40] 88 bis boulevard de Latour-Maubourg, Paris; 5, Place Bellecour, Lyons; 28 rue Belliard, Brussels.

[41] Headquarters: 67 rue Boissière, Paris.

[42] General Secretary: M. l'Abbé Gremand, Collège Saint-Michel, Fribourg, Switzerland.

[43] International Headquarters: Drift 22-24, Utrecht, Holland. French Headquarters: 5 rue Cadet, Paris.

[44] Headquarters: 1 rue des Flamands, Louvain, Belgium.

" International Union of Social Studies ";[45] " International Secretariat of Catholic Youth ";[46] and " International Union of Women's Catholic Leagues." [47]

Internationalism, then, is inculcated in France by both " Right " and " Left " by many agencies. With regionalism, it serves to mitigate and modify the effects of simultaneously inculcated nationalism. There is a national psychology in France. The vast mass of Frenchmen are supremely patriotic. But responsibilities as well as privileges constitute a part of patriotism as it is taught in France; and among the responsibilities of patriotism, that of a regard for the good opinion of the world is a conspicuous mark of French national psychology.

[45] General Secretary: M. Defourny, professeur à l'Université, Louvain, Belgium.

[46] Headquarters: 70 via de la Scrofa, Rome.

[47] Headquarters: Hoogt, 1, Utrecht, Holland.

APPENDICES

APPENDIX A

DIGEST OF TYPICAL TEXTBOOKS IN FRENCH SCHOOLS FOR INSTRUCTION IN HISTORY, MORALS AND CIVICS, GEOGRAPHY, AND READING

I. For Use of Children Aged 6–7 during " Preparatory " Year in Elementary Primary (Maternal) Schools

1. **Augé, Claude,** and **Petit, Maxime,** *Livre Préparatoire d'Histoire de France,* 111th edition (Paris, Larousse, n. d.), 108 pp.

Sketch of political and military history from ancient Gaul to the Great War with attention to national heroes such as Vercingetorix, Clovis, Charlemagne, Roland, Philip Augustus, Saint Louis, Du Guesclin, Joan of Arc, Bayard, Henry IV, Richelieu, Louis XIV, and Napoleon (12 pages on the last-named). Two pages on the Third Republic and one on the Great War. Numerous illustrations, almost all of which are military in character.

The preface addressed to " my dear children " is as follows:

" France has not always been as educated, as rich, and as prosperous as to-day. She was formed slowly, she has grown little by little, and she has ended by becoming one of the greatest states in the world. In studying history you will learn to know all those who have made the French fatherland: the generals who have won battles, the men who have governed our country, the writers and artists who have immortalized the genius of our race. You will see that if France is powerful and respected it is because she has never despaired after the most trying experiences. The glory of France has been slowly and dearly acquired: you have the right to be proud of it, but you have the duty to be worthy of it. And that is why you should learn none too soon, by examples of history, to acquire love of work and devotion to the fatherland."

The causes of the Great War are stated in these words: " The Germans had become very rich and very powerful by their commerce and industry. They wished to be still more rich and powerful and, as they had a redoubtable army, they declared war against France and Russia."

2. **Bedel, Jean,** *L'Année enfantine d'Histoire de France,* 24th edition (Paris, Colin, 1926), 71 pp.

Sketch of political and mainly military history from ancient Gaul to the Great War, with attention to national heroes. Illustrations chiefly of ways of living, though some of battles.

Begins with the sentences: " About 2,000 years ago, France, our dear country, was called Gaul. Gaul was conquered by the Roman general Julius Caesar in spite of the fine defense of the Gallic chieftain Vercingetorix."

The causes of the Great War:

" France remembered 1871; but, generous, she desired only peace. William II wished war. On 28 June 1914, the Archduke and heir of Austria and his wife were assassinated by an anarchist. Austria, where the old Emperor Francis-Joseph reigns, holds Serbia responsible for this murder and declares war against her. However, Russia must help Serbia and France is the ally of Russia. *Both seek to avert the conflict and England endeavors to maintain peace.* But Germany *wills* war, for which she has prepared for 43 years. William II invents pretexts and declares war against us."

The account of the Great War is devoted largely to German atrocities:

" Little children, women and old men, mutilated, tortured, enslaved; villages destroyed, cities martyred, Arras and Reims razed by incendiary bombs; all our factories pillaged, our trees cut down, our coal mines rendered long useless. How recall the ships sunk by submarines, the raids of Zeppelins and Gothas, the bombardment of long-range cannon, the use of asphyxiating gas, inventions of modern German science. . . . [And yet] our heroic soldiers got the better of Germany."

3. **Blanchet, Désiré,** and **Pinard, Jules,** *Premières Leçons d'Histoire de France,* 209th edition (Paris, Belin, 1926), 141 pp.

Sketch of political and military history from ancient Gaul to the Great War with attention to national heroes. Illustrations chiefly of fighting.

Begins: " France, our fatherland, was formerly called Gaul, from the name of its first inhabitants, the Gauls."

Very brief account of Great War:

" After 1871 France, without forgetting Alsace and Lorraine, consecrated herself to peace. It was to assure peace that she concluded an alliance with Russia and established an entente cordiale with England. But Germany let loose the terrible war of 1914–1918. Conquered by France and her allies, Germany had to return us Alsace and Lorraine by the treaty of Versailles. The greatest French generals were Joffre, Foch, and Pétain."

There follow pages on the French colonies, on letters and arts, and on inventions (with tribute to Pasteur). The whole concludes with these words: " To love passionately our country, to respect her law, to submit in good spirit to all obligations which she imposes upon us, to work with courage, such is our duty. It is in the accomplishment of this duty that we shall show ourselves worthy of our glory and our greatness."

4. **Blanchet, Désiré,** and **Toutain, Jules,** *L'Histoire de France à l'École. Premières Notions* (Paris, Belin, n. d.), 24 pp.

Consists of 129 very brief paragraphs surrounded by numerous colored illustrations telling the story of France from Gallic times to 1920.

Begins: " *To the children of France.* France is our fatherland. It is a beautiful and a sweet country. It produces grain, wine, fruits, rich pastures. The French, our ancestors, have made France great and beautiful. Children, learn to know France and to love her. Be good Frenchmen."

A few paragraphs:

104. " Too ambitious, Napoleon made unfortunate wars in Spain and Russia. Conquered at Leipzig, he abdicated at Fontainebleau and withdrew to the Island of Elba."

119. " A great patriot, Gambetta, organized the national defense against the Germans."

123. " The Republic has created our army, opened schools everywhere, conquered vast colonies."

124. " In 1914–1918 France, victorious over Germany, who had attacked us, regained Alsace-Lorraine."

125. " Our France is in the first rank among the nations of the world. She is richer than formerly by reason of her agriculture, her industries, her commerce, and her colonies."

5. **Laclef, A.,** and **Bergeron, Eugène,** *Histoire de France des tout Petits,* 20th edition (Paris, Delalain, n. d.), 118 pp.

Sketch of history of France from prehistoric man to the end of the Great War with attention to national heroes; obviously anti-monarchical and critical of war. Illustrations, but few of them military.

On Napoleon: " After the Revolution, the French were free; they might be happy, but they were not wise. An ambitious general, who had helped to defeat the enemies of France, wished to govern the whole

346 DIGEST OF FRENCH TEXTBOOKS

country and be master quite like the old kings; he had himself crowned *emperor* under the name of Napoleon I. The French let him do it, but they soon regretted it. Napoleon deprived them of their liberties and, in continual wars, caused the death of thousands upon thousands of men. . . . Even more than Louis XIV, Napoleon I left our country completely exhausted." There follows a " reading " from Maupassant on the " Horror of War."

The account of the Great War (7 pages) is headed " Germany wishes to destroy France " and comprises two readings from Maurice Barrès on " The German Crimes " and " Children during the War," and a third on " Our re-found brothers of Alsace-Lorraine." It states that: " The German Emperor, William II, declared war, without cause. Germany wished to crush, to destroy our country. We were without reproach; we proceeded without fear." It is filled with references to the " Boches," the " barbarians."

6. *Syllabaire Langlois, 2e Livret,* 17th edition (Paris, Colin, 1925), 156 + 73 pp.

A primer. It is not at all nationalist in the present edition, but earlier editions of the same book contained such passages as these:

" Remember, little French children, that it was Germany which attacked France and forced her to wage the Great War. Remember that, for more than four years, Belgium and northern France were occupied by the Germans. Our enemies behaved like barbarians, robbing the factories of machinery, the houses of furniture, and the museums of beautiful masterpieces. Cities were destroyed by them, and villages razed. They poisoned well-water and cut down fruit trees. The Germans committed atrocious crimes, mutilating or killing children, shooting women and old men. With their airplanes they bombarded our cities, causing numerous deaths. Their submarines sank merchant-ships and even hospital-ships. Conquered, the Germans asked for peace. Our soldiers went into their country to occupy it, but they behaved humanely, respecting the inhabitants and their goods. Eternal shame to Germany! Eternal glory to sweet France and her Allies! "

II. For Use of Children Aged 7–9 during Two-Year " Elementary Course " in Elementary Primary Schools

1. **Aulard, A.,** and **Debidour, A.,** *Récits familiers sur les Grands Personnages et les Faits principaux de l'Histoire nationale,* 13th edition (Paris, Rieder, n. d.), 112 + 94 pp.

Sketch of French history from prehistoric age to end of nineteenth century with attention to national heroes and state of civilization. Illustrations chiefly of persons.

Tendency to exalt the Revolution and the Republic. " The soldiers of the Republic were heroic soldiers. . . . They conquered the Kings of Europe and saved the fatherland." On the other hand Napoleon is spoken of in these words: " He persecuted the republicans. . . . He was a man of genius, but his pride and ambition worked much evil for France. . . . He abused popular confidence by undertaking ruinous wars, he ruined France and caused her to lose the *frontier of the Rhine,* which the Convention [Republic] had given her."

The war of 1870 is blamed on the Empress Eugénie. " Gambetta wanted nobly to continue the war, but the country was tired of it and asked for peace. . . . Germany took from us those dear provinces of Alsace and Lorraine, whose population, so French at heart, have not ceased to love us."

Because of its anti-clerical tendencies the book has been condemned by the French bishops and may not be used in Catholic schools.

2. **Blanchet, Désiré,** *Histoire de France, Cours élémentaire,* 256th edition (Paris, Belin, 1926), 168 pp.

Sketch of military and political history of France from the Gauls to the end of the Great War with attention to national heroes. Illustrations, chiefly of warriors.

Only the glories of Napoleon are discussed. There is no mention of the causes of the war of 1870, beyond the statement that " France was not ready." The Great War is briefly commented upon as follows: " France wished to live at peace with all nations. But in 1914 Germany provoked a general war. With the allies, England, Russia, and the United States, France fought valiantly for right and justice. Victorious in 1918, she imposed on Germany, in 1919, the treaty of Versailles, which returned Alsace-Lorraine to us."

The book concludes with a " Moral of History " in these words:

" Children, you have read the history of your country, the recital of its victories and defeats, its prosperity and adversity. Love your country as citizens and soldiers. As citizens you will fulfil all your duties and remain attached to the institutions which the Republic has founded. As soldiers you will perform with zeal your military service and, if the fatherland appeals to your devotion, you will be ready to shed your blood for it. Thus France will follow the path of its glorious destiny if all citizens are united in the same sentiment, love of the fatherland."

3. **Blanchet, Désiré,** and **Toutain, Jules,** *L'Histoire de France à l'École: Cours élémentaire et moyen,* 19th edition (Paris, Belin, 1926), 64 pp.

Sketch of history of France from the Gauls to 1919. Illustrations mainly military. The text is paralleled by brief anecdotes chiefly of a military character.

Twice the Great War is mentioned in almost identical words: " In 1914 Germany unchained a terrible war against France, Russia, and England. But vanquished on the Marne in 1914, pushed back at Verdun in 1916, she had to capitulate in 1918. The Treaty of Versailles (1919) returned Alsace-Lorraine to France."

4. **Brossolette, L.,** *Histoire de France: Cours élémentaire,* new edition, 158th thousand (Paris, Delagrave, 1926), 160 pp.

Sketch of history of France from time of the Gauls to 1610 with special attention to wars and national heroes. Numerous bellicose illustrations. In the last few pages of the book there is a very brief pictorial history of France since 1610, and these pictures are of civilization rather than of fighting.

The first lesson is summarized as follows: " Our country was formerly called Gaul. The inhabitants were Gauls. More than anything else the Gauls loved war."

The book is critical of monarchy, laudatory of the Republic, and anti-clerical in tendency. It has been condemned by the French bishops and may not be used in Catholic schools.

5. **Charrier, Ch.,** *Nos Lectures: Cours élémentaire,* 2d edition (Paris, Hatier, 1923), 228 pp.

A reader, comprising seventy short, simple selections — seven for each month.

Fifteen selections deal with patriotic episodes of the Great War and others deal with such topics as " Roland at Roncevaux," " Siege of Paris by the Normans," " Battle of Bouvines," " Saint-Louis," " Du Guesclin." About half the selections have no special nationalist implication.

One of the war-tales tells how two little French children (aged eight and ten) outwitted a detachment of Germans and saved the lives of thirty French soldiers.

6. **Fournier,** *Les Lectures des Petits: Premier Livre de Lecture courante,* 11th edition, 500th thousand (Paris, Gedalge, n. d.), 128 pp.

A reader comprising forty-two short, simple selections, interspersed with pictures and specimens of writing.

Pretty and familiar stories and fanciful descriptions. Not at all nationalist.

7. **Gauthier** and **Deschamps**, *Cours d'Histoire de France: Cours élémentaire,* new edition (Paris, Hachette, n. d.), 97 pp.

Sketch of history of France from time of the Gauls chiefly to 1610 and, more briefly, to 1919. National heroes are stressed and the illustrations are mainly of persons.

The tone of the book may be perceived from the following account of the battle of Bouvines (1214):

" Bouvines. . . . It was a great victory. *1214.* . . . A happy date in the history of the fatherland, for Bouvines was our first national victory. All classes: knights, burgesses, clergy; united in face of peril. They had to drive the enemies from France: English, Germans. All France was happy over the victory of Bouvines."

On the Great War: " It was willed by Austria and above all by Germany." There is a glowing tribute to Guynemer, " the valiant aviator ":

" He is the Roland of our epoch. Like Roland, he was very valiant; and like Roland he died for France. His life is more beautiful than can be imagined. . . . Roland was the example of knights of olden time. Guynemer is the example of Frenchmen of to-day. . . . I shall never forget him, because he died for France like my papa."

8. **Guyau,** *L'Année préparatoire de Lecture courante,* 86th edition (Paris, Colin, 1926), 214 pp.

A reader, comprising sixty-five selections, illustrated and designed to afford moral and civic training as well as to supply useful information of a very simple sort.

One selection treats of the War of 1870 and seven treat of the Great War. The first on the Great War tells how a young school teacher died an heroic death for the fatherland and explains the cause of the war as follows:

" After the conquest of Alsace and of a part of Lorraine, the ambition of the German Emperor and his people did not cease to grow. Now they must have quite a section of France because our fatherland possesses a mild climate, a fertile soil, numerous mines, sources of wealth. The Germans resemble certain criminals who await a favorable opportunity to throw themselves on those whom they wish to despoil.

William II felt sure of victory because of the number of his soldiers and the terrible arms which his factories produced, and he tried to bring on a war. But France desired peace; she opposed only patience to his provocations. Then William II had Austria pick a bad quarrel with Serbia. As soon as Russia mobilized to support Serbia the Emperor of Germany seized the occasion to declare war against Russia. Through our defensive alliance with this Empire we were thus drawn into the conflict, which William II willed."

9. **Laclef, E.,** and **Bergeron, E.,** *Notions essentielles d'Histoire de France: Cours élémentaire,* 26th edition (Paris, Delalain, n. d.), 186 pp.

Sketch of history of France from prehistoric times to the end of the Great War, with special attention to legends, anecdotes, and national heroes. Illustrations chiefly of persons.

In a section on modern science lauding Pasteur, appears the following:

" It was likewise a French scientist who contributed to the invention of wireless telegraphy; another who, after fifty years of tireless toil, conferred upon our country the marvellous discovery of refrigeration. . . . The first submarine was also due to a Frenchman. It is in France that the automobile industry made the greatest progress; it is to France that aviation owes most."

No mention of any scientific achievements elsewhere.

On the causes of the Great War:

" For a long time Germany desired and prepared a new war against France, and the Kaiser Wilhelm II did not cease to threaten us. In 1914 the occasion for an attack against us presented itself in the following circumstances: Austria, allied with Germany, sought a bad quarrel with a little neighboring nation, Serbia, and declared war on her. Russia wished to protect Serbia, but the Kaiser opposed it and declared war first against Russia and then against France, allied with Russia.

" The peace of Versailles is a peace of justice. It marks the triumph of right over might."

No mention of the League of Nations.

10. **Lavisse, Ernest,** *Histoire de France, Cours élémentaire* 1832d thousand (Paris, Colin, 1926), 184 pp.

Sketch of history of France from the time of the Gauls to the end of the nineteenth century, with special attention to national heroes.

and with some closing general reflections, of a highly emotional character, on the Great War. Illustrated.

The French are invariably pictured as brave and noble, willing and glad to die for the fatherland. The whole book is intensely, passionately patriotic.

After describing in moving words some of the horrors of the Great War, the author states:

" All these terrible things happened because Germany wished to become mistress of the world. Therefore, she desired to destroy France. . . . My dear little ones, you will remember your fathers and brothers who have suffered so much during the five years of the war, who in so great numbers have fallen on the field of honor. To the very end of your life you will think of them every day."

11. **Lavisse, Ernest,** *Les Récits de Pierre Laloi* (Paris, Colin, 1925), 179 pp.

A book of readings for the classes in moral and civic training. The selections are grouped under such headings as health, temperance, love of labor, sincerity, courage, fraternity, conscience, the family, the school, the fatherland, the duties of all citizens, the social life, and the Republic.

Mottos in heavy type are printed at the end of each selection, including: " Nothing is more beautiful than a numerous family well united " (with a picture of the father and mother and twelve children); " Let us remember those who have died for the fatherland "; " The fatherland is the whole of France "; " Obedience to law is the first duty of the citizen "; etc.

The selections on patriotism deal with the noble behavior of Frenchmen, especially young Frenchmen, in the face of German invasion. One of them concludes: " Children, listen attentively to your teachers when they speak to you of the fatherland. Your teachers are patriots; by example as well as by word they teach you devotion to France."

12. **Mathieu, l'Abbé,** *La Lecture expliquée au Cours élémentaire,* 7th edition (Paris, Hatier, 1925), 240 pp.

A reader comprising eighty-six short selections — eight or nine for each month. Used chiefly in private (Catholic) schools.

More than half the selections are of familiar stories and poems. A fourth deal directly or indirectly with religion, such as " Vocation," " Angel and child," " Counsels for a first Communion," " Evening Prayer," " Christmas Night," etc. The remainder are patriotic, several treating of the heroic attitude of Belgium towards the Germans, one describing duties to France, another idealizing the French flag, etc.

One selection inculcates the forgiveness of enemies, even after war. A eulogy of Marshal Foch contains these words: " The English were ready for flight. Foch sought General French. Dialogue: ' If you leave me, I shall die with my Frenchmen.' General French regained courage." An instruction to pupils to tell " what the Germans did in the occupied territories " is accompanied by two pictures, the one showing a seizure of children by brutal German soldiers and the other representing a burning of a house in which a father and his daughter perish before the crazed eyes of a wife and mother. There are three or four other pictures of a similarly revolting character in the book. The book concludes with Alphonse Daudet's famous story of " La Dernière Classe."

13. **Mironneau, A.,** *Choix de Lectures: Cours élémentaire,* 25th edition, 913th thousand (Paris, Colin, 1926), 300 pp.

A reader comprising numerous brief selections.

A third of the selections are stories and descriptions. Another third seek to give moral and social training and deal with the family, the school, qualities and faults, social duties, and the fatherland. The selections in the last third are historical or geographical or refer to the Great War.

On the fatherland are seven selections: the little peasant boy of Lorraine; the child-soldier; the refusal of the peasant to leave his land except to fight for the common fatherland; the Greek boy; the killing of a French patriot by the Germans in the war of 1870; a tribute to the French flag; and the little drummer boy. The historical selections, fifteen in number, and four of the five selections on the Great War are intensely patriotic. The fifth, an extract from the Bulletin of the Armies, relates a story of mutual chivalry between Germans and English in the midst of the fighting about Ypres.

14. **Pierron, R.,** and **Pruvot, G.,** *L'Évolution française: Histoire de France du Certificat d'Études* (Paris, Lesot, n. d.), 103 pp.

A sketch of French history, very brief up to 1610, and a bit more detailed since 1610. Many illustrations and charts in color and numerous pictures in black and white.

The book is zealously democratic and republican and patriotic. Considerable attention is given to social and economic developments.

On the Great War:

" Brusquely in 1914 we had to undergo a terrible war, which lasted until 1918, a war provoked by Germany, who wished to dominate the world and to create markets. She brought into the war Austria and

Turkey. On our side we had as allies the Belgians, the English, the Russians, the Italians, the Americans, etc."

The League of Nations is mentioned and a section entitled " After the War " reads as follows:

" Externally, we have had to recall Germany constantly to the execution of the treaty of Versailles, which the Dawes Plan now seems to assure. We have been obliged, moreover, to make great sacrifices in order to reconcile our interests with those of our allies. Finally the troubled equilibrium of Europe is maintained only by dint of prudence and firmness. Internally the reconstruction of the devastated regions, the stabilization of the franc, and the struggle against the high cost of living have constituted the constant preoccupation of our Government."

15. **Plique-Rogeaux, Mme.,** and **Sion, Ch.,** *La Politesse en Action,* 2d edition (Paris, Belin, 1925), 96 pp.

A book of readings for the inculcation of politeness.
One of the first readings:

" French politeness has always been famous throughout the world. It is a heritage of our ancestors, of which we can be proud and which we must preciously preserve, for it contributes to make France loved. To-day when all Frenchmen are equal before the law and are free citizens they ought more than ever to show to one another the regard which testifies to their mutual esteem and to the sentiment of their dignity."

Otherwise, the book is not at all nationalist.

16. **Pomot, Henri,** and **Besseige, Henri,** *Petite Histoire du Peuple français* (Paris, Les Presses Universitaires, 1928), 179 pp.

A sketch of French history, very brief up to 1610 and somewhat more detailed thereafter. Emphasizes social life and economic development. Critical of Napoleon I and Napoleon III, and laudatory of the Revolution and the Republic.

The causes of the Great War are explained as follows:

" The Germans had a *powerful army* with many machine-guns and heavy cannons. They were allied with the *Austrians.* Their Emperor *William II* delivered threatening speeches; he said, for example, that his powder was dry and his sword very sharp. France, on her side, did not wish war. But she had not forgotten Alsace and Lorraine. To defend herself against the Germans, she was obliged to have a numerous army. Besides, she was allied with *Russia*, equally menaced by Germany. The *English*, jealous at seeing the Germans too powerful, had become our friends. *War had to be expected*."

The brief narrative of the War is very restrained and matter-of-fact, and concludes with these words in bold-faced type: " While admiring the heroism of the ' poilus,' reasonable people began to detest war and to put forth every effort to prevent its recurrence."

A final chapter on the League of Nations comprises paragraphs headed as follows: " The horrors of war make it hateful; nations have need of one another; peoples, like individuals, ought to regulate their disputes in court; the League of Nations; the Assembly and Council; the League of Nations has already accomplished much for peace; France has played a great rôle in the League; the Germans have joined the League; necessity of aiding and supporting the League." As a whole the book is written in the spirit of humanitarianism and internationalism.

III. For Use of Children Aged 9–11 during Two-Year " Middle Course " in Elementary Primary Schools

1. **Aulard A.,** *Éléments d'Instruction civique: Cours moyen,* new revised edition, 120th thousand (Paris, Rieder, 1922), 61 pp.

Comprises sixteen lessons: one on France, one on the French nation one on patriotism, one on France and other countries, one on the League of Nations, and the other eleven on the organization and functioning of the French government.

The first lesson begins: " France is our *country*, it is our *nation* it is our *fatherland;* " and then proceeds to define each of these terms

Patriotism is defined as " the solidarity among all members of the great French family."

" In civilized humanity " [the author goes on to say], " the French nation is the only one which strives to give an example of a society aspiring to govern itself by reason, only by reason, without invoking the aid of a superhuman authority. The French have the duty of defending France by arms, if, unfortunately, foreigners make war on us. . . . We must love ourselves and aid each other and let every individual live not only for himself, but for France, for the nation, for the Republic. That is what we mean by patriotism.

" The *rôle* of France in the world, as the French Revolution has defined it, is to proclaim the right of people to govern themselves, to give the example of fraternity among peoples by the pacific diffusion of the *principles of 1789*. . . . There is the *historic rôle*, the true grandeur of France among all the nations. Therefore, let us love France and let us not hate other nations."

On the army:

" If it were not for the army, France would be conquered and would become German or Russian. But, we wish to *remain French,* and, besides, the existence of France is useful to humanity. Therefore, let us perform our military service with *good humor* since it is necessary. Let us perform it with *zeal,* complying fully with the *military regulations,* since it is for the sake of France."

The lesson on the League of Nations is the last in the book. It concludes: " All Frenchmen have duties not only to France, but also to the League of Nations. They must realize that people, to live happily, are obliged to aid one another. There is a *solidarity* of peoples as there is a solidarity of individuals."

On account of the anti-clerical tone of the book, it has been condemned by the French bishops and may not be used in Catholic schools.

2. **Aulard, A.,** and **Debidour, A.,** *Histoire de France: Cours moyen,* 31st edition entirely revised (Paris, Rieder, n. d.), 288 pp.

A brief summary of the history of France from Gallic times to 1610 and a somewhat more extended treatment of French history from 1610 to 1919. It is anti-royalist, decidedly pro-republican, and so anti-clerical that it has been condemned by the French bishops and may not be used in Catholic schools. It pays some attention to science and art as well as to politics. It is vigorously patriotic.

The beginning of the Great War is described in these words:

" From 1906 to 1914, under the presidency of M. Fallières and then under that of M. Poincaré, France worked in peace, when she was attacked by Germany. On August 3, 1914, the German Emperor, William II, declared war against us, falsely alleging that French airplanes had bombarded the city of Nuremberg and other German districts. This was completely false. But the Emperor of Austria-Hungary sought unjustly to quarrel with a little nation, Serbia, which he wished to rob of independence. Russia, our ally, supported Serbia, its friend. Germany, which supported Austria-Hungary, wished to crush us with a rapid blow in order to turn next against Russia and crush her in turn. That is why Germany declared war against us on a falsehood."

Speaking of the Treaty of Versailles, the authors say:

" A League of Nations has been instituted. Let us strengthen it in order to ensure peace forever. If peoples govern themselves they cease to hate one another, and if they behave like brothers, there will be no more war, and *the heroes of national defense* will not have shed their blood in vain."

3. **Bayet, Albert,** *Leçons de Morale: Cours moyen,* new revised edition (Paris, Rieder, n. d.), 182 pp.

A book of readings on altruism, health, courage, honesty, politeness, tolerance, duties towards one's family and friends, etc. The readings are adaptations from the writings of Marcus Aurelius, La Fontaine, F. Buisson, Maupassant, Tolstoi, Pestalozzi, Victor Hugo, Pascal, Rousseau, Voltaire, Condorcet, Anatole France, etc.

Not at all nationalist. There is observable, however, some anti-Catholic bias, and the French bishops have condemned it.

4. **Blanchet, Désiré,** *Histoire de France: Cours moyen,* 256th edition entirely revised (Paris, Belin, 1925), 280 pp.

A brief review of French history from Gallic times to 1610 and a more detailed treatment since 1610. Illustrations chiefly of political personages and soldiers. Nationalist almost to the extent of jingoism. Extracts:

"Napoleon died May 5, 1821. 'I attribute,' he said, 'the opprobrium of my death to the reigning house of England.' . . .

"The war of 1870, which was so cruel for our country, must inspire us with patriotic thoughts. To defend the fatherland, if ever it should be again attacked, we must fulfill all our duties and particularly our military duties. Peoples that lose their military prowess are peoples condemned to perish. History pronounces against these the final sentence: 'Woe to the vanquished.' Let us not forget the war of 1870. . . .

"The frightful conflict provoked by Germany in 1914 has aroused unusual indignation. It is to avoid such catastrophes in the future that the Treaty of Versailles has provided for the creation of the League of Nations, whose purpose is to maintain peace throughout the world. The courage, the tenacity, the spirit of sacrifice, of which France has given proof from 1914 to 1918, have given her an incomparable prestige among all people. She must now get back to work with a new energy."

5. **Blanchet, Désiré,** and **Toutain, Jules,** *L'Histoire de France à l'École: Cours élémentaire et moyen,* 19th edition (Paris, Belin, 1926), 64 pp.

(For description, see II, 3 above.)

6. **Bruno, G.**, *Les Enfants de Marcel, Instruction morale et civique en Action, Livre de Lecture courante: Cours moyen*, 137th edition (Paris, Belin, 1924), 286 pp.

Very widely used before the Great War, it is now much less used. The present edition does not differ perceptibly from the edition analyzed and discussed by Professor Reisner in his *Nationalism and Education since 1789* (New York, Macmillan, 1920). An intensely nationalist book.

7. **Bruno, G.**, *Le Tour de la France par deux Enfants: Devoir et Patrie: Cours moyen*, 392d edition entirely revised and supplemented with an epilogue (Paris, Belin, 1926), 322 pp.

For moral and civic instruction. A fanciful trip of two children, cast in story-form and told in such a way as to inspire ardent patriotism and to give school children some lively notions of correct personal and social behavior and much useful knowledge of the geography and political institutions of France.

The little heroes of the story are two boys of Lorraine who cannot bear to live under German rule. As one of them exclaims: " Beloved France! We are thy sons and all our lives we will be worthy of thee." And they remain, throughout their travels and experiences, most proper little boys, paragons of virtue. And among their many virtues patriotism stands foremost.

The author says in her preface: " In grouping all moral and civic instruction around the idea of *France,* we have desired to present to children the fatherland under its most noble features and to show them that it is great in honor, in labor, in profound respect for duty and justice."

8. **Bruno, G.**, *Le Tour de l'Europe pendant la Guerre, Cours moyen*, 10th edition supplemented with an epilogue (Paris, Belin, 1926), 315 pp.

A reader. A continuation of the author's story of travel, this time outside of France.

The countries are taken up in the following order: " Our allies " (England, Belgium, Russia, Japan, Serbia); Germany; Austria-Hungary; Ottoman Empire; " the neutrals " (Switzerland, Scandinavia, Holland, Balkan States, Italy, Spain, Portugal). Later in the book, Italy declares war upon Austria and is therefore given a new write-up; and in the epilogue (comprising thirty-nine brief chapters) the United States is given considerable attention. The whole closes with the "entry of our troops into Mayence — the passage of the Rhine " and " memory of the past — hope for the future."

The whole book is militantly patriotic. Suffice to quote the last sentence: " I shall go happy because I have seen Alsace delivered, our France greater than ever, and the dawn of the covenant of universal peace."

9. **Calvet, C.,** *Histoire de France: Cours moyen,* new edition entirely revised (Paris, Bibliothèque d'Éducation, n.d.), 320 + 16 pp.

A brief summary of the history of France to 1610 and a somewhat more detailed treatment of French history from 1610 to 1900 with a sixteen-page supplement on the Great War. Illustrated. Strongly anti-royalist and pro-republican; so anti-clerical that it has been condemned by the French bishops; anti-Napoleon, patriotic.

On " France To-day ":

" France is no longer the vanquished of 1870. She has recovered Alsace-Lorraine, favored the reconstitution of Poland, aided in the liberation of countries formerly oppressed by the Austro-Hungarian Monarchy. . . . By her efforts, which her allies of the Great War seconded, a sort of equilibrium, confessedly still insecure, tends to be established in Europe, and she thus contributes to the maintenance of general peace. But, however anxious she may be to avoid any conflict, she intends to have the Treaty of Versailles of 1919 executed and to defend her independence against an offensive return of German nationalism: whence the necessity of keeping a strong army."

On the responsibility for the Great War:

" To realize the wish of his people, which was to put " Germany above everything," William II did not hesitate to unchain a European struggle. The pretext was supplied by an unexpected incident, the assassination of the heir-apparent of Austria, an assassination in which a Serb took part. The Austrian government, urged on by William II, pretended to hold Serbia responsible for the crime. It was to provoke Russia, the natural protector of the Slavs. France ranged herself on the side of her ally."

10. **Chadeyras, F.,** *Belles Lectures françaises: Cours moyen,* 75th thousand (Paris, Delagrave, 1925), 280 pp.

A reader, comprising 135 selections, of which 29 deal with patriotic subjects and one deals with the League of Nations.

Most of the 29 selections of a patriotic sort are of battles or episodes of the Great War; others are from writings of Lavisse, Victor Hugo, Quinet, Barrès, Clartie, etc.

The final selection, on the League of Nations, is an eloquent indictment of war and a plea for international peace.

11. **Charrier, C.,** *Nos Lectures: Cours moyen et supérieur,* 4th edition (Paris, Hatier, 1924), 390 pp.

A reader comprising 150 selections, of which 35 deal with patriotic subjects.

Most of the 35 patriotic selections treat of battles or episodes of the Great War; others tell how the Marseillaise was written or praise the tricolor or extol patriotism or celebrate national achievements.

One — number 147, by E. Moselly — is headed " After the War " and is written around two refrains of " we shall never forget " and " we shall never forgive." The last paragraph is as follows:

" We shall never forget. The time will come when the German, perpetual traveller, attracted by sweet France, will take his way among our fields and our vines. Child of my country, shepherd lad of the Garonne or of the Meuse, thou wilt recognize his crafty face, the feather in his hat, and also, I think, the little cloth notebook wherein he furtively writes down, behind the hedge, poetical effusions and notes for the general staff. Child of my country, if this traveller extends his hand to thee, do not take it. Look well into his heart; thou wilt see there an ineffaceable stain, that of the blood of thy father and of thy elder brother."

12. **De la Vaulx, Henri,** and **Galopin, Arnould,** *Un Tour du Monde en Aéroplane,* revised and annotated by a group of teachers with a preface by G. B. Tartière, new ed. (Paris, Albin Michel, n. d.), 492 pp.

A reader telling a highly fanciful tale of an international aeroplane race from France to America, Australia, Asia, Africa, and back to France. The French aeroplane, bearing a very brave and most resourceful French boy, wins the race, outdistancing its English and American rivals and outwitting and foiling the sinister plots of its German rival. The German pilot, after a most villainous career, finally incites a rebellion of Moroccans against the French, but is captured and put to death. " Justice is done," as the French pilot remarks.

The descriptions of foreign countries are meagre and often inaccurate; they are subordinated to the story-interest of German villainy and French heroism. A large amount of space is given to an account of the French colonies in Africa.

13. **Dès, Madame,** *Jean et Lucie, Histoire de deux jeunes Refugiés, La Guerre racontée aux Enfants: Cours moyen et supérieur,* preface by Henri Havard (Paris, Fernand Nathan, n. d.), 360 pp.

A highly emotional and colorful account of the Great War, in story form, as a reader.

The general tendency of the book is shown in the following passages:

" Our gratitude would be sterile if we should forget that the enemy has been inhuman and disloyal, that he has conducted the war in a horrible manner, that not only the soldiers but the German civilians, even the women, have applauded the atrocities ordered by the chiefs, the very thought of which fills our heart with disgust. . . . Do not forget that, little Frenchmen. To forget it would be an insult to our dead. It would be likewise a menace for the future. It is dangerous to go to sleep with a snake at our side, and Germany has lied too much for us to be able ever to have faith in her word.

" You must, my dear child, be worthy of this patrimony of honor. You must continue to practice the virtues of your ancestors and become better every day. Thus you will contribute, you, little student, to the greatness and glory of *Immortal France.*"

14. **Devinat, E.,** and **Toursel, A.,** *Histoire de France: Cours moyen,* new edition (Paris, Martinet, n. d.), 114 pp.

A survey of French history since 1610 with an introductory review of earlier history. Strongly republican and patriotic. Illustrated.

On the responsibility for the Great War:

" Proud of her strength, Germany wished not only to grow, but to dominate other peoples. And she had not satisfied against our country in 1871 all the thirst for vengeance which burned in her since Jena. In June 1914 an archduke of Austria was assassinated in Serbia, a Slavic nation. Austria demanded harsh reparations, which that little country accepted. In spite of everything, Austria, urged on by Germany, would attack Serbia, but Russia, ' mother of the Slavs,' opposed it. France and Russia *proposed to submit the difficulty to arbitration.* The Central States refused and the Emperor of Germany, William II, allied to Austria, declared war against Russia and then, under a false pretext that French airplanes had bombarded a German city, the Kaiser attacked us. France had done everything to avoid war."

France after the war:

" We are victors and our dear provinces of Alsace and Lorraine have been recovered. . . . In the German Republic the warlike spirit of revenge has not yet disappeared. . . . And we must not forget that five times in a little more than a century our country has been invaded by Germans: 1792, 1814, 1815, 1870, 1914. France would wish no more war, but does that suffice to keep us from being attacked? "

A page is devoted to " Arbitration and the League of Nations." A paragraph on the Locarno agreement ends: " With compulsory arbitration, is the era of European peace really beginning? "

On account of its anti-clerical tone the book has been condemned by the French bishops and may not be used in Catholic schools.

15. **" Fédération de l'Enseignement,"** *Nouvelle Histoire de France: Cours moyen* (Quimper, Librairie Goanach, n. d.), 352 pp.

A sketch of French history prepared by a group of teachers affiliated with the Communist Party. Half of the book deals with the period since 1789. It emphasizes class-conflicts between the nobility and the bourgeoisie and between the bourgeoisie and the proletariat. It devotes considerable attention to politics, particularly to political revolutions, but more to economic transformation and the living and working conditions of peasants and laborers.

Praise is accorded to the Republic for many achievements, but it is pointed out that much remains to be accomplished. The treatment of the Great War is brief and critical. It concludes:

" The world ought now to live at peace. But peace depends not merely on political conditions. It depends above all on economic conditions, on industrial and commercial agreement throughout the world. It depends also on the will of peoples. When the peoples, better instructed, shall know each other better they will cease to hate one another, and governments will no longer be able to hurl some against others. As Anatole France said once to teachers: ' The union of the laborers will bring peace to the world.' "

16. **Gauthier** and **Deschamps,** *Cours d'Histoire de France: Cours moyen,* new edition (Paris, Hachette, n. d.), 161 pp.

A survey of French history, very brief up to 1610 and more detailed thereafter. Comprises 176 paragraphs of historical text chiefly of a political or military nature, interspersed with " readings " on such topics as " For the Fatherland even unto death," " Our national hymn," " The soldiers of the Republic," " The insult of the Bey of Algiers," " The Siege of Paris in 1870," " The Colonies," " The Marne — Glory to the Victors." The book is intensely republican and nationalist. Its anti-clericalism has been condemned by the French bishops.

The account of the Great War is headed: " William II prepares his War." Twelve pages are devoted to the story of French courage and German atrocity from 1914 to 1918. No mention of the League of Nations.

17. **Giraud, Jean,** *Histoire de France de 1610 à 1919,* 3d edition (Paris, De Gigord, 1925), 167 pp.

A political and military history with some attention to the Church and to social and economic conditions. Used chiefly in private (Catholic) schools. Less nationalist than some of the others.

On the War of 1870: " Prussia, ready for war, caused France to declare it."

On the military law of 1913: " This law was vigorously opposed by the radicals and socialists, whose dangerous ' pacifism ' did not envisage the war quite near."

The immediate causes of the Great War are set forth with some attempt at judiciousness. The treatment of the military operations of the war is relatively brief, though space is found for a special reading on " The crimes of Germany," and for another on " The triumph of France."

The League of Nations is mentioned.

18. **Habert, P.,** and **Bouillot, V.,** *Lectures choisies d'Auteurs contemporains: Cours moyen,* 3d edition (Paris, Hachette, n. d.), 412 pp.

A reader, comprising 129 selections, of which 53 are patriotic or nationalist, and of these all but two deal with aspects of the Great War.

Most of the numerous selections on the Great War treat of French bravery or German cruelty, and the " atrocity " stories are reinforced with disgusting pictures. To cite only a few of the many which might be mentioned, there is (p. 35) a poem by Miguel Zamacois about a little French boy of seven years whom the Germans had killed while he was playing with a toy gun, with a sad picture of the dead boy; there is (p. 60) a poem by Jean Aicard about another horrible German atrocity, with a gruesome picture showing a dead Frenchman in a ditch and a young French boy killing a German officer; there is (p. 368) a story by Benjamin Valloton about still another German atrocity, with a picture showing a line of middle-aged German soldiers shooting down a brave, honest little boy, who has been stood up against a wall.

19 **Huguet, G., Jouannon, E.,** and **Brestau, A.,** *Petits Français, n'oubliez pas. Livre de Lecture: Cours moyen,* 2d edition (Paris, Delagrave, 1920), 256 pp.

A reader, comprising 86 selections, all about the Great War.

The following are typical titles of the selections: " The Horror of the War," " In Alsace," " A letter from the Front," " The dead," " School in mourning," " Story of a crime," " Slavery," " How women make war," " Under the bombs," " Germany conquered."

There are numerous illustrations and these are harrowing and moving. A typical picture is that (p. 94) of a man showing a boy some awful ruins with the inscription: " Look, child, and remember."

From the author's " Preface to Children ":

" *Forgetting would be treason.* . . . Listen. If you forgot that one day a proud and brutal people, after 44 years of deceitful peace, had thrown itself on your country to establish its domination, if all the French acted like you, our enemies would profit therefrom to forge new arms and to unchain another war wherein France that time would go down vanquished and abased. France would be betrayed by the heedlessness of her children. But you will not desire that it be so, and, after having read this book, you will watch carefully for any new danger which may threaten your country, you will keep a perpetual memory of the sublime heroism of our soldiers, of great suffering valiantly borne by all the French, and you will love still more your Fatherland."

20. **Laclef, A.**, and **Bergeron, E.**, *Histoire de France essentielle: Cours moyen:* 27th edition (Paris, Delalain, n. d.), 308 pp.

A survey of French history, brief up to 1610 and more detailed thereafter to 1900, ending with a fairly detailed account of the Great War. Illustrations of political personages and battles. Mainly a political and military history.

Every other page is devoted to a rather simple and straightforward narration of facts, selected and told with some calm and judiciousness. Alternate pages are filled with " readings," most of which are intensely patriotic. For example, there are stirring " readings " on the conquest of Algeria, the Crimean War, the sorry treatment of French prisoners by the Germans in 1870, the suffering of the Parisians during the siege, the sad fate of Alsace-Lorraine, France to-day, patriotism, etc.

The origins of the Great War are described with greater fullness and judiciousness than in most books of the same grade, but a " reading " makes a terribly emotional indictment of " the crimes of Germany " and another, from the pen of Ernest Lavisse, exalts the triumph of France in 1919. There is no mention of the League of Nations.

21. **Lavisse, Ernest**, *Histoire de France: Cours moyen,* 25th edition, 2004th thousand (Paris, Colin, 1926), 272 pp.

A survey of French history, brief up to 1610 and more detailed thereafter, with a concluding chapter on the Great War. Illustrations chiefly of persons. A warmly republican and democratic "liberal" book pervaded throughout with the most ardent and emotional patriotism.

The text is interspersed with such italicized paragraphs as the following: "There is perhaps not a country in the world which would have shown so much courage in a like situation as France in 1870"; "France does not believe that one has the right to treat men like beasts, who change their masters without being consulted"; "The terrible year (1870) was one of the saddest moments in our whole history"; "France is the freest country in the world — that is a great honor"; "France has contributed more than any other country to the progress of aviation."

The account of the Great War begins with "ambition and pride of Germany" and ends with a glowing tribute to the Peace of Versailles. "The peace of Versailles, peace of justice, is also a peace of humanity. . . . May the Great War, whence France and the Allies have issued victorious, be the last of wars."

The book concludes with "General Reflections," from which two passages are here quoted:

"At the commencement of the war, we were almost alone in face of the enemy. By halting his advance, we gave time to England to increase her military forces and to Italy and the United States to join us. At the end, when the Allies understood the necessity of a single military command, it was a Frenchman, Marshal *Foch*, whom they chose to lead them to victory. . . .

"For almost fifty years, since the disastrous treaty of Frankfurt, I have lived in a France defeated, dismembered, humiliated. I have suffered defeat, dismemberment, humiliation. I have seen, because France was defeated, Germany imagine that she might do anything; her pride and ambition menaced the human race. But, without desiring war, I have always hoped that a day would come when France would take her just revenge and when humanity, thanks to her, would be assured of its liberty and dignity; for France and humanity are not two words in opposition to each other; they are conjoint and inseparable. Our Fatherland is the most human of Fatherlands. Vive la France."

22. **Lavisse, Ernest,** *Les Récits de Pierre Laloi* (Paris, Colin, 1925), 179 pp.

(For description, see II, 11 above.)

23. **Lavisse, Général E.,** " *Tu seras Soldat,*" *Histoire d'un Soldat français,* 24th ed. (Paris, Colin, 1916), 320 pp.

Readings and patriotic lessons for military instruction. Very widely used between 1880 and 1900, but latterly much less used.

Its character is clearly indicated in the preface:

" This book is destined for the youth of the schools. About imaginary personages, the heroes of the book, I have grouped numerous true stories, chosen as far as possible from times nearest to our own [the Franco-Prussian War of 1870–1871]. In speaking to young people of all the griefs inflicted upon France in 1870, when she was subjected to foreign invasions, in acquainting them with what the defeat has cost us, I have desired to show them to what frightful misfortunes a people is exposed which does not keep on guard and is not sufficiently armed to defend its frontiers *always menaced.* In exposing as simply as possible the organization of our armed forces on land and sea, I have wished to prove that they are powerful and well organized and to create in the soul *confidence.* In explaining the noble mission of the army, in demonstrating its utility and its necessity, in citing examples of discipline and devotion afforded by its officers and men, I have desired to teach the children to love it and to prepare them to fulfil a sacred duty, that of *military service.* To sum up my thought, I would wish that in all the schools of France the teachers would repeat often to each of his or her pupils the words which I have inscribed in large letters at the head of this modest little book: You will be a soldier."

The whole volume is thoroughly militarist. There is not a hint of any means of avoiding war or of any distinction between a just war and an unjust war.

24. **Miraton** and **Farges,** *L'Éducation Morale et Civique par la Suggestion artistique et littéraire: Cours moyen et supérieur* (Paris, Delalain, n. d.), 162 pp.

A book of moral and civic instruction. Comprises eleven chapters — school-life, family-life, animal-life, labor, the country, great figures of the past, our person, others, the Great War, social life and nature — each divided into sections and each section including a picture and a special reading.

Chapter V has six sections headed respectively: " The power of our country," " The wealth of our country," " The beauty of our country," " The nobility of our country," " The sacrifice to country," and

" The dead as immortal counsellors to the living "; all the readings are intensely patriotic selections from such writers as Michelet, Gambetta, Erckmann-Chatrian, Poincaré, and Barthou; the chapter opens with a picture of Rouget de l'Isle singing the Marseillaise and closes with a reprint of the words of the Marseillaise.

Chapter VI presents four " great figures of the past ": Socrates, symbolizing by his death obedience to the laws; Jeanne d'Arc, signifying love of France; Victor Hugo, love of the Republic; and Pasteur, devotion to science and love of humanity.

Chapter VII on the Great War is very interesting: it teaches at some length that war is " not fresh and joyous " and offers an eloquent plea for " Peace, the hope of the world." The accompanying poems are " The Song of Nations " and " The Song of Peoples."

25. **Mironneau, A.,** *Choix de Lectures: Cours moyen, Ier degré,* 9th edition, 271st thousand (Paris, Colin, 1924), 355 pp.

Reader comprising 112 selections, of which 23 deal with patriotic subjects. Of these 10 deal with the Great War and most of them are nationalist.

The majority of the selections in the book seek to tell interesting or instructive stories or to inculcate the love of nature and good conduct.

In one of the war stories it is stated that " one Frenchman is worth ten Germans." In another a French hero dons the clothes of a German sentry, whom he has killed, mounts guard a short distance from the enemy trench, and thus enables a detachment of French colonials to decimate and capture a Bavarian company. There is the story of the standing dead, and several stories of German atrocities.

26. **Pierron, R.,** and **Pruvot, G.,** *L'Évolution Française* (Paris, Lesot, n. d.), 103 pp.

(For description, see II, 14 above.)

27. **Plique-Rogeaux, Mme.,** and **Sion, Ch.,** *La Politesse en Action,* 2d edition (Paris, Belin, n. d.), 96 pp.

(For description, see II, 15 above.)

28. **Pomot, Henri,** and **Besseige, Henri,** *Petit Histoire du Peuple Français* (Paris, Les Presses Universitaires, 1928) 179 pp.

(For description, see II, 16 above.)

29. **Roux, Franz,** and **Vincent, Ad.,** *Les Belles Histoires: Cours moyen et supérieur* (Paris, Imprimeries Reunies, n. d.), 301 pp.

A reader comprising 114 selections on subjects of morals, history, geography, useful knowledge, the Great War, prose and poetry, with illustrations.

Thirty-nine selections are warmly patriotic or nationalist, and of these, nineteen deal with episodes of the Great War, the character of which may be inferred from the following titles: " The Calvary of the evacuated regions," " A seventeen-year-old heroine," " Tricks of War," " The destruction of Louvain," " The dead standing," " France, the Liberator," " A brigadier in a tank," " A corner of martyred Lorraine," " The martyrdom of Cambrai," " The entry of the French into Colmar," etc. Some of the pictures accompanying these war stories are calculated to inspire children with hatred of the Germans.

A few selections in the book deal with scenes or events in foreign countries and they are mainly unobjectionable. But one, on New York City, is impressively derogatory of New York and of Americans in general. On the other hand, there is a kindly selection on Layfayette and the American War of Independence, and another on Chateaubriand's visit with Washington.

30. **Vast** and **Jalliffier**, *Histoire de France: Cours moyen*, new edition revised by Ch. L'Hôpital, 42d thousand (Paris, Delagrave, 1925), 218 pp.

A survey of French history, very brief up to 1610 and more detailed thereafter up to 1900, with a supplementary chapter on the Great War. Illustrations of political personages and soldiers. Mainly a military and political history with an occasional brief section on society and science.

Warmly patriotic and ardently republican. Thus Napoleon's wars are described at considerable length, but he is criticized for his autocracy.

" So many victories, so many armies sacrificed, served only to render France *weaker* and *more endangered*. It is the *punishment* of peoples who abandon themselves to one man, to one conqueror, instead of *governing themselves with wisdom* and *defending themselves with moderation*."

On the other hand, the authors in their treatment of the period from 1871 to 1900, written apparently before the Great War, inculcate hostility to Germany and preparedness for a war of revenge:

" *Let us remember that we are envied and feared and that we must be on the alert to defend the fatherland. It is the national duty which is imposed on us.* The French Republic is not aggressive. *But she has the duty of guarding her security and her honor and of not forgetting her sons of Alsace and Lorraine, torn away, in spite of themselves, from the French fatherland.* Let us recall always that Prussia prepared for sixty-four years to avenge the disaster of Jena, which Napoleon inflicted upon her."

This section concludes with a statement of " our duties, our rights," " our duties " being " to the fatherland first and, after the fatherland, to humanity."

The Great War is treated at some length in an appendix. Germany is held solely responsible and " the German people, as much as their Kaiser, must bear the whole responsibility." The treatment concludes: " Let us keep the *soul of conquerors* and impose upon Germany, by incalculable energy, the full execution of the treaty of Versailles. Thus we shall win the peace as we have won the war and shall prove ourselves worthy of our ancestors."

31. **Vial-Mazel** and **Cusset,** *Histoire de France: Cours moyen* (Paris, Les Presses Universitaires de France, n. d.), 178 pp.

A survey of French history, one-third of the space being given to the period prior to 1610, and two-thirds to the period since 1610 (with the Great War). Illustrations chiefly of persons. Mainly a political and military history. Thus, three pages are given to the war of 1870– 1871; three pages, to peaceful developments from 1871 to 1914 (including the construction of the colonial empire); then seven pages to the Great War; and finally brief chapters on French colonies, French marine, French army, and French architecture.

On the cause of the Great War:

" It was on the subject of a Balkan question that the conflict broke out in 1914. *On June 28th the heir-apparent of Austria was assassinated* in the course of a visit to Bosnia, at *Serajevo.* Austria demanded a reckoning with Serbia. Negotiations ensued and France and England counselled peace when *Austria, urged on by Germany,* who had already called her reservists to the colors, *sent* an ultimatum, *then a declaration of war to Serbia.* Russia, protector of the Slavs, *mobilized. On August 3d the ambassador of Germany,* M. de Schoen, *presented at Paris a declaration of war.*"

In the account of the peace terms two paragraphs are devoted to the League of Nations. The second says:

" Several conflicts of interest have already been adjusted by it and numerous conventions have been drafted, but to play the real rôle which its authors have assigned to it, there must be ' a new state of mind, a new morality among nations,' as M. Painlevé has said. While waiting for the new mind France must, by instinctive devotion and reasoned effort of all her children, continue to face her obligations as a continental and colonial Power."

IV. For Use of Children Aged 11–13 during Two-Year
" Higher Course " in Elementary Primary Schools

1. **Ammann, A.,** and **Coutant, E. C.,** *Histoire de France: Cours
supérieur, Cours complementaire, Écoles supérieures,* 306th thousand
(Paris, Fernand Nathan, 1922), 448 pp.

A general account of French history with special attention to the
development of civilization in France, divided into three equal parts:
(1) from the origins to 1494; (2) from 1494 to 1789; and (3) from
1789 to 1920. Illustrations, chiefly of architecture and the other arts.

In a relatively brief treatment of the achievements of the Third
Republic the acquisition of colonies is conspicuous. " The Republic
not only has conquered colonies but seems to have made the nation
understand the advantages of *colonial politics:* it is the necessary condition for the future greatness of France."

A fairly detailed account of the causes of the Great War is summed
up as follows:

" From the end of the nineteenth century France had retaken her
place among the Great Powers. To the Triple Alliance of Germany,
Austria, and Italy, formed against her, she had opposed her alliance
with Russia; then she concluded an *entente cordiale* with England
(1904). Also Germany resolved on a new war, in which she would
crush forever her rival and likewise ruin Russia. Thenceforth she
consecrated herself exclusively to preparing a struggle which would
subject the world to her. In 1914 she found a pretext to declare war."

Of the eight pages devoted to the story of the war, two are given to
a harrowing account of " German crimes." The story ends: " France
went through the worst experience; she came out bruised and impoverished, but she came out with an incomparable prestige. She had
reconquered her national integrity and, with her allies, saved the freedom of the world."

No mention of the League of Nations.
The book closes with this paragraph:

" We may finally derive from the teaching of History a legitimate
pride: it acquaints us with what place our fatherland has occupied in
the world, what services she has rendered to humanity. If European
civilization should be deprived of what France has furnished, what an
immense void would result! "

2. **Baudrillart, Alfred,** *Histoire de France et Notions d'Histoire
générale: Cours supérieur,* published with the collaboration of J. Martin
(Paris, Bloud & Gay, 1927), 791 pp.

A history of France from earliest times to 1923 with considerable attention to economic and intellectual developments and to the history of other countries in Europe and throughout the world. Much used in Catholic schools. Comprises thirteen " books," of which the first treats of ancient Gaul and the Roman Empire; the next three, of the Middle Age; the next four, of the period from 1494 to 1789; the next four, of the years from 1789 to 1914; and the last, of the Great War and its aftermath.

A strikingly straightforward and fair-minded history. Although its central theme is French history, it gives fairly detailed and pretty unprejudiced accounts of the internal development especially in the nineteenth and twentieth centuries of Germany, Austria, Italy, England, Russia, the United States, etc. It also treats of modern imperialism as a world movement.

The account of the Great War is exceptionally judicious. There are no harrowing or romantic tales of German atrocities. There is a full account of the peace-treaties of 1919–1923 and the paragraph on the League of Nations reads as follows:

" A League of Nations has been established on the initiative of President Wilson. The seat is at Geneva and its mission will be to secure the reduction of armaments of the various Powers and to maintain peace and security in the world by regulating, through arbitration, the conflicts which will arise in the future among the Powers. Germany will become party to this League only after giving guarantees, of which the principal one will be the execution of the clauses of the treaty."

3. **Blanchet, Désiré,** and **Toutain, Jules,** *L'Histoire de France à l'École: Cours du Certificat d'Études primaires et Cours supérieurs,* 30th edition (Paris, Belin, 1926), 127 pp.

A survey of French history from ancient times to 1920. Illustrations, mainly of national personages and of the growth of civilization in France. Nearly half the book is devoted to the period since 1789. The whole book is marked by ardent patriotism.

The work of the Revolutionary Convention (1792–1795) is summarized thus: " The Convention had saved France and given her her natural frontier, the Rhine. ' I shall never forget,' said the great orator Berryer, fervent royalist, but sincere patriot, ' I shall never forget that the Convention has saved my country.' "

The war of 1870–1871 is discussed at considerable length and there are stirring supplementary readings on " Was France ready? " " Gambetta," " Alsace-Lorraine," " Woe to the vanquished," " Hope," etc. The account of the Great War opens as follows:

" Victorious over France in 1870–1871, Germany ever after dreamed of dominating the world. Her policy became more and more dangerous for France, England, and Russia. Austria-Hungary, in accord with Germany, sought a quarrel with Serbia in 1914. In spite of all efforts of France, England, and Russia to preserve peace, war was declared by Austria-Hungary against Russia and France (July-August 1914)."

A whole lesson is devoted to " Characteristics and consequences of the War ": most of it centres in the statement that " The Germans and their allies paid no heed to the rules of war. Their whole purpose was to spread everywhere terror and devastation." The League of Nations is barely mentioned.

4. **Charrier, Ch.**, *Nos Lectures: Cours moyen et supérieur*, 4th edition (Paris, Hatier, 1924), 390 pp.

(For description, see III, 11, above.)

5. **Dalliès, J.**, and **Guy, C.**, *Précis d'Histoire de France à l'Usage du Cours supérieur des Écoles primaires élémentaires, des Écoles primaires supérieurs*, 13th edition (Paris, Gedalge, 1915), 348 pp.

A narrative of French history from earliest times to 1900, with a chronology of events from 1900 to 1915, and a 14-page supplement on the French colonial empire.

The book is fervently republican and patriotic. As the authors say in their preface:

" They have concluded that the Republic is not only the legal form but also the necessary form of our government, and they have not hesitated to say so. It is the Republic, which, after the fall of the Second Empire and the defeats of 1870, has saved the honor of our country. It is the Republic which has repaired our disasters, remade a new France, and conquered a vast colonial domain. It is the Republic, which, grouping under the national flag the Frenchmen of all parties, has mustered them, the heroes, against the barbarous invader, in the month of August 1914, in order to defend our traditions, our hearths, and our independence. It is the Republic or rather it is France as a whole, which will recover Alsace-Lorraine and break down the criminal force of Germany."

From the " Conclusion " of the book:

" We shall add a last word to show, by comparison, how much we ought to felicitate ourselves on being children of this country, France. First, no other nation in Europe possesses such remarkable territorial unity; in no other is to be encountered such perfect unity of legislation and language. All the citizens with us are equal before the law: all, without other condition than that they have not forfeited their honor, are with us electors and eligible to office; all offices, from the most modest to the most exalted, are with us open simply to merit."

Then the authors proceed to point out defects in England, Austria, and Germany, and to reëmphasize the lack of defects in France.

6. **De la Vaulx, Henri,** and **Galopin, A.,** *Un Tour du Monde en Aéroplane,* new edition (Paris, Albin Michel, n. d.), 492 pp.

(For description, see III, 12, above.)

7. **Dès, Mme.,** *Jean et Lucie, Histoire de deux jeunes Refugiés, Cours moyen et supérieur* (Paris, F. Nathan, n. d.), 360 pp.

(For description, see III, 13, above.)

8. **Gauthier** and **Deschamps,** *Cours d'Histoire: Antiquité, Histoire de France, Histoire générale: Cours supérieur,* new edition (Paris, Hachette, 1925), 273 pp.

The first thirty pages afford a hurried glance at ancient and medieval history. The rest of the book is devoted to a survey of French history to 1920 with only such glimpses of general history as are directly connected with French history, especially with the wars of French history. Illustrations, about half of political and military personages and about half of the growth of civilization in France. Much use of black-faced type and supplementary readings. Ardently patriotic. On account of its anti-clericalism, it has been condemned by the French bishops and may not be used in Catholic schools.

All the readings on the Revolutionary era from 1790 to 1797 are of a very patriotic sort: " The Festival of the Federation," " Mirabeau at the Tribune," " The Marseillaise," " Vive la Nation," " The Defiance of Europe," " Danton," " The Generals of the Republic."

On Napoleon: *" Napoleon is incontestably the greatest warrior of the world. It is by war that he has covered France with incomparable glory.* But it is also by war that he delivered the nation to the hatred and vengeance of the vanquished peoples."

Fifteen pages are devoted to the war of 1870–1871; five pages, to the pacific work of the Third Republic from 1871 to 1914; sixteen pages, to the Great War; and part of one page, to the League of Nations.

The account of the Great War is prefaced by a reading entitled " William II prepares ' his ' war." The " distant " causes of the war are described as follows:

" It is *Germany, even more than Austria, which is responsible for the immense cataclysm, which has upset the world.* Since her misfortunes at Jena in 1806, all Germany had turned towards war like Prussia. The Hohenzollerns, and above all William II, caused their criminal ambitions to be shared by the Germans, or more exactly, by the governing classes."

The " pretext " for the war is thus set forth: " Germany, faithful to Bismarck's lessons, only yearned to find a pretext for war. The pretext was the assassination at Sarajevo of Francis-Ferdinand, heir to the Austrian throne. Austria-Hungary, urged on by her ally, *Germany,* contrary to all good faith, held Serbia responsible for the assassination. On July 21, she addressed to Serbia an unacceptable ultimatum, but *accepted* by the little Slav nation in accordance with the counsels of Russia and France. In spite of this acceptance Francis Joseph broke off the negotiations and *mobilized all his forces.* From July 25, *France, Russia, England,* and *Italy,* which loyally desired peace, were insistent that the dispute be submitted to a congress of arbitration. At this moment everything depended upon the Emperor of Germany. William II would have had to say only one word and Austria would have accepted arbitration. But that word, which would have spared so many human lives and would have saved him his empire, he did not say. On July 28 the Austrian army invaded Serbia, the protégé of Russia. It was only then that Russia mobilized. War could no longer be avoided."

All that is said about the peace is that Alsace-Lorraine was returned to France, that Poland was freed, that Belgium regained her independence, and that the League of Nations was organized.

The cover of the book bears a likeness of Gambetta with the mottos: " France sums up everything for me," and " Liberty of Reason, Justice, Progress. That is why nothing in my heart is above France."

9. **Guirbal, Jean,** *La Grande Guerre en Compositions françaises: Cours supérieur* (Paris, Fernand Nathan, 1915), 104 pp.

A reader and composition guide. Comprises thirty-two stories, twelve essays, six models of correspondence, and eight descriptions of pictures.

The spirit of the whole book is indicated in the author's introductory remarks: " More than ever our school children must be associated with the great thought and action of the present hour, and consequently more than ever all intellectual efforts required of them must be oriented towards the *exaltation of the patriotic sentiment.*"

The stories are on such themes as " The torn flag," " The Battle of the Marne," "How a French officer dies," "Dead while singing the Marseillaise," "The soldier-child," "German barbarism," "The heroism of a French girl," etc.

The essays are on such themes as "Let us love France," "The wounded," "German prisoners," etc.

The model letters include "A letter to a soldier at the front," and "Reply to a soldier."

The pictures are all of war and fighting.

10. **Lavisse, Ernest,** *Histoire de France et Notions d'Histoire générale: Cours supérieur,* with the collaboration of Pierre Conard, 2d edition, 110th thousand (Paris, Colin, 1925), 312 pp.

Comprises six "books" (1) Antiquity (64 pp.); (2) The Middle Age (64 pp.); (3) Renaissance and Reformation (44 pp.); (4) Absolutism (64 pp.); (5) Louis XVI, Revolution, Empire (82 pp.); (6) 1815–1920 (88 pp.). Some general history appears in the first "book," but elsewhere is very incidental to French history. Some attention is given to society, art, and literature.

The author says in the preface: "The teaching of history at school is of no use if it does not tell the student whence comes Humanity and at what point in its progress it has arrived. Properly understood, the greatest place, the preëminent place will be given to the Fatherland. No country has rendered so many services to Humanity as France."

The work is ardently patriotic and republican.

The Great War is treated with some restraint and the account of the Peace of 1919–1920 concludes with a brief description of the organization of the League of Nations and with these italicized words: "After having killed millions and millions of men, the terrible war of 1914 will finally have killed war, the worst of the scourges from which Humanity has suffered during its long past."

11. **Lavisse, E.,** *"Tu seras Soldat," Histoire d'un Soldat français,* 24th edition (Paris, Colin, 1916), 320 pp.

(For description, see III, 23, above.)

12. **Lemmonnier, Henry, Schrader, F.,** and **Dubois, Marcel,** *Cours de Géographie: Cours supérieur et complémentaire,* 14th edition, 515th thousand (Paris, Hachette, 1924), 176 pp.

A geography and atlas, comprising fourteen pages on "general ideas of geography"; eighty pages on the five continents of the Earth, with twenty coloured maps, physical and political.

On France, a matter-of-fact account of physical features — mountains, rivers, sea-coast, plains, climate — administrative and political divisions, population, communications, agriculture, industry, commerce, and resources.

13. **Lomont, A.,** *Histoire de la Grande Guerre 1914–1918,* with a preface by Paul Painlevé, 2d edition (Paris, Gedalge, 1921), 264 pp.

Paul Painlevé in his preface says of the author: " Inspector of primary education, member of the Higher Council of Public Instruction, he has written as an historian and an educator. No trace of polemics in his recital; not a word which can wound; not a line which can be contested."

The book opens with this statement: " The war of 1914 was willed by Germany directed by Prussia." He then explains how a German soul was created between 1871 and 1914, a soul which was marked by " the pride of might and the covetousness of a brutal and envious race." Germans spied on France and repeatedly provoked her to war.

" At length, quite determined on war, William II, to reach his ends, seized the pretext furnished to him by the murder of the heir of Austria, at Sarajevo, on June 28, 1914. Pushed on by Germany, Austria pretended to hold Germany responsible for this crime and declared war against her. In vain France, England, Russia, and Italy sought to maintain peace. On August 1, Germany declared war against Russia, which had mobilized to defend Serbia. On August 3, she declared war against France, who, faithful to her alliance, had declared her solidarity with Russia."

The account of the war itself is vehemently nationalist. The French are always brave and gallant. The Germans are barbarous. The book contains numerous special readings, all intended to extol the French cause and conduct or to belittle the Germans; some of the accompanying documents are of doubtful authenticity.

In the fairly detailed account of the peace-settlements from 1919 to 1921 the League of Nations is barely mentioned.

14. **Melinand, Camille,** *Sois Juste, Premiers Éléments de Morale* (Paris, Delalain, 1921), 152 pp.

Treats of human nature, will, and reason; of justice, truthfulness, and love of work; of duties toward one's self; and of duties toward others.

The duties toward others are: " respect for rights, respect of life, respect of property, respect of liberty, respect for others' feelings, respect for moral personality, politeness, cheerfulness." Each of these is discussed in a brief chapter. " The family " and " the school " are also discussed, but not " the fatherland."

With the exception of an occasional mention of " the fatherland " as a motive for doing this or that, there is nothing nationalist in the book.

15. **Miraton** and **Farges**, *L'Éducation morale et civique par la Suggestion artistique et littéraire: Cours moyen et supérieur* (Paris, Delalain, n. d.), 162 pp.

(For description, see III, 24, above.)

16. **Pagès, G.**, *Histoire sommaire de la France de 1610 à nos Jours*, 10th edition (Paris, Hachette, n. d.), 283 pp.

A sketch of the political and military history of France from 1610 to 1920. Illustrations, chiefly of personages and fashions. The text is accompanied by special " readings," most of which describe battles.

Fifty-two pages are devoted to the career of Napoleon: 3 pages to his reforms in France and 49 to his wars. Twenty-six pages are devoted to the internal history of France from 1815 to 1870; 5 pages, to the conquest of Algeria; and 25 pages, to the wars of Napoleon III. Four pages are devoted to the internal history of the Third French Republic; 9 pages, to its colonies and foreign relations; and 7 pages, to the Great War.

The causes of the Great War are set forth as follows:

" The *Triple Entente* had no other purpose than peace. But *Germany* wished peace only on condition of imposing it herself and reaping its rewards. She was disquieted and irritated as soon as her *hegemony* was menaced. She armed herself still more. She levied, in 1913, a *war-tax* of a billion marks. Then *William II* egged on the Emperor of Austria, Francis-Joseph, to attack Serbia, a little Slav state protected by Russia. *The aggression of Austria against Serbia* rendered the European War inevitable."

No mention of the League of Nations.

17. **Perron, J.**, and **Lomont, A.**, *Les Grandes Questions de l'Histoire de France* (Paris, Gedalge, n. d.), 273 pp.

A survey of the history of France from Gallic times to 1924 with some attention to the growth of civilization, but with principal emphasis on politics and war.

The War of 1870–1871 fills ten pages; the internal history of the

Third Republic, ten pages; the Great War, nine pages; and the League of Nations, two pages.

The book is staunchly republican and patriotic. The Republic is represented as having always pursued a *" loyal and pacific policy "* and at the same time as having " desired peace, not peace at any price, but a peace by which we would be respected and which, if necessary, we could impose."

On the Great War: " It was willed by Germany directed by Prussia."

On the occupation of the Ruhr: " The evil intention of Germany led France to occupy the basin of the Ruhr in January 1923, occupation which lasted a year without inducing the conquered nation to make the payments that it owed as reparations."

The account of the war is followed by a reprint of the eloquent tribute of the French Parliament to the dead warriors of France.

Two pages are devoted to a summary of the organization and activity of the League of Nations, closing with these words: " Thus, for five years the League of Nations has secured in the world a great moral authority and given the impression that its rôle will be in the future only for the greatest good of peoples and for general peace."

The last " instruction to students " in the book is to study " the German menace; to seek in history, since the earliest Germanic invasions, the epochs in which France has had to struggle against German peoples: Germany, Austria."

18. **Roux, Franz,** and **Vincent, Ad.,** *Les Belles Histoires: Cours moyen et supérieur* (Paris, Imprimeries Réunies, n. d.), 301 pp.

(For description, see III, 27, above.)

19. **Segond, E.,** *Histoire de France et Notions d'Histoire générale: Cours supérieur,* edition revised and completed by Maurice Tessier (Paris, Hatier, 1923), 762 pp.

Treats of ancient Oriental peoples (20 pp.), ancient Greece (23 pp.), ancient Rome (23 pp.), the Middle Ages (233 pp.), modern times to 1789 (241 pp.), and 1789–1920 (217 pp.). The treatment of medieval and modern history centres in the history of France, but there are brief chapters on England and Germany in the Middle Ages, on the English Revolution of the seventeenth century, on Russia under Peter and Catherine II, on Prussia and Austria in the seventeenth and eighteenth centuries, and on German and Italian national unification in the nineteenth century. Some attention is devoted, moreover, to religious, economic, and intellectual developments. Illustrations mainly of persons.

On French history since 1870, 14 pages are devoted to the War of 1870–1871; 11 pages, to domestic events from 1870 to 1914; 11 pages, to colonial expansion; 25 pages, to the Great War.

On the Great War, after a bald statement of how the struggle began, there is this statement:

" The war, willed, prepared, and provoked by Germany, assumed from the first a special character. It was the struggle of *European civilization* against German barbarism. The destruction of Louvain, the systematic bombardment of the cathedral of Reims, the inexcusable bombing of *Senlis,* the murder of civil hostages, the deportations from the district of *Lille,* the piratical acts of German submarines, testified to the baseness to which the German soul descended: all of which must be remembered and denounced in history in order to permit us to judge Germanic culture."

Five pages are given to a glowing description of the return of Alsace-Lorraine to France, and two pages to the peace terms of 1919–1920. There is a paragraph on the League of Nations.

V. For Use of Adolescents Aged 13–16 in Higher Primary Schools

1. **Aimond, Ch.,** *Histoire de France du XVIᵉ Siècle à 1774: Cours supérieur,* 3d edition, 53d thousand (Paris, De Gigord, 1924), 287 pp.

A history of France from 1500 to 1774, beginning with an account of the rise of the modern nations of western Europe, the great inventions, and the maritime discoveries, and closing with the intellectual movement of the eighteenth century and external politics of France.

A clear and unprejudiced history. Wars are discussed, but they are subordinated to the story of economic, social, religious, and intellectual development.

2. **Aimond, Ch.,** *Histoire de France: Cours supérieur: 1774–1851,* 3d edition (Paris, De Gigord, 1925), 264 pp.

Fourteen chapters on the history of France from 1774 to 1851 with attention chiefly to politics, although one chapter is devoted to literature, art, and science in the first half of the nineteenth century. Illustrations, mainly of persons.

Not particularly nationalist. Somewhat pro-Catholic.

3. **Aimond, Ch.,** *Histoire de France: Cours supérieur: 1852–1920, avec Notions d'Histoire générale,* 2d edition (Paris, De Gigord, 1923), 280 pp.

Comprises eighteen chapters, of which three treat of the internal history of France since 1852 (including one chapter on science, literature, and art), one treats of the French colonies, nine of the history of other European countries, one of the Far East, one of the United States, one of South America, and two of the Great War and the contemporary world. Emphasizes the rôle of the Catholic Church.

In the chapter on German history the author devotes a page to Pan-Germanism, saying that " the remarkable progress of Germany developed more and more, in the German soul, the *cult of force,* with this idea, already familiar to Bismarck, that, in international conflicts, force creates right."

On the Great War:

" It has *indirect origins* and *immediate causes:* all involve the *responsibility of Germany.* We have already explained the *indirect causes* when we have spoken of German *militarism,* of the dream of world domination, in which *Pan-Germanism* was cradled, and finally of the intimate *disposition* of William II and his people. . . . As for the *German people,* from the great industrialists to the socialists, they were ready to follow with enthusiasm their emperor against France, ' the hereditary enemy,' as well as against England, their dangerous rival in the economic sphere. . . . The immediate cause, or rather the *pretext* of the rupture, must be sought in the East."

There follows a fairly detailed account of the events of July and August 1914, which, if somewhat biased in fact, shows the author's desire to be judicious. There is no mention of German atrocities in the twenty-page story of the war, except a sentence and a picture of " the burning of the Cathedral of Reims by the Germans."

A page and a half are devoted to the League of Nations ending with these words: " The League of Nations enjoys only a *moral authority* and it possesses no armed force to make its decision respected. Besides, it includes neither the papacy, that is the highest moral authority in the world, nor the United States, which has disavowed the creation of President Wilson. This, despite the League's praiseworthy activity in favor of general peace, is a real source of weakness."

The book closes with this paragraph:

" Doubtless the recent collapse of Germany, Russia, and Austria has made France the *foremost military power* in Europe. But it would be unjust to tax with " imperialism " France's legitimate care to prevent the offensive return of Germany. In reality a strong France is necessary to the maintenance of the peace of the world, and on the contrary it is her weakening or disappearance which would give the signal for new catastrophes.

4. **Ammann, A.,** and **Coutant, E. C.,** *Histoire de France: Cours supérieur,* 306th thousand (Paris, F. Nathan, 1922), 448 pp.

(For description, see IV, 1, above.)

5. **Baudrillart, Alfred,** *Histoire de France et Notions d'Histoire générale: Cours supérieur* (Paris, Bloud and Gay, 1927), 791 pp.

(For description, see IV, 2, above.)

6. **Dalliès, J.** and **Guy, C.,** *Précis d'Histoire de France,* 13th edition (Paris, Gedalge, 1915), 548 pp.

(For description, see IV, 5, above.)

7. **Driault, E.,** and **Randou, M.,** *Précis d'Histoire de France depuis le Début du XVIe Siècle jusqu'à nos Jours et Notions d'Histoire générale* (Paris, Alcan, 1925), 394 pp.

A survey from 1500 to the present, with attention primarily to politics and secondarily to economics and society. It is mainly French history, but out of a total of 71 brief chapters, 18 deal with the history of other countries. Most of the chapters are provided with special " readings."

On French history since 1870 five pages are devoted to a judicious and restrained treatment of the Franco-Prussian War; twenty-two, to political, social, and intellectual developments under the Third Republic; five, to the colonial empire; and seven, to the Great War. The cause of the Great War is set forth as follows:

"About 1914 Germany dreamed of *organizing the world under her sway.* She would reduce France to the condition of a second-rate Power and would take new territories from her; she would supplant England in the dominion of the seas; she would unite under her own rule all the European colonies. Only a war would permit her to realize these designs. She found the pretext for it in the assassination of the heir-apparent of Austria, Franz Ferdinand, killed at Serajevo (Bosnia) on June 28, 1914, by a Serbian student. Serbia, in no way guilty, made excuses, however, but she could not entirely accept *the humiliating conditions* of an ultimatum, which Austria, urged on by the Emperor William II, addressed to her. *Russia,* faithful to the policy of defending *Slavic interests,* took the part of Serbia. *Germany,* deaf to all proposals of arbitration, declared war against Russia on August 1, 1914, and on the third against France."

The account of the war is simple and straightforward. " Atrocities " are not mentioned. The chapter closes with a " reading " on the valor of the French soldier. Three pages are devoted to the League of Nations — its organization and functioning and an eloquent plea of Léon Bourgeois on its behalf.

There is a concluding section on " The rôle of France in the World," in which it is vigorously contended that " France is the country of justice and generosity " and that " France is the exemplar of order, peace, and labor." The chapter on contemporary Germany closes with a pessimistic " reading " on " Our ideas of Germany," centring in these words: " As for us, we do not know what Germany of the future will be, and we do not deny the possibility of an evolution on its part in the sense of a true liberalism, but what we do know in certain fashion is that Pan-Germanism is always alive." One chapter is devoted to special pleas against depopulation, tuberculosis, and alcoholism; and the contrast between the growing population of Germany and the stationary population of France is impressively pointed out.

8. **Faubert, Charles,** and **Guedel, Jean,** *Histoire, troisième Année, d'après H. Vast et R. Jalliffier* (Paris, Delagrave, 1923), 355 pp.

An account of French and general history from 1852 to 1920. Comprises twenty-three chapters: five on strictly French history; thirteen on the history of other countries; one on the Great War; two on the contemporary world; one on the French colonies; and one on the rôle of France in the world.

The general cause of the Great War is traced to the " armed peace " of 1871–1914, for which " Germany alone was responsible "; and the immediate cause is attributed to " William II, perfidious counsellor of the old Emperor of Austria, Francis-Joseph." The story of the war (9 pages) recounts no German " atrocities." The accompanying account of the peace treaties (4 pages) makes no mention of the League of Nations and ends with this paragraph:

" France, faithful to her civilizing mission, has largely contributed to the advent of a régime of liberty and justice. She has regained in the eyes of all other people her prestige as a great nation, invincible in combat, generous after victory. She can find to-day among new states of eastern Europe, grouped in a *Little Entente*, the diplomatic assistance which is necessary to her, together with that of her great allies, in order to require of Germany the reparation of the destruction caused on her soil by the barbarism of the invaders."

In the second chapter on the contemporary world a final section (one page) is devoted to an exposition of the organization of the League of Nations, concluding as follows: " This organ does not seem likely to produce all beneficent effects. . . . It still lacks any permanent international force to sanction its decisions in the face of recalcitrant states. Nevertheless it has the germ, precious indeed, of an institution of peace and justice, the development of which we should labor to expand, and which, in the troubled period that the world experiences, inspires the largest hopes."

The last chapter — a strongly patriotic chapter — concludes: " We still pass through difficult hours; after having won the war, we have still to win the peace; but the past of France is to us a guarantee of the future, and at the end of this study it is an act of ardent faith in the destinies of our fatherland with which its history inspires us."

9. **Fèvre, Joseph,** *Le Livre d'Instruction civique de Droit usuel, d'Économie politique,* 6th edition, revised and brought up to date, (Paris, Belin, 1925), 419 pp.

Comprises three " parts ": (1) 19 lessons on the French Government; (2) 23 lessons on private law — persons, property, contracts, inheritance, courts, commercial law; and (3) 16 lessons on political economy — production, distribution, and consumption, of wealth.

Of the 19 lessons on the French Government, the first two treat of " the individual rights of French citizens: civil equality and liberty and property "; the third, of natural sovereignty and universal suffrage; and the last of military service.

The lesson on military service begins with a section entitled " A modern state cannot get along without a permanent army, the guarantee of its security "; and the last paragraph of this section reads as follows: " A State which, under pretext of consecrating all its resources to works of peace, should neglect military effort, would draw upon itself the envy of its rivals and undergo invasion, dismemberment, and ruin. The *surest guarantee of peace is military power.*" The lesson is supplemented by a " reading " from Paul Doumer on " France must have an army."

There is no mention of the League of Nations or of international duties.

10. **Lomont, A.,** *Histoire de la Grande Guerre,* 2d edition (Paris, Gedalge, 1921), 264 pp.

(For description, see IV, 13, above.)

11. **Malet, Albert,** and **Isaac, Jules,** *Histoire de France et Notions d'Histoire générale de 1852 à 1920,* 3d edition (Paris, Hachette, n. d.), 320 pp.

An account of French and general history from 1852 to 1920. Comprises seventeen chapters: three on strictly French history; ten on the history of other countries; one on the French colonies; one on the Great War; one on the contemporary world; and one on French vitality and the rôle of France in the world. Emphasizes military history.

On the Great War:

" The Great War's direct cause was the *policy of Austria-Hungary in the Balkans,* its premeditated aggression against Serbia, principal obstacle to its projects of expansion. The occasion of the conflict was the *murder of the heir-apparent of Austria at Serajevo* on June 28, 1914. But Austria-Hungary could engage in such an enterprise only with the support and urging of her powerful ally, Germany. Therefore the basic and determining cause of the war was the *vast ambition of Germany,* her pretensions to hegemony, the necessity in which she found herself, in order to achieve her ends, to subjugate or break her principal adversary, France."

A page is devoted to a description of " German mentality," by no means flattering, and another page to a picture of German " atrocities " at Ypres. The story of the war, altogether, covers 33 pages.

The account of the peace-treaties of 1919–20 (7 pages) contains eight lines on the League of Nations, concluding; " *the new institution had only moral force:* the Council of the League had at its disposition no material force to make its decisions respected."

The last section in the chapter on the contemporary world deals with " international life " and treats of the principle of nationalities, pacifism, the Hague Conference, and (in pessimistic vein) the League of Nations.

In the final chapter France is highly complimented on her " natural resources," on her " colonial resources " (her colonial policy of " education, collaboration, friendship "), and on her " intellectual influence." It is summed up in the italicized and repeated phrase that " *France has incarnated the cause of liberty and justice.*"

12. **Melinand, Camille,** *Sois Juste, Premiers Éléments de Morale* (Paris, Delalain, 1921), 152 pp.

(For description, see IV, 14, above.)

13. **Métin, Albert,** *Cours d'Instruction civique et Notions de Morale sociale,* 8th edition entirely revised by André Siegfried (Paris, Masson, 1924), 229 pp.

A book of civic and moral instruction. Comprises one chapter on the nation and patriotism, fourteen chapters on the central and local government, the rights and duties of citizens, and the judiciary, and two chapters on the relations of nations to one another.

The fatherland and patriotism are defined as follows:

" *The fatherland is the country where one is born, of which one is a citizen.* When we say that France is our fatherland we mean also that it is the country whose social life, manners, civilization, and national ideals accord best with the profound tendencies of our being. We express in a word the idea that there is perfect harmony between this land of France and its children. Patriotism, in the circumstances, flourishes naturally: it is love of the fatherland with rights of solidarity which it involves, and duties to which it impels. . . . *The integrity of the fatherland must be maintained.* . . . It is a duty, among states, to respect one another. It is above all, on the part of the citizens, a sacred duty to defend, at the risk of their lives, the frontiers of the country to which they belong."

The noble qualities of patriotism are developed and stressed, but none of its possible faults are mentioned.

Most of the book is given to a clear and straightforward exposition of the government of France. The two concluding chapters deal with (1) international rights and duties and (2) international law, international arbitration, and the League of Nations. It is maintained that " the love of humanity ought to be reconciled with the love of the fatherland."

" If humanity had arrived at a better degree of material and moral organization any such conflict would not exist any more than there is a serious conflict between the family and the State; . . . it is by improving the fatherland, by raising the level of morality of nations, that most will be achieved for a better humanity."

There is an eight-page account of the League of Nations, clear, accurate, and eulogistic.

14. **Pagès, G.,** *Histoire sommaire de la France de 1610 à nos Jours,* 10th edition (Paris, Hachette, n. d.), 283 pp.

(For description, see IV, 16, above.)

15. **Sieurin, E.,** *Cours d'Histoire pour le Brevet élémentaire depuis le Début du XVIᵉ Siècle jusqu'en 1920,* 8th edition (Paris, Masson, 1923), 586 pp.

A survey from 1500 to 1920, with attention primarily to politics and secondarily to economic and intellectual development. It is chiefly French history, but out of a total of fifty-two chapters thirteen treat of the history of other countries.

On French history since 1870, eight pages are devoted to the war of 1870–1871; twenty-five, to political and intellectual developments under the Third Republic; six, to the colonial Empire; and twenty-seven, to the Great War.

There is a fairly detailed and judicious account of the causes and beginning of the Great War. The military operations are sketched in some detail, but there is no mention of " atrocities." The Russian withdrawal from the war is labelled " treason " and in a concluding paragraph the war of 1914–1918 is summed up as " the struggle between civilization and barbarism."

A page is devoted to the League of Nations, which is described as " the greatest moral authority which has ever existed; it will work for the reconciliation of peoples. It will seek to avert conflict among the nations. It promises to guarantee the territory of every State, great or small, which is a member."

The final chapter is on " The rôle of France in the World," and it is very patriotic. Under " political rôle," it extols the principles of 1789 and adds " that the principle of nationality is of course essentially French." Under " social rôle," it stresses the abolition of serfdom and slavery, the establishment of the right to work, the disinterested character of French science, and the benefit of French civilization conferred upon fifty million colonial subjects. Under " intellectual rôle," it praises the " French spirit," the " French language," " French disinterestedness," and " French humanitarianism." The chapter concludes:

" France has never been an egoistic nation. She has always worked as much for others as for herself. She has always tried to assure in the World the reign of the ideas of justice and fraternity. During the torment of 1914–1918 she has struggled for world civilization against German barbarism. It is thanks to her above all, thanks to her generosity, to her disinterested devotion, to her gold and to her blood, which she has lavished without counting, that, finally, Right has triumphed over Might."

16. **Sieurin, E.**, and **Chabert, G.**, *Histoire de France et Notions d'Histoire générale de 1852 à 1920*, 11th edition (Paris, Masson, 1923), 419 pp.

An account of French and general history from 1852 to 1920. Comprises nineteen chapters: two strictly French history; twelve on the history of other countries; one on the French colonies; one on the Great War; one on the contemporary world; and two on French vitality and the rôle of France in the world. Emphasizes economic development.

The chapter on German history stresses Pan-Germanism. The account of the causes of the Great War is strikingly judicious in spirit and content. The story of the war, which fills 37 pages, is also restrained and does not mention " German atrocities." The account of the peace treaties (7 pages) mentions the League of Nations.

A section in the chapter on the contemporary world is devoted to a favorable three-page account of the organization and functioning of the League of Nations.

The concluding chapter on the rôle of France in the world emphasizes the following: (1) France's political role — universality of the principles of 1789, the principle of national self determination; (2) her social rôle — peasant proprietorship, free labor, freedom of writing, public education, social laws, disinterested French science in world service; (3) her economic rôle — very honorable place of French agriculture, great progress in metallurgical, textile, and chemical industries, and development of means of communication; (4) her intellectual rôle — universality of the French language and diffusion of the French spirit and ideas.

17. **Thouverez, Émile,** *Le Livre de Morale des Écoles primaires supérieures,* 4th edition entirely revised (Paris, Belin, 1926), 250 pp.

A book of moral instruction. Comprises 45 brief chapters, of which the first 32 treat of personal conduct and of general, personal, and social virtues, and the last 13 deal with such topics as the nation, the fatherland, the state, the republic, democracy, the national idea, social justice, socialism, feminism, and international duties. Each chapter is supplemented by a brief " reading."

" The nation possesses a double unity: a moral unity and a legal unity. The moral unity of a nation constitutes what is called the *fatherland*. The fatherland is the country which has given us birth, it is the language we speak, it is the history of ancestors, and the tombs of elders, and the dreams of glory, and everything which a great emotion confers upon us when, returning from a trip to a foreign country, we find anew our fatherland. The State is the legal unity of a nation. . . . All Frenchmen respect the French laws, the French flag."

Military service is declared to be the first duty to the fatherland.

The chapters on the nation and patriotism are accompanied by readings on " Thermopylae," " France," " Sentiment of the Fatherland," " Dead for the Fatherland," and " Military duty."

The chapter on international duties treats very briefly of the interdependence of nations, of their reciprocal duties of justice and charity, and of a few examples of international arbitration. There is a bare mention of the League of Nations. The accompanying readings are extracts from Ruskin's *Crown of Wild Olive*, Epictetus, and Kant.

18. **Vinson, Paul,** *Instruction civique, Droit usuel, Économie politique* (Paris, Hatier, 1923), 223 pp.

Comprises three parts: (1) 22 chapters on government; (2) 7 chapters on private law; (3) 8 chapters on political economy.

In the introduction the author says: " Our country, formed by ten centuries of original civilization, transformed by the Revolution and by the methodical mind of Napoleon, has characteristics which are peculiar to it. However much its administration may be decried, it is superior from this point of view to all foreign countries. It is important therefore that every citizen should know on what its organization rests."

Of the 22 chapters on government the first four treat of " the nation," " the solidarity of generations and the continuity of national life," " patriotism," and " the State," and chapters 5–12 of " personal liberties and national sovereignty," while chapter 16 deals with " military obligations " and chapter 22 with " relations of states among themselves."

On patriotism:

" We conceive of our country as a living being, all of us desire its welfare, its progress, its independence. All of us wish that its moral and economic development may be continual. Our patriotism makes us suffer ills, accidents, or injuries, which weigh on its rights and interests. Its glory is dear to us and we rejoice in belonging to it. We seek, each of us in our way, in common with the rest, to facilitate the progress of the nation. Each of us feels himself an element in this force, whose greatness we desire. We therefore comprise the national life. The idea of nation is linked to the idea of fatherland and to that of solidarity. . . .

" *Patriotism* consists in loving one's country and the nationals of this country and in making all one's efforts in behalf of their greatness. It does not consist in loving it blindly or in wishing to conceal its faults or imperfections."

On military service: " It is an *honor*." " *Rebels* and *deserters* are dishonored for life and commit a crime, which is punishable by death."

The chapter on " relations of states among themselves " treats of the rights and duties of states, abuses committed by certain states (Austria's attack on Serbia in 1914 is cited as an example), neutral states and the right of intervention, of " international solidarity," and of " how love of humanity should be reconciled with love of the fatherland."

This section of the chapter closes with a paragraph entitled " Fatherland before everything." These are its final words: " We do not have to hate the Germans because they are Germans, but we cannot forget the evils they have caused us, which obliges us to distrust them. And then, too, we would find ourselves well off only in France. We can be only proud of her history, of her sufferings, and of her glory. We must love before every one our French brothers, to whom everything unites us and we shall not hesitate to take arms like them and defend even to the sacrifice of our life the menaced fatherland."

The chapter then goes on to treat of " international law," " international arbitration," and " the League of Nations." The two-page section on the League of Nations, after mentioning its organization and purpose, closes with these words:

" The League of Nations is of a moral purpose and intent of which we may approve unanimously. It will contribute to surpress war. But no means has yet been found to force a recalcitrant State to submit to the League's decisions. It has no army to defend one of its members unjustly attacked. Also, while having confidence in its future and in its action to bring about the reign of peace, we must continue to count only upon ourselves to defend the French soil against all aggression."

There is added a " reading " from Ferdinand Brunetière, in which pacifism is denounced as " cultivating laziness in men's hearts."

VI. For Use of Young Persons in Secondary Schools (Lycées and Collèges)

All the eighteen books listed in V, above, and, in addition, the following:

19. Blanchet, Désiré, and Toutain, Jules, *Histoire contemporaine de 1815 à nos jours*, 8th edition (Paris, Belin, 1925), 524 pp.

An account of French and general history from 1815 to 1920. Comprises six parts: (1) Europe from 1815 to 1848; (2) Europe after 1848; (3) Contemporary Europe; (4) Economic Development of Europe and Colonial Expansion; (5) Europe and the World from 1914 to 1921; and (6) General Features of Contemporary Civilization. Mainly political and military.

The first chapter of Part V is entitled " The War of 1914–1918 " and begins: " In 1914 Europe was recovering somewhat from the worries and preoccupations which the Balkan Wars of 1912–1913 had caused. But at the end of July and beginning of August broke out the conflict the most terrible, the most bloody, the most disastrous, which the world has ever experienced. This war, which was to last for more than four years and accumulate ruins of every kind, has as its only cause the criminal ambition of Germany and its Emperor William." Then follows a lengthy account of military operations, ending with a violent section on German cruelties and crimes.

A brief chapter is devoted to the peace-treaties of 1919–1921; the League of Nations is barely mentioned. The chapter concludes: "France cannot, must not, forget the martyrdom which her départements of the north and northeast have been forced to undergo by Germany. She cannot, must not, renounce the reparations which have been solemnly promised her. The sacrifices which she has experienced are too great and too grievous for her to forgive a conquered foe who does not repent and who will not repent."

A chapter on "General Features of Contemporary Civilization" speaks of the armed peace, the Hague conference, economic rivalries, and world commerce, but not of the League of Nations. Its last section "The Situation in 1921" ends with this: "The nations vanquished in 1918 have not renounced the idea of taking revenge for their defeat and on the other hand the economic rivalries have become more lively than ever — France must guard vigilantly her security and not let her might be the least diminished."

20. **Challeye, Félicien,** *Philosophie scientifique et Philosophie morale,* 3d edition revised and corrected (Paris, Fernand Nathan, 1927), 652 pp.

Comprises two parts: (1) Scientific Philosophy — ten chapters on general science and on the particular sciences of mathematics, physics and chemistry, biology, psychology, sociology, and history; and (2) Moral Philosophy — sixteen chapters on the moral conscience, morality and science, the moral obligation and sanction, a historical sketch of various systems of ethics, and special treatment of moral duties to one's self, to the family, to the nation and fatherland, to the state, to humanity, justice, property, and charity. A positivist rather than a Christian tendency is evidenced.

In the chapter on the nation and the fatherland, there is a thoughtful and judicious explanation of the rise of modern national patriotism, a condemnation of the type of extreme nationalism preached in Germany by Treitschke and in France by Barrès, a condemnation of anti-patriotism, a plea for the harmonizing of patriotism and internationalism in the service of humanity, and an exposition of the individual's duties to the fatherland. "The first, the most important, of our duties towards the fatherland, is that of acting for the good of our compatriots," and this involves, in particular, "social justice": . . .

" We have also the duty of defending, in case of invasion, the national soil and, even before, the duty of preparing ourselves to defend it. . . . This duty can be imposed in certain circumstances, even on the man who is most deeply convinced that violence is morally bad and that war is criminal. . . . As it is necessary to prepare one's self to defend the national soil in case of invasion, so it is necessary to strive to impose a policy of peace which would save the country from the dreadful sufferings and absurd ruins of war."

There follows a study of " peace and war," and the chapter closes with an exposition of international and colonial duties. The League of Nations is mentioned. And the last words are: " One day all the peoples of all races, equally free, will unite fraternally in pacified humanity."

21. **Driault, E.,** and **Hennemann, M.,** *Nouvelles Leçons d'Histoire de 1815 à nos Jours* (Paris, Alcan, 1925), 344 pp.

An account of French and general history from 1815 to 1920. Comprises nineteen lessons: seven on strictly French history, including two on art and French civilization and one on French colonies; ten on the history of England, Belgium, Germany, Austria-Hungary, the Balkans, Russia, the Far East, the United States, and Latin America; one on the Congress of Vienna and the Holy Alliance; and one on the Franco-German War of 1870–1871 and the Great War of 1914–1918. Illustrations wholly of works of art.

The lesson on the French colonies closes with these words: " By a magnificent effort France has known how to conquer and reconstruct in a century a colonial empire of more than twelve million kilometres area, peopled by more than fifty-seven million inhabitants, and whose annual commerce exceeds seven billion francs. Public opinion, too long indifferent or hostile, has come to appreciate during the war the great services rendered by our colonies and to pay homage to the sacrifice of the native troops who fought for the French cause. France must continue her civilizing task and see to it that the French name is loved wherever her flag is planted."

To the lesson on Belgium is appended a copy of the treaty of 1908, by which Belgium gave to France the right of preëmption of the Belgian Congo.

The lesson on Germany concludes with a paragraph on " Pan-Germanism " and an extract from Bernhardi.

The account of the Great War distinguishes between " the causes " and " the pretext." The causes are set forth, with a serious attempt to be judicious, as the " armed peace " from 1871 to 1914 and the

economic and imperialist rivalries.   Only five pages are devoted to
the military operations of the war.   Four pages are given to the peace-
settlement, in which the League of Nations bulks large.   The author
is insistent that " whatever may be the faults of its organization, the
League of Nations has one great merit: it exists and it is, in
fine, our only guarantee against an always possible recourse to armed
violence."

The last lesson extols *French* civilization, stressing " national unity,"
" social harmony," " French historians," " French scientists," " French
philosophy," and " France's civilizing mission."   It closes: " France
has a passion for labor and for peace.   If you have faith, young teachers of to-morrow — and you have faith because you are young — you
have before you the finest apostolate which has ever been proposed
to educators."

This book is widely used in Normal Schools.

22. **Guibert, J.,** *Cours de Morale, théorique et pratique,* 14th
thousand (Paris, De Gigord, 1922), 399 pp.

A Catholic work with ecclesiastical approbation, for use chiefly in
Catholic schools.   Comprises six " parts ": (1) eleven lessons on goodness, duty, money, degrees of freedom, moral effort, fruits of moral
action, the moral sanction, etc.; (2) seven lessons on the duties of
religious and private life; (3) two lessons on the duties of family life;
(4) eight lessons on the duties of social life — professional virtues,
respect for life, liberty, honor, property, and charity; (5) seven lessons
on the duties of national life — the fatherland, the state, the law, the
government, and citizenship; and (6) one lesson on international law.
Each lesson is provided with three or four questions for review or writing
and with two or three " maxims."

The lesson on the fatherland teaches the moral duty of patriotism
and its questions for review are these: " Show why it is needful to
love and serve the fatherland "; "Why is the flag the sacred symbol
of the fatherland, before which we should uncover? "   The accompanying maxims are three: " To die for one's country is not a sad fate;
it immortalizes one by a beautiful death " (Corneille); " It is the
ashes of the dead, which created the fatherland " (Lamartine); " A
flag is some bunting at the end of a pole, but a pole which lives, a
bunting which speaks, and where the soul of thirty millions of men
has passed with all its history and all its virtue " (Lacordaire).

The duties of citizens are set forth under these headings: (1)
obedience to the laws; (2) respect for magistrates; (3) taxation; (4)
voting; and (5) patriotism.   On the last it is stated: " Every citizen
must be patriotic.   However much one's heart may turn towards all

humanity — and certainly we would make a merit of that — there is due no less a very particular love and devotion to the national group to which one belongs. . . . In time of war, true citizens should not have such a horror of war as to compel the public authorities to submit to all indignities, all damages, and all invasions rather than to defend by war the honor and interests of the country. Then, too, once war is declared, true citizens should not be so stingy of their blood as to refuse to go against the enemy and encounter with courage the danger of death. Finally, both in order not to be overwhelmed in war and in order to make peace lasting, true citizens should gladly accept the obligation of military service, for thereby young men prepare themselves to defend the fatherland and form permanent armies, which serve as a bulwark."

The lesson on international law condemns " offensive war " as immoral and repeats the moral obligation of " defensive war." Some attention is devoted to the underlying principles of international law and to the practice of arbitration, but the League of Nations is not mentioned. An eloquent plea is made for the joint cherishing of nationalism and internationalism.

23. **Hauser, Henri,** *Histoire contemporaine,* 10th edition (Paris, Vuibert, n. d.), 113 pp.

An account of French and general history from 1815 to 1889. Comprises five parts: (1) 1815–1848; (2) 1848–1870; (3) Europe 1870–1889; (4) Economic Development and Colonial Expansion; and (5) Contemporary Civilization.

A special " conclusion " sums up " the rôle of France ": " Without denying the political and commercial rôle of England and the philosophical rôle of Germany, we must recognize that France has occupied a great place in the history of this century. She has had the glory of seeking to realize the ideas of humanity, liberty, and justice preached by the philosophy of the eighteenth century. With the armies of the Republic, even with the conquering armies of Napoleon, it is French ideas which have spread everywhere. . . . The civilizing mission of France is not achieved. She has not yet succeeded in effecting the complete triumph in Europe of the ideal of justice which she carries within herself. Outside of Europe she has painfully reconstructed a colonial empire, in which now lives a population greater than ours. These peoples she has the duty of governing with mildness and equity, of transmitting progressively to them her ideas. After having been the preceptress of Europe, it remains to her, for her part, to teach the world."

24. **Isaac, J.,** and **Carrère, J.,** *Les Institutions actuelles de la France, Supplément au XIXe Siècle par A. Malet et P. Grillet* (Paris, Hachette, 1925), 68 pp.

A brief account of French government under four heads: the sovereignty of the people and the electoral system; the public liberties; the public powers and the parliamentary system; and the administrative organization. The book contains five constitutional documents. A matter-of-fact summary.

25. **Malet, Albert,** *L'Époque contemporaine,* 12th edition (Paris, Hachette, n. d.), 718 pp.

An account of French and general history from 1789 to 1914. Comprises twenty-eight chapters: the first fifteen on strictly French history from 1789 to 1870; the next three on Italy, Germany, and the Balkans to 1870; the next two on economic and imperialist developments throughout the world; the next six on the Far East, England, Germany, Austria, Russia, and the United States from 1870 to 1914; and the last two on French history from 1870 to 1914 and on French government in the nineteenth century. The chapter on later French history includes a two-page account of the Great War.

The book is concerned primarily with political history; as such, it is thorough and judicious and not strikingly nationalist.

26. **Malet, Albert,** *XVIIIe Siècle, Révolution, Empire, 1715–1815,* 8th edition (Paris, Hachette, n. d.), 752 pp.

An account of French and general history from 1715 to 1815. Comprises eighteen chapters: eleven on the period from 1715 to 1789, and seven on the Revolution and the career of Napoleon.

The book is concerned primarily with politics and war and secondarily with the development of general civilization. It is objective and not particularly nationalist.

27. **Malet, A.,** and **Grillet, P.,** *XIXe Siècle: Histoire contemporaine 1815–1920,* new edition containing the history of the Great War by Jules Isaac (Paris, Hachette, n. d.), 1184 pp.

An account of French and general history from 1815 to 1920. Comprises twenty-five chapters: the first six, to 1850; the next eighteen, to 1914, and the last on the Great War. Of these chapters four deal with strictly French history; four, with intellectual, social, and religious developments; four, with economic development and with the history of non-European countries; and thirteen, with international relations and the history of various European countries.

Most of the book is scholarly and judicious and not strikingly nationalist.

The last chapter, on the war, covers 115 pages. In its introductory summary we are told that: " The Great War had as essential *cause the pretensions of German hegemony.* It had as direct cause *the policy of Austria-Hungary in the Balkans,* her aggression against Serbia, which constituted an obstacle to her." Developing these points, a whole section (18 pages) is devoted to " The Origins of the War." The outstanding headings in this section are: " German Responsibility," " The German Mentality," " The Struggle for Hegemony," " The German Preparations in 1913," etc. The section concludes with a paragraph headed " The meaning of the War " and containing these words: " The struggle was between German militarism and Occidental liberalism."

The account of military operations is straightforward, but it closes with a two-page summary of German " atrocities ": " From 1914, in fact up to the last minute of the war, the Germans had pursued in France methodical devastations. . . . Over vast spaces, the richest fields had been transformed into a veritable desert. In the zone of combat entire villages had disappeared without leaving any traces. Large cities like Reims, Arras, Soissons, Verdun, Saint Quentin were only heaps of ruins."

Thirteen pages are devoted to an account of the peace-negotiations and an exposition of the terms of the peace-treaties of 1919–1920, and ten pages are devoted to post-war developments. The League of Nations is discussed on two pages, the discussion closing on a pessimistic note: " The League of Nations, which would be the keystone of the new international edifice, obtained only a precarious existence; it existed, however, and weak and imperfect as it was, it contained precious germs susceptible of an ' infinite development.' "

Much is made of the failure to execute the Treaty of Versailles: " Put in check at Washington, the treaty has been repeatedly broken by Germany. *The judicial clauses have not been executed.* . . . By every means Germany has sought to elude or to nullify the clauses on disarmament: *military formations camouflaged* or *safety police* and *civic guards* have been organized all over the German territory. But above all Germany has sought to escape the *execution of the financial terms,* under pretext that they surpassed her capacity to pay. . . ."

The book closes with a three-page account of the " Organization of the German Republic " and " The new Germany." Its note may be gathered from the following concluding words: " In all Germany, with rare exceptions, *the directing classes of society have remained monarchist*. Thus the German Republic, established by accident, seems to have only a precarious existence. But its consolidation would appear indispensable to the maintenance of world peace."

28. **Miroux, Camille,** and **Bruneteau, L.,** *Précis d'Histoire contemporaine pour le Baccalaureat* (Paris, Colin, 1920), 216 pp.

A summary of French and general history from 1815 to 1920, mainly political and secondarily economic.

A chapter (20 pages) is devoted to the Great War. The causes are indicated by the headings of the first three paragraphs: " The German Government, pushed on by the Pan-Germanists, has the ambition of world hegemony, which it thinks it can realize only by war "; " From an Austro-Serbian dispute, deliberately aggravated by Austrian and German diplomatists, Germany brings on an European conflict "; " The invasion of Luxembourg and Belgium by German troops compels France, then England, to go to war."

Five pages are devoted to the peace settlement, in which the League of Nations is mentioned; and the book closes with these words in black-faced type: " Thus humanity proceeds grievously wounded from the most frightful crisis in its history, and the political and economic primacy of Europe seems to have received a rude set-back to the profit principally of the United States and Japan. At least we can hope that henceforth the right of peoples to dispose of themselves will not be contested and that the League of Nations, sufficiently strengthened, will be able to prevent such conflicts as were always to be feared under the régime of the ' armed peace,' which Germany had imposed on the world after 1871."

29. **Nouvel, E.,** *Histoire contemporaine, 1815–1923* (Paris, Delagrave, 1923), 282 pp.

A summary of French and general history from 1815 to 1923, mainly political and incidentally intellectual and economic.

A chapter (19 pages) is devoted to the Great War. The " fundamental causes " of the war are found " in the German mentality, in the belief of the German people in the superiority of its culture and its divine mission, and in its ambitions, which, in 1913, reached the stage of paroxysm. It dreamed of a vast customs-union (Mittel Europa), including the Ottoman Empire as far as the Persian Gulf, and of the seizure of the colonies of decadent peoples. Germany, certain of her might, made haste to use it."

The " pretext " for the war is set forth thus: " The assassination at Serajevo, on June 28, 1914, of the Archduke Francis Ferdinand, heir to the crown of Austria-Hungary, by a young Herzegovinian student, Prinzip, provides an opportunity to Austria to accuse the Serbian government of complicity. An *ultimatum* of insensate violence is addressed to Serbia; but this country, on the pacific counsel of Russia and France, humilitates herself and accepts the Austrian demands with insignificant reservations. Austria, at the instigation of Germany, promptly breaks with Serbia and rejects the proposals of the English minister, Sir Edward Grey, for an accommodation and declares war on Serbia on July 28. Russia, who does not wish to let Serbia be crushed, replies to a beginning of Austrian mobilization on her frontier by a partial mobilization of her own. Austria then reconsiders and shows a disposition to enter into negotiations, but Germany intervenes to prevent any accommodation and summons Russia to suspend preparations; the ultimatum being rejected, Germany declares war upon Russia on August 1. Against France, obstinately pacifist, who refuses, however, to promise neutrality, Germany declares war also, August 3, for quite ridiculous reasons."

Eight pages are devoted to the peace settlement, and the book closes with these words: " If the war has aroused heroism and an admirable spirit of devotion and sacrifice, it has also unchained instincts of violence and rapine. It has left in our minds the disturbance which always follows great commotion and which is ordinarily betrayed by an immoderate thirst for money and pleasures; it has multiplied the examples, always demoralizing, of fortunes too easily acquired. At the same time, by its very atrocities, it has called into being in our souls a sentiment of horror against war and the hope that that war at least would be the last. It would be necessary in order to realize this hope that such a will to peace should be common to all peoples, that the League of Nations, which, for its beginnings, has already rendered good services, should become, by the sincere adherence of all, a powerful and active organism. This moral progress is not yet obtained, but it represents the ideal toward which humanity must proceed."

VII. Miscellaneous Supplementary Texts

1. **Bazin, René,** *La Douce France,* 32d thousand (Paris, De Gigord, 1924), 347 pp.

A book of supplementary readings for the schools, especially for Catholic schools. The author states in his preface: " I thought it would be good always, a necessity to-day, to show to little Frenchmen and little Frenchwomen why we should love France and never despair of her, for already the subject which I should treat, appeared to me. . . . Yes, I would write for the school children of France. I would tell them what is the soul of this country, its character, its vocation, its national form. The title came of itself. It would be *The Sweet France,* magnificent words, in which all the tenderness of our fathers is enveloped and which was living since the twelfth century in popular poems and in hearts long before that."

The book comprises fifty readings. Not all are of directly patriotic import: thirteen deal with as many different professions and occupations; and several are religious in subject and treatment, such as " Our Nuns," " An evening at Saint Denis," " All Saints," " Christmas," " The Patron of French Curés," etc.

The majority of the readings, however, are patriotic — very sentimentally patriotic. And their character can be imagined from the following topics of which they treat: " France is quite beautiful "; " France is varied "; " France is a country of resurrection "; " The Great War "; " Marvellous sayings of Frenchmen during war "; " Alsace and Lorraine "; " Two Alsatian stories "; " The return to the fatherland "; " Overseas France — our Canadian brothers "; " Some colonial pioneers."

2. **Baudrillart, J.,** *Livret de l'Histoire de la Guerre 1914–1918,* 24th thousand (Paris, Delagrave, 1920), 48 pp.

For use of children in Elementary and Higher Primary Schools as supplement to other textbooks. Comprises six lessons: (1) From the beginning to the Marne; (2) Verdun; (3) The war in the East; (4) The war in the East and on the Italian sector; (5) Submarine warfare and the fluctuations of 1917–1918; (6) The victory and the peace.

From the preface: " The moment has come to incorporate the recent war into the history which we teach our pupils. . . . Let us give to our pupils the impression that France, in five years, has run the greatest danger of its whole history and that it has escaped disaster only by a heroism, an endurance, and a tenacity, of which past centuries offer no example."

On the causes of the war: " Here is the true cause of the war. *The will of a people and its rulers to dominate the world."*

From the conclusion: " *In 1871, in reality, we had been attacked as we were in 1914. But if the first attack succeeded, the second has failed. The new treaty effaces that of Frankfort and, by the reorganization of Europe and of the world, which it realized, it is the most considerable event which history has registered."* The League of Nations is not mentioned.

The text is interspersed with "readings" on the nobility of the *poilus* and the atrociousness of the Germans.

3. *Chronologie et Géographie illustrées de l'Histoire de France* par une Réunion de Professeurs (Paris, Librairie Générale, n. d.), 384 pp.

A chronological account of French history from earliest times to 1920, with a few supplementary notes on world history, for use as a supplement to textbooks of history for the schools. Mainly political and military, with some attention to the Church and art and science.

The account of the Great War covers twenty-five pages. Its causes are described thus:

" (1) German imperialism, which wished to dominate the world; the Germans believed in a divine mission of universal hegemony; to this end they have developed excessively their military and naval power. They supported throughout Europe, above all in France and Belgium, active agents of propaganda; they implanted their ideas, expanded their culture, and imposed their commercial, economic, and scientific tutelage;

" (2) The age-long hatred of Germany for France, hatred manifested in 1870 by the annexation of Alsace-Lorraine and by the repeated threats of war in 1875 and 1887 and, on the subject of Morocco, in 1905 and 1911. The *immediate causes* were:

" (1) The attack on Serbia by Austria, following the assassination of the heir-apparent, an attack which led Russia to mobilize in order to defend Serbia;

" (2) The intervention of Germany to support her ally Austria and to profit from the conflict; she declared war against Russia, then against France under the false pretext that French airplanes had bombarded Carlsruhe and Nuremberg;

" (3) The violation of Belgian neutrality, which provoked the intervention of England."

The account of the peace-treaties fills three pages. The League of Nations is not mentioned.

4. **Vast, H.,** *Petite Histoire de la Grande Guerre* (Paris, Delagrave, 1919), 272 pp.

A book for supplementary reading in connection with classes in contemporary history in the schools. Comprises sixteen chapters: the first three, labelled respectively " Race and Pan-Germanism," " William II and Europe," and " The Responsibility for the War," deal with the background and beginnings; the next ten deal with military and naval operations; and the last three treat of peace settlement.

The book is extremely one-sided. In all the international difficulties prior to the war Germany is black and France is white. All British ministers are " confirmed pacifists." The responsibility of the war must be laid upon " the German people " quite as much as upon the " Kaiser."

The " first " and " chief " result of the war is set forth in these words: " France breathes. Alsace and Lorraine are restored to us. All the sorrows of the invasions and mutilations of the past are effaced. The radiant dawn of 1918 dissipates the shadows which obscure our sky from 1814 and 1815 and above all from 1870. Doubtless our territory has not its natural frontier of the Rhine, which Hoche, Kleber, and Jourdan gave us. But in revenge our Republic possesses its magnificent colonial empire, the hope of to-morrow, which renders it more powerful in the world than was the Republic of our ancestors. The French henceforth will dare to raise their heads with legitimate pride."

A section is devoted to " The fiction of a democratic Germany " and another to " The shameful flight of William II." This chapter closes with these words: " The Germans are vanquished; they are not convinced; their pride must be pricked so that they may know how to live and let live. The German at home has great qualities, a worker, a disciplined person, an organizer of the first order. In respect of his neighbors he is disdainful, quarrelsome, always ready to invoke the right of the sword. Adversity will doubtless make him reform. But we shall never forget the evil he has done us. Let us always distrust his advances as tricks. Until now the German has always been for the Frenchman only the crook who deceives, the brute who robs and kills."

The account of the peace-settlement contains no reference to the League of Nations. The appended bibliography lists numerous French works and no others, and most of the French works are war propaganda.

APPENDIX B

GUIDE TO TEACHER–SOCIETIES

I. General Societies of Public-School Teachers

1. French League of Education (*Ligue Française de l'Enseignement*).

Founded in 1866. It is a confederation of associations interested in the French public school system and its problems. Teachers, parents, and politicians seek pedagogic information from the League and in turn lend their support to its attempted solution of current problems. It has markedly Radical tendencies.

The original purpose of the League was to work for the general development of state education in France. During the World War the League carried on an active propaganda in order to strengthen French morale. After the war the League began a campaign for the realization of the *école unique* reform. It proposed the abolition of primary instruction in the lycées and collèges, suggesting that it be concentrated in free public schools, and the creation of scholarships for needy students. The League has also agitated in favor of night schools for those who do not receive secondary education. At its congresses it has studied the question of hygienic school conditions, especially as regards tuberculosis. It has considered the problem of school attendance and has resolved to seek means for enforcing the law of obligatory education. It has studied new pedagogic methods and has recommended the use of moving pictures.

Organ: *L'Action Laïque*. Officers: President, François-Albert; General Secretary, A. Salzèdo. Headquarters: 3 rue Récamier, Paris. Membership: over 500,000.

2. Friends of the New University (*Compagnons de l'Université Nouvelle*).

A small society which seeks better conditions for the teachers and studies new pedagogic reforms. It is in favor of *l'école unique*.

Organ: *L'Université Nouvelle* (monthly). Officers: President, H. Laugier; Vice-President, Mme. Alice Jouenne; General Secretary, G. Grelois. Headquarters: 13 rue Froment, Paris.

3. The International League for the New Education (*Ligue International pour l'Éducation Nouvelle*).

Founded in 1921. " The new education prepares the child not only to be a citizen able to fulfill his duties toward his neighbors, his nation, and humanity, but also to be a human being conscious of the responsibilities of man."

The League supports the League of Nations and its tone is on the whole international.

Organ: *Pour l'Ère Nouvelle* (monthly). Nine reviews are published by the different national branches. Officers: President for France, Mlle. J. Hauser. Headquarters: 11 Tavistock Square, London, England; for France, 11 rue de Cluny, Paris.

4. National Syndicate of Public School Teachers of France and her Colonies (*Syndicat National des Institutrices et Instituteurs de France et ses Colonies*).

Founded in 1901. Its original title was *Fédération des Amicales d'Instituteurs*. In 1920 it was reorganized as a trade union, much to the displeasure of the Government. Legal action was started against it but this procedure proved futile. Many of the individual members joined the *Confédération Générale du Travail* and the Syndicate itself became affiliated to this organization in 1925.

The Syndicate is composed of elementary school teachers. It aims are:

(1) To strengthen the fraternal bonds which unite its members;

(2) To facilitate the exchange of educational ideas;

(3) To defend the material and moral interests of the elementary school teachers, individually and collectively, in public life, in relations with the higher authorities, and before the courts;

(4) To collaborate with the organized working class by means of the C. G. T.

In the years immediately following the war the Syndicate had its hands full in fighting for existence and in defending its members. After 1922 the persecution became less severe and the Syndicate broadened its sphere of action. In this year it began an active campaign for the *école unique*. The question of salaries has attracted the attention of the Syndicate and it has been insistent in demands for higher wages. At the annual Congress in 1922 the problem of Alsace-Lorraine was discussed. Since that time the Syndicate has opposed the special conditions which allow religious instruction to be given in the public schools of Alsace-Lorraine. The introduction of the lay French system is demanded. In addition, the Syndicate has favored the creation of night trade-schools for those who do not get the regular secondary instruction, has opposed the idea of military instruction in primary and normal schools, has recommended the creation of special schools for backward children, and has produced a series of lantern-slide lessons as an aid to teachers.

In 1923 a member of the Syndicate, G. Clemendot, began a campaign against chauvinist history in the primary schools. This question was discussed at the Congresses of 1923 and 1924. At the latter date the Syndicate adopted the following resolutions:

" (1) The instruction of history will remain a part of the elementary school curriculum, for it is necessary in order to train the child to be an enlightened worker and an informed citizen of to-morrow, instructed as to his rights and conscious of his duties;

" (2) The instruction should be truthful and should repudiate the falsehoods which too often dishonor it;

" (3) The instruction will try to show human evolution towards progress and justice — and will pay much attention to the economic and social life of the past. It will show the rôle which France has played in this evolution and indicate what France owes to other peoples and what she has given to the world. It will be absolutely pacifist and will reject all that would tend to instill in the young a hatred for foreigners. It will have no other object than to teach the truth and human fraternity. It will in this way prepare the child for a greater, yes, international society.

" (4) It will be necessary to modify the methods which have been used up to the present time. For example, one should try:

" (a) to stress as much as possible general or national rather than local history which might be given too much attention, thus deforming and overloading the curriculum;

" (b) to stress in the general history of civilization the rôle of the workers, and material, intellectual, and social evolution;

" (c) to limit to a minimum the number of facts to be treated."
The Congress demands the creation of an instruction for those who have completed the requirements of obligatory education. This instruction should bear the chief burden of history teaching. The Congress authorizes the Pedagogic Commission to write and to publish new textbooks at the expense of the National Syndicate."

Organ: *Bulletin Mensuel*. Officers: General Secretary, Roussel; Secretary of propaganda, Glay. Headquarters: 73 rue Notre-Dame de Nazareth, Paris. Membership: 78,000.

5. National Syndicate of Lycée Professors and of the Personnel of Feminine Secondary Instruction (*Syndicat National des Professeurs de Lycée et du Personnel de l'Enseignement Secondaire Féminin*).

Founded in 1905. Its principal aim is to better the material conditions of its members. It favors the *école unique*, the centralization of primary education, which is now divided between the primary schools and the primary classes of the lycées, into one gratuitous primary system and desires the same reform for secondary education, which is now divided between the collèges and the lycées. The Syndicate favors the League of Nations (*Bulletin*, Oct. 1926, p. 31) and the teaching of German in the schools (*Bulletin*, Jan. 1927, p. 300), and endorses the attitude of the Congress of the International Bureau of National Federations on the teaching of history.

Organs: *Bulletin Officiel* (monthly); *La Quinzaine Universitaire* (fortnightly). Officers: President, Cope; General Secretary, Lacroix; Administrative Secretary, Bellette. Headquarters: 246 rue St. Jacques, Paris. Membership: 8,000.

6. The Educational Workers' International (*L'International des Travailleurs de l'Enseignement*).

Founded in 1919. It is a Communist group and has close relations with Moscow. It preaches the dictatorship of the proletariat, internationalism, war against imperialism, and freedom of instruction. It believes in a centralized public school system. It demands better conditions for teachers.

Several articles concerning the instruction of history appeared in the International's *Bulletin* for February 1927. The following quotations are characteristic: " The objective point of view is the proletarian point of view because the working class represents the reality of the productive forces and the struggle for a new social order " (p. 17).

" The two essential tasks are to teach the youth to understand the most important elements of the world to-day: to analyze at least in a general manner important forces and to trace in broad lines the historical evolution that has resulted in the present world situation " (p. 26).

" The history taught in the schools ought to become authentic, i.e., the history of class struggles " (p. 26).

Organ: *L'Internationale de l'Enseignement* (monthly) published in French, Russian, English, German, and Spanish. Officers: General Secretary, L. Vernochet. Headquarters: 33 rue de la Grange-aux-Belles, Paris.

The French section of the Educational Workers' International is known as the Federation of Syndicates of Instruction (*Fédération des Syndicats de l'Enseignement*). It is affiliated with the *Confédération Générale du Travail Unitaire*. Inspired by the words of Anatole France, " Burn all the books which teach hate," the Federation has been waging a war on chauvinist textbooks. A model history text was published in 1927. (See above, p. 361.)

Organ: *L'École Émancipée* (weekly). Secretary: L. Vernochet. Headquarters: 33 rue de la Grange-aux-Belles, Paris.

7. National Union of Members of Public Instruction (*Union Nationale des Membres de l'Enseignement Public*).

Founded in 1925. It is open to elementary, secondary, and university teachers. It is interested in all sorts of pedagogic questions and in the material conditions of its members.

For its attitude on historical textbooks, see above, p. 60.

Organ: *Bulletin* (six times a year). Secretary: Charmailloux. Headquarters: 9 rue de Provence, Versailles. Membership: 3,000.

8. The University Entente (*Entente Universitaire*).

Founded in 1920 as the *Comité d'Entente Universitaire*. The Entente aims to unite all the officials who are employees in the Ministry of Public Instruction and Fine Arts. This is partially realized, for more than forty associations are affiliated with the Entente. The question of salaries has been the predominating subject at the meetings of this organization. The Entente has no definite policy as regards other problems, not even as regards *l'école unique*.

Officers: Secretary, J. Corrot. Headquarters: Lycée Louis-le-Grand, rue St. Jacques, Paris.

9. The International Bureau of National Federations of the Personnel of Secondary Public Instruction (*Le Bureau International des Fédérations Nationales du Personnel d'Enseignement Secondaire Public*).

Founded in 1912, but not well organized until after the war. According to the by-laws the aims of the Bureau are as follows:

" (1) To unite the members by ties of international friendship and solidarity;

" (2) To contribute to the progress of secondary education;

" (3) To study the means by whch young men studying abroad may continue work without prejudice and without losing time;

" (4) To consider ways of bettering the material and moral conditions of the personnel;

" (5) To collaborate with other institutions, either public or private, which have the same aims."

At the annual congress of 1926, held at Geneva, the following resolutions concerning the teaching of history were adopted:

" (1) The study of history in secondary education ought not to have as its essential purpose either the moral edification of the pupils or even exclusively the formation of the mind by the study of the evolution of humanity. Above all else it ought to explain and make known events and men in order that they may be impartially judged.

" (2) The teaching of history can and ought to be conceived of in all countries as the most efficacious means of moulding future citizens. To this end national history ought to be the basis of the instruction, especially in the lower classes, but on the formal condition that, consciously or unconsciously, it should not systematically glorify one country and methodically attack all others.

" (3) The study of history in secondary education ought, especially in the higher classes, to stress phenomena of an economic nature and the interdependence of all civilized nations. It ought to throw light on the development of human solidarity and the rôle of international bodies which are the result of this solidarity and which include among others the League of Nations, that ought, in this study, to occupy the place to which its importance and its activity entitle it."

Organ: *Le Bulletin International.* Officers: General Secretaries, J. Clavière, and A. Bellette. Headquarters: 2 rue Montpensier, Paris. Membership: 42,000, representing 14 nations.

10. The National Confederated Syndicate of Members of Secondary and Higher Instruction (*Le Syndicat National Confédéré des Membres de l'Enseignement Secondaire et de l'Enseignement Supérieur*).

Founded in 1922 as an outcome of the development of the trade-union movement among the secondary and university teachers. The Syndicate favors the *école unique,* demands social insurance and higher wages for its members, and advocates the professional equality of sexes. It is anti-chauvinistic. Its membership is small, but its influence is considerable.

Organ: *Bulletin* (monthly). Secretary: Zoretti. Headquarters: 15 rue Malfilatre, Caen, France.

11. Society of *Agrégés* (*Société des Agrégés*).

Founded in 1914 by men who had passed the difficult state examinations for prospective teachers — the so-called *agrégation.* The Society is mainly interested in material questions. It has nevertheless preached coöperation with pacifist German teachers, and its delegate to the Congress of the International Bureau of National Federations at Geneva voted in favor of the resolution concerning the teaching of history.

Organ: *L'Agrégation* (monthly). Officers: President, Dorolle;

Secretary, Mohé. Headquarters: 147 rue de Rome, Paris. Membership: 1,800.

12. Society of *Agrégées* (*Société des Agrégées*).

Founded in 1920. It is composed of women who have passed the *agrégation* examinations. It has the same aims and takes the same position regarding the teaching of history as the Society of *Agrégés*.
Organ: *Les Agrégées* (monthly). Officers: President, Mme. Flobert; General Secretary, Mlle. S. Collette. Headquarters: 7 Place Jussieu, Paris.

13. Society of History and Geography Professors of Public Instruction (*Société des Professeurs d'Histoire et de Géographie de l'Enseignement Public*).

Founded in 1910. It is an association of professors who have adopted resolutions against chauvinism and against the devoting of too much attention to military history.
Organ: *Bulletin* (quarterly). Officers: President, Marizet; General Secretary, Weulersee. Headquarters: 20 rue de la Terrasse, Paris.

14. National Syndicate of "*Collège*" Professors (*Syndicat National des Professeurs des Collège*).[1]

Founded in 1905. Its principal preoccupation is the material betterment of its members. It favors *l'école unique*, demands that German be taught under the same conditions as English, and opposes the chauvinist teaching of history. It is affiliated with the *Confédération Générale du Travail*.
Organ: *Le Journal des Collèges* (monthly). Officers: General Secretary, E. Espié; Director of *Le Journal*, M. Dupont, 6 rue Antione Carro, Meaux. Headquarters: In care of the Secretary, 11 bis Avenue Gambetta, Chermont (Oise).

15. The Friendly Association of Monitors of the National Lycées (*L'Association Amicale des Censeurs des Lycées Nationaux*).

Founded in 1907. Its members are disciplinary and administrative officials. The Association's chief aim is to seek the material betterment of its members.
Organ: *Bulletin* (quarterly). Officers: President, Piobetta; Secretary, L. Aubert. Headquarters: Lycée Lalande, Bourg.

[1] "Collège" in French refers to a secondary school which is supported by the municipality.

16. Federation of War Veterans of Public Instruction (*Fédération des Anciens Combattants de l'Enseignement Public*).

Founded in 1919. Its purposes are: " To preserve the worship of our comrades who died for France and to aid their families; to maintain and to strengthen the bonds of friendship created by the War among the veterans; to obtain special reparations for the veterans; to defend their professional rights; to realize an intimate and cordial union among the members of the different grades of schools; to aid the veterans to express their ideas concerning post-war instruction and the reforms to be realized."

Organ: *Bulletin.* Officers: President, Dubuc; General Secretaries, Maurice Randoux and André Jacques. Headquarters: 37 rue des Bordonnais, Paris. Membership: 10,000.

II. General Societies of Private-School Teachers, Especially of Teachers in Catholic Schools

1. General Society of Education and Instruction (*Société Générale d'Éducation et d'Enseignement*).

Founded in 1870. It is the largest Catholic educational association and tends to centralize the diocesan educational system. Its offices serve as a bureau of documentation and of propaganda. The Society is definitely opposed to the *école unique* which would make education in the lycées and collèges gratuitous.

The Society has no definite nationalist program, although articles such as the following are to be found in its *Bulletin:*

" In closing let me say that I believe: (1) That the teaching of history, and particularly the history of France, should be stressed more than ever in the Catholic schools in order to foster the intellectual, moral, and social development of the child, to develop his patriotic sentiments, to instill in him a deep sense of gratitude towards those who for twenty centuries have contributed to the grandeur of the country, and to inspire him with a desire to continue their work by serving France and the Church — nation of souls. (2) That the professors should try to make the teaching of history as attractive and real as possible; that in the lower classes history as it is usually taught should be replaced by the biographies of the greatest figures of the past. (3) That the professors should separate philosophy from history, stress great forces, and put emphasis on the action of the Divine Providence who governs the world." (*Bulletin,* July 1925, pp. 617–618.)

Organ: *Bulletin* (monthly). Officers: President, Colonel Kelber;

General Secretary, Antoine Lestra. Headquarters: 14 bis, rue d'Assas, Paris.

2. The Syndicate of the Directors of Christian Educational Institutions (*Syndicat des Directeurs des Maisons d'Éducation Chrétienne*).

Founded in 1872 as the *Alliance des Maisons d'Éducation Chrétienne*. Its name was changed in 1926. The purpose of the Syndicate is to strengthen Catholic educational institutions and to defend them from the encroachments of the state schools. The Syndicate studies new pedagogic methods, proposes the use of textbooks suitable for Catholic education, and unites the leading Catholic secondary schools " in a sort of brotherly legion."

Organ: *L'Enseignement Chrétien* (monthly). Secretary: Canon Mouchard. Headquarters: 15 rue Cassette, Paris. Membership: 440 French schools; 100 foreign schools.

3. Association of Private School Male Teachers (*Association des Instituteurs Privés*).

Founded in 1910. It is a Catholic organization. Its members are teachers in the archdiocese of Paris. It is particularly interested in pedagogic questions. It is opposed, of course, to the *école unique*.

Headquarters: 76 rue des Saints-Pères, Paris. President: F. Laudet. Membership: 600.

4. Parisian Union of Private School Female Teachers (*Union Parisienne des Institutrices Privées*).

Founded in 1910. Its program is the same as the Association of Private School Male Teachers.

Headquarters: 76 rue des Saints-Pères, Paris. Membership: 350.

APPENDIX C

SELECT LIST OF FRENCH PERIODICALS (OTHER THAN DAILIES) WHICH ARE IMPORTANT BECAUSE OF THEIR WIDE CIRCULATION OR BECAUSE THEY ARE REPRESENTATIVE OF SIGNIFICANT POLITICAL, SOCIAL, OR RELIGIOUS FORCES IN FRANCE.

Total number, 108. Unless otherwise noted, the place of publication is Paris. The list is of January 1928.

ACTION FRANÇAISE AGRICOLE (L') **Weekly**
" Weekly of rural defense." Founded 1925 by the Action Française.
Editor-in-chief: Henri de Castillon de St. Victor.
Directors: Léon Daudet, Charles Maurras, Ambroise Rendu.
　Newspaper format. Political articles and review of the press of same type as those in the daily *Action Française* (see below, p. 431). Articles on agriculture, market quotations of farm products. Financial columns.

ACTION NATIONALE (L') **Monthly**
Founded 1908.
Managing Editor: Théodore Steeg, senator and former minister.
　Magazine. Contains valuable political documentation, especially from point of view of parliamentary reform.

ANNALES POLITIQUES ET LITTÉRAIRES (LES) **Fortnightly**
Founded 1883.
Director: Pierre Brisson.
　Magazine. Announces a circulation of over 100,000 paid subscribers. Illustrated literary periodical, featuring popular French writers. Regular contributors: Gustave LeBon, on current events; M. de St. Aulaire, on foreign affairs; Jacques Seydoux, J. Natanson, la Comtesse de Noailles, Paul Bourget, Mme. Gérard d'Houville, Roland Dorgelès.

ATTAQUE (L') **Weekly**
Founded 1888. " Weekly independent journal " — motto: " Straight to its aim."
Director: Ernest Gegout.
　Newspaper format, single sheet. Eugène Lautier, " Radical-

Socialiste" deputy, is a leading contributor. Front page devoted to political propaganda — anti-Catholic, anti-Communist. Back page mainly financial notices.

AUX ÉCOUTES Weekly
Founded 1918.
Direction not named.
> Thirty-page weekly pamphlet, colored illustrated cover. No signed contributions. Consists principally of paragraphs of barbed comments on society, art, drama, and politics, with pen-and-ink sketches scattered liberally throughout. Anti-Poincaré, but also anti-Cartel. Large news-stand sale.

BATAILLE (LA) Weekly
"Syndicalist and Social." Founded 1915.
Director: F. Marie.
> Single page newspaper format. Published by "Publicité Populaire," syndicalist organization. Contains political comment from syndicalist viewpoint, appeals for civic justice, and financial information for bondholders. Claims to have 10,000 circulation.

CAHIERS DES DROITS DE L'HOMME Fortnightly
Official Organ of the *Ligue des Droits de l'Homme,* which corresponds to the American Civil Liberties Union, though with a pronounced Jacobin and "anti-clerical" tone. Founded 1900. (See above, pp. 337–338.)
Director: Henri Guernut.
> Pamphlet. Motto: "Review of ideas for battle — review of battle by ideas." News of groups of the League all over France and the League's activities in behalf of citizen's liberties. Contains full reports of resolutions voted at congresses of the League. Reported to have 15,804 subscribers (1927).

CAHIERS DU BOLCHEVISME Fortnightly
"Organ of Theory of the Communist Party." (S. F. I. C.)
Founded 1924. Editors not named.
> Under the administration of the daily *Humanité* and edited at the headquarters of the Communist Party. Of small magazine format, it contains articles on economic, social, and political problems in Europe; book reviews and news of Communist Party groups in France, as well as a "tribune of discussion" open to readers.

CAMBRONNE Monthly
Founded 1926.
Editors not named.
> Magazine illustrated with cartoons. Satirical articles treating politics, society, literature, and the arts. Criticizes severely the Union

Nationale and Clemenceau, ridicules President Doumergue, and at the same time is bitterly antagonistic to certain representatives of the Left, such as L. O. Frossard of the C. G. T. Much personal " mud-slinging " both in special articles and in pages of nearly unprintable anecdotes.

CANARD ENCHAINÉ (LE)   Weekly

Founded 1916.

Director: Maurice Maréchal.

Four-page satirical newspaper, containing many caricatures and illustrated jokes, mainly political. Radical tendencies, especially anti-Poincaré. Large sale at news-stands.

CANDIDE   Weekly

Founded 1924. " Great Parisian and literary weekly."

Eight to ten pages, newspaper format. Drawings and cartoons by Sennep and Hermann-Paul. News of the literary and artistic world, with short stories, essays, playlets, and musical, dramatic, and artistic criticism. Weekly section on theatre written by Sacha Guitry, current events by Pierre Veber, articles and light political comment by Stéphane Lauzanne; many Academicians are regular contributors. Very widely read.

CARNET DE LA SEMAINE (LE)   Weekly

Founded 1915.

Editor-in-chief: Albert Dubarry.

Clever satirical pamphlet, covering all phases of Paris life — boulevards, theatres, clubs, courts, Parliament. Rather liberal in politics.

CHARIVARI (LE)   Weekly

" Illustrated Satirical Weekly." 97th year.

Editors and contributors not named.

Pamphlet illustrated with small comic cuts between paragraphs and making a specialty of full-page cartoons by Bib. Concentrates on political affairs, making extremely bitter comment on the activities of Left politicians, but not sparing certain Conservatives. Large circulation.

CLARTÉ   Monthly

Founded in 1919, under the inspiration of Henri Barbusse, publication suspended in 1924. Has reappeared since December 1926, but Barbusse is no longer connected with it. No editors named, but Pierre Naville is probably in charge.

Articles on international political and revolutionary movements, with special attacks on France's " imperialism " and " militarism." Of Communist sympathies, but not an official organ.

COMMENTAIRES   Weekly
Founded in 1921.
Manager: Louis Prévot.   Contributors anonymous.
Political and financial pamphlet, specializing in satirical comment
and small cartoons criticizing both Left and Right.   Much space
is given to financial gossip.

CONFERENCIA   Fortnightly
"Journal of the *Université des Annales.*"   Founded 1907.
Directress: Madame Yvonne Sarcey.
Illustrated magazine publishing popular lectures given by leading
men of letters, artists, scientists, etc.   Under same management
as *Les Annales.*   Has a large circulation, especially in the provinces.

CORRESPONDANT (LE)   Fortnightly
Founded 1829.   The oldest French review still in existence.
Director: Édouard Trogan.
Literary, artistic, historic, economic, and political articles.   Con-
servative and Catholic in domestic policy; quite liberal in foreign
policy.   Very high intellectual standards.

COSMOPOLIS (formerly L'INDISCRET)   Fortnightly
" Humorous gazette of society, the fine arts, literature, finance, and
travel."   Founded 1906.
Director: Édouard Aullier de Better.
Anonymous caustic comment on doings of politicians, especially
venomous criticism of Herriot and the Cartel des Gauches, but at
the same time not too lenient with Poincaré.   Contains some book
reviews and news of society at French resorts.

COURRIER DE LA IVᵉ RÉPUBLIQUE (LE)   Weekly
Organ of the political organization " IVᵉ République " (Republican
Party of National Reorganization) founded by war-veterans in 1919.
It controlled the " Groupe de l'Action Républicaine et Sociale " in
the 1919 legislature.
Director: Jean de Goitisolo.   Editor-in-chief: Charles Rousseau.
Political writers: Fernand Hauser and Raoul Sabatier.   Collabo-
rators: George Lecomte (French Academy) and Joseph-Barthélemy.
Six-page newspaper, chiefly concerned with politics (hostile to
Cartel and to Socialists.)   A page devoted to literary criticism and
an unusually large percentage of space — 50 per cent — to retail
advertising.   Announces its circulation as 25,000.

COURRIER DU PARLEMENT ET DES ASSEMBLÉES
    DÉPARTMENTALES   Weekly
"Independent Republican."   Founded 1905.

Director: Robert LeCouret. Contributors: Mario Roustan and Louis Martin, senators; Edouard Crocikia.

Single newspaper sheet. Specializes in parliamentary gossip, and keen political forecasting. Sympathetic to Cartel des Gauches in its clever cartoons and write-ups of personalities and directs its sarcasm especially against Louis Marin and the " die-hards " of the Right. Financial news also featured.

CRAPOUILLOT (LE) Monthly
Founded 1915.
Director: Galtier-Bossière.

Illustrated magazine devoted to the fine arts, literature, and the theatre, publishing critical articles by the younger literary lights, such as Pierre MacOrlan, Jean Oberlé, Michel Vaucaire, and cosmopolitan rather than French in its artistic preferences.

CRI DE PARIS (LE) Weekly
Founded 1897.
Editors and contributors not named.

Sixteen-page pamphlet of political and Parisian gossip, extremely patriotic and pro-Poincaré. Attractively presented and embellished with clever cuts. Nearly all its articles unsigned. Wide sale on news-stands.

CRI DU JOUR (LE) Weekly
Founded 1926.
Editor-in-chief: Jacques Landau. Parliamentary comments by Ferdinand Lop.

Sixteen-page pamphlet of political comment, Left in sympathy, and " anti-militarist." Articles mostly unsigned. Announced circulation 20,000.

CROIX DU DIMANCHE (LA) Weekly
Founded 1888.

Same editors and direction as daily La Croix, which publishes it in combination with Le Laboureur, a section dealing with agricultural questions.

Four-page newspaper format, its editorials and features of the same type as La Croix (see below, p. 433). Very large circulation in all French rural communities. Fights against the de-Christianization of rural and urban working-class.

CYRANO Weekly
Founded 1924.
Editor-in-chief: Léo Marchès.

One of the most important satirical weeklies, containing articles by such celebrated wits as Clément Vautel, Henri Béraud, Colette, Pierre Veber, etc. Numerous cartoons and vignettes. Specializes in political comment, leaning slightly to the Left, and in Paris gossip in general. Large sale on news-stands.

DÉMOCRATIE (LA)   Monthly
8th year, new series.
Director: Marc Sangnier.
Part of propaganda of " La Jeune République " (see above pp. 328– 329). Catholic in religion, pacifist in program for national de- velopment, international in scope, dealing with historical, political, and literary topics. Georges Hoog writes monthly chronicle of foreign and domestic politics.

DÉMOCRATIE NOUVELLE (LA)   Weekly
Founded 1918 by Lysis (M. Letailleur) who died in 1927.
Fontenoy, General Cordonnier, E. Mittler, Biard d'Aunet.
Editors: H. Hilaire and Girard. Contributors: Édouard Blanc, Pamphlet, organ of the " Party of the New Democracy " (" Parti de la Démocratie Nouvelle "), founded by Lysis, who, like so many French conservatives, began his career in the columns of *Humanité*. The Party aims (1) to eliminate politicians from politics; (2) to reorganize the government on a more democratic and efficient basis. Very patriotic and pro-army, but unfriendly to Poincaré. Articles are political, economic, and financial, with a few book reviews.

DÉMOCRATIE RURALE (LA)   Weekly
" Journal of National Solidarity."   39th year.
Director: Kergall.
Small one-page sheet, concerned with agricultural and financial announcements.

DIMANCHE–ILLUSTRÉ   Weekly
Founded 1924.
Tabloid newspaper format, with numerous photographic illustra- tions.
Issued by the daily *Excelsior*. Under same financial direction as *Le Petit Parisien*. Very strong American influence: translated editorial by Frank Crane, two comic pages from the *Chicago Trib- une*, including Andy Gump, and stories and feature articles translated from English, of the same type as those which appear in any Sunday magazine section of an American newspaper. In format, arrangement of reading matter and advertisements, it is the nearest approach to an American newspaper to be found in the French press.

DIVAN (LE)   **Monthly**
Founded 1919.
Director: Henri Martineau.
Small magazine of literary and artistic discrimination, containing criticism, poems, and essays by lesser known but able writers.

DOCUMENTS POLITIQUES, DIPLOMATIQUES ET FINAN-
CIERS (LES)   **Monthly**
Founded 1920.
Director: R. Mennevée.
Magazine. International documentation on political and financial questions. Specializes in studies on the origins and responsibilities of the Great War. Especially valuable for information on the financial background of European politics. Circulation at least 1,000 per month.

DOSSIERS DE L'ACTION POPULAIRE (LES)   **Fortnightly**
" Review of Religious and Social Action." Founded 1921.
Edited by Éditions Spes.
A Catholic magazine which informs the clergy and laity on religious, economic, social, and political questions. Some of the articles are written by the clergy, but many are by laymen, and all are carefully organized and well documented for serious study of social reform by church groups.

ÉCHO MUNICIPAL (L')   **Weekly**
" Political and News Weekly of Paris and of the Département of the Seine." Founded 1923.
Director: Jean Pausader.
Four-page small newspaper format. Gossip of municipal politics and news of city public works and other public departments. A few cartoons and photographs of civic development. News on taxation and market quotations.

ÉTINCELLE SOCIALISTE (L')   **Weekly**
" Organ for the defense of International Socialism." (S. F. I. O.).
Founded 1925.
Editor-in-chief and political director: Maurice Maurin.
Marxian Socialist newspaper, containing articles on international as well as French politics and economics.

EUROPE NOUVELLE (L')   **Weekly**
Founded 1918.
Editor: Louise Weiss.
Devoted to international affairs, publishes original diplomatic documents and special issues making exhaustive inquiries into

European economic problems.   Large circulation in French intellectual circles and abroad.

ÈVE   Weekly
Founded 1920.
Editor-in-chief: R. Manevy.
Illustrated tabloid newspaper for women, appearing Sundays. Also sold as supplement to twenty-one provincial newspapers. Movies, theatres, sports, fancy-work, fashions, literary news, short stories and novelettes — all treated with a " feminine slant." Very large news-stand sale.

ÉVOLUTION   Monthly
Founded 1926 by Victor Margueritte.
Secretary-general: Armand Charpentier.
Calls itself " Monthly review of questions concerning international conciliation and the *rapprochement* of peoples."
Contributors to this little magazine are prominent in the pacifist movement in France and Europe, and write much on war guilt — including George Demartial, Baron Baudran, L. Laurent, Alcide Ebray.   Treats questions of past wars and future peace.

FANTASIO   Fortnightly
Founded 1906.
Editors not named.
Humorous magazine, illustrated in colors.   Political and domestic satire, society scandal, with what is presumed to be typical Gallic flavor.   Large sale on news-stands.

FRANCE NOUVELLE (LA)   Monthly
Founded 1916.   " Union makes France."
Director: Paul Gaultier.
Organ of the " French Union " (" L'Union Française "), which is composed of men of prominence in all fields for the purpose of carrying on French propaganda abroad.   Informative articles on national institutions, social, juridical, commercial, and diplomatic problems.   The avowed aim of the publication is to foster a sympathetic understanding of France in allied and other friendly nations.   Magazine format.

FRANCE VIVANTE (LA)   Weekly
Founded 1918.   " The Renovators' Journal."
Editors: E. A. Fourmond and E. Boucly.
Pamphlet founded by " Probus " (J. Corréard) as organ of the " Federation of Republican Renovators " (" Fédération des Républicains Renovateurs "), which advocates a program of social,

economic, and administrative reform along conservative and national lines.

FRONT REPUBLICAIN (LE) Weekly
Founded 1925. "Neither Bolshevism nor Fascism."
Director: Roger Cluzeau.
Organ of political organization, "The Republican Battle-front" ("Le Front Républicain"), founded in 1925. Rather small body, of which the leading spirit is the deputy Jean Goy (Seine) independent of groups in the Chamber. This newspaper represents moderate radical opinion, with an extensive program of parliamentary reform.

FROUFROU Weekly
Founded 1922.
Editors not named.
Newspaper format, illustrated with black and white drawings. Devoted exclusively to the humorous side of "amour," and advertisements related thereto. Very large sale on news-stands.

GAZETTE FRANÇAISE (LA) Weekly
Founded 1923.
Editor: M. Piedvache (pseudonym, Amédée d'Yvignac).
Organ, newspaper format, of "Christian politics." Royalist and Catholic, but has submitted to authority of the Vatican and is therefore hostile to Action Française, of which it was originally an off-shoot. Contributors include: Comte J. du Plessis, Pierre Bordes. Specializes in political and religious news and publishes some literary criticism.

GENS QUI RIENT Weekly
Founded 1923. "Journal of Humor and Love."
Eight-page pink newspaper. Many illustrations. Cf. Froufrou. Large sale.

GRAND GUIGNOL (LE) Monthly
Founded 1922.
Editor: Georges Anquetil.
Large volume, over 200 pages, devoted to scandal, "moeurs," politics, finance, drama, literature — in each case seeking the sensational. All the most lurid events of the month described with zest and illustrated by realistic drawings, many in color. Attacks on politicians, especially those of the Right, often verge on libel. Although its avowed aim is to improve society by exposing vice in all its forms, it seems, by its treatment of the subject, to pander to the very tastes it deplores.

GRIFFE (LA) Weekly
Founded 1918. " Republican Journal of Combat."
Director: Jean Laffray. Editor-in-chief: J. M. Renaitour.
Newspaper format. Well-written financial, political, and literary
journal, pro-Caillaux. Its financial and economic page is headed
by a quotation from Caillaux and its policies are his inspiration.
Markedly " anti-clerical."

HUMBLES (LES) Monthly
Founded 1913. " Monthly Literary review of Primary School
Teachers."
Editor: Maurice Wullens.
Small magazine, containing contributions by school-teachers of
radical tendencies, often verging on anarchism. Essays, sketches
and poetry of able, thoughtful writers, who are anti-imperialist
and pacifist in so far as political opinions are expressed.

HUMOUR (L') Weekly
Founded 1917.
Editors not named.
Newspaper format, in subject matter and illustrations similar to
Froufrou. Wide sale on news-stands.

ILLUSTRATION (L') Weekly
Founded 1843.
Director: René Baschet.
Large magazine, printed on glazed paper, numerous illustrations,
photographs and some colored plates. News of the day, fine arts,
travel (especially in the interests of French tourist trade) pictured with short write-ups. *La Petite Illustration,* weekly supplement, is a pamphlet containing French plays and novels which are
popular successes. Large circulation in France and abroad.

IMPARTIAL FRANÇAIS (L') Weekly
Founded 1923.
Director: Gaston Grémy.
Small newspaper format. Political, literary, and social criticism;
" no news, but opinion," is the aim. A few cartoons and much
lively comment on all matters civic, and on national and international politics. Reviews current periodicals and gives large
excerpts of leading articles. Keen parliamentary reports, and
lucid accounts of foreign affairs and their relation to French policy.
An interesting department, " In the religious world," gives news
of all cults. Financial and literary notes, and a regular supplement,
Les Cahiers de l'Impartial, which contains studies in economic
and political problems.

INFORMATEUR–EXPRESS DE LA FINANCE, DU PARLEMENT
ET DES TRIBUNAUX **Weekly**
Founded 1912.
Director: H. Hamard.
Single-sheet news bulletin, printed on only one side. Foreign
and domestic politics in short articles, as well as financial news.
Typical of the news-financial bulletins which are posted daily by
banks and other financial houses for the guidance of clients.

INTERNATIONALE COMMUNISTE (L') **Fortnightly**
Founded 1927.
Editors not named.
Magazine. " Fortnightly organ of the Executive Committee of
the Communist International." Contributors are from all nations,
and subjects discussed are international in scope — political, economic, and social conflicts in Europe and Asia. A few book
reviews. There are no illustrations, but the cover is strikingly
decorated with Communist emblems.

JE SAIS TOUT **Monthly**
Founded 1905.
Editor: Pierre Lafitte.
" The Great Popular Scientific Review." Illustrated popular scien-
tific magazine, in format more American or English than French.
Pays much attention to scientific military preparations for future
warfare and gives much prominence to material on French inven-
tions. Large circulation and news-stand sale.

JEUNE RÉPUBLIQUE (LA) **Weekly**
Founded 1920.
Director: Marc Sangnier. Editor: Georges Hoog.
Organ (newspaper format) of the " Jeune République," a Catholic
pacifist political organization (see above, pp. 328–329). Supports
the Bloc National on most domestic questions, and labors for a
rapprochment with Germany. Among contributors are Louis Rolland, Fabien France, Leroy-Debasan.

JOURNAL AMUSANT (LE) **Weekly**
Founded 1847. The oldest of the French humorous magazines.
Director: Jean Pascal.
Drawings and cartoons, short stories and anecdotes in a rather
restrained " Gallic " vein.

JOURNAL DES MUTILÉSET REFORMÉS   **Weekly**
Founded 1916.
Director: André Linville.

Newspaper format. Protects interests of wounded war veterans of the " Federated Union of French Associations of Wounded and Crippled War-Veterans and their Wives, Orphans, and Families " (" Union Fédérale des Associations Françaises de Mutilés Reformés, Anciens Combattants et de leurs Veuves, Orphélines et Ascendants "). More than 80,000 subscribers. Non-political, but presents liberal views on events of the day.

JOURNAL DU PEUPLE (LE) **Weekly**
Founded 1916. " A free tribune for all free men."
Director: Henri Fabre.
Newspaper format. Left in politics, sympathetic to Caillaux and all Radical movements. Political articles, especially those criticizing the Bloc National, are very well written by such contributors as Georges Yvetot, René Maran, René Valfort. Good literary page and financial columns.

LAROUSSE MENSUEL ILLUSTRÉ **Monthly**
Founded 1907 by Claude Augé.
Political editor: Jules Gerbault.
Magazine, illustrated. All important events of the month, in France and abroad, are written up in alphabetical order, with special attention to literature, science, art, and foreign and domestic politics, with photographs. French achievements in the world of commerce, industry, and science are given much space. A day-by-day chronicle of world events is an especially useful feature. Aims to be impartial.

LECTURES POUR TOUS **Monthly**
Founded 1898.
Editors not named.
Format that of popular English or American magazine, colored illustrated cover. Short stories, pages of photographs, feature articles, popular scientific expositions — attractively presented for entertainment of average reader. Large circulation.

LETTRES (LES) **Monthly**
Founded 1913.
Director: Gaëtan Bernoville.
Literary magazine published by Éditions Spes — liberal Catholic organization. Religion, philosophy, literature, and art are emphasized, with little reference to politics. Eminent contributors include many members of the French Academy .

LIBERTAIRE (LE) **Weekly**
Founded 1895. " Weekly Organ of the Anarchist-Communist Union."
Director: Pierre Mualdes.

Newspaper, issued semi-weekly also, when events are important enough to demand it, as in case of Sacco-Vanzetti affair. Anti-religious, anti-government, anti-bolshevist, anti-militarist, anti-American, anti-etc. Large headlines and violent comment on events of the week.

MERCURE DE FRANCE   Fortnightly
Founded 1890.
Director: Alfred Vallette.
Literary magazine, treating French and international drama, fine arts, history, sociology, science, travel, archaeology, bibliography. " Fortnightly Review " gives all current events in world of literature, art, and politics. Large circulation.

MERLE BLANC (LE)   Weekly
Founded 1919.
Editor-in-chief: Bernard Gervaise.
Newspaper format. Abounds in comic cartoons. Parodies articles in serious journals and publishes humorous sketches of everyday events and some clever political skits, ridiculing mainly the Right. Page for children. Large sale on news-stands.

MONDE ILLUSTRÉ (LE)   Weekly
Founded 1857.
Director (politics): Jacques Stern.
Large magazine, illustrated with news pictures and treating all subjects of current interest, stage, cinema, sports, races, literature, finance, in conservative, unsensational manner.

NATION (LA)   Weekly
Founded 1926.
Bulletin of the " Republican Federation of France " (" La Fédération Républicaine de France "), a political organization of the Bloc National. Fights the Cartel des Gauches exclusively, and is extremely national, especially in foreign affairs. Among its contributors are Louis Marin, Minister of Pensions, " Trygée," and François Coty, deputy and editor-owner of Le Figaro (see below, pp. 435–436).

NATIONAL (LE)   Weekly
Founded 1926. " Organ of the Young Patriots and French Nationals."
Motto: " Hierarchy, Discipline, Order."
Director: Pierre Taittinger, deputy.
Newspaper format. National in every sense of the word. Anti-Poincaré, who is considered too gentle with radicals. Leopold

Marcellin, Émile Bergeron, Le Provost de Launay, Léon Treich are well-known contributors.

NOUVEAU SIÈCLE (LE) Weekly
Founded 1925.
Director: Georges Valois. Political editor-in-chief: Jacques Arthuys.
" Organ of the Cohort of Fighters, Producers, and Heads of Families." Newspaper format. Political and economic propaganda. Against Poincaré and Action Française, with which it has been in active physical combat. Nationalist and Fascist. Features news of war-veterans.

NOUVELLE ÉGALITÉ (LA) Semi–Weekly
Founded 1909.
Director and editor-in-chief: G. Guary and Cesar Lainé.
" Political, literary, colonial, feminist, agricultural, industrial, economic, commercial and financial organ of social demands."
Newspaper format. Independent Socialist in politics, which is principal topic of discussion. Also has financial page and sport column.

NOUVELLE LANTERNE (LA) Monthly
Founded 1927.
Director: René de Planhol.
Literary and political booklet, written entirely by the director, a former court reporter of *Écho de Paris*. Nationalist in foreign policy. Anti-Poincaré. Sympathetic to Léon Daudet and the Action Française.

NOUVELLE REVUE FRANÇAISE (LA) Monthly
Founded 1909.
Director: Gaston Gallimard. Editor-in-chief: Jean Paulhan.
Marcel Proust, André Maurois, André Gide, Paul Valéry, Julian Benda are some of the most prominent contributors to this purely literary review, which holds itself aloof from the politics of the day. Short stories, essays, poetry, dramatic and artistic criticism are primarily concerned with French productions, but foreign works are studied.

NOUVELLE REVUE SOCIALISTE (LA) Monthly
Founded 1924.
Editors: L. O. Frossard and Jean Longuet. Political editor: " Bracke."
" Monthly review of the International Socialist Movement." Contributors include Emile Vandervelde, Romain Rolland, and internationally known Socialists. Discusses the problems of theoretical

socialism, C. G. T. events, and affairs in the international labor movement. Regular department of book reviews and a serial novel.

NOUVELLES LITTÉRAIRES, ARTISTIQUES ET SCIENTIFIQUES Weekly

Founded 1922.
Directors and founders: Jacques Guenne and Maurice du Gard.
Editor-in-chief: Frédéric Lefèvre.
Newspaper format. Contributors are some of the best known literary personalities in France and abroad. Photographs and sketches. Point of view is international, rather than purely French. Reproduces articles and stories from other periodicals noted for high literary quality. Excellent book reviews. The announced circulation is 100,000, and it is probably the most widely read of literary weeklies.

ŒUVRES LIBRES (LES) Monthly

Founded 1921.
Editors not named. Published by Fayard.
250-page book devoted to the publishing of complete novels, plays, short stories, chronicles, essays, and articles of unusual literary value, written for the most part by noted French authors and occasionally by foreigners. Each issue contains on the average one play, one or two novels, a short story, and a long essay on a subject of exotic interest or on a much discussed social problem. Contributors include Eugène Brieux, Maurice Maeterlinck, Sacha Guitry, Henri Duvernois, Stephane Lauzanne, Maurice Rostand, Pierre Mille, Binet-Valmer. Has devoted considerable space to translations from contemporary Russian literature.

OPINION (L') Weekly

Founded 1908.
Editor-in-chief: Jacques Boulenger. Director: Maurice Colrat, deputy (Right Centre).
Magazine format. Politics, economic and financial affairs, foreign relations, art, literature, sports, and current events treated in dignified but popular style. Leans to the Right. Good sale on news-stands.

OPINION RÉPUBLICAINE (L') Weekly

Founded 1925. " Political, social, literary, and artistic weekly."
Founder: Louis Antériou, Republican Socialist deputy.
Principal contributors: Oualid, Roger Picard, Georges Scelle, Ernest Charles, Yvonne Netter, Maurice Bourdet.
Slender magazine format. Republican Socialist in politics. Devotes much space to intellectual life and literary discussion.

PARIS–FLIRT   Weekly
Founded 1921.
Editors not named.
Pink newspaper.   Many drawings and short stories of " Gallic "
flavor.

PARIS–RADICAL   Weekly
Founded 1922.
Political director: André-Grisoni.   Editor-in-chief: Edouard Crocikia.
Newspaper format.   " Radical-Socialiste " in politics; the organ
of the party in Paris.   Collaborators include: Moro-Giafferri, Antériou, Nogaro, Queuille, Delbos, Berthod, and all the other prominent " Radicaux-Socialistes " in Parliament.   Mostly party news.
Features a " tribune of war-veterans."   Back page contains news
of especial interest to suburban branches of the party.

PARLEMENT ET L'OPINION (LE)   Weekly
Founded 1910.
Editors not named.
Magazine format.   Clever cartoons and cuts.   Specializes in anonymous caustic comment on parliament and its personalities from
point of view of Bloc National.   Also gossip of stage, society, and
sports.   The financial pages and book reviews are sprightly.

PARLEMENTAIRE (LE)   Weekly
Founded 1906.   Amalgamated with LA DÉPÊCHE PARLEMEN-
TAIRE.
Director: Adrien Rinder.   Editor-in-chief: Edgar Lebrun.
Unimportant newspaper of liberal tendencies, emphasizing French
colonial mismanagement.   Political articles predominate, with
many " fillers " in the shape of miscellaneous news items, oddities,
and gossip.

PAX   Weekly
Founded 1926.   " Weekly independent organ of international eco-
nomics and politics."   Published in Paris, Madrid, and Geneva.
Director and founder: Paul Girard.   Political director: Jacques
Seydoux.
Newspaper format.   News of whole world, especially from political
and social point of view.   Economic and financial pages with an
international outlook.   Book reviews are international in scope.

PÉLÉRIN (LE)   Weekly
Founded 1877.   Published by La Bonne Presse, publishers of La
Croix.
Director: Léon Berteaux.

Catholic illustrated weekly, for family reading. Gives brief summaries of religious, political, and other events of the week, both in France and abroad, a certain number of caricatures and jokes, and a few stories, and altogether furnishes varied Sunday reading for Catholic homes. Sold in churches on Sunday all over France and is reputed to have the largest circulation of all illustrated weeklies in France. All political news is viewed from Catholic standpoint.

PENSÉE FRANÇAISE (LA)   Fortnightly
Founded 1921.
Editor: Alain Ducreux.
Full title: " French Thought and National Energy " (" Documentary and critical review of intellectual and economic activity "), sometimes appears with the description " Organ of French expansion." Magazine format. The most nationalist periodical in France from every point of view. Devoted to the development of French spiritual and material influence abroad, with emphasis on the colonies; combats foreign ideas and commerce in France; " boosts " all French achievements, advocates discrimination against foreigners in France in prices charged by French tradesmen — in short, is aggressively nationalist. A Belgian edition was issued for three months in 1926 but went bankrupt.

PETIT DÉMOCRATE (LE)   Weekly
Founded at Limoges, 1905. Removed to St. Denis, 1912.
Director: Robert Cornilleau.
Newspaper format. " Popular democratic journal." Organ of the " Popular Democratic Party " (" Parti Démocrate Populaire "). Catholic. Politically keeps a central course, criticizing both Right and Left groups. Pacifist tendencies and broad international outlook. Good literary section. Announced circulation, 15,000.

POTINS DE PARIS (LES)   Weekly
Founded 1917.
Director: R. D'Arger.
Pamphlet. Parliamentary, theatrical, literary, society, and financial gossip, all anonymous. Politically leans to Bloc National, but spares neither Right nor Left. Cover carries political cartoon.

PROGRÈS CIVIQUE (LE)   Weekly
Founded 1919.
Director: Henry Dumay, same management as *Le Quotidien* (see below, pp. 451–452).
Editor-in-chief: Henri Bellamy.
Magazine format. " An Honest Journal for Honest People,"

"Solely for Public Service," "Never sectarian, never neutral." Active organ of the Cartel des Gauches. Political affiliations mainly "Radical-Socialiste." Announced circulation 85,000. Very lively weekly, arranged for popular consumption — boxed quotations scattered throughout. Numerous cartoons, political and comic. Articles of general interest, literary criticism, form for readers, etc. Anti-clerical.

PROGRÈS PARISIEN (LE) Weekly
Founded 1903.
Director: Paul Roger. Editor-in-chief: Emile Meiffredy.
Newspaper format: "Political, economic, financial, and literary journal." Conservative, financial newspaper, especially antagonistic to Communists and any social reform which may increase burdens of the taxpayer. Primarily devoted to market and stock exchange information.

QUESTIONS ACTUELLES (LES) Weekly
Founded 1887.
Director: Léon Berteaux.
Magazine of about 32 pages, containing exact documentation on all current matters — religious, political, legislative, diplomatic, social. Issued by the organization "La Documentation Catholique" of which it is a part, and announced as indispensable to all Catholics who wish to participate usefully in the life of the Church and the State. Both French and international problems are studied.

RENAISSANCE POLITIQUE, LITTÉRAIRE, ARTISTIQUE (LA) Weekly
Founded 1913.
Directress: Madame Henry Lapauze.
Magazine format. Literary critic: Fortunat Strowski; political collaborators: Georges Bonnet, Henry Bérenger, Jean Montigny, Charles Pomaret, etc., politicians of the moderate Left. Much attention given to literature and art as well as to current political events.

RÉPUBLIQUE DÉMOCRATIQUE (LA) Weekly
Founded 1902. "Organ of the Republican-Democratic Alliance" ("Parti Républicain Démocratique et Social").
Director: A. Mamelet.
Politically, moderate Right wing of the Union Nationale, supports Poincaré. Nearly all space devoted to political articles, criticizing the Left. Among its regular contributors are Charles Reibel, Georges Lachapelle, Jean Fabry, and other noted parliamentarians. Announced circulation: 18,000.

REVEIL FRANÇAIS (LE) **Weekly**
Founded 1924.
Director: Émile Bergeron.
Newspaper format. Illustrated with a few photographs and cartoons. Mainly anti-Masonic propaganda, but also attacks Communists and Cartel des Gauches in general. Some jokes and puzzles.

REVUE BLEUE **Fortnightly**
Founded 1863.
Director: Paul Gaultier.
" Political and literary review." Magazine devoted to literary, artistic, and musical criticism, articles on current economics, sociology, and science. A few short stories. Fortnightly review of political events in France and abroad.

REVUE DE FRANCE (LA) **Fortnightly**
Founded 1921.
Literary director: Marcel Prévost, French Academy.
Political director: Raymond Recouly. Dramatic and literary critic: Fernand Vanderem.
High literary quality is the outstanding feature of this review, which has a large circulation for its type. The department " La Vie Courante " is written by leading Academicians. Politically liberal, with certain conservative influences, favoring Poincaré and the Union Nationale.

REVUE DE PARIS (LA) **Fortnightly**
Founded 1894.
Secretary-general: Marcel Thiébaut.
One of the outstanding literary and political reviews. Among the regular contributors are Henri de Régnier, the Comtesse de Noailles, Paul Souday, Madame Gérard d'Houville. Articles on political questions are written by the Comte de Fels regularly, and the fortnightly review of current politics, for many years under the direction of André Chaumeix, is now in the hands of Georges Suarez. Treats politics with a sense of humor, steering a middle course between Right and Left.

REVUE DES DEUX MONDES (LA) **Fortnightly**
Founded 1829. " The Highest Expression of the French Mind."
Director: René Doumic, permanent secretary of the French Academy.
Literary and political review of international reputation. Publishes novels, short stories, and poems by leading littérateurs of France and often of other countries, including America. The political chronicle of the fortnight is written by René Pinon. Has

published articles by Poincaré and is a stronghold of conservatism. Has a large circulation and wide influence.

REVUE DES VIVANTS (LA)   Monthly

Founded February 1927. " Organ of the War-Generations."
Directors: Henry de Jouvenel and Henry Malherbe. Secretary-general: Jean Thébaud, who is president of the " General Association of Wounded War-Veterans " (" Association Générale des Mutilés de la Guerre ") founded in 1915 to aid all French war victims. Has been especially prominent in protesting against the payment of the war debt to the United States.

Contributors include Pierre Bénoit, Henri Béraud, Claude Farrère, Georges Suarez, and Lucien Romier. A regular feature, " International Life " (" La Vie Internationale "), is very militant and national, under the signature of René Cassin, honorary president of the " Federated Union of War Cripples " (" Union Fédérale des Mutilés "). This new review is developing a large circulation because of its notable contributors and attractive magazine format.

REVUE HEBDOMADAIRE (LA)   Weekly

Founded 1891.
Director: François de Grix. Editor-in-chief: Jean d'Elbée.
Regular contributors, Louis Latzarus, Jean-Louis Vaudoyer, Guy de Portalès, Lucien Fabre.

Small magazine format, can be put in coat-pocket. Section at end of each number devoted to photographs of current interest. Mostly literary material, but contains a weekly commentary on politics and finance, conservative in outlook.

REVUE MONDIALE (LA)   Fortnightly

Founded 1890. Formerly *Revue des Revues*.
Editor-in-chief: Louis-Jean Finot.
" Few words, many ideas." Small magazine. Gives much prominence to foreign as well as French literature, science, art, and politics.

REVUE POLITIQUE ET PARLEMENTAIRE (LA)   Monthly

Founded 1894.
Directors: Fernand Faure and Édouard Julia.
Review devoted to articles on social, economic, political, and legal problems in France primarily. Historic studies on same topics. Contributors are professors and savants of international repute. Monthly chronicle of domestic and foreign political affairs and policy, naval and military questions, and the syndicalist movement in France.

REVUE UNIVERSELLE (LA)   **Fortnightly**
Founded 1920.
Director: Jacques Bainville, active in Action Française organization
and a writer of editorials for the daily.
Magazine, its program as follows: " to remake the public mind
by means of intelligence, to attempt an intellectual federation of
the world through French thought." Politics, economic, literary
and dramatic criticism; well written. Royalist and nationalist.

RIRE (LE)   **Weekly**
Founded 1895.
Editors not named.
Humorous magazine. International and domestic politics reviewed
with appropriate cartoons and a certain proportion of " Gallic "
wit. Large circulation and news-stand sale.

SIFFLET (LE)   **Weekly**
Founded 1921.
Director: André Bordessoule.
" Satirical and Political." Small magazine. Nearly all devoted to
comments of the editor on current parliamentary and other political
events, leaning toward the Left. A few good cartoons.

SOURIRE (LE)   **Weekly**
Founded 1898.
Director: L. Querelle.
Magazine format, with colored plates and numerous cuts. Gossip,
drawings, jokes in " Gallic " vein. Some political comment, but
negligible.

TABARIN (LE)   **Weekly**
Founded 1894. " Political — Financial — Independent."
Director: R. Richaud-Gaillat.
Four-page small sheet. Some conservative political comment.
Most of paper devoted to financial news and advertisements.

VERS L'UNITÉ
" Review of Spiritual Synthesis " combined with *France-Europe,*
" Independent organ of the New Right," founded in 1922 in Geneva,
recently moved to Paris, where it has become the organ of the " New
Right " (" Droite Nouvelle "), a small party of conservative tradi-
tions, but with an international outlook.
Directors: Madame Th. Darel and Marquis de Casa Fuerte.
Political director: Baron Robert Fabre-Luce.
This magazine has a German edition, and advocates a reconcilia-
tion with Germany, denouncing French chauvinism and calling

for an international organization for world peace. *Vers l'Unité* is a review of international scope concerned with literature, fine arts, and philosophy, discussed by contributors of all nationalities. The section *France-Europe* is edited by Fabre-Luce and is devoted to articles on international *rapprochement*.

VIE JUDICIARE (LA)   **Thrice-Weekly**
Founded 1902. Formerly *Les Échos Parisiens*.
Director: Lucien Thiboust.
Newspaper format. News of courts and municipal and national politics. Numerous articles on court cases and legal gossip. Half issue is devoted to legal notices.

VIE POLITIQUE ET LITTÉRAIRE (LA)   **Monthly**
Founded 1915. " Independent Review."
Director: G. O. Maugard de Wandel.
Rather insignificant and undignified monthly with pretensions. Contributors are neither well known nor distinctive in their offerings. Politically uncertain, but seems sympathetic to Poincaré.

VIENT DE PARAÎTRE   **Monthly**
Founded 1922.
Director: Marius Boisson.
Magazine of literary and artistic criticism, not only of French but of significant foreign productions.

VOIX PAYSANNE (LA)   **Weekly**
Founded 1922. " Weekly organ of the French Peasant Council."
Director: Renaud-Jean, Communist deputy from Lot-et-Garonne.
Newspaper format. Communist agricultural weekly. A few cartoons and photographs, generally political. Front page almost exclusively political articles, other pages have news of interest to various agricultural localities, articles on practical farming, prices of farm products in the provinces and in Paris. Sale of farm implements and other farm necessities at factory prices by the weekly.

APPENDIX D

GUIDE TO DAILY NEWSPAPERS OF PARIS

[As of January 1928.]

ACTION FRANÇAISE (L') **Morning**
Founded 1908 as a daily.
The Committee of the Action Française was formed in 1898 by a group of Royalists, and published the weekly *Action Française* from 1899 to 1908. For doctrines and program of Action Française see above, pp. 202–205.
Founder: Henri Vaugeois.
Political directors: Léon Daudet and Charles Maurras.
Editor-in-chief: Maurice Pujo.
Principal contributors: Jacques Bainville, Bernard de Vesins, Pierre Héricourt, J. LeBoucher, Hervé le Grand, Abel Manouvrier, Eugène Marsan, Sennep (caricaturist).

" Organ of integral nationalism "; " Everything that is national is ours " (Duc d'Orleans): with these mottoes the most nationalist newspaper in France brands itself. Its format is attractive from the typographical point of view: conservative headlines, few illustrations. The *manchette* (reading-matter at the top of front page beside the heading) is changed daily and contains a trenchant paragraph on some event of the day or a retort to comment from another newspaper. It is ordinarily four pages, the first page containing editorials by Daudet and Maurras — political events dominating; page 2, foreign and miscellaneous news; page 3, press review and serial; page 4, letters, arts, theatres. The review of the press is especially important for its caustic interpolations by the editor. A very small proportion of advertising. Circulation is estimated at 50,000 paid subscribers, and street sale of 100,000 or more copies, depending on the sensational quality of the day's events. Two very important turning points in the recent career of the Action Française have had considerable effect on these circulation figures: on August 27, 1926, Cardinal Andrieu, Archbishop of Bordeaux, condemned the Action Française for its un-Christian influence on Catholic readers; Pope Pius XI, on September 7, 1926, endorsed this condemnation and on December 29, 1926, ordered the paper to be put on the Index. A letter of March 10, 1927, signed by nearly all Cardinals,

Archbishops, and Bishops of France supported the Pope. It is impossible to estimate how many devout Catholic readers were lost to the newspaper by this act. The second *coup* which gave the paper the utmost publicity and undoubtedly reacted very favorably on its circulation figure was the sensational escape of Léon Daudet from the Prison de la Santé on June 25, 1927, where he had begun to serve a sentence of six months and fine for libel in connection with his son's death. The paper is strenuously Royalist and Nationalist.

AVENIR (L') **Morning**
Founded 1918. (Amalgamated with *L'Éclair*)
Director-editor-in-chief: Émile Buré. Literary critic: Leon Treich.

" All the news in complete independence." This newspaper is chiefly political, and strongly supports the Bloc National. Since Millerand was forced to resign from the presidency after the victory of the Cartel in 1924, it has been his organ. It is pro-Fascist (Italian) and Catholic in sympathies. Prominence is given to political news and foreign and colonial affairs, all discussed from a distinct Right bias. Four pages regularly, with rather forceful headlines, especially on the front page, but no photographs, and cartoons are rare. Page 1 is devoted exclusively to political editorials and news; page 2, literary criticism, serial, official news items; page 3, latest news, especially foreign; page 4, sports, theatres, financial bulletin, a few want advertisements.

COMŒDIA **Morning**
Founded 1907.
Director: Gabriel Alphaud.
Editor-in-Chief: Gabriel Boissy. Musical critic: Pierre Lalo; parliamentary critic: Jules Verau.

Ordinarily six or eight pages, illustrated copiously with photographs and cartoons and attractively arranged. While giving the essential news of the day, it is primarily the newspaper of those who are more interested in the theatre, music, cinema, music-halls, cabarets, popular literature, school and university life, sports, fashions, social and diplomatic functions — in short, the *vie mondaine* of the *boulevardier*. On the more serious side, there is the financial bulletin and news of the courts. While the main interest is in French and especially Parisian artistic achievements, the public is kept posted on foreign developments by correspondents who write of the theatrical and artistic world abroad with knowledge and sympathy. The daily radio section is especially complete for foreign programs. Although little attention is paid to grave political problems, the Poincaré régime is supported, while at the same time M. Herriot's efforts as Minister of Public Instruction are appreciated. In format and headlines *Comœdia* is nearer the English or American than the French tradition.

CROIX (LA) **Evening**
Founded 1880.
Director: (in charge of all publications of La Bonne Presse) Léon Berteaux.
Director of *La Croix*: Paul Féron-Vrau.
Editors-in-chief: Canon Bertoye (Franc) and Jean Guiraud.
Principal editors: Pierre L'Érmite, Pierre Dauchez, Théry, Abbé Lavigne, Hervagault, Abbé Finaert, René Johannet, Commandant Boell, etc.

The leading Catholic newspaper of France, published by La Bonne Presse, which issues twenty-five diverse Catholic periodicals. *La Croix* has an enormous influence on members of the Church not only in Paris but all over France, where it is issued with local supplements in 104 départements or arrondissements, and sold under the protection of the Church. In appearance it is sober and impressive, its heading always bears the figure of Christ on the Cross, with the legend: " Adveniat Regnum Tuum." There are a few photographs or cartoons on the front page. Ordinarily six pages, the front page contains a concise summary of the most important events of the day, and political and religious editorials. Other pages contain provincial and Church news, letters from its special foreign correspondents, which are well written and documented; a large section of comments from the French and foreign press; news of patriotic ceremonies, one or two serial novels; sporting news (but *not* races); radio (but no theatres). Politically one of the bitterest enemies and one of the most powerful which the Cartel des Gauches had to face, it has fought against the principle of " laicity " and against the alleged control of the government of France by Freemasonry. Sympathizes with the smaller nations which are Catholic in sentiment, especially Poland, and looks at every domestic or foreign political problem from the religious point of view. Gives prominence to projects for social and economic reform, and has published some noteworthy articles on the financial problems of France.

ÉCHO DE PARIS (L') **Morning**
Founded 1884.
Director: Henry Simond. Principal editorial writers: General de Castelnau, Pertinax (M. Giraud), Henry de Kerillis. Regular contributors: Serge de Chessin, Gaston Japy, Joseph-Barthélemy, Louis Marin. Cartoons by Sennep on political questions.

One of the " Big Five " (the others being *Le Petit Parisien*, *Le Matin*, *Le Journal* and *Le Petit Journal*), *L'Écho de Paris* is unique in that it is both a powerful political organ of definite convictions and at the same time a newspaper of wide circulation. Conventional in format, sober and dignified in style, calling itself a " political, literary, and morning newspaper," it typifies the aggressive respectability of its large bourgeois reading-public. It represents the conservative, anti-socialist middle classes and members of the academic, clerical, and military world in particular. It has always been in the foreground, if not the actual inspiration, of all patriotic manifestations and military displays since its founding. Until his death the leading editor was Maurice Barrès, a name which is symbolic of all that is connected with the word " patrie." After the death of Barrès on December 6, 1923, the torch was carried on by General de Castelnau, at that time a deputy and president of the Commission on Military Affairs, who later became president of the " Ligue des Patriotes." Topics connected with the development of a bigger and better army, navy, and colonial empire are treated by experts and are regularly given prominence in special articles or on a special weekly feature page. In foreign policy, it condemns the Locarno pacts and the mild-mannered diplomacy of Briand, and demands a " strong " hand with Germany, towards which its attitude has not appreciably changed since 1914. Ordinarily comprises six to eight pages, with rather striking front-page headlines, some photographs and a few good cartoons during the week. There are weekly feature pages of interest to women, children, lovers of the fine arts and literature, etc., all written with a national outlook, a love for everything belonging to the traditional France and an undisguised dislike of all foreign innovations, ideas, and influences in France. Its circulation is from 150,000 to 200,000, a great proportion being regular subscriptions, especially in the provinces.

ÈRE NOUVELLE (L') **Morning**

Founded in 1919 under the editorship of Yvon Delbos (deputy) by the Radical minority in the Chamber elected that year.

Manager: Édouard Hégu.

Parliamentary collaborators: L. Antériou, Émile Borel, P. Bastid, Georges Bonnet, Frédéric Brunet, G. L. Chastanet, Henri Michel, A. Milhaud, de Moro-Giafferri, F. Merlin, L. Proust, M. Roustan, etc. Contributing editors: Georges Ponsot, Ferdinand Buisson, A. Aulard, Albert Bayet, François-Albert, Henri Guernut, Victor Augagneur, Louis Laloy, Albert Noret, etc.

The pride of *L'Ère Nouvelle* is that it organized and led the Cartel des Gauches to victory in the elections of May 11, 1924. Since then it has bent all its efforts to carrying out the program of the Cartel, and has been especially active in denouncing "imperialism," advocating heavier direct taxation, urging greater coöperation with the League of Nations. Strongly in favor of the reduction of military service and expenditures, it has, nevertheless, displayed interest in various patriotic demonstrations, and has published sentimental editorials on, for example, the burial of the Unknown Soldier. It is of smaller size than ordinary French news-sheets, and rarely more than four pages. Politics of course is the *raison d'être* of the newspaper, which is read not for its news but for its propaganda. There are no striking headlines or illustrations. Page 1, editorials and articles on economic, political, and social questions, generally written by Left politicians; page 2, small news items, feature articles; page 3, foreign news, and a very complete review of the press; page 4, sports, races, theatres, Bourse, "Tribune of War Veterans," serial novel.

EXCELSIOR Morning

Founded 1910.
Editor-in-chief: H. de Weindel. Operated by *Le Petit Parisien*.

The most illustrated daily in France, issued on six or eight pages, at least half of which are completely covered with news photographs, including the first and last pages. *Excelsior*, in format and style, and in its appeal to conventional bourgeois families, women and youths especially, resembles the American daily. Headlines, make-up, arrangement of photographs, and classification of advertisements copy American models. A noteworthy characteristic is the absence of editorial comment or signed articles with a political bias, the paper being more impersonal in tone than any other in France. Its circulation is reported to be 25,000 subscribers, and 250,000 daily sale on news-stands. Weekly feature pages on sports, fashions, radio. Daily features: arts, theatres, cinema, society, " Bloc notes " — a column of impersonal comment on happenings of the day. On Sunday a magazine appears as supplement (also sold separately) *Dimanche Illustré*, which is made up largely of Chicago Tribune Syndicate features, a great many articles being devoted to write-ups of American millionaire philanthropists, American inventions, etc. (See p. 414.)

FIGARO (LE) Morning

Founded 1826. Reorganized 1854.
Director: François Coty (perfumer and deputy).
Literary director: (until his death, August 1927) Robert de Flers of the French Academy. Former political editor: Lucien Romier.
Contributors: Marcel Prevost, Henri de Regnier, Louis Barthou,

Léon Bérard, Marcel Boulenger, André Chaumeix, Abel Hermant, J. & J. Tharaud, Raymond Recouly, Admiral Ratyé, etc.

Le Figaro has a world-wide reputation as the spokesman of " le monde des salons," the academic world, and political personalities of conservative tendencies. By virtue of the high place in the literary and social world which its editors have occupied, the attitude and opinions of *Le Figaro* have a prestige and authoritativeness far in excess of that warranted by its small circulation. In format the newspaper has not changed in scores of years — it was the first French newspaper to publish as many as six pages, which is still the ordinary size. In addition, there are valuable weekly supplements, *Le Figaro Littéraire, Le Figaro Artistique Illustré,* and special editions, *Le Figaro des États-Unis* and *La Page Coloniale.* Well documented articles on economic subjects are regular features, and from time to time special studies of the economic and political problems of foreign countries are published in instalments. While thus displaying an active interest in international affairs, *Le Figaro* is none the less one of the most patriotic organs in France, the superiority of French culture in every field being admitted, sometimes tacitly, often with much ostentation. Its carefully edited pages, printed on white glazed paper instead of the usual grayish stock, seem to be weighted with the honor and responsibility of carrying French propaganda to the foreign hinterland. Page 1 is devoted to the leading editorials, " Echoes," a daily literary essay or discussion of some topic of erudition, and a few of the most striking news items; page 2, miscellaneous news, society, literary criticism; page 3, foreign news, press comment; page 4, sports and Bourse; page 5, theatres, advertisements; page 6, advertisements mainly of fashionable hotels in France and abroad, and serial novel.

GAULOIS (LE) Morning

Founded 1865. (Amalgamated in 1929 with *Le Figaro.*)
Director: René Lara. Former director: Arthur Meyer, 1844–1924.
Contributors: Most of the French Academy — very much the same type as those who write for *Le Figaro.*

" Journal of social defense — the most Parisian of the great dailies," *Le Gaulois* calls itself the organ of the aristocracy, upper bourgeoisie, and men of affairs. In 1914 it was reported to have more than 40,000 subscribers in the ranks of the old French nobility, but in 1927 the estimate dwindled to 22,500 subscribers of all classes. In politics it is ultra-conservative — Royalist, Catholic, and extremely patriotic, but always courteous to its enemies and never indulging in the mud-slinging for which vehemently nationalist journals have been notorious. Its format, heavy and solemn, has not changed in years — few headlines and no illustrations, and rarely more than four pages. A literary supplement, reviewing all French publications, appears each Saturday and is read by many who are more interested in the intellectual valuations of *Le Gaulois* than in its political opinions.

HOMME LIBRE (L') **Morning**
Founded 1913 by Georges Clemenceau. On September 29, 1914, it was suspended for eight days for publishing an editorial of Clemenceau contrary to the decision of the censors. The following day *L'Homme Libre* became *L'Homme Enchaîné,* under which title it was published until its editor was made head of the Government on November 16, 1917, when it changed management and resumed its original title.

Editor — since 1919: Eugène Lautier (Radical deputy from Guyane), who is a leading figure in French journalism. For twenty years Lautier was editor of foreign news for *Le Temps,* and from 1905 to 1909 wrote on foreign affairs for *Le Figaro.*
Director: Auguste Bernier.
Contributors: Paul Lombard, literature, drama, music; Barbelieu, artistic criticism; Jousset, parliament; Charles Briand, courts.

Politically, this newspaper represents the Right wing of the Cartel des Gauches. Eugène Lautier, who is a member of the Commission on Foreign Affairs of the Chamber, specializes in foreign and colonial problems, and is much quoted in other journals for his independent views and moderately nationalist outlook. While the views of Eugène Lautier, one of the most influential of the moderates in the Cartel, are of considerable importance, his paper is otherwise of limited interest — four small pages, without illustrations. Its circulation has been estimated at less than 5,000. Page 1 contains the signed political and economic articles of the day, with conservative, unalarming headlines; page 2, literature, serial novel, brief news and special articles; page 3, Bourse, races, theatres; page 4, sports, advertisements.

HUMANITÉ (L') **Morning**
Founded in 1904 by Jean Jaurès as organ of the Socialist Party. Since the Tours Convention of December 1920, it has been in the hands of the Communist Party (S. F. I. C.).
Director: Marcel Cachin.
Literary director: Henri Barbusse.
General secretary: Vaillant-Couturier.

L'Humanité is the best known radical newspaper in France, and has always represented the extreme Left. After the control of the journal passed from the Socialists to the Communists, at the end of 1920, the tendency to sensationalism increased, all familiar journalistic tricks — huge headlines, grotesque photographs and cartoons, heavily emphasized reading matter — being used in the interests of Bolshevist doctrine. The appearance of the paper, the generous use of illustrations, special features, the size of the issue (six pages or more), and the general vitality of its make-up show that there must be ample funds in the treasury of the Communist Party to finance so elaborate an undertaking. Its circulation is estimated at 200,000 to 250,000 and comprises not only the working-class districts of Paris proper, but many proletarian communities in the suburbs of Paris and certain large industrial cities such as Lille in the North and Lyons in the South. Its general policy is that of the " Communist International " — anti-imperialist, anti-militarist, anti-capitalist, anti-clerical. Marcel Cachin's editorials take first place in prominence and in trenchant criticism of the Government, with special attention to foreign relations, political campaigns, and colonial scandals. André Marty, Jacques Doriot, and Paul Vaillant-Couturier are the best known of the group of Communist deputies whose articles in *L'Humanité*, especially " anti-militarist " and " anti-imperialist," have exposed them to prosecution by the Government and to jail sentences for inciting to sedition, etc. Reports of Communist activities all over the world and especially of the Communist organizations of France occupy a large amount of space; of late the journal has given much attention to sporting activities, such as the motor-cycle " raid " from Moscow to Paris, and bicycle races in France, with the hope of interesting the youth. Other regular features are designed for teachers, women in the home and the factory, young men in military service, etc. Page 1 is composed so as to catch the eye with striking headlines, grotesque cartoons, and news photographs, and contains a large proportion of news as well as the leading editorials; page 2, miscellaneous news; page 3, international news and serial novel; page 4, feature page; page 5, " The Labor Front," news of C. G. T. U., theatres; page 6, labor news and advertisements.

INFORMATION (L') **Noon and Evening**
    Founded 1902.
    Director-editor: Léon Chavenon.
    Contributors: André Antoine, theatres; Georges Scelle, foreign news; Paul Ginisty, Parisian chronicle; Henri Duvernois; Jacques Ancel.

The political edition of this newspaper appears at noon, and the financial edition, containing all the Bourse transactions of the day, comes out in the late afternoon. The financial edition has a very large sale around the Bourse; the political edition, with a circulation of about 75,000 is also important, especially in time of financial crises, when political rumors may strongly influence the price quotations. Of moderate Left tendencies, the political editorials are written not for the purpose of propaganda, but for the information of investors. *L'Information* consists of four small-size news pages, without photographs or cartoons, and with well-emphasized, but not sensational, headlines. Page 1, political articles, especially foreign affairs, and leading news items; page 2, a very detailed review of the press, sports and brief comment on the news of the day; page 3, financial and economic information; page 4, races and advertisements.

INTRANSIGEANT (L') Evening
Founded 1880.
Director: Léon Bailby.
Editors: Jean Fabry (deputy) and Fernand Divoire.
Principal contributors: J. H. Rosny, Sr., Lucien Descaves, Gerard Bauer, Pierre Mac Orlan, H. de Montherlant, Paul Morand.

" *L'Intran.*," as it is familiarly called, has the largest circulation of all Paris evening papers, about 450,000, and publishes several editions each evening, often sold on the streets by special newsboys as well as on the regular news-stands. In politics it is strongly conservative, and has actively carried on campaigns against the menace of Bolshevism and against the recognition of Russia. On all occasions it is a strong upholder of national and military interests. Patriotic celebrations are given a large amount of front-page space, with numerous photographs. The regular edition is from six to eight pages. A significant feature is the concentration of all the latest and most sensational news on the front page, with headlines designed to " sell " the issue to the public — much in the same manner as the headlines of the popular evening newspapers in America. Photographs are liberally used on the front page, and there are some political editorials, but everything is subordinate to news events of the day. On the inside pages a very small size of type is used, which is hard to read. Perhaps the editors of " *L'Intran.*" are aware of the general practice, to read the first page and barely glance at the others — at any rate, there is little to catch the eye or mind. At least two full pages are devoted to advertisements, including columns of want advertisements of interest to working people and the lower bourgeoisie, the bulk of the paper's clientèle.

JOURNAL (LE) Morning
Founded 1892.
Director: F. Mouthon.
Editor-in-chief: T. de Marsillac.

Contributors of feature articles and special inquiries: Henri Béraud, who made a sensational survey of post-war Germany; Jacques Deval, social conditions in United States; Jacques Kessel, Pierre Bénoît, Géo London, etc.

One of the "Big Five," *Le Journal*, which is surpassed in popularity only by *Le Petit Parisien*, has a circulation of at least 1,000,000, and reaches a class of readers which prefers its morning paper to be entertaining rather than argumentative. Of the "great journals of information" it has for many years had the reputation of being the most literary, and has published the short stories and serial novels of French popular writers of wide fame. Aside from fiction, it provides entertainment in the form of special investigations in France and abroad, from the pen of professional men-of-letters rather than seasoned news correspondents, so that the point of view is never impartial or neutral, but always related to the personality and prejudices of the writer. For example, a series of articles on America by Jacques Deval, popular playwright and novelist, during the winter of 1926–1927, told the French very little about America but a great deal about the life of Americans as a young literary lion might see it from Broadway or Palm Beach, seasoned with misquoted statistics on divorce, etc. "Mon Film," a daily chat by Clément Vautel on everything and nothing in and about Paris, is one of the best known features in the entire Parisian press, and carries on the traditions of earlier French journalism. The political views of *Le Journal* are negligible; its large circulation among both Left and Right groups makes a middle course necessary, with moderate support of the Government. From time to time it publishes articles by nationalist parliamentarians and military experts which place it in the forefront of the chauvinist press, but these are not sustained over long periods, as in *L'Écho de Paris*.

JOURNAL DES DÉBATS (LE)   **Evening**
Founded 1789.
Director: Étienne de Nalèche.
Contributors: René Bazin, E. Doumic, Henri de Régnier, of the French Academy; Georges Lechartier, Jacques Bardoux, Auguste Gauvain, A. Liesse, of the Institute; A. Albert-Petit, H. Bidou, Pierre Bernus, R. de Caix, A. Chaumeix, etc.

Le Journal des Débats Politiques et Littéraires, the oldest daily newspaper of France, carries the prestige and dignity of its years on every page. In politics it is classed as "liberal republican," with, however, a distinct conservative outlook in respect of labor agitation and financial rehabilitation. Its articles on foreign affairs, written by Auguste Gauvain for many years, are famed in France and abroad for their vigor and independent judgment. On several important occasions it has held opinions contrary to the prevailing " French " sentiment — as in its approval of President Wilson's attitude on Fiume in 1919 and its pro-Greek sympathies in the fall of 1922. Its format, which remains unaltered, no matter what the nature of the event, is not designed to attract the masses — inconspicuous and brief headlines, never more than a column wide, no cartoons or photographs. Until 1926 it appeared regularly on four pages, but has recently become a six-page daily, which permits more articles of a purely literary nature. The limited public of *Le Journal des Débats* is important in the academic and political world as well as in financial circles — a public which reads the *Débats* to be informed and which does not need to have its opinions dictated. On the whole there is probably less " nationalist " sentiment in this newspaper than in any other in France of the conservative type.

JOURNÉE INDUSTRIELLE (LA) Morning
Founded 1918.
Editor-in-chief: C.-J. Gignoux. Former editor, Lucien Romier.

" Journal of Industry, Commerce and Agriculture," *La Journée Industrielle* is the organ of French commercial and industrial activity, and is read mainly by business men and manufacturers. Of its six pages, only the first is of interest to all the various types of French *industriels* — a compact account of the news events of the day, a review of the press at home and abroad, latest economic and industrial developments, articles on fiscal policy, and an editorial which concerns itself with the economic significance of current political reactions, interpreted from the conservative point of view of the investor. The other pages are devoted to news of various industries, latest price quotations from world markets, advertisements — all of interest to the business executive.

LIBERTÉ (LA) Evening
Founded 1865.
Editor-in-chief: Camille Aymard.
Contributors: Jacques Bainville, Jean de Bonnefon, Pierre Taittinger, Charles Omessa, Le Provost de Launay, Raoul de Nolva, etc.

An evening journal which is second in popularity to *L'Intransigeant*, politically of the Right, with pro-Fascist leanings, and a strongly patriotic viewpoint. There are four pages regularly, the first containing political editorials, news of the morning, a few photographs; page 2, sports, fashions, brief items; page 3, foreign news, serial novel; page

4, advertisements and a rather full press review. Altogether the news sections are rather colorless; the editorials on the other hand are fiery — against either the Left or Germany, which is regarded with war-time hatred.

MATIN (LE) **Morning**
  Founded 1884.
  Director: Bunau-Varilla.
  Editors: Henry de Jouvenel, Stephane Lauzanne.
  Contributors: Jules Sauerwein, Henri Duvernois, Louis Forest, Raymond Poincaré.

Of the five newspapers of large circulation, *Le Matin* is the most cosmopolitan. Its system of foreign correspondents and provincial representatives is probably the most complete of all French journals, while a special arrangement with the *London Daily Mail* gives it all the resources of that organization. With its prominent and provocative headlines, liberal display of photographs, fac-similes and cartoons, the front page is far removed from the conventions of the older French dailies. While the majority of the special articles and editorials are unsigned, save when they come from the pen of a celebrity such as Poincaré, Stephane Lauzanne, or Henry de Jouvenel, there is even in the news items a feeling of definite personal bias, an injection of editorial opinion. *Le Matin* has long been regarded as one of the " official " journals, giving to the public any information which the Government in power wished it to have. With regard to national spirit, it has been recognized, even by the French, as one of the most active belligerents against Germany, long before the war. As A. de Chambure [1] states: " A patriotic fervor, perhaps even chauvinism, permissible in war-time, pervades it [1918]. Some day, when, amid the peaceful joys of victory, the historian will set down those who engineered the great struggle against Germany, *Le Matin* will be in the vanguard. It did not await the war to take its stand. It was mobilized long before August 2, 1914; it lacked neither supplies nor munitions. During the preceding ten years it had already begun firing. It has carried on its campaign incessantly with the most ardent patriotism, boring through the lines of the enemy, unmasking him, laying bare his snares and ambuscades, giving new courage to the faltering, proclaiming its confidence and faith [in France], penetrating everywhere like a vigilant quartermaster, lending a helping hand to the weary, caring for the sick, advising the perplexed, grappling with traitors, exalting heroes. And if, now and then, in the impatience

[1] *Quelques Guides de l'Opinion en France pendant la Grande Guerre* (Paris, 1918).

of its elation and self-confidence, it somewhat outstripped the pace of events and published good tidings prematurely, hailing Victory before she had completely unfurled her banners: if it announced, for example, ' Russians five stages from Berlin ' or ' Famine in Germany,' it is because it felt the need of reassuring its readers, of restoring their enthusiasm in a dark moment, and of galvanizing them into finding the strength to follow to the end the long and arduous trail which they had yet to mount." Since the war it has maintained its " strong " attitude towards Germany, and has conducted a campaign for the breaking off of diplomatic relations with Russia. Its circulation is estimated at from 700,000 to 1,000,000. The readers who take *Le Matin* pride themselves on being on a higher social plane than the readers of other popular dailies, as for example *Le Petit Parisien*, which is called " the janitor's paper." The articles in *Le Matin* presuppose a fairly good educational background, and their literary quality appeals to the discriminating. In religious matters it is impartial, but for various reasons it is the favorite daily of the Jewish population of France — as a perusal of the society column will indicate.

ŒUVRE (L') **Morning**
Founded 1893.
Director: Gustave Téry.
Editor-in-chief: Jean Piot.
Collaborators: André Billy, G. de la Fouchardière, Henry Barde, Jean Hennessy.

L'Œuvre is the best known of the newspapers of the Cartel des Gauches, largely through the personality of its editors, Gustave Téry and Jean Piot, whose trenchant criticism of the Government prior to the Left victory in 1924, and defense of the Cartel since 1924, have been widely quoted in the French and foreign press. In addition, André Billy and Jean Piot are authorities on French journalism, and pride themselves on making *L'Œuvre* the leader in all phases of news-production. It is a small six-page issue (somewhat larger than an American tabloid in dimensions), containing very few advertisements and a minimum of " filling." There is a liberal use of photographs and humorous cartoons. Without being sensational, the headlines are full of life, and often terse wit. To Gustave Téry is due the credit, if there be any, for the invention of the *manchette*, the daily " bright thought " or slogan which appears in large letters beside the heading. This practice, invented during the war, was rapidly adopted by the other popular newspapers, notably *Le Matin* and *L'Action Française*. While there is a daily signed political editorial, the aim of *L'Œuvre* is not so much to provide direct propaganda for the Cartel as to present the news in so vivid a fashion and with such caustic comments that the reader will be influenced by the Left without being aware of it. "*L'Œuvre* is not read by imbeciles," is the editorial watchword. G. de la Fouchardière writes a daily column of "Hors d'Oeuvre," in which he treats curious happenings with whimsey and keen satire. Some of his best shots are directed at certain patriotic manifestations, as when he holds up to ridicule the national ceremonies each day at the tomb of the Unknown Soldier: "Every day this laborer, this peasant, this shopkeeper, this clerk — this civilian who was torn from his peaceful life to be led to slaughter, is awakened from his eternal slumbers by some military ceremonial which renews his martyrdom with memories of the frightful nightmare" (July 29, 1927). It is noteworthy that General Verraux, one of the contributors to *L'Œuvre*, as early as 1922 urged a pacific *rapprochement* between France and Germany. The paper, however, does not lack patriotism.

PARIS–MATINAL **Morning**
> Founded May 13, 1927.
> Director: Eugène Merle (Also editor of the satirical weekly *Le Merle Blanc*, now discontinued, and founder of *Paris-Soir*).
> Editor-in-chief: Raoul Alexandre. The literary editor, Henri Béraud, well known for his investigations for *Le Journal*, recently resigned.

Advertises itself: "The great newspaper, three editions, six and eight pages, of absolutely new ideas, of radically novel conception, of strikingly original format. . . . The modern journal for modern people." There are so far three phases to the brief career of *Paris-Matinal*, which resembles that of a sky-rocket. First, preparation to go off: for several months preceding its initial appearance, there were huge billboards on the Grands Boulevards, flaming posters all over Paris, and a large-scale advertising campaign in the provincial press, offering two watches (a gentleman's and a lady's) to each annual subscriber at 85 francs per year. Before a single issue of the paper had been printed, it boasted of 57,127 paid subscribers (indicating the distribution of 114,254 free watches!). Second, the explosion, with considerable éclat, of a daily with many original features, most important being the front page, an illustrated and heavily headlined résumé of all the news of the day which is treated at greater length on the inside pages. This page has therefore the appearance of an American illustrated tabloid, except that its size is that of a large newspaper. The paper is well written and well presented throughout, and enlivened by good cartoons and many photographs. There are very few advertisements, showing that the paper must finance itself through other channels. Politically it favors the Cartel des Gauches and sympathizes with Radical movements in other lands. At the same time its viewpoint is extremely pro-French, i.e. in behalf of French industries, the cinema, colonial development. The back page, which is devoted to latest foreign news and financial items (an innovation, considering that in most papers this page is given to advertisements or unimportant matter), contains a spicy résumé of the leading foreign news. After its impressive send-off, *Paris-Matinal* has now entered the third phase, which seems to be the fade-out. It has stopped delivering the paper to its paid subscribers, on the pretext that it is reorganizing its mailing department, and has only its news-stand sale, which has hardly had time to become extensive. There are indications that the original capital back of the paper is nearly exhausted, and that the high hopes of rapid success have not materialized.

PARIS–MIDI Noon
Founded 1911.
Editor: L. Parsons.
Political editor: Marcel Lucain.

Paris-Midi, politically independent, pro-Poincaré, had as its first editor Maurice de Waleffe, a noted journalist, and during the war was famous for its daily bulletin, " Où nous en sommes ce matin," which he conducted in a most optimistic vein. He was succeeded in 1918 by Albert Milhaud, who in 1924 became a deputy. Henry Bérenger (senator) has had a large interest in the paper until recently. The front page is designed to catch the eye and exploit the latest rumors of the afternoon. Page 2 is concerned with literature, art, and society, while half a page is allotted to a review of the morning press, well digested and annotated. The two most important features of the paper, which are responsible for its large sale in the city (about 60,000) are the financial bulletins and the racing news, the latter extremely detailed, so that *Paris-Midi* serves as a program for the afternoon races in competition with the special racing sheets. Altogether, the paper is designed for the urban male population, mainly preoccupied with the Bourse and sports.

PARIS–SOIR Evening
Founded 1923.
Editor-in-chief: Paul Reboux.
Contributors: Henry de Forge, Louis Aubert, Bernard Gervaise, Georges Gombault, Gaston Vidal, Henri Prété.

Paris-Soir, of clearly defined Left tendencies, is a rather sensational journal of the lower middle-class. It is said recently to have been purchased by *Le Journal* and to be undergoing a reorganization. In the meantime its literary and journalistic standards are very low, its best features being a good sporting page and radio section.

PETIT BLEU (LE)   Morning
Founded 1900.
Editor-Director: Alfred Oulman (before the war Oulmann).

Le Petit Bleu, printed on bluish-green heavy paper, and sold at 20 centimes instead of the universal price of 25 centimes, is one of the most distinctive journals of Paris. It calls itself " the most Parisian of Paris journals," and in its terse and clever comment, its interest in gossip of " Gallic " flavor, its illustrated jokes and spicy anecdotes it reproduces faithfully the mentality of the *boulevardier* — the man-about-town of narrow views and inherent conservatism. From another standpoint the term " Parisian " is equally applicable — it specializes in municipal scandal and the intrigues of a political and financial nature which emanate from the Hôtel de Ville. The paper has a relatively small circulation and carries very little advertising. *Le Petit Bleu* is always exposing some sensational outrage to the public treasury or morals, and the vitriolic pen of Alfred Oulman is well known and thoroughly feared. There are generally only four pages: page 1, carrying a large black-faced type quotation below the title, and photographs of prominent figures on either side, and a large political cartoon in the centre of the page, is devoted to exposés, denunciations, and the daily editorial, " Petits Bleus du Matin," signed by Alfred Oulman. Page 2 carries miscellaneous news, including foreign items and a very careful review of the press, which gives especial attention to comments from papers of the opposite side, and to the " manchettes " which appear on the most important dailies. A characteristic feature is a small box entitled: " Affairs no longer talked about," listing the recent scandals which seem to have blown over, or mysteries not yet unraveled by the French police and almost forgotten by the public. Page 3 is entitled " Le Petit Bleu économique et financier." On the back page is assembled the lighter section of the paper, gossip, jokes, photographs, society notes, theatres, book reviews.

PETIT JOURNAL (LE)   Morning
Founded 1863.
Owned by Louis Loucheur.
Editor: Marcel Ray.

Although classed as one of the " Big Five," *Le Petit Journal* seems to be relying on past glories for its prestige. Originally it was the first French newspaper to pass the million mark in circulation, and while it still boasts of " five million readers," publicity experts fix its daily issue between 400,000 and 600,000 copies. It is suggested, moreover, that the newspaper is just breaking even in its finances — if it is not actually losing money — but it is at the same time a profitable investment for Louis Loucheur's political career. The paper has always been directed and edited by prominent political figures; before the war Senator Charles Prevet (died February 1914); during the war and until his appointment as Minister of Foreign Affairs in the Clemenceau Cabinet, Stephen Pichon was editor and was responsible, through his daily articles, for a great deal of the popular enthusiasm which called Clemenceau to the premiership. Senator Gomot and the former minister Clémentel were Pichon's political and editorial aides. A. de Chambure [2] gives the following estimate of Pichon's contribution to war psychology: " In proclaiming his patriotic devotion, his literary efforts were most happy, and one may say that, side by side with such journalists as Clemenceau, Capus, Berthoulat, Sembat, Hervé, Téry, Barrès, Maurras, Daudet, and Bailby, he ranks among those who will have made their voices resound most eloquently during the war." Other political collaborators during the war and post-war period were Méline, Herriot, Mourier, Raoul Péret, and Henry Bérenger. In politics to-day it is classed as " independent republican," and has pursued a middle course, always protecting the interests of the " petit bourgeois," the backbone of its reading public. In its literary quality, composition of pages, and features, there is little to distinguish *Le Petit Journal* from *Le Petit Parisien*. The front page is liberally illustrated with small and large photographs and at least one comic cartoon; the headlines are not strikingly original or aggressive; the news of the day is given for the most part briefly and without editorial comment. Among the most prominent contributors are to be noted Eugène Brieux, Daniel Blumenthal, Raphael-Georges Lévy, Edmond Haraucourt, Madame Marcelle Tinayre, and Albert Londres, famous for his sensational investigations. A weekly, widely read in the provinces, is *Le Petit Journal Illustré*, and other periodicals published by the same organizations are: *La Mode, La Musique, Le Petit Journal Agricole et la France Paysanne Réunis*, and *Le Plein Air*.

PETIT PARISIEN (LE)   **Morning**
  Founded 1876.
  Editor-in-chief: E.-J. Bois.

[2] *Op. cit.*, p. 188.

Director: Pierre Dupuy, deputy, Commissioner of Merchant Marine in Clemenceau Cabinet and President of the Chamber Commission on Military Marine, 1919–1924. Until his death in the spring of 1927, Senator Paul Dupuy was co-director, and at the same time prominent in the Senate as one of the Commission on Foreign Affairs and the governing committee of the " Groupe de l'Union Démocratique et Radicale," leader of which is Paul Strauss. Another co-director is François Arago, their brother-in-law, who was president of the largest group of the Bloc National in the Chamber, 1919–1924, the " Entente Républicaine," and president of the political organization, " Action Nationale Républicaine." Paul and Pierre Dupuy were the sons of Jean Dupuy, who became director of Le Petit Parisien in 1888, and was senator and minister.

The most important thing about Le Petit Parisien is that it has the largest circulation of all French newspapers, and, according to the device which never fails to appear below the heading, " the largest circulation in the whole world." In 1927 it announced its circulation as 1,700,000. That this figure is probably no exaggeration may be assumed from a study of the circulation statistics given by A. de Chambure in A Travers la Presse: [3] 1903, average circulation 820,000; 1909 — 1,100,000; 1912 — 1,362,000; 1913 — (average January 19–February 2) 1,362,485. The aim of Le Petit Parisien is impersonality and complete objectivity; there are extremely few signed articles (these are mainly those of its editor, E.-J. Bois, when he discusses foreign affairs), and no opinions are injected into the news items unless these are entirely political. A study of the front page explains the popularity of the paper among the masses. (It is called by the others " le journal des concièrges " or " Le Petit Idiot "). First of all, the great variety of small photographs and comic cartoons or caricatures — on the average, about ten separate illustrations. Second, more than any other French paper, it plays up the crime element and especially sanguinary accidents, giving these in more detail and with greater front-page attention than elsewhere in the press. Sports are treated at length and vividly, while at the same time a weekly, Le Miroir des Sports, which has the largest circulation of all sporting weeklies, is issued by Le Petit Parisien. Of the regular six-page issue of Le Petit Parisien, at least two full pages are completely filled with advertising, one page of which is a classified " want-ad " section, designed for the needs of working-people and the lower middle class. There is an abundance of cheap fiction — two serial novels and one short story — each day. From the national point of view, Le Petit Parisien has consistently resisted foreign influences in France, has maintained popular interest in a strong army

[3] (Paris, 1914), p. 130.

and navy, has conducted campaigns against depopulation, and has kept before its readers the opportunities which awaited the citizens of France in the development of the colonial empire. Politically, in spite of the Bloc National background and activities of the directors, *Le Petit Parisien* has maintained a middle course: it found a great deal to say in favor of the diplomatic activities of the Herriot Government, although it never approved of the recognition of Russia. Emphasis is given to utterances of politicians actually in power, important speeches of the opposition, whether Left or Right, being relegated to inside pages. A very important activity of *Le Petit Parisien* is its operation of one of the most powerful radio broadcasting stations in France, which is becoming a national institution. The programs are mainly devoted to French music of a sentimental, semi-classical sort, and short talks on the news of the day, sports, drama, all of which is publicity for *Le Petit Parisien*.

PEUPLE (LE) Morning

Founded 1921.
Director: Francis Million.
Contributors: Léon Jouhaux, Secretary-General of the Confédération Générale du Travail, Paul-Boncour, Paul Faure, Henry Fontanier, and other leaders in the Socialist labor movement.

The official daily newspaper of the Socialist General Labor Federation (C. G. T.), *Le Peuple*, published regularly on four large pages, gives every evidence of being alive with news, as well as information on the activities of the C. G. T. and the foreign labor movement. Page 1 contains the same news items as in any other morning paper, with one or two photographs and forceful but not sensational headlines. The first and last columns are devoted to political editorials, written in rather elevated style by C. G. T. leaders or prominent Socialists, evidently designed for workers of some knowledge of economics and some intellectual background. Page 2 contains miscellaneous news, radio, sporting notes, and either a short story or a selection from a recent publication on political or social science, and serial novel. Page 3 gives foreign news, the labor items being emphasized, political meetings, and news of C. G. T. activities. On page 4 appears another serial novel (often a reprinting of a forgotten classic — George Sand or Zola's minor works), official C. G. T. notices, news of theatres and movies, and a few advertisements. The paper is at present striving to attain a subscription list of 25,000. It is evident that *Le Peuple*, with its high literary and journalistic standards, appeals chiefly to the intellectual élite among the large membership of the C. G. T.

POPULAIRE DE PARIS (LE)   **Morning**

Founded 1918.

Director: Léon Blum, secretary and leader of the group of the Socialist Party in the Chamber.

Administrator, Compère-Morel, deputy.

Contributors: All leading parliamentarians of S. F. I. O., and Jean Longuet, Bracke, Maurice Delepine, André Pierre, etc.

Le Populaire, the Socialist daily, has led a precarious existence, especially after the Congress of Tours, December 1920, when it was reduced to a fraction of its former importance, since about 60 per cent of the Socialist Party adhered to Moscow and took over *L'Humanité* as its official organ. After the elections of 1924 and the victory of the Cartel, with which it had made common cause, *Le Populaire* became a weekly, and it was only in 1927 that, after much argument pro and con, it reappeared as a daily. It is still a feeble sheet of small size, four pages, with practically no cuts or photographs, and makes little attempt to compete with daily newspapers. The first page is nearly entirely devoted to propaganda, accounts of Socialist and labor congresses all over the world, and a short editorial on domestic politics. The inside pages contain miscellaneous news items gleaned from other papers, international news dispatches, with especially complete League of Nations accounts, a rubric, " The Labor Movement," and a serial novel, which happened in 1927 to be a translation of *David Copperfield*. The last page is filled with miscellaneous items, notices of Socialist Party meetings, results of races, sporting news, market and commercial quotations, radio programs, and theatrical notes. That the official daily of the Socialist Party is not well on its feet financially is seen by the publication of subscription lists for its support. It claims a circulation of 220,000 (1927 *Annuaire de la Presse*), but in that case it would not need to beg for donations.

PRESSE (LA)   **Evening**

Founded 1833.

Director: André Payer, deputy, who belongs to no parliamentary group, but is Bloc National in sympathies.

La Presse and *La Patrie* (established in 1842, " organ of national defense ") are the same papers. In 1914 *La Patrie* independently had one of the largest circulations of the evening papers, due to the collaboration of the famous journalist Henri Rochefort, who died that year. During the War *La Presse* and *La Patrie* had the same editor, Émile Massard, and were prosperous because of their publication of " extras " in the early afternoon. After the war both papers were acquired by André Payer, a contractor and municipal councillor of

Paris, who has been a deputy since 1919. *La Presse* is practically a one-man paper in spite of the fact that nearly every news item or commentary is signed by such journalists as J.-F. Louis Merlet, Pierre Chassagnac, Henry Montbrun, Pierre Humbourg, Pierre Demours, Raymond Saladin, etc., etc.: the one man whose influence dominates the paper is the owner, André Payer, who writes a daily front-page editorial (in italics) in involved language, preaching in general the same type of national doctrine, especially in foreign affairs, as may be found in *L'Écho de Paris*. The front page carries large and sensational headlines, often a page wide, a few photographs, the early afternoon news, and André Payer's editorial. Page 2 has miscellaneous news, echoes, financial information, and serial story; page 3 is "La Presse Sportive," with a section on theatres; page 4 is almost entirely racing news, with the program for the day's events.

QUOTIDIEN (LE) **Morning**
Founded February 1923.
Director: Henri Dumay.
Editor-in-chief: Pierre Bertrand.
Leading contributors (1927): Dr. Toulouse (alienist), Tristan Bernard, Michel Georges-Michel, Pierre Mille, Henry Bellamy, J. Ernest Charles, etc.

Le Quotidien, "an honest paper for honest people," "created by more than 60,000 French men and women to defend and perfect republican institutions," has had a curious history. In June 1922, Henri Dumay, who had received his journalistic training on the staff of *Le Petit Parisien*, and had in 1919 founded the very successful Radical weekly, *Le Progrès Civique*, made an appeal in that weekly for a newspaper which would be entirely free of the corrupt and occult influences surrounding the bourgeois press and which would maintain the same "rigorous probity and ferocious independence" of *Le Progrès Civique*. From every part of France came the response of school-teachers, office-workers, small tradesmen, etc., who invested savings to the extent of 12,000,000 francs in bonds and 9,900,000 francs in stock in the new venture. The career of *Le Quotidien* from its launching in 1923 to the fall of 1926 was phenomenal in the annals of French journalism — its attractive format, able editing, and the renown of its collaborators gave it a firm hold on a large section of the reading public, and placed it first or second in circulation after the "Big Five" morning papers, disputing this position with *L'Humanité*. Among its best-known contributors were several Socialist leaders, such as Léon Blum and Pierre Renaudel; other Radical leaders, including Herriot, Jean Hennessy, François-Albert; Ferdinand Buisson, president of the "Ligue des

Droits de l'Homme "; A. Aulard, the historian; Jean de Pierrefeu (author of *Plutarch a Menti*); Dr. Héricourt, etc. During 1925 and the fall of 1926 rumors were current in Paris insisting that the huge and luxurious office-building of *Le Quotidien,* the numerous motor-cars and new château of M. Dumay, etc., were being financed not from the sale of the paper or its direct publicity, but by the banks, the railways, insurance companies, etc., who had purchased the silence of *Le Quotidien.*[4] When an accounting was asked of M. Dumay and M. Bertrand on November 18, 1926, by M. Georges Boris, the General Secretary, the reaction was such that MM. Buisson and Aulard resigned from the board of directors, and shortly afterwards eight other collaborators resigned and eight of the leading members of the staff were ousted. In spite of the storm which raged during the winter of 1926–1927, *Le Quotidien,* directed by Dumay and Bertrand, seems to be as popular as ever, and its pages do not appear to have suffered from the loss of its eminent collaborators. It specializes in " reform " — social and economic, and to this end has conducted some inquiries into the sale of " lots " in the suburbs, the settlements of foreigners in and about Paris, the fate of " filles-mères," of chorus-girls, of domestics, etc., which have been good journalistic " stunts " as well as careful studies of social problems. Many of these have been written by women writers, with a talent surpassing that of the highly-paid " sob-sisters " of American syndicates. The front page is well illustrated by photographs and staff cartoonists, and always made impressive by a boxed quotation of great dignity — Voltaire by preference. There is always a signed special article on a social or moral issue, and an editorial written by Pierre Bertrand in a terse, epigrammatic style that recalls Arthur Brisbane. Politically the Cartel des Gauches is supported, although certain personalities, such as Caillaux and Maurice Sarraut, do not seem to be on the good books of *Le Quotidien,* which often leans towards the Socialist Party. A large proportion of the public of *Le Quotidien* is connected with the public-school system, and a great deal of space is given to the discussion of the problems of the *école unique* and laicity, *Le Quotidien* being distinctly " anti-clerical." Of the six pages issued regularly, at least two are filled with advertisements, while space is found for two serial novels, a weekly woman's page, literary columns, etc., and an abundant supply of foreign news. The circulation of the paper, which recently raised its price from 25 centimes to 30, is estimated at 250,000.

RAPPEL (LE) (Same as *La Lanterne*) **Morning**
Founded 1869 by Victor Hugo and Auguste Vacquerie.
Director: Edmond du Mesnil;[5] editor-in-chief: Charles Gallet.

---

[4] See above, p. 152.   [5] Died in 1928.

Edmond du Mesnil, whose personality dominates *Le Rappel*, has long been considered the *enfant terrible* of the Radicals, with whom he is nominally classed. It is difficult to assign to M. du Mesnil the label " Left " or " Right " — the Left finds him too reactionary (he was a confirmed " militarist " before the War and active in the campaigns for national defense and for the three-year military service law); while the Right finds him too Radical in various projects for social reform which he advocates from time to time. Of late, however, the Right has had less and less to dispute with M. du Mesnil, who is solidly behind Poincaré and the Union Nationale, and extremely sceptical of Locarno and other pacific efforts of Briand. Non-political news finds little place in *Le Rappel;* the front page is filled with editorials by du Mesnil, Charles Gallet and others (notably Pierre Dominique), with a few news items; there are no photographs or cartoons, as a rule, but the short headlines are trenchant and arresting. Page 2 contains news items (most of them political) and comments from other pages; page 3 is devoted to literary and artistic life, book reviews and artistic criticism, anecdotes, echoes, which are well written and attractively presented; theatres, and a serial novel. The fourth page (there are never more than four pages) is filled with miscellaneous bulletins — Bourse, races, sports, radio, etc. *Le Rappel* is also issued as *La Lanterne,* which in this way preserves its identity and ownership of the title, though no longer possessing an editorial staff of its own. *La Lanterne,* founded in 1877, was perhaps the most discussed newspaper in France as the organ of the " Radicaux-Socialistes," " anti-clericals," and " anti-militarists," in the last quarter of the nineteenth century. Among the young Socialists who wrote fiery editorials was Alexandre Millerand, whose radical doctrines, as expressed in *La Lanterne* in the late nineties, were quoted with much effect by Renaud-Jean (Communist) in the Chamber of Deputies in June 1924, when the Left drove Millerand, as an arch-conservative, from the Elysée. In 1898 Aristide Briand was director of *La Lanterne;* it gradually veered from the extreme Left to a moderate Radical position under René Viviani, and later under Gaston Doumergue, who used it as his organ until he became Premier in December 1913. During the war it was under the direction of Alexandre Israel (later Herriot's " chef-de-cabinet ") and Marcel Sembat, the Socialist, and while its main activity was bitter criticism of the Government (especially that of Clemenceau) it was none the less imbued with patriotism and a win-the-war spirit. The acquisition of *La Lanterne* by du Mesnil and its union with *Le Rappel* snuffs out a journal of historic importance.[6]

[6] A fortnight after the death of Edmond du Mesnil, *Le Rappel* suspended publication (March 15, 1928). Its founders had endowed it with a special sustaining

SOIR (LE) **Evening**
Founded in 1864, revived by present management in 1925.[7]
Director: Alexis Caille.
Editors-in-chief: L. O. Frossard and Robert Tourle.
Political advisers: Georges Bonnet and Édouard Daladier (former ministers, both Radical-Socialists).
Collaborators: François-Albert, Vincent Auriol, Jean de Pierrefeu, Victor Méric, Paul Louis.

Le Soir, which advertises itself "the only evening paper of the Left," appears the latest of the newspapers of the evening — about eight o'clock, and thus, when there is any important development which the other evening papers have been unable to exploit, it sells well on the boulevards. Its front page is arranged to catch the eye with provocative headlines, many illustrated jokes, and some small photographs. Mingled with news items are clever little squibs signed by young journalists who are endeavoring to build up a reputation. Literature and the theatre are given especial attention on two full pages, while a page is devoted to latest foreign news bulletins and racing results. A good sporting page is a regular feature, and the back page is filled with advertisements and radio programs. In spite of its designation as a Left paper, *Le Soir,* in the entire newspaper, does not give more than three or four columns to political propaganda or subjects affected by it. Paul Louis, formerly an active Socialist, writes short editorials which appear in a special box in the right-hand corner of the front page. In policy it often sides with the Socialists, but gives the impression of being more interested in entertaining the public and thereby increasing the sale of the paper than in conducting any bitter political campaigns.

TEMPS (LE) **Evening**
Founded 1861.
Political director: Adrien Hébrard, son of Adrien Hébrard who directed *Le Temps* from 1867 to his death in 1914. The direction then passed to the elder son, Émile Hébrard, and in 1925 to the present director. (In 1929 the Hébrards sold their interests to a corporation of financiers.)
Political editors: Paul Merlin, E. Julia, Achille Perreau, Gaston Deschamps, L. Chênebenoit, Raymond Recouly, Roland de Marès, Maurice Réclus, Rémy Roure, etc.

---

fund, designed to preserve its existence, but post-war financial disturbances made survival impossible.

[7] Amalgamated with *Paris-Soir* in 1928, and now (1929) published under that title.

Parliamentary correspondent: Albert Bazerque. Staff economists: Paul Delombre (was Minister of Commerce in 1898) and Jenny. Foreign and colonial affairs: E. Roels, André Ganem, Lindenlaub, Jacques Bardoux, René Puaux, Guilaine, de Jessen, A. Duboscq, W. d'Ormesson, Lt. Col. Reboul (also military questions).

Specialists: military affairs, General Nudant; naval affairs, Edmond Delage; university life, Parigot; drama, Pierre Brisson; music, Henry Malherbe; literature, Paul Souday; medicine, Dr. Logre. Other contributors of special features are Abel Hermant (recently elected to the French Academy); Vuillermoz (music); Myriam Harry; Pierre Mille (essays, *En Passant*); Émile Henriot; Georges Suarez, etc.

Le Temps is a French national institution. It is almost as much a part of the literary, intellectual, social, and political life of France as the French Academy. Founded under the Second Empire by A. Nefftzer, its principles were republican from the start: it fought the Empire and every attempt at the restoration of a monarchy, and has steadily defended the republican tradition, against the Royalists and parties of the extreme Right on the one hand and against the Socialists and later the Communists on the other. When *Le Temps* is considered the " official " representative in France and the world of French public opinion, it is not only because it has always taken the point of view of the existing Government on foreign and domestic problems (notable exception being the " Socialistic " propositions of the Left Government of 1924–1925) but because it has made itself the champion and protector of national interests at home and abroad — a sacred mission which the Hébrard family feels is the divine right of its newspaper. For instance, the controversy which the editors carried on in 1927 with Albert Mathiez because of his book on the Terror, brought out the idea that *Le Temps* believed Mathiez was unpatriotic in repainting the Terror in more attractive colors — unpatriotic because the nation, which was facing a new terror in the shape of Bolshevism, might be deceived into thinking Terrors were not as fear-inspiring as conventional history had depicted them. For national glory as well as for financial gain, France's colonial empire receives careful and daily attention; and it is interesting to note that more space is given to territories not yet completely in the power of France from a military point of view (such as Morocco), where much work remains for the army, than to less troublesome possessions. Towards Germany *Le Temps* has maintained a defiant and distrustful attitude which has not evolved appreciably from the hatred of ten years before. Army and naval affairs, particularly reorganization, are treated with expert thoroughness by seasoned warriors, and no attempt is made at dissimulating France's preparedness for trouble. In the world of literature, the fine arts, and the sciences, *Le Temps* is the standard-bearer of French tradition and its critics start with the *a priori* assumption that France is the most civilized nation in the world and that they are their country's spokesmen and prophets. Certain regular contributors, however, notably Paul Souday, have been conspicuously "international-minded," have fought for the appreciation of foreign art, music, and literature in France, and have paid homage to great writers like Romain Rolland and Anatole France in spite of their pacifist and Communist views. For a generation the format and features of *Le Temps* have been unchanging — except for the date (and the subject-matter), an issue of 1927 is the exact counterpart of an issue of 1900; the short headlines have not become more sensational with the speeding-up of the world's pace; there are the same number of columns to a page, the same styles of type, the same rubrics, the same absence of photographs or cartoons. The issue is six to eight very large pages, depending on the activities of French national institutions such as the French Academy or the Institute, which are generally reported in full (especially speeches of admission to the Academy, which embody some of the most nationalist statements ever printed in *Le Temps*.) Similarly, *Le Temps* publishes in full the speeches at all patriotic ceremonies in Paris and those of national personages at such ceremonies in the provinces. From the religious point of view, the *Temps*, while respecting Catholicism as the spiritual background of the nation, has distinctly Protestant sympathies and pro-Jewish tendencies. Its society column, for instance, notes primarily the activities of the Jewish financial aristocracy. In general it may be said that *Le Temps*, the London *Times*, and the *New York Times* perform the same functions for their respective nationals. It is interesting, however, to note the small amount of advertising in *Le Temps* beside the enormous importance of the English and American *Times* as advertising media. Perhaps this fact is to be explained by the limited circulation of *Le Temps*, which, in spite of being admittedly the best documented and most informing newspaper in France, does not interest itself in the everyday happenings of Paris and rarely treats events or personalities with the impressionist touches of modern journalism. In spite of its inherent and ostentatious patriotism, *Le Temps*, by the emphasis and large amount of space devoted to foreign relations and foreign news, gives the impression of an international bulletin-board. It was the first newspaper in France to be connected by its private wires to the principal cities of Europe, and has maintained its place as the authoritative source of foreign news and of the attitude of the Quai d'Orsay on questions involving France — an attitude in most cases identical with that of the editors of *Le Temps*. To-day it has telephone as well as telegraph lines with special correspondents in Berlin, Vienna, Rome, London, Madrid, and Brussels; while telegraphic services keep its correspondents in Constantinople, Sofia, Belgrade, Budapest, Geneva, Stockholm, Bucarest, Tangiers, etc., in constant touch with the Paris office. In addition to its regular correspondents, *Le Temps* sends special envoys or groups of correspondents to report exceptional foreign events.

An important publicity bureau estimates the circulation of *Le Temps* as between 50,000 and 80,000.

VICTOIRE (LA) **Morning**
Founded as daily, August 1914. Previously appeared as a weekly, *La Guerre Sociale*, founded in 1912.
Director-editor: Gustave Hervé.

As the editor of the weekly, *La Guerre Sociale*, Gustave Hervé, an ex-professor and revolutionary Socialist, had made a reputation as an " anti-militarist " and " internationalist." Writing of this paper in 1913, A. de Chambure [8] dismissed it as " the journal of ' General ' Hervé, seconded by several lieutenants who are even more violent than their chief." The outbreak of the war produced a striking *volte face:* over night *La Guerre Sociale* became the daily *La Victoire*, and Hervé, the pacifist, became Hervé, the ultra-fire-eating patriot. M. de Chambure, in his *Quelques Guides de l'Opinion en France pendant La Grande Guerre*, now refers to M. Hervé in most respectful terms as one of those journalists " whose brutal and popular originality is the surest means of success " and describes the joy of the nationalists at Hervé's sudden conversion: " People wanted to know what the man who had insulted the tricolor would have to say. His first article, even the first word of that article, produced stupor, astonishment, delight. M. Hervé had become a patriot, a single night had sufficed to revive in him the love of the flag he had profaned. . . . The appeal of the clarion-warning of danger had caused to reverberate within him that patriotic sentiment — dormant, not dead — which sees only that France must be defended, and her soil saved from ruin and disgrace. To gain a full understanding of this sentiment, Hervé's deposition at the trial of Malvy, July 30, 1918, should be read. His entire life-story, his complete rôle of militant internationalist redeemed by the war, is laid bare therein without reservations. And, in fact, he came to make a public and oral profession of his faith at the very bar of the political and judicial tribunal which was sitting in judgment on a minister." Since the war Hervé has continued to win the plaudits of the nationalists by his fiery editorials, which are written in a vivid, slangy, personal, direct-to-the-man-in-the-street style which is peculiar to Hervé. He

[8] *Cf. À Travers La Presse*, p. 141.

calls his paper the " Organ of the Authoritative Republic," and " National Socialist Daily," and explains these designations by a paragraph which appears always in a box beside the title. Here is a specimen: " Our program: To combat, in all extreme Left sympathizers, among our people, that Prussian Socialism which was developed in France immediately after our defeats of 1870, under the influence of Karl Marx and the German social-democracy, and which has lined them up stupidly as implacable foes of the ' capitalist régime.' . . . To replace this Socialism of Prussian inspiration, which aims to absorb the individual into the State and force all Frenchmen, workers or not, to a goose-stepping march, with a French Socialism which does not annihilate either individual liberty, or the Fatherland, or civilization." Hervé is especially bitter against the Communists and an enthusiastic supporter of Millerand, whose political career contains certain parallels to Hervé's editorial career. *La Victoire* is a medium-sized four-page paper, with a number of cuts and photographs on the front page, especially when patriotic ceremonies occur. Hervé's editorial, headed in heavy type, always fills the first two columns of page 1, while his short commentaries (three or four lines) are inserted here and there on this page between other articles. The other pages contain the usual rubrics, and many advertisements for new subscribers and funds for propaganda. In 1925 *La Victoire du Dimanche,* an illustrated weekly, was founded, which publishes a special edition for workers and one for peasants. It is an open secret that certain captains of industry are giving Hervé financial encouragement in his campaign against industrial unrest and Communist doctrines.

VOLONTÉ (LA)　**Morning**

Founded October 1925.
Director: Albert Dubarry.
Editor-in-chief: Aimé Méric.
Contributors: Bernard Lacache, Émile Arène, Valmy-Baysse, André Germain, J.-F. Louis Merlet, etc.

La Volonté is a new paper of Left affiliations already widely known as the organ of the followers of Joseph Caillaux. It is a venture of Albert Dubarry, the director of the satirical weekly *Le Carnet de la Semaine,* the monthly *La Vie Aérienne et Sportive,* the stage fortnightly *La Rampe,* and the provincial daily *La France de Nice et du Sud-Est.* M. Dubarry, well known during the war as a " defeatist " and archenemy of Léon Daudet, uses *La Volonté* to convey his political ideas, which are allied to the revisionist program of Georges Valois in his most recent metamorphosis. He engages in long-winded controversies with other political editors who enjoy this form of contest, notably Edmond du Mesnil of *Le Rappel*, who takes issue with Dubarry almost daily, not bitterly but with the friendly consideration shown to a respected sparring-partner. Holding himself aloof from the stereotyped Radical party-lines, Dubarry sides on some issues with the Socialists, on some with the Communists, especially on questions of foreign policy. It is a four-page newspaper, the front page enlivened by a few photographs and exceptionally clever headlines. Literary, artistic, and theatrical news form a large proportion of the reading matter, and there is a very thorough review of the press. It is noteworthy that *La Volonté* is one of the journals of Paris which is extremely critical of French " nationalism " and which insists that France cannot have peace within her borders until she has coöperated with other nations to reduce tariffs and other obstacles to international harmony.

NOTE: Since the compilation of the above guide, two new dailies have appeared: *L'Ami du Peuple* (founded in 1928 by François Coty), and *La Rumeur* (founded in 1928 by Georges Anquetil).

APPENDIX E

GUIDE TO LEADING DAILY NEWSPAPERS OF PROVINCIAL FRANCE

Classified by cities, in alphabetical order. Population figures for the cities are from the census of 1921. The Guide is of January 1928.

Bordeaux (*Gironde*) *Pop. 267,409.*

FRANCE DE BORDEAUX ET DU SUD–OUEST (LA)
Founded 1887.
Director: P. Astier.
Political collaborators: Senators Cuminal and Roustan; Deputies Albert Milhaud and Pierre Renaudel; Georges Ponsot (former deputy and editor of *L'Ère Nouvelle* at present).
Contributors: Edmond Blanc, Max Carrère, Henri Guernut (Secretary " Ligue des Droits de l'Homme "), Dr. Laumonier, Longemer, G. de Pawlowski.

Organ of the Left; Jacobin. Reports its average circulation as 335,000. 6–8 pages; 22 regional editions. Private wire to Paris.

LIBERTÉ DU SUD–OUEST (LA)
Founded 1911.
Editor-in-chief and director: Abbé Daniel-Michel Bérgey, deputy.

Right; Catholic; calling itself a newspaper of " combat and action." Very lively front page, designed for popular reading. Private wires to Paris and Toulouse.

PETITE GIRONDE (LA)
Founded 1872.
Director: Marcel Gounouilhou (former deputy).

One of the six leading provincial dailies of France, with probably the largest circulation of all regional newspapers (219,580 certified circulation in 1927). Represents the conservative bourgeois element of the southwest, Bloc National in politics and very patriotic in all phases of activity. Twenty-two different editions take care of local news in the entire southwest region of France, with special correspondents who furnish the political, commercial, agricultural, and industrial information on each district. Private wire to Paris, and large Paris offices for editing news and receiving advertisements. Many photographs and cartoons make the paper most attractive, and its literary standards are as high as *Le Matin* or *Le Journal*. Its contributors are well-known Paris journalists and men of letters. Special maritime and commercial section daily, and a weekly section devoted to the interests of wine-growers.

Lille (*Nord*) *Pop. 200,952.*

DÉPECHE (LA)
Founded 1882.
Director-editor: H. Langlais.

6 to 12 pages; the only paper in Lille with a private wire to Paris. Republican and conservative.

ÉCHO DU NORD ET LE GRAND ÉCHO DU NORD DE LA FRANCE (L')
Founded 1819. *Écho du Nord* (evening) and *Grande Écho* (morning)
Directors: Émile Ferré and Jean Dubar. Ferré was reprisal hostage in Lithuania during the war and in consequence received a prize from the French Academy.

One of the six great regional dailies. From six to ten pages daily, twelve editions, with special correspondents in outlying localities and Belgium. Conservative republican in politics, paying especial attention to the interests of the metallurgical, spinning, and other great industries in the region — advocating, in consequence, very high tariff rates to protect these manufactures. Claims to have a circulation of 225,000 and the largest of the region, but this is disputed by the *Reveil du Nord*, its leading rival. Considered one of the best advertising media in provincial France.

RÉVEIL DU NORD (LE)
Founded 1899.
Director: E. Guillaume. Editor-in-chief: Lucien Le Masson.

Conservative, popular journal, with very energetic management. Six to twelve pages daily, and ten editions, covering the northern départements. The first French daily to register its circulation with the "Office de justification des tirages." Certified circulation, 1927: 180,000. Also publishes weekly: *Le Reveil Illustré*, a family magazine with many photographs, cartoons, serial stories, etc., and the weekly: *Les Sports du Nord*.

Limoges (*Haute-Vienne*) *Pop. 90,187.*

COURRIER DU CENTRE (LE)
Founded 1851.

Liberal republican, but with very little personality. Specializes in giving news most speedily in the region, goes to press at 2 A.M. with latest news from Paris of the hour before, and thus appears with information ten hours ahead of other regional papers which send editions to Limoges. Ten special regional offices and 250 correspondents in eleven départements.

GAZETTE DU CENTRE (LA)
Founded 1881.

Conservative bourgeois journal, appearing in the evening.

Lyons (*Rhône*) *Pop. 561,592.*

LYON RÉPUBLICAIN
Founded 1878.
Director: Georges Soustelle.
Editors: Paul Sigrist, Georges Sabatier, Paul Boissonnet, Georges Dron, etc.

One of the six great regional dailies. Moderate republican, with large bourgeois circulation claimed to be 200,000. Nine separate daily editions to cover twenty-seven départements.

NOUVELLISTE DE LYON (LE) (See special study below, pp. 469–470.)

PROGRÈS (LE)
Founded 1860.
Directors: Léon and Henri Delaroche.

Organ of the moderate Radicals.

SALUT PUBLIC (LE)
Founded 1848.   Director: Lucien Henriet.   Editor-in-chief: Marius Gonin.

Liberal Republican. The organ of the economic, industrial, and financial interests of the southeast. Private wire to Paris.

Marseilles (*Bouches-du-Rhône*) *Pop. 586,341.*

PETIT MARSEILLAIS (LE)
Founded 1868.
Directors: J.-B. Samat and G. Bourrageas.

Bloc National in politics; one of the six leading provincial dailies, and claims to have a circulation of 350,000. Private wire connection with Paris. Twelve editions per day. Conservative in format. Among its contributors is Mermeix, foreign and political expert of *Le Gaulois* of Paris. As in most of the large provincial dailies, the greater half of the six to eight pages is devoted to advertisements.

PETIT PROVENÇAL (LE)

Founded 1876.
Director: Paul Carrère.
Editor-in-chief: Camille Ferdy.

Radical Socialist. Twelve regional editions. Specializes in departments of interest to the entire family: fashions, cinema, sports, etc. Claims a circulation of 300,000.

RADICAL DE MARSEILLE (LE)

Founded 1869.
Director: Vincent Delpuech.
Editor-in-chief: L. Boudouresque. Contributors: music, Gabriel Marie; literature and art, P. Gavary and Charles Fromentin.

Le Radical is the newspaper of the working-classes of pronounced Left tendencies, though not out-and-out Socialist. Specializes in a Sunday sporting edition.

SÉMAPHORE DE MARSEILLE (LE)

Founded 1827.
Director: Paul Berlatier.

Conservative newspaper defending the interests of the industrial, commercial, financial, and especially the maritime world. Especially valuable for its colonial studies. One of the most widely read of French papers in the French colonies and in the shipping world. Six to eight pages daily, very few photographs, very sober format.

Nancy (*Meurthe-et-Moselle*) *Pop. 113,226.*

EST RÉPUBLICAIN (L')

Founded 1889.
Director: V. René Mercier.
Contributors: Theatres, G. Boulay; Arts and Letters, H. Hunziger, etc.

Moderate conservative; claims the largest circulation of the newspapers of the east of France. Publishes eight to sixteen pages daily in seven editions. Circulation estimated at 120,000.

Nantes (*Loire-Inférieure*) *Pop. 183,704.*

PHARE DE LA LOIRE, DE BRETAGNE ET DE VENDÉE (LE)
Founded 1815.
Director-Proprietor: Maurice Schwob.

Conservative daily of Republican, ultra-patriotic traditions. Publishes ten day and night editions covering the west of France, and is the most powerful political and commercial journal of the west.

POPULAIRE DE NANTES (LE)
Founded 1873.
Political director: Gaston Veil.
Editor-in-chief: J. Tallandeau.

The leading paper of Left tendencies of the west, calling itself " Organ of the Democracy of the West." Among its regular contributors are the most prominent Radical intellectuals of France, including Professor Aulard, Guy Lavaud, François-Albert, Professor Bouglé, etc.

Nice (*Alpes-Maritimes*) *Pop. 155,839.*

ÉCLAIREUR DE NICE ET DU SUD–EST (L')
Founded 1883.
Director: Léon Garibaldi.
Contributors: Henry Bordeaux, Gabriel Hanotaux, C. Mauclair, Fernand Hauser, etc.

Calling itself " Républicain indépendant," *L'Éclaireur* leans to the Right, and is one of the most patriotic of all provincial journals. It has a circulation of about 115,000.

Rennes (*Ille-et-Vilaine*) *Pop. 82,241.*

NOUVELLISTE DE BRETAGNE, ANJOU, MAINE, NORMANDIE ET VENDÉE (LE)
Founded 1901.
Director-Editor-in-chief: Eugène Delahaye.

Founded by a group of Breton Catholics, of Bloc National sympathies, to be the organ of a " Catholic and liberal policy." Has a private wire to Paris. Publishes ten départemental editions. Six to eight pages daily.

OUEST–ÉCLAIR (L')
Founded 1899.
Political director: Emm. Desgrées du Lou.

Editor-in-chief: A. Moraux.
Paris editor: Louis-Alfred Pagès.

Conservative Republican journal of Catholic sympathies. Certified circulation of 177,343 in 1925. Especially defends army-interests. Covers twelve outlying départements and also publishes seven regional weeklies, *Le Petit Breton, Le Vie Rennaise, L'Ille-et-Vilaine, Le Morbihan, Les Côtes du Nord, L'Avenir de la Mayenne,* and *Le Calvados.* Private wire to Paris.

Reims *(Marne) Pop. 76,645.*

ÉCLAIREUR DE L'EST (L')
   Founded 1886.
   Director: Paul Marchandeau.
   Editors-in-chief: Paul Dramas and René Benedetti.

" Organ of the reconstitution of the northeast," *L'Éclaireur* was the only paper in Reims to continue publication during the bombardment. Steers a middle course in politics, extremely patriotic — a tendency which is readily explained by the history of the region which it serves. In 1926 its certified circulation was 52,240. Publishes seven daily editions.

Rouen *(Seine-Inférieure) Pop. 123,712.*

JOURNAL DE ROUEN (LE)
   Founded 1762.
   Directors: Jean and André Lafond.

One of the six great provincial dailies, *Le Journal de Rouen,* after *Le Journal du Havre* (founded 1750), is the oldest newspaper in France. (Not the oldest daily from its inception, however, as the Paris *Journal des Débats,* founded in 1789, holds that distinction.) In politics it calls itself " Républicain progressiste," which is rather an inappropriate designation for a very conservative journal, defending the interests of the commercial, industrial, and agricultural proprietors. A serious journal, with special feature articles regularly covering maritime and colonial questions, economic problems, etc. From six to twelve pages daily, four editions covering all Normandy.

Saint-Étienne *(Loire) Pop. 167,967.*

TRIBUNE RÉPUBLICAINE (LA)
   Founded 1899.
   Director: A. Gintzburger.
   Editor-in-chief: René Grumbach.

The only great regional daily of the Centre, with twelve départemental editions covering twenty départements. Has recently increased in importance and size, due to the post-war developments of St. Étienne and Roanne, etc., as industrial centres. Leans to the Left politically. Six to sixteen pages daily, with a great amount of advertising.

Strasbourg (*Bas-Rhin*) *Pop. 166,747.*

DERNIÈRES NOUVELLES DE STRASBOURG (LES)
Founded 1877.

Four editions daily, eight to thirty-two pages, one in French, one in German, one for Colmar and one for Sélestat. It claims to have the largest circulation of any newspaper in Alsace-Lorraine, the certified figure being 115,000. Publishes special supplements weekly on the arts and sciences, the cinema, fashion, sport, tourism, and economic and financial studies. Conservative in politics.

JOURNAL D'ALSACE ET DE LORRAINE (LE)
Founded 1787.
Director: Edmond Degay.
Editors: Daniel Blumenthal, Paul Bourson, Étienne Chichet (parliamentary editor).
Contributors: Senator Tauflieb; Deputies Albert Milhaud, André Mallarmé, Bertrand Nogaro; ex-deputy Camille Simonin.

Before the war *Le Journal d'Alsace et de Lorraine* was the stronghold of French influence under the German occupation; since the recovery of the provinces it has become the official government organ, i.e. the spokesman for the functionaries. Politically it is moderate Left. Announced circulation is 20,000. There are two editions.

Toulouse (*Haute-Garonne*) *Pop. 175,434.*

DÉPÊCHE (LA)   (See special study below, pp. 467–469.)

EXPRESS DU MIDI (L')
Founded 1891.
Editor-in-chief: Gaston Guèze.
Contributors of political articles: Ambroise Rendu, ex-deputy; Henri Auriol, deputy, Marquis de Palaminy, Comte d'Antin de Vaillac, and Jacques Bainville.

L'Express du Midi is the leading Royalist Catholic paper in southern France, and calls itself an organ of " social and religious defense " and of " patriotic union." Private telegraph and telephone to its Paris office; 800 correspondents in the region and 3,500 sales dépots, serving 18 départements.

MIDI (LE)
Founded 1908.
Directors: Vincent Auriol, deputy; Albert Bedouce, deputy; Ellen Prévot (former Socialist deputy, now general councillor).
Editor-in-chief: Charles Hudelle.

Organ of the Socialist Party in the south, publishing six daily editions read by workers and peasants of fifteen départements.

TÉLÉGRAMME (LE)
Founded 1884.
Director: Albert Cuvilliez.
Political collaborators: Turrel (Minister of Public Works 1896–1898); Reille-Soult, Duc de Dalmatie (ex-deputy), Henri Auriol, Dr. Jean Molinié, Coucoureux, etc.

Calling itself " Social Republican," *Le Télégramme* represents the conservative, Catholic class which does not subscribe to the more extreme Right doctrines of the Royalist *Express du Midi*. Publishes fifteen editions, covering twenty départements. Six to eight pages. Private telephone and telegraph to Paris.

STUDIES OF TWO REPRESENTATIVE PROVINCIAL NEWSPAPERS:
1. *La Dépêche de Toulouse*.
2. *Le Nouvelliste de Lyon*.

DÉPÊCHE DE TOULOUSE (LA) **Morning**
Founded 1870.
Directors: Arthur Huc (editorial pseudonym, Pierre et Paul); and Maurice Sarraut, senator and president (1926–1927) of the Radical Socialist Party. Political editor at Paris: François de Tessan.
Political contributors: François-Albert, A. Aulard, C. Bouglé, Paul-Boncour, Victor Bérard, Léon Jouhaux, Yvon Delbos, Guglielmo Ferrero, Édouard Herriot, Paul Painlevé, Albert Sarraut, Aimé Berthod, Dr. Toulouse — all notable Jacobins of the Left.
Economic contributors: E. Barthe, Professor Nogaro (deputies); Émile Borel (deputy, former Minister of Marine, Member of the Institute); Gaston Jèze and Georges Scelle (professors).
Literary contributors: Paul Souday (literary critic of *Le Temps* and correspondent of the *New York Times*), Édouard Haraucourt,

Camille Mauclair, Pierre Mille, J. H. Rosny, Octave Uzanne, Jean de Pierrefeu, Maurice Dekobra.

Of all the dailies published outside of Paris, *La Dépêche de Toulouse* holds first place in importance, and has standards and equipment which make it the equal of any of the " Big Five " daily newspapers in Paris in the presentation of news and the extent of its influence. Calling itself " Journal de la Démocratie," it is the recognized oracle of Radical thought in France, and has been the power which has maintained its director, Maurice Sarraut, as the spokesman of the Moderate Left and the recent president of the " Parti Radical-Socialiste." In the dignified columns of *La Dépêche* all the members of the Governments of the Left have for many years given their programs to the public; the " brains " of the Cartel des Gauches — the professors, scientists, economists, and men of letters, have been regular contributors of articles which are exclusively the property of the provincial *Dépêche,* though quoted in the great Paris press. Eighteen daily editions carry the paper into thirty départements of southern and central France, from the Gironde on the Atlantic coast to the Spanish border, east to Marseilles, and as far north as the départements of Indre and Allier: covering an area which is almost one-third of the Republic. Each of these editions is in effect two distinct journals: one a great metropolitan daily, edited and made up in Paris at the office of *La Dépêche,* telegraphed to Toulouse and printed there without further editing; the other a local newspaper, written by a regional agency and local correspondents, and edited at Toulouse, with all the flavor of home-town news and even local advertising, for each of the eighteen regions. The special features, such as sporting page, women's page, popular science, parliamentary gossip, children's stories, literary notes, are sent from the Paris office. A survey of any issue of *La Dépêche* shows how much more interested its public is in world events and the doings of Paris than in the life of its own region — even if the region be a large and active city like Toulouse. Page 1 is a front page that could appear on a newspaper anywhere in France — it may be considered a cross-section of the mentality of the typical Frenchman of Radical views and good education, whether of Lille, Paris, Strasbourg, Lyons, or Toulouse or any other region. The first two columns bear the heading " Ideas and Doctrines," and always contain the leading political article, signed by a national Radical personage. To balance, the last two columns, headed " Men and Things," carry the literary, historic, or sociological views of a well-known man of letters or learned specialist. Sandwiched between are the leading international news, the principal event of the day in France, a few small photographs, and always a small comic cartoon of non-political interest. Nothing on the front page except the address of the paper would indicate its relationship to Toulouse. The same is true of page 2, which contains the continuation of news articles of the front page, miscellaneous news items from all over France, a regular section, " The Political Greenroom," and a serial novel. Page 3 is devoted to late news dispatches from all over the world, the quotations of the Paris Bourse of the day before, and sporting notes, in which we find racing news of Paris with some notices of sporting events around Toulouse, and a few miscellaneous news items of Southern France. Finally, on page 4, or a later page, is given the news of the city or section for which the special edition is issued. No effort is made to present such news in an attractive or striking manner, no local photographs are used or local personalities interviewed. Paragraphs of advertisements of local shops are used as fillers throughout the page, inserted as news items. Of the remaining pages (the regular edition varies from eight to ten pages) at least two and a half are covered with advertisements. The regular feature pages are, as already indicated, of interest to all classes of readers, whether urban or rural. The weekly agricultural chronicles are among the best published in France, and show the efforts of *La Dépêche* to please its farming clientèle. From the point of view of patriotism, it is apparent that no extreme sentiments on the " patrie " or appeals to chauvinist instincts are made; at the same time patriotic ceremonies, especially those commemorating French savants' centenaries, etc., are fully reported. The circulation of *La Dépêche*, certified, was 200,084 in 1925.

NOUVELLISTE DE LYON (LE) **Morning**

Founded 1879.
Director: Régis Rambaud.
Editor-in-chief: Ernest LeClerc.
Editors: F. Garcin, N. Sapin, J. Cherbut, A. Michot, J. Giraud, etc.
(No nationally known names.)

Le Nouvelliste calls itself a " Daily Political Journal " and announces its political program, from its foundation, to be the following: " To defend order, liberty, and the religious and social principles essential to any well-organized society." It believes itself entitled to the distinction of being the most important organ of the conservative and Catholic press in France — a self-appraisement which it is hard to reconcile with the importance of the Catholic daily, *La Croix*, which covers not only Catholic Paris but every département of France. The achievements of *Le Nouvelliste*, however, are imposing. Nine editions daily cover twenty-five départements, and the total circulation, guaranteed, is 230,000. While *La Croix* places its emphasis on the Church,

Le Nouvelliste is primarily interested in politics, with, of course, the problems of Catholicism uppermost. At the same time it makes no effort at moral censorship — unlike *La Croix*, it prints racing results and the programs of movies, theatres, and music-hall revues. While *La Croix* features signed contributions from the pens of prominent clerics or laymen noted for their devotion to Church activities, *Le Nouvelliste* rarely indulges in signed articles, and has no members of the clergy on its editorial staff. The first page of *Le Nouvelliste* is striking because of its numerous photographs, reproduced by a special reddish rotogravure process which is a vivid contrast to the drab black type in which the reading matter is printed. Six or seven large photographs, featured on a rather small-sized news-sheet, give the paper an immediate popular appeal which may be comparable to that of the English or American tabloid. There are no cartoons, and the inside pages have neither photographs nor cuts nor feature articles to attract the reader. The front page, as in the case of *La Dépêche de Toulouse,* is composed and telegraphed from the Paris office of *Le Nouvelliste,* where several editors cover all important Parisian events and receive foreign news from agencies and newspapers of Paris. On the front page, as in *La Croix,* appears a summary of the important events, international and French, of the previous day, which are treated at greater length in regular news articles. Below is regularly printed a political editorial (unsigned) of a column or two in length, dealing in general with the Catholic view of current problems. Foreign news receives considerable attention on the front page and in the late news dispatches on page 3, with main emphasis on questions connected with Vatican activities. Local news, as in all the other provincial papers, appears on an inside page — a mere chronicle of civil notices, court cases, and other official items, Church notes, parish activities, etc. There are at least two full pages of advertisements in every six to eight page normal issue. From the standpoint of patriotism, it is to be noted that *Le Nouvelliste* combats most aggressively the " anti-patriotic " influences of its political enemies, the Left, whether moderate or extreme. Much attention is given to the alleged teaching of internationalism by " Communist " teachers in the lay schools, and to the influence of " Moscow " in counteracting the influence of French traditions in the minds of the young. Towards Germany the attitude of the journal is as bitter as that of *L'Écho de Paris.* All patriotic manifestations, all decorations of war heroes, unveiling of monuments anywhere in France, speeches of noted patriots, congresses of veterans, etc., are given front-page attention and detailed photographic descriptions. To stimulate subscriptions and popular interest, various competitions are frequently organized, mostly based on the serial novels which occupy at least two-thirds of a page in each issue.

INDEX

SOCIAL AND ECONOMIC STUDIES
OF POST–WAR FRANCE

EDITED BY
CARLTON J. H. HAYES

VOL. I. **The Public Finances of Post-War France.** By ROBERT M. HAIG, Professor, School of Business, Columbia University. 8vo, cloth, pp. xxviii + 463. $5.50 net.

VOL. II. **The Process of Inflation in France, 1914-1927.** By JAMES HARVEY ROGERS, Professor of Economics in the University of Missouri. 8vo, cloth, pp. xx + 378. $5.00 net.

VOL. III. **The Economic Development of Post-War France: A Survey of Production.** By WILLIAM F. OGBURN, Professor of Sociology in the University of Chicago, and WILLIAM JAFFÉ, Assistant Professor of Economics in Northwestern University. 8vo, cloth, pp. xii + 613. $6.00 net.

VOL. IV. **The Labor Movement in Post-War France.** By DAVID J. SAPOSS, Professor of Trade Unionism in the Brookwood Labor College, and A. D. MEURIG EVANS, Fellow of the Social Science Research Council. 8vo, cloth. *In press.*

VOL. V. **France: A Nation of Patriots.** By CARLTON J. H. HAYES, Professor of History in Columbia University. 8vo, cloth, pp. x + 487. $4.50 net.

VOL. VI. **The French Parliamentary System.** By LINDSAY ROGERS, Professor of Public Law in Columbia University. 8vo, cloth. *In press.*

VOL. VII. **The Foreign Policies of Post-War France.** By PARKER THOMAS MOON, Professor of International Relations in Columbia University. 8vo, cloth. *In press.*

COLUMBIA UNIVERSITY PRESS
COLUMBIA UNIVERSITY
NEW YORK

FOREIGN AGENT
OXFORD UNIVERSITY PRESS
HUMPHREY MILFORD
AMEN HOUSE, LONDON, E.C.